Using Multiethnic Literature in the K–8 Classroom

ᨠ ᨠ ᨠ ᨠ ᨠ

Violet J. Harris
University of Illinois
at
Urbana–Champaign

Christopher-Gordon Publishers, Inc.
Norwood, Massachusetts

Credits

Every effort has been made to contact copyright holders for permission to reproduce borrowed material where necessary. We apologize for any oversights and would be happy to rectify them in future printings.

Chapter Two:
Quotes from *Sam and The Tigers* used with the permission of Dial Books for Young Readers, a division of Penguin USA.

Chapter Seven:
Shadow & Substance, Copyright 1982 by the National Council of Teachers of English. Reprinted with permission.

Quotes from **"Allison's Adventure: Tosa Girl finds Famous Pen Pal."** Reprinted with permission of the Milwaukee Journal Sentinel.

Chapter Nine:
"Who Has Set This Table" Copyright © 1993 by Joyce Carol Thomas

Christopher-Gordon Publishers, Inc.
480 Washington Street
Norwood, MA 02062
1-800-934-8322

Printed in the United States of America

10 9 8 7 6 5 4   02 01

ISBN: 0-926842-60-9

Using Multiethnic Literature
in the K–8 Classroom

 જી જી જી જી જી

Contents

Preface

ಬಿ ಬಿ ಬಿ ಬಿ ಬಿ

This volume exists for several reasons. First, many people have told the chapters authors in one fashion or another that they lack information about the literature. They want titles, names of authors and illustrators, sources for ordering the books, and ideas for using the literature in school or a home. Others requested an updated version of an earlier volume, *Teaching Multicultural Literature in Grades K–8*.

Second, the literature's status is improving and becoming institutionalized through regular reviews in journals such as *Horn Book Magazine,* inclusion in textbooks, and growing, albeit segmented, availability in chain bookstores. Such institutionalization warrants critical analysis of the literature as creative artifacts and its appropriation by individuals who support competing pedagogies and ideologies.

Third, while the book's authors share many ideas in common, they also differ. The authors display, in the postmodern jargon of the day, "multivocality." However, some consistent elements are found in the chapters that examine the literature of a specific group: brief historical overview, current status, contemporary trends, analysis of problematic texts, exemplary texts, treatment of multicultural issues such as the elderly, and teaching strategies.

Fourth, questions about authorship, authenticity, insider/outsider perspectives, and political correctness continue to confound. I am especially vexed by a variation on these issues which I label "nostalgic literary racism or blindness." Racism is not a term I use frequently or in a cavalier manner. So, it is with considerable concern that I label pleas for the republication of books such as *Epaminondas* as examples of this racism or blindness. Or, at the very least, the calls for resurrecting dead, stereotypical texts, reveals an unwillingness to view books of this ilk within the racially charged and oppressive social, political, and cultural milieus which nurtured them. Labeling the books "classics" or excellent examples of humor and adaptations of folkloric motifs does not erase the considerable hurt they cause or diminish their roles as reinforcers, intentionally or unintentionally, of systematic oppression.

Most importantly, some wonderful literary voices continue to be heard and others have emerged: Virginia Hamilton, Rita Williams-Garcia, Walter Dean Myers, Laurence Yep, Marie Lee, Nicholasa Mohr, Gary Soto, Michael Dorris, and Gayle Ross, among many. Similarly, the artistic work of Tom Feelings, Allen Say, Jerry Pinkney, and Ed Young continue to forge a path for emerging artists such as Dave Diaz, David Soman, Brian Pinkney, Pat Cummings, and Meloyde Rosales. This volume attempts to encourage those involved with children to read and share the literature so that girls and boys, as well as women and men, might experience the joys, pains, passion, tears, and laughter in the fictive and non-fictive worlds created by the authors, poets, and illustrators.

Two issues in the book need to be addressed: definitions of critical terms and the role of Whites. Terms such as race, ethnicity, multicultural, multiethnic, culture, and cultural diversity are defined in the same manner by some authors and in different ways by others. I chose not to impose shared conceptions or definitions for these terms because that would result in unwanted conformity and limitations on the visions and ideas of the authors. No consensus exists about the definition(s) of multicultural or multiethnic. Only three markers of identity—race, gender, and class—are routinely included under its umbrella. I decided to focus on the salient marker of racial or ethnic identity, fully aware of its limitations and the criticisms about the concepts. Other elements of identity, for instance, gender, class, language, gays and lesbians, disability, age, and so on are examined through the prisms of race and ethnicity.

Where does this leave Whites (or Caucasians, European Americans, Anglos) and are they excluded? Whites are not a central focus because a genuine need exists for on-going and extensive analysis of the role of race and ethnicity in children's literature.

Whites are, however, encouraged to read and debate the ideas included here. Most importantly, they are urged to read, share, and evaluate the literature discussed within these pages.

I wish to acknowledge and thank all those individuals who contributed to this volume.

VJH
December 1996

Foreword

Carl A. Grant

ಬಿ ಬಿ ಬಿ ಬಿ ಬಿ

> We write, because we believe that the human spirit cannot be
> tamed and should not be trained. (Niki Giovanni, 1988, p. 67)

I was an admirer of Violet Harris's scholarship in literature long before I
had the opportunity and pleasure to meet and work with her. I was particularly impressed with her analysis, critique, and suggestions for teaching
multicultural literature. I also had great appreciation and respect for her
insights about the history of African American literature and its importance to students of color, especially African American children.

The challenging task of providing teachers and teacher educators with
the very best ideas and materials so that they can educate students to live
in a culturally diverse society and be good citizens in our global village is
being significantly aided with the publication of *Using Multiethnic Literature in the K–8 Classroom*. This powerful book is a *must* read for teachers
and teacher educators interested in the history, purpose, and influence of
literature on people in general and on students in particular. Also, the book
complements, supports, and adds to the excellent collection of work produced by the contributors in Harris's earlier publication, *Teaching
Multicultural Literature in Grades K–8* (1992).

In *Using Multiethnic Literature in the K–8 Classroom*, educators concerned or reluctant about the purpose and role of multicultural literature
in the classroom will find excellent reasons to begin a re-education that can
lead them from a monocultural perspective on literature to a multicultural
perspective. The organizational structure of the book enhances the understanding of multicultural and multiethnic literature: five of the ten chapters provide general insights and observations about multicultural literature, with discussions of race, class, gender, power, and otherness, and the
dynamics of interactions between the forces that shape personhood; and
the other five chapters focus directly on literature from the perspective of a
particular ethnic group (that is, African Americans, Puerto Ricans, Asian
Pacific Americans, Mexican Americans, and Native Americans).

Harris (1996) distinguishes between "multicultural" and "multiethnic"
literature as follows:

> Race and ethnicity are not synonymous. However, the historic
> development of academic studies that focused on race issues
> resulted in their being tagged with the label "ethnic." The
> conflating of race and ethnicity is evident also in the terms
> multiethnic and multicultural. Here multiethnic refers to
> groups such as those of African, Asian/Pacific Islander,
> Latino/a, or Native American ancestry. In contrast,
> multicultural can include race, ethnicity, gender, class, and
> other elements that denote difference. (p. 109)

Harris's distinction between multicultural and multiethnic is useful because it points out why there is a need for literature that offers discussions on race, gender, and class; illuminates the problems caused by racism, sexism, and/or classism (for example, James Baldwin's *The Fire Next Time*); and argues for literature that accurately informs and celebrates the history and circumstances of various ethnic groups.

Harris has gathered an outstanding group of scholars and practitioners to discuss multicultural and multiethnic literature and propose how to successfully implement this literature in the classroom. The chapter authors offer teachers and teacher educators rich ideas about the importance and practical inclusion of multicultural and multiethnic literature in their teaching. The chapter authors also challenge ethnocentric arguments about discussions of race, class, and gender in literature; they illuminate the history and driving forces behind the publication of literature for children; they give an insider's view on how different ethnic groups view the past and current status of children's literature; and they explain what it means to develop and read multiculturally. Harris's book makes a significant contribution to the educational community for another reason: it reconfigures the debate about teaching multicultural/multiethnic literature from discussions of inclusion and/or omission of some literature to a paradigm shift in the studying and teaching of literature.

Literature is one of the foundational subject areas of multicultural education. For more than twenty-five years, key questions, sources of evidence and support for challenges to multicultural education have been located in discussions of literatures—for example, What should students read in school? What should be done about non-traditional literature (e.g., writings by and about people of color, females, people with disabilities, and those living at or below the poverty line)? Should (or how should) some "classics" that became controversial during the Civil Rights era (e.g., *The Adventures of Tom Sawyer* and *The Adventures of Huckleberry Finn*) be used? While the discussions are important to becoming multiculturally and multiethnically literate, they only touch the surface of exploring multicultural and multiethnic literature for the classroom because the arguments center around inclusion or exclusion of certain works and writings within a single tradition (specifically, the Western tradition). Harris and her chapter authors have moved the literacy debate to discussions of multiple perspectives and voices in literary creation, study, and teaching. They make visible and vital the observations of Gates (1992) of "the Other" and argue that there should be no "Other." Instead, the literature from all groups must be in the mainstream of literary creation and study. In addressing "the Other," Gates states:

> The question of place of the texts written by "the Other" (be that odd metaphor defined as African, Arabic, Chinese, Latin American, female, or Yiddish authors) in the proper study of "literature," "Western literature," or "comparative literature" has, until recently, remained an unasked question, suspended or silenced by a discourse in which the "canonical" and the Noncanonical stand as the ultimate opposition. "Race," in much of the thinking about the proper study of literature in this century, has been an invisible quality, present implicitly at best. (p. 45)

Similarly, the chapter authors explain how literature effects and affects what Egan-Robertson has termed the "personhood" of students. Egan-Robertson states:

> In school, young people form feelings, beliefs, roles, and relationships, in part, through the way written materials are used to organize activity in the classroom. Hence literacy practices and especially literacy instruction affect adolescents' sense of personhood. The established purpose for using literacy, the chosen texts, the content encoded in written texts, and the interpretations built on them all shape adolescents' sense of personhood including both affiliation and alienation. (In review, p. 3)

Egan-Robertson's observations on the importance of literacy practices influencing personhood makes a significant contribution to the study of literacy. One literacy practice that may contribute to the positive development of personhood is reading and discussing literature that represents the diversity of our society. Egan-Robertson's position, therefore, supports and complements Harris's ideas on the importance of an instructional program that includes the reading of multicultural and multiethnic literature.

As a teacher in Chicago and professor at the University of Wisconsin-Madison, multicultural and multiethnic literature has played and continues to play a very prominent role in helping me to teach. In Chicago, where I taught in all African American classes, literature by people of color and women and literature that explained the nature and function of racism, classism, and sexism excited the students and inspired them in their pursuit of knowledge. At the University Wisconsin-Madison, where I teach predominantly all-White classes, multicultural literature plays a significant role in helping students not only to understand abstractly but also to put into "context" how issues of race, class, gender, power, and privilege influence students' education. The multiethnic literature that I use has played a significant role in helping me introduce to the students a "new" and important body of literature that they had been previously denied.

A few days before I started to write this foreword, I happened upon James Baldwin's autobiography on PBS. Baldwin is one of my favorite authors and I often use his essay *A Talk to Teachers* in my "Introduction to Education" class. Also, I had the privilege of corresponding with him about this essay while he was living in France. What is particularly meaningful to our discussion here is his deliberation about the political and social nature of his work, that is, how he believes that the writings and literature of African Americans and people of color are politically and socially motivated by their life experiences and their personhood. During the broadcast, Baldwin also points out that his political and social motivation is not born out of a desire to mystify but to de-mystify and explain how race, class, and gender are such powerful determinants of life events and opportunities. In *Notes of a Native Son*, Baldwin (1955) states:

> I have not written about being a Negro at such length because I expected that to be my only subject, but only because it was the gate I had to unlock before I could hope to write about anything else. (p. 8)

Baldwin's comment parallels Egan-Robertson's argument concerning the development of personhood, because he could not write about anything else until he wrote about who he was. As I learn about the life and work of Violet Harris, I recognize that her writing and work is also politically and socially motivated. The Afro-American literature she spent her allowance on as a young girl, and the family members and teachers who introduced her to literature have greatly shaped the nature of her work, leading her to argue in this book that

> I became convinced that the literacy achievement of African-American children would improve if they could see themselves and their experiences, history, and culture reflected in the books they read. I still hold firmly to that belief. I want children to discover African-American literature and the literature of other people of color in a more systematic fashion. I want it to become an integral component of schooling. (p. xvi)

Coupled with Baldwin's experience showing the role writing plays in the development of personhood, Harris's argument for literature becoming an integral aspect of learning should help readers to understand that multiethnic literature plays a role not only in literacy development but also in the development of their total being. Teachers and teacher educators can gain from Baldwin and Harris's belief that all students need to participate in literary practices (e.g., reading about their history and culture and the history and culture of other racial/ethnic, gender, and social class groups). With the publication of *Using Multiethnic Literature in the K–8 Classroom*, Harris and her chapter authors provide teachers and teacher educators with the tools to make multicultural and multiethnic literature important and meaningful in every school and classroom in the United States.

REFERENCES

Baldwin, J. (1955). *Notes of a native son.* Boston: Beacon.

Baldwin, J. (1963). *The fire next time.* London: M. Joseph.

Baldwin, J. (1988). *A talk to teachers.* In Rich Simonson and Scott Walker (Eds.), *Multicultural literacy.* Saint Paul: Graywolf Press.

Egan-Robertson, A. (in review). Exploring personhood: Constructing intertextual links between academic and community literacy practices. *Journal of Literacy Research.*

Gates, Jr., H. L. (1992). *Loose cannons: Notes on the culture wars.* New York: Oxford.

Giovanni, N. (1988). *Sacred cows . . . And other edibles.* New York: Morrow.

Harris, V. J. (Ed.). (1992). *Teaching multicultural literature in grades K–8.* Norwood, MA: Christopher-Gordon.

Harris, V. J. (1996, Spring). Continuing dilemmas, debates, and delights in multicultural literature. *The New Advocate,* 9 (2), 107–122.

Twain, M. (1920). *The adventures of Tom Sawyer.* New York: Bantam Books.

Twain, M. (1923). *The adventures of Huckleberry Finn (Tom Sawyer's comrade).* New York: Harper.

Chapter 1 ——————————————————

Selecting Literature for a Multicultural Curriculum

Rudine Sims Bishop

ဆ ဆ ဆ ဆ ဆ

PART I.   A DEFINITION AND A RATIONALE

The teacher seeking to incorporate multicultural literature into the class-room and the curriculum faces a number of issues that need to be clarified, not the least of which is what is meant by the term "multicultural litera-ture." How one defines the concept determines, in part, what kind of books one chooses and how one uses those books in a classroom setting. The first part of this chapter attempts to clarify the concept, to affirm the impor-tance of multicultural literature, and to suggest some of the functions it might serve in a classroom. The second part of the chapter suggests some ways multicultural literature can be evaluated for classroom use.

What Is Multicultural Literature?

The concept of multicultural literature is related to the concept of multicultural education, a label that names a variety of different educa-tional practices and strategies. Although many American ethnic groups can likely trace their struggle for educational equity back many decades, James Banks (1993), one of the educational experts most closely associated with multicultural education, traces its roots to the African American Civil Rights Movement of the 1950s and 1960s. Among the demands of African Ameri-cans was the elimination of discrimination in education, to be achieved, in part through reforming school curricula so that it includes and reflects the history, culture, and perspectives of African Americans. The desired effect was to increase educational achievement of students who seemed too often marked for school failure, and ultimately to fulfill the promise of a truly democratic egalitarian society by making possible full meaningful partici-pation of all its citizens, without regard to race. By the late 1980s, accord-ing to Banks, this call for societal and curricular reform had been joined by a number of diverse groups, including Latinos, American Indians, Asian

Americans, women, the disabled, gays and lesbians, and the elderly, all of whom felt victimized, oppressed, or discriminated against in some way by the dominant majority. The aspect of this push for equal rights that relates to schools and schooling, known currently as the multicultural education movement, has come to be one of the most widely discussed current issues in our society.

Sonia Nieto (1992), in her book *Affirming Diversity*, places multicultural education in a sociopolitical context. Her comprehensive definition of multicultural education provides an appropriate context for defining multicultural literature and a useful framework for discussing the issues raised in the first part of this chapter.

> Multicultural education is a process of comprehensive school reform and basic education *for all students*. It challenges and rejects racism and other forms of discrimination in schools and society and accepts and *affirms the pluralism* (ethnic, racial, linguistic, religious, economic, and gender, among others) that students, their communities, and teachers represent. Multicultural education *permeates the curriculum* and instructional strategies used in schools, as well as the interactions among teachers, students and parents, and the very way that schools conceptualize the nature of teaching and learning. Because it uses critical pedagogy as its underlying philosophy and *focuses on knowledge, reflection, and action (praxis)* as the basis for social change, multicultural education furthers the democratic principles of social justice. (p. 208, emphasis added)

In its affirmation of pluralism, Nieto's interpretation of multiculturalism would appear to lead to a definition of multicultural children's literature as that which represents all the diversity to be found in this society. No literature, then, would be excluded from the body of multicultural literature. Ideally that should be the case; but, in actual practice, only a subset of children's literature is labeled "multicultural" by most experts who speak and write about the topic. Although the composition of that subset varies from individual to individual, in common practice the label "multicultural children's literature," like multicultural education, is rooted in the call for inclusion and curricular reform by groups who have traditionally been marginalized in this society, and generally is used to refer to literature by or about people from such groups. Virtually all published definitions of multicultural children's literature, therefore, include literature about African Americans, Asian Americans, American Indians, and Latinos. Most include a variety of other groups as well—women, religious groups, regional groups, gays and lesbians, the disabled. In an effort to connect with various ethnicities, many tacit or explicit definitions of multicultural children's literature include literature that originated in or is set in places outside the United States, generally those places from which people emigrated or were brought involuntarily to this country, such as Eastern Europe, China, or

Africa. Others, in an effort to place multiculturalism in a global context, include literatures that emanate from or pertain to anywhere outside the United States.

The label, then, is inadequate as a descriptor. Identifying multicultural literature as literature of or about "The Other"—people other than white middle-class citizens of the United States—helps to reinforce and maintain old social patterns by setting up the American white middle class as the norm, and all others as "multicultural," an obvious misuse of the term. On the positive side, it focuses attention on those groups whose histories and cultures have been omitted, distorted, or undervalued in society and in school curricula. In the absence of a more accurate, widely accepted term, each "expert" creates her own definition of multicultural literature. I believe that multicultural literature should be defined in a comprehensive and inclusive manner; that is, it should include books that reflect the racial, ethnic, and social diversity that is characteristic of our pluralistic society and of the world. In my own work, however, and in this chapter, I choose to focus on literature by or related to people of color. This is because I believe that race—or color—is one of the most—if not *the* most—divisive issues in this society, and that, until recently, the absence of such literature has constituted one of the most glaring omissions in the canon of children's literature. The prophetic turn-of-the-century dictum of the African American intellectual leader W. E. B. Du Bois (1903) still resonates: "The problem of the twentieth century is the problem of the color-line—the relation of the darker to the lighter races of men in Asia and Africa, in America and the islands of the sea" (p. 54). Nearly a hundred years later, the problem remains a serious one. Multicultural children's literature in and of itself will not make that problem go away, but it is the hope of educators who espouse multiculturalism that it may contribute in a small way to alleviating its effects.

Why Is It Important to Include Multicultural Literature in the Classroom and Curriculum?

As Nieto's definition notes, multicultural education is *for all students*. So is multicultural literature. Underlying this assertion is the idea that, if our society is to meet the challenges of democratic pluralism, all students need to recognize the diversity that defines this society, learn to respect it, and see it in a positive light. In schools that appear to be increasingly segregated along lines of color and class, literature, television, and other media may present some of the few opportunities for *all* students to encounter people of different racial, ethnic, and socio-economic groups. Literature, then, becomes one of the ways in which schools can affirm pluralism, one of the tenets of Nieto's definition of multiculturalism.

Moreover, when students are exposed exclusively to literature in which they see reflections of themselves and their own lives, they are miseducated to view themselves and their lives as "normal," to interpret their own cultural attitudes and values as "human nature," and to view other people and other lives as exotic at best, and deviant at worst. Students who retain such a perspective, because they have learned to take their privilege as a given and have not been taught to question the status quo, are likely to perpetuate the discrimination and oppression that multicultural education is supposed to help eliminate.

On the other hand, students who do not see any reflections of themselves or who see only distorted or comical ones come to understand that they have little value in society in general and in school in particular. Self-esteem develops from a number of sources, not the least of which is the social context in which children grow up, including the context beyond family and community. As a part of the social and scholastic context, literature can contribute to the development of self-esteem by holding up to its readers images of themselves. When children are invisible in the literature sanctioned by the schools, or when the images they see are distorted or laughable or inaccurate, the effect on their self-esteem is likely to be negative. Thus, it is possible for literature to contribute to children's understandings of how they are viewed and valued by the school and the society of which schools are reflections. Ultimately, to the extent that school achievement is tied to a sense of self-worth, multicultural literature can have a beneficial effect on the school achievement of children who have historically been denied realistic images of themselves and their families, community, and culture.

What Do We Want to Accomplish with Multicultural Literature in the Elementary Classroom?

An important factor in determining what literature to select and how to assess that literature is the function(s) one expects the literature to fulfill. For example, a teacher who views literature about people of color as a vehicle for sensitizing other children to the inequities in our society may be led to choose different books and employ different teaching strategies than the teacher who wants merely to "expose" children to literature about people different from themselves. The former may seek out books like Mildred Taylor's *The Gold Cadillac* (1987); the latter may choose any book that features someone who appears, in that teacher's view, to be different. A different teacher, with yet another goal in mind, may search for books in which children of color can see positive reflections of themselves. Keeping in mind—to reiterate Nieto—that multicultural literature is for *all* students, and that it needs to *permeate* the curriculum, literature about people of color can serve at least five broad functions: (1) it can provide knowledge or information, (2) it can change the way students look at their world by offering varying perspectives, (3) it can promote or develop an appreciation for diversity, (4) it can give rise to critical inquiry, and (5) like all literature, it can provide enjoyment and illuminate human experience, in both its unity and its variety.

Nieto's definition asserts that knowledge is one of the bases for social change, which is the ultimate goal of multicultural education. Multicultural literature can contribute to that knowledge. Indeed, part of the motivation behind the current emphasis on multicultural literature is the perceived need to counteract a tradition of distortions, inaccuracies, and omissions of the histories, heroes, literatures, and cultural traditions of people of color. Many new or recent nonfiction books—history, biography, photo-essays—help to fulfill that need. For example, in *Undying Glory* (1991), Clinton Cox tells the story of the Massachusetts 54th Regiment, an African American military unit that fought in the Civil War. Many students—and teachers—are unaware that such a unit existed.

Fiction can provide another kind of knowledge—insights into some aspects of the culture—values, attitudes, customs, the ways of living, believing, and behaving; the design for living—of a social group. A book of fiction should not be treated as a factual instructional text, and no one such book can be expected to accurately portray or represent an entire group of people. Recurring themes, topics, and motifs in a group's literature, however, can offer insights into aspects of the culture that seem to have a particular significance to members of the group. Recent picture books by both African American and Latino writers, for example, frequently feature relationships between young children and older members of their extended family [e.g., *Aunt Flossie's Hats* (Howard, 1991), *Abuela* (Dorros, 1991), *Uncle Jed's Barbershop* (Mitchell, 1993), *A Birthday Basket for Tía* (Mora, 1992)], suggesting that maintaining ties with the extended family is important in those cultures, and that older people are respected, valued, and honored as wise mentors and companions for the young and the passers-on of stories and traditions.

Secondly, literature by and about people of color can offer varying perspectives, different ways of viewing the same or similar phenomena. Traditionally, for example, the history of the United States is told from the perspective of the Europeans who began arriving in the late 15th century. Seldom is that history seen from the perspective of the people who were occupying the land at the time. Virginia Driving Hawk Sneve has written *The Navajos* (1993) and *The Sioux* (1993) for inclusion in a series called First Americans Books. They provide introductory overviews of those groups, their past and present ways of life, and how they were affected by their encounters with Europeans. For another example, Laurence Yep's fictional treatment of the building of the transcontinental railroad, *Dragon's Gate* (Harper, 1993), offers a rare portrait of that event from the perspective of the Chinese workers whose labor under adverse conditions was sorely needed and little appreciated.

Multicultural literature can also engender an appreciation for the diversity that occurs both within and across social groups. Simply including, as a matter of course, multicultural literature in the classroom library implicitly makes a statement about the normality of diversity. That alone, however, does not constitute a multicultural literature program. Actively incorporating such literature into the curriculum—all year, throughout the curriculum—can help students come to respect and value diversity as natural and enriching.

Diverse literature, written from a number of perspectives, also offers opportunities to examine critically the values, attitudes, and points of view it appears to convey or promote. Some questions may derive from specific books: Why would Holiday House and Virginia Driving Hawk Sneve call their series "First Americans?" What does that mean in relation to the Mayflower and Jamestown? Is Mildred Taylor's *The Gold Cadillac* relevant to today's world or is it simply of historical interest? Others may be more general, and come from wide experience with books. What function do stereotypes serve? For whom? Is an author trying through a book to persuade readers to adopt a particular attitude? To what end? What literary devices does she employ? Whose voices are being heard in the literature in the classroom? Which voices are missing? Why might that be so? Questions like these may be raised by teachers as they consider how multicultural literature can be the starting point for reflections on what it means to live in a democratic society. The same issues can be discussed at varying levels with students as they are given ample opportunities to read and respond to multicultural literature.

Finally, it is well to remember that reading literature, especially fiction, no matter what culture it reflects, ought to be an aesthetic experience. In our search for social significance and our desire for social change, we dare not forget that a well-written piece of literature is a work of art. It may be serious and cause readers to reflect or to become angry or to see something familiar in a new way; it may be informative and diminish ignorance; but it does so through readers' engagement with the literary work. In classrooms where multicultural literature is to have an effect, that experience is primary. Other goals can be achieved when readers are given the time and the opportunity, with a knowledgeable teacher as facilitator, to make thoughtful responses to their reading and to enrich their own readings by interacting with others whose responses may or may not be similar.

PART II.   SELECTING AND EVALUATING MULTI-CULTURAL LITERATURE: ISSUES AND CONCERNS

When it comes to actually selecting multicultural literature for a classroom—particularly literature by and about people of color—some problems and limitations become immediately apparent. For one thing, even though the numbers of such books have increased significantly in the past few years, the proportion of such books remains quite small. For another, the output is not balanced across genres and topics. A large portion of what passes for multicultural literature is folktales from within and without the United States, related to people of color—that is, folktales from American Indians and from Africa, Asia, and Latin America. Few fictional books portray contemporary lives of Latinos, American Indians, or Asian Americans. Very little poetry from those groups is available, and biographies are limited as well. Nevertheless, recent increases in the numbers of books published annually have made available a quantity of books about people of color and other under-represented groups sufficient for teachers to begin to make multicultural libraries a reality for all classrooms.

Even so, thoughtful selection of books for classroom use can be complicated. Given the sociopolitical underpinnings of multicultural education, it is not surprising that controversies arise over the ways people who have historically been overlooked or denigrated are portrayed in books charged with helping to create social change. Such controversies often swirl around issues such as visual and verbal stereotyping, authenticity and authority, perspective and world view, and underlying ideology. Selection is further complicated by the lack of clarity about what is meant by multicultural literature, who its primary intended audience is, and the ostensible underlying purposes which the books may have been written to serve.

A discussion of four picture books featuring young Black girls—*Secret Valentine* (Stock, 1991), *Amazing Grace* (Hoffman, 1991), *The Best Bug to Be* (Johnson, 1992), and *Tar Beach* (Ringgold, 1991)—can focus attention on some of the literary and extra-literary concerns that often become a part of discussions of literature by and about people of color, and that come into consideration as part of the selection process.

Secret Valentine is a slight book, aimed at pre-school children, part of author/artist Catherine Stock's collection of holiday stories. Told in the first person present tense, it describes the Valentine's Day preparations of an unnamed Black girl who, with the help of her mother, makes cards for the members of her family and for a lonely older woman who is her next-door neighbor. On Valentine's Day she receives cards from everyone in her family, plus one that smells of lavender and is signed "From Your Secret Valentine."

For the most part, this is an innocuous little book that might possibly be useful as Valentine's Day approaches. Although its prose is unremarkable, its themes—that Valentine's Day is a day to express love, that appropriate expressions of love can be created by the giver, and that reaching out to someone can be the beginning of a friendship—can engender useful discussions with young children.

Secret Valentine is representative of one type of book that is generally included under the multicultural umbrella. It falls into the category because its characters are Black, presumably North American, given the description of Valentine's Day customs. (The discussion that follows assumes that the characters are intended to be African Americans—as opposed to Africans or Black British or Europeans, for example). The specific setting, however, is unclear and not important to the story. This is a book in which the race or color of the characters is entirely a visual phenomenon. Nothing in the text would identify the characters as African American, and the author/artist could have chosen to portray them as White Americans without changing a word.

What then, was the point of making the characters Black? It is, of course, impossible to know the answer with certainty. A strong possibility is that, in presenting an apparently middle-class Black mother and child participating in a familiar American holiday experience, the author is making a case for inclusion, stressing the idea that many cultural experiences are shared across racial and social lines. A book like *Secret Valentine* can serve to integrate visually a book collection, and help White children "meet" children of color on shared cultural terrain. Many such books also are appealing to children of color because the books offer positive portraits of people who look like them, and whose experiences are similar to their own, or close enough to make the story appealing.

It is unlikely, however, that *Secret Valentine* would be appealing in that regard to African American children, and it is almost certain to provoke objections from African American adults. The difficulty is with the illustrations, and in a picture book, that is at least half the story. The little girl is shown wearing braids. While her hair is neatly parted, the braids are sticking straight up into the air, in all directions, all over her head. It is a hairstyle with a history. For many years, the dominant portrait of the Black child in American children's literature was the comic pickaninny, and part of what made him or her comical was the hair, which was usually shown braided and sticking out from the head in all directions. From the time of Topsy of *Uncle Tom's Cabin* and continuing for almost a century, this stereotyped image has been a source of laughter and embarrassment. In the 1990s, the echo of the pickaninny image is unfortunate and does not reflect current reality; a visit to any urban kindergarten would reveal numerous examples of current hairstyles being worn by little Black girls.

The portrait of this little girl is further clouded by artistic inconsistencies in the way she is depicted throughout the book. Her age seems to vary; that is, in some pictures she looks quite young, and in others, two or three years older. That general inconsistency is further complicated by what has to be an inaccuracy. By the end of the story, the little girl has changed hairstyles and is wearing two pony tails. The problem is that, given the length of those braids, her hair is not long enough to pull into pony tails, and it could not have grown so long over the course of a week. Nit-picking though that point may seem, it signals a lack of background and a kind of color-me-brown approach to producing a book with Black characters.

Such details serve to illustrate some of the points of discussion engendered by the current emphasis on multicultural literature. One is the issue of authenticity, or whether the portrayal of the characters and their cultural experiences ring true, especially to readers who have been acculturated in the group being represented. On one level, since *Secret Valentine* does not purport to highlight or illuminate any distinct African American experience, and since the little girl likely is meant to represent Everychild, or at least EveryAmericanChild, it cannot be called to account for its portrayal of an African American cultural reality. On the other hand, in opting to make the characters visually African American, the artist stepped into a sociopolitical arena in which she obligated herself to make the images as authentic as possible. This is not always easy because it may involve tacit knowledge of which the artist may be unaware. For example, an adult African American reader would question whether an African American woman— especially one young enough to be the mother of a pre-schooler—who, in the 1990s, wears her hair in the old-fashioned bun worn by the mother in this book, would be likely to have her child wearing the kind of braids pictured in this book. That bun suggests that the mother subscribes to a standard of beauty and a conservative sense of style that would reject those braids as unattractive at best, a point that may not be apparent to someone unfamiliar with some aspects of African American life and culture. It takes more than brown paint to portray a realistic African American character.

In terms of the functions multicultural literature may be expected to serve, *Secret Valentine* becomes a questionable choice. No matter how innocent the story, and how well-meaning the author, it cannot be divorced from the sociocultural and political environment out of which it grew and the one into which it is released. While it may well serve the purpose of calling attention to Valentine's Day and its social opportunities, it does so at the expense of possibly helping to perpetuate a long-standing stereotype. Its potential for visually integrating a book collection is thus overshadowed by its failure to help change the way its readers see the world.

Amazing Grace is aimed at a somewhat older age group than *Secret Valentine*. Grace loves stories and loves to act them out, always giving herself the best part. When her teacher announces that the class play will be *Peter Pan*, Grace wants to play the role of Peter. When her classmates tell her she can't be Peter because she is a girl and because she is Black, Grace is upset. Her grandmother, however, helps her discover that she can do anything if she puts her mind to it. Predictably, Grace wins the role and is "amazing" as Peter Pan.

Although the Library of Congress cataloging information classifies *Amazing Grace* under "Afro-American," there is reason to believe that it might have been set in England, and that its characters are, therefore, Black British. It was originally published in Great Britain, and both the author and illustrator live in London. For the most part, however, the setting is generally urban and otherwise non-specific. For this story, the specific setting does not matter, although in a different story it might. As with any large group of people, there is great diversity among people of African descent, particularly those living in different places with different climates and different social and political systems, such as the United States, the Caribbean, and Great Britain. Some books set in different locales would need to accurately reflect the social and cultural realities of people living in those settings.

The illustrations in *Amazing Grace* are much more successful than *Secret Valentine* in making the characters seem realistic and contemporary. Like the little girl in *Secret Valentine*, Grace wears braids, but usually just two, neatly arranged, and often with ribbons to match her outfit. Her mother and grandmother both wear their hair natural and unstraightened, in what is called by some an Afro hairstyle. The portrayals are consistent throughout the book. Each major character is presented as a unique individual. Part of the difference between the portraits in *Amazing Grace* and *Secret Valentine* can be attributed to differing artistic styles, but in any case, *Grace* gives the impression that its characters are real people.

On the other hand, *Grace* has been criticized, not for its portrayal of Black people, but for the portrait of Grace playing Hiawatha. Grace is shown bare-chested, wearing face paint, a feathered headband and two long braids, seated on a colorful rug with her legs and her arms crossed. It is a familiar Indian stereotype, and an example of the way stereotypes work as easy shorthand. One could discuss whether the picture is a statement about the artist's concept of "American Indian" or the artist's concept of how a little (British?) girl of Grace's age would convey that she was role-playing a mythical American Indian character (and what difference it makes). At the very least the picture lends itself to a critical discussion of stereotyping and its consequences.

In terms of multicultural literature, *Grace* is an exemplar of a second type of book that falls under the umbrella; it is a book with a clear social agenda. It intends to affect attitudes. Unlike the girl in *Secret Valentine*, Grace is not Everychild; her race and gender are both important to the story, as are her personal characteristics. The multi-racial (or multi-colored, if you will) classroom is important as well. The message is this: you can be or do anything you want if you put your mind to it. Nana states it at least twice, and Grace repeats it to herself at least once. The message seems aimed primarily at Grace and children like her, but it is also aimed at children who believe, as do Natalie and Raj, that race and gender are limitations.

Two questions can be raised about a book that is so heavily didactic. One is the extent to which the message is true or believable. One implication of the message in *Grace* is that gender and race are not factors in determining achievement; it is simply a matter of "putting your mind to it" and working at it. In that world view, achievement is a matter of individual effort. This is an encouraging message to offer primary grade children, and to the extent that it proposes that one should not allow oneself to be defeated or limited by racism and sexism, a positive one. But there is another relevant truth. In the real world, race and gender *do* matter. Sometimes the limitations other people and institutions impose on women and people of color (doubly on women of color) cannot be overcome by hard work alone. In selecting books for a curriculum designed to foster social change, it might be well to consider *Grace* as a launching pad for a critical examination of its underlying messages, if not by young primary grade children, then by teachers and librarians. It is interesting to note, for example, that Grace's mother reacts with anger, but Nana prevents her from transmitting that anger to Grace, leaving the reader with the impression that anger is an inappropriate response. An interesting exercise for teachers might be to examine the books and stories that Grace knew and acted out: *Hiawatha*, *Joan of Arc*, *The Jungle Book*, Anansi, the story of the Trojan horse, and various adventure stories and fairy tales. How typical is that fare for American primary grade children? (The publisher designates the book as appropriate for children from 4 to 8). Does the list reflect a canon? An American or British one? Is it "classical?" Is it multicultural?

A second question raised by the overtly didactic nature of *Amazing Grace* is the extent to which the message may overwhelm the art. Taken to an extreme, a book heavy with a message could become a tract. Although it leans slightly in that direction, *Grace* does not, in my opinion, fall into that trap. Its language is lively, its major character is well-defined within the parameters of a picture book, its artwork is aesthetically appealing, and the art complements and extends the text. In addition to the strong message about self-empowerment, *Grace* celebrates story and imagination. The ending is satisfying, if predictable.

In *Secret Valentine*, race is made irrelevant, a matter of coloring. In *Amazing Grace*, it is an important element in the story. But beyond questions about credible visual representation and whether race plays a role in the plot is the question of whether or not the portrayal of the character and her family rings true in terms of their membership in a particular group with shared values, attitudes, behaviors, beliefs, and other aspects of a culture. Because Grace is portrayed as a unique individual, and because the story in part involves her family life, *Amazing Grace* can be examined in terms of the credibility of its representation. Grace lives with her mother and her grandmother, who hails from Trinidad. Theirs appears to be an all-female household, a not uncommon situation in today's world. Nana's speech accurately reflects some features of Black English vernacular, as in ". . . another one who *don't know nothing*," and "She's always *asking me do I want* tickets . . ." and "If *Grace put* her mind to it, she can do anything *she want*" (emphasis added). The relationship between Grace and her grandmother seems close, echoing a theme—and a value—often found in African American children's literature. With the exception of Anansi, Grace's role-playing derives from non-Black literary traditions, but the focus on story is plausible. To the extent that her family life is depicted, it seems both believable and realistic.

Amazing Grace, then, can contribute positively to a multicultural curriculum. Indirectly, the depiction of racial diversity in Grace's classroom and community suggests that such diversity is normal and natural. The strong message about empowering oneself is worth discussing, and may increase some students' awareness of the possible effects of discrimination based on race or gender. The book also offers opportunities for critical inquiry into the truth of its message. In spite of the somewhat heavy-handed way it makes its point, *Grace* offers an engaging story about a likable and believable contemporary young Black girl.

The Hiawatha picture, however, is problematic. If the book is to be used, that portrait needs to be confronted. At best it offers a chance to discuss the practice of stereotyping and its possible effects; at worst, it can serve to reinforce some of the very ideas multicultural literature is meant to change.

The Best Bug to Be presents another aspiring actress and another multiracial classroom. Kelly tries out for the school play, and like Grace, she wants to be the star. She is assigned, however, to be a bumblebee, a part that seems particularly lowly when her friends brag about their ostensibly more exciting roles. Kelly takes her parents' advice to work at being the best bumblebee she can, and in the end she steals the show and becomes the envy of her friends.

This lively story is sparked by humor, both situational and linguistic. It is likely to appeal to primary age children, who will find the situation believable, and the resolution both funny and satisfying. The watercolor paintings capture the action and emotions of the story. As a read-aloud book, it could offer an enjoyable experience.

On one level, *Best Bug* resembles *Secret Valentine* in that no mention of race or color is present in the written text. A common misconception among a number of adult readers has been that, unless a book of contemporary fiction portrays Black people as urban and poor, or unless racism or discrimination is central to the plot, or the characters speak in Black dialect, that work does not qualify as African American children's literature, but should be considered "universal." (Even the Library of Congress Cataloging-in-Publication Data on the verso of the title page does not list "Afro-

Americans" as a subject category for *Best Bug*, as it does for *Amazing Grace*). The same misconception holds regarding books about other people of color. Such readers fail to understand the great diversity to be found within any group, and that many middle-class African Americans and other American people of color are generally bicultural, leading lives that in many respects are indistinguishable from those of other Americans, but at the same time maintaining distinctive ethnic cultural patterns.

In the case of *The Best Bug to Be*, Kelly is not an Everychild, and race is a given, not an issue. The pertinent question here is the extent to which the portrayal of this African American girl and her family carries the ring of truth. In that regard, it may be useful to examine *Best Bug* in terms of its underlying themes and values and attitudes. Kelly's family includes a father who is present in the home and actively involved in his child's care, reflecting the high value traditionally placed on family and relationships in the African American community and in African American children's literature. When Kelly announces to her parents that she has been given the disappointing role of a bumblebee, their advice to her—and the theme of the book—is to take the role she has been given and transcend it. ("Whatever you're asked to do, sweetheart, you should do your absolute best". . . "You've got so much talent, and you're so smart, you can make your bumblebee the best role on the stage.") It is advice that echoes historical and current reality for many African Americans and others as well. In terms of film, for instance, many Black actors and actresses historically were limited to roles such as maids, mammies, and comic sidekicks. Donald Bogle, in his seminal work, *Toms, Coons, Mulattoes, Mammies & Bucks* (1992) asserts that what many such actors did was to turn the "roles inside out and to come up with personal statements that moved and affected audiences in ways that they still cannot explain" (p. 302). Although the comparison between the bumblebee role and African American film history may be a bit of a stretch, the same principle has, of necessity, been applied across many aspects of African American life.

Another important literary and cultural aspect of *Best Bug* is the way the author uses language. Readers familiar with African American linguistic styles will recognize the bragging—Sharon with hand on hip (". . . I'm the Queen of the Butterflies. When I do my special dance, . . ."), Kelly's indirect request ("I really wouldn't mind it if you made me the star . . ."), the teasing that occurs between certain of the children (". . . everyone knows, ladybugs are the cute bugs")—as suggestive of African American discourse styles. African American writers often incorporate such discourse styles into their work either as dialogue or as narrative style.

As part of a multicultural literature program, *The Best Bug to Be* offers an appealing story played out on what African American playwright August Wilson (1990) called "the common cultural ground" (p. A15). At the same time, it is flavored with elements that mark it as an example of African American children's literature for young readers. Like *Amazing Grace*, it presents a racially integrated classroom (with a Latina teacher) as an unremarkable occurrence, and, like *Grace*, it presents an opportunity for a critical discussion of the truth of its message or theme. A comparison between the two in terms of their themes and the extent to which the presentations of the themes cross a line between teaching and preaching could stimulate further critical discussion.

In *Tar Beach*, Cassie Louise Lightfoot is eight years old and living in Harlem. She and her family picnic on the rooftop of their building, humorously referred to as tar beach. As the stars come out, Cassie imagines herself flying over the city, powerful and free, claiming for herself the Brooklyn Bridge and righting wrongs inflicted on her father and other men of color. Through the power of her imagination, she is free to go wherever she wants.

The written text is a spare, first person narrative of Cassie's magical escapades. The most important feature of *Tar Beach* is its artwork, which is based on a story quilt that the artist completed in 1988. The pages are bordered by reproductions from the original story quilt, the effect of which is echoed in the paintings of city buildings. The use of the quilt as an art form is a tribute to a craft that was practiced from the time of slavery by many African American women, who incorporated African designs and patterns into the quilts.

The flying motif appears frequently in African American literature. Stories of slaves flying to freedom—literally and figuratively—are part of African American folklore. Thus, *Tar Beach* fits into a continuing literary tradition. *Tar Beach* also exemplifies another practice prevalent in African American children's fiction: the incorporation of some aspect of African American history, in this case discrimination by the trade unions practiced against African Americans and Native Americans.

Tar Beach is a unique work of art, an unmistakable representation of an African American experience. In a multicultural literature program, it is the kind of book that adds a distinctive voice, a distinctive world view. It is set in an African American neighborhood and features African American characters exclusively. It incorporates motifs from African American history and literature. Although *Tar Beach* is fictional, it is also partly autobiographical, and therefore provides some historical information about racial discrimination in unions. Its depiction of an African American family rings true. It is the sort of book that is generally touted as an example of authentic African American children's literature.

CONCLUSION

The foregoing discussion of four picture books was intended to point to some of the criteria that might be considered when assessing multicultural literature for classroom use. Unfortunately, there is no quick and easy checklist that can be applied to evaluate such literature, but, in general, concerns fell into three overlapping categories: literary, sociopolitical, and educational.

The four books were examined for their literary and visual artistry, although some of that discussion was, of necessity, intertwined with other issues. For example, the question of the artwork in *Secret Valentine* is related to both aesthetic and sociocultural issues, and the discussion of the language in *Best Bug* was also both literary and cultural. The issue of didacticism in relation to *Grace* is a literary concern. Any book being considered for classroom use needs to be looked at in terms of its literary and, in the case of picture books, its visual artistry. Any standard children's literature textbook can be a resource for those who want to brush up on traditional ways of thinking about and evaluating children's literature in general. (A particularly useful one is the sixth edition of *Children's Literature in the Elementary School* by Charlotte S. Huck, Susan Hepler, Janet Hickman, and Barbara Kiefer [1997].)

The discussions of *The Best Bug* and *Tar Beach* demonstrated that certain readings or interpretations of some works require understanding of the literary and cultural traditions out of which that work arises. It is unreasonable to expect that busy teachers will become expert on the cultures and literatures of numerous diverse social groups. Nor is it necessary to attempt an in-depth reading of *every* book as an exemplar of a literary or cultural tradition. *The Best Bug to Be,* for example, can be enjoyed for its story, its theme, its humor, its character portrayal, and its art. The language can be explored for its humor and its liveliness, even without an awareness of its debt to Black discourse styles.

On the other hand, it is not unreasonable to expect that teachers committed to multicultural education will, as they incorporate diverse literature into their classrooms, make an effort to increase their knowledge about those related cultures and literary traditions with which they are unfamiliar. *Tar Beach,* for example, can be better understood if the reader has some background knowledge about the author and certain aspects of African American history and literature. That is why the publisher provides an explanatory afterword. As a practical matter, those kinds of notes, coupled with critical reviews by knowledgeable reviewers may provide enough background to enrich the reading of a particular book. Anthologies with explanatory notes can be another useful resource for teachers who want to understand something of the literary traditions of a group with whose literature they are not familiar.

Concerns about the literary traditions of particular groups are related to other types of issues. When controversies arise in relation to multicultural literature, they generally center on sociopolitical concerns. Probably the most controversial current issue swirling around literature about people of color is that of authenticity, and closely related to that, whether or not authentic literature about people of color can be created by people who are not members of the group being portrayed. I have tried to define authenticity in terms of whether or not the depiction of the characters seems accurate or rings true in relation to their physical appearance, and to their behaviors, attitudes, values, language, beliefs, their way of life—in short, their culture. Authenticity becomes an issue in relation to books about people of color because of the record of distortion and omission of the literatures and histories of disenfranchised groups in the school curriculum. The reasoning goes like this: multicultural literature is to help correct misconceptions and eliminate stereotyped thinking and if it is to help readers gain insight into and appreciation for the social groups reflected in the literature, then the literature ought to reflect accurately those groups and their cultures.

Judging authenticity is neither an exact science nor an objective exercise. Teachers can bring to the reading of a book only their own individual backgrounds and life experiences. The more effort teachers have made to learn about other people and their cultures and their literatures, therefore, the more likely they are to make reasonable assessments of individual books. If a teacher lacks background knowledge of the historical, cultural, or literary traditions of a group being depicted, one recourse is to turn to knowledgeable critics and reviewers. When examining books that ostensibly attempt to illuminate a distinct cultural experience or to relate factual information about a person, a group, or an event, another consideration is the credentials of the author. This is an accepted criterion in the case of nonfiction, but a controversial one when it comes to fiction.

The issue of authority, or whether someone who is not acculturated in a group can create authentic literature (especially fiction) about people in that group (for example, can white people write authentic literature about people of color?) is a complex one. It is partly a political question and therefore tied to issues of power, ownership and definition. Given the history of race relations in this country, people who see themselves as members of oppressed groups are not always willing to trust people whom they identify as members of the oppressing group to tell their stories, particularly in light of a history of stereotyping, distortions, and patronizing of such groups in literature for children. One question might be, for example, that if, as Camille Yarbrough (1989) declares through a character in her novel *The Shimmershine Queens*, "a people's story is the anchor that keeps them from drifting, the compass to show the way to go, and it's a sail that holds the power that takes them forward" (p. 21), then who ought to be telling a people's story? Whose story is it anyway? Put another way, if there is such an entity as African American children's literature, for instance, is it by definition created by African Americans? Johnson (1990) defines African American children's literature as "literature written by African Americans that seeks to represent, interpret, and envision the lives, real and imagined, of African American people" (p. 3). This definition, with which I concur, excludes non-African American writers from that particular canon.

That does not mean, however, that non-Black writers cannot create accurate and realistic depictions of African Americans, or more generally, of people from groups distinctly different from them culturally. Obviously there is no one-to-one relationship between ethnicity and accuracy or authenticity. It is a matter of sensibility and perspective. Problems do arise when writers do not adequately prepare themselves to bridge the cultural gaps between their own backgrounds and that of their subjects. Some authors insist that, because our human likenesses outweigh the specifics of our cultural differences, it takes only craft, imagination, and possibly knowledge of or research into factual matters to write authentic literature about any human character or life experience. Others recognize that the farther a writer's background, knowledge, and experiences are from the culture of the person or people about whom he or she is writing, the greater the necessity for the author to fill in the cultural gaps, the greater the effort needed to do so, and the greater the risk of mistakes. For example, over fifty years ago, Florence Crannell Means (1940), a white writer whose career was largely built on writing fiction about people of color, had this to say: "It is obvious, too, that the writer must herself deeply know the people she's writing about. She must go to them—when they are of her day—and be of them as well as among them" (p. 35). "To be sure, it's dangerous business to try to interpret other peoples" (p. 40).

Teachers trying to make informed selections of books about people of color will need to examine individual books for their own merits. Two of the four books examined in this chapter were created by white authors; one is largely successful, the other is not. The others represent two different African American perspectives. The important consideration for the teacher is to make certain that voices from within the parallel cultures that have historically been excluded from the curriculum and from the literary canon will not continue to be excluded in favor of work that is only visually representative of people of color, or work that seems preferable because its world view and its perspective is familiar, even if inaccurate.

Another recurring concern related to both literary and sociopolitical issues is stereotyping. In regard to stereotypes, little need be said beyond the admonition that they should be avoided. An issue often arises, however, in relation to books such as *The Story of Little Black Sambo* or *Dr. Doolittle*, which are considered to be "classics," but which contain both visual and verbal images that have long been known to be derogatory. In my view, those too, should be avoided. This is not a call for censorship, but for careful selection of books that can help fulfill the goals of a multicultural curriculum, which include the equitable treatment of so-called minorities. Books are selected and rejected daily by teachers and librarians for a variety of sound educational reasons, and elementary and middle school literature programs are generally not built on the premise that certain specific books must be read by every child. When such books show up in classrooms unbidden, however, they can offer opportunities for careful, sensitive, critical discussions of their derogatory images and the purposes they serve.

One of the ways for a teacher to alleviate some concerns about evaluating multicultural literature is to try to select a varied and balanced collection of books. Obviously, the collection should be pluralistic, including works by and about people from many diverse groups. Within the literature of any one group, the collection should strive to reflect the diversity that is a part of all groups—people of varying socio-economic circumstances, occupations, and lifestyles. Books should be sought that will offer differing perspectives on issues and events, or themes that can be compared or contrasted across a set of related books. Various genres such as poetry, folklore, historical fiction, nonfiction, biography, and realistic fiction should be represented in the collection. An effort needs to be made to include books that span the range of literary multiculturalism, from picture books that simply include people of color, to novels that illuminate a distinctive cultural or historical experience, to nonfiction that provides factual information about a people and their way of life. A diverse and balanced collection, incorporated purposefully and thoughtfully into the curriculum, makes it more likely that no one book will bear the burden of being the only experience a child has with literature about a so-called minority group, and may relieve teachers of the worry that the one book they select will be charged with representing an entire group of people to their students.

Ultimately, multicultural literature for the classroom should be evaluated on the basis of the educational purposes it is intended to serve. The discussions of the four picture books focused on such issues as the apparent intended purpose of the book; the implied audience for it; and its potential to provoke or promote critical discussion. Other considerations might include the book's usefulness as a part of a curricular focus such as a language arts program (for example, as a read-aloud choice or as a model for writing), or a thematic study, or in a particular content area. The main purpose of a literary work, however, is to encourage its readers to reflect on the human condition. The function of multicultural literature is to ensure that students have the opportunity to reflect on it in all its rich diversity, to prompt them to ask questions about who we are now as a society and how we arrived at our present state, and to inspire them to actions that will create and maintain social justice.

REFERENCES

Banks, J. A. & Banks, C. M. (1993). *Multicultural education: Issues and perspectives*. (2nd ed.). New York: Allyn and Bacon.

Bogle, D. (1992). *Toms, coons, mulattoes, mammies and bucks: An interpretive history of Blacks in American films*. (New Expanded Ed.). New York: Continuum.

Du Bois, W. E. B. (1903/1969). *The souls of Black folk*. New York: New American Library.

Huck, C. S., Hepler, S., Hickman, J., & Kiefer, B. (1997). *Children's literature in the elementary school*. (6th ed.). Madison, WI: Brown & Benchmark Publishers.

Johnson, D. (1990). *Telling tales: The pedagogy and promise of African American literature for youth*. New York: Greenwood.

Means, F. C. (1940). Mosaic. *The Horn Book, 16*, 35–40.

Nieto, S. (1992). *Affirming diversity: The sociopolitical context of multicultural education*. New York: Longman.

Wilson, August. (1990, September 26). I want a Black director. *New York Times*, p. A15.

Children's Books

Cox, Clinton. (1991). *Undying glory: The story of the Massachusetts 54th Regiment*. New York: Scholastic.

Dorros, Arthur. (1991). *Abuela*. Illus. by Elisa Kleven. New York: Dutton.

Hoffman, Mary. (1991). *Amazing Grace*. Illus. by Caroline Binch. New York: Dial.

Howard, Elizabeth Fitzgerald. (1991). *Aunt Flossie's hats (and crab cakes later)*. Illus. by James Ransome. New York: Clarion.

Johnson, Dolores. (1992). *The best bug to be*. New York: Macmillan.

Mitchell, Margaree King. (1993). *Uncle Jed's barbershop*. Illus. by James Ransome. New York: Simon and Schuster.

Mora, Pat. (1992). *A birthday basket for Tía*. New York: Macmillan.

Ringgold, Faith. (1991). *Tar beach*. New York: Crown.

Sneve, Virginia Driving Hawk. (1993). *The Navajos: A first Americans book*. Illus. by Ronald Himler. New York: Holiday House.

Sneve, Virginia Driving Hawk. (1993). *The Sioux: A first Americans book*. Illus. by Ronald Himler. New York: Holiday House.

Stock, Catherine. (1991). *Secret valentine*. New York: Bradbury.

Taylor, Mildred. (1987). *The gold Cadillac*. New York: Dial.

Yarbrough, Camille. (1989). *The shimmershine queens*. New York: Knopf, Bullseye Books.

Yep, Laurence. (1993). *Dragon's gate*. New York: Harper.

Chapter 2 _____

Children's Literature Depicting Blacks[1]

Violet J. Harris

₡ ₡ ₡ ₡ ₡

Quite literally, we are in the midst of a renaissance and an aesthetic revolution in children's literature depicting Blacks. The new enlightenment is not necessarily the result of increased numbers of books featuring Blacks. Rather, the renaissance and aesthetic revolution evolve from the increasing excellence of many works, text and art, the willingness to engage in artistic risks, less emphasis on didacticism, and a growing desire to entertain and intellectually challenge readers. Equally important, multifaceted views are apparent.

Consider the following titles which may evoke powerful responses among child and adult readers. Sometimes the titles will evoke crying, laughter, or screams. On occasion, they may cause a reader to jump for joy, rage at humans and the heavens, seek comfort in some form or fashion, or remain mute for minutes on end. Most of all, you want to read the books. Share these titles and book covers with a group of 5th or 8th graders, monitor their responses, and determine how many remain unaffected: *The Middle Passage* (Feelings, 1995), *Her Stories* (Hamilton, 1995), *Daddy, Daddy Be There* (Boyd, 1995), *Glory Field* (Myers, 1994), *From the Notebooks of Melanin Sun* (Woodson, 1995), or *Like Sisters on the Home Front* (Williams-Garcia, 1995). These titles evoked powerful responses within me. I placed orders for them with my local bookseller, knowing that some would arrive several months later. I waited with great anticipation; they were more than worth the wait.

Many readers might experience responses comparable to mine. Other readers, especially children, might not. My responses are affected by my knowledge of literature and history, age, gender, race, the setting in which the initial reading occurred, and numerous other interacting factors. A recounting of my experiences with one book may illuminate the responses of other readers.

The Middle Passage[2] (Feelings, 1995), in particular, generated a tremendous amount of fear, curiosity, and trepidation. The book depicts one of the most horrific examples of human cruelty, the African slave trade. Several times, I approached the book and could not remove the shrink wrap. Slave narratives, autobiographies, and adult novels such as *To Be A Slave* (Lester, 1968), *Our Nig* (Wilson, 1983), and *Beloved* (Morrison, 1988) provided me with unvarnished insights into slavery. Still, I was unprepared for the emotions *The Middle Passage* evoked.

Anger, hurt, pain, fear, and pride (for Feelings' achievement) were some of the emotions. I wondered how Feelings coped with similar emotions as he labored for over 20 years to produce the book. Some answers were provided in an article Feelings wrote nearly a decade ago.

> Art, like literature, has the power to move beyond the limits of facts to a deeper understanding that is personal and emotional. Art jumps over our defenses, beyond the walls we have erected that protect us from pain. Art can bring us an understanding that is deep and fresh. It can move beyond the concrete limits of words (p. 73).[3]

Art and its creation, then, provide insights and emotional anchors which other creative processes or artifacts may not.

Writing specifically about the paintings in *The Middle Passage*, Feelings wrote:

> There is a bittersweet duality in the project, which I term a mutuality of consciousness. For pain and joy never simply exist side by side. Rather, they interact with each other and build on each other. The pain of the Black experience has always been tempered by the strength of Black people and the joy has always been tempered by the pain. This is, again, evident in Black music where the lyrics are sometimes raw and mournful, while the rhythm is almost joyful—so joyful that one is moved to dance. The powerful joy of the rhythm is not an evasion of the sorrow, but an affirmation of the presence of life.[4]

Feelings' aesthetic and political philosophies affirm the hope that many need to overcome the middle passage, slavery, segregation, and other "isms" of today. The decision to include an introduction written by John Henrik Clark, but omit text to accompany the illustrations, creates a context for a shared book experience in many languages. It also suggests that this is an issue which affects many throughout the world. Members of the 1996 Coretta Scott King Award committee of the American Library Association recognized the power of the book and awarded Feelings its award for illustration.

Because the book presents historical truth in an unrelenting fashion, I wondered whether adults would deem it inappropriate for children and not have the courage to share Feelings' masterpiece. This concern is warranted. Censorship is on the rise and it is not unusual to have a parent or teacher question the merit of exposing children to controversial topics.[5] Other children's books about slavery, *Amos Fortune, Free Man* (Yates, 1950), *The Slave Dancer* (Fox, 1973; 1984), and *Meet Addy* (Porter, 1993), generated considerable discussion about and opposition to their depiction of slavery.[6]

The other previously mentioned titles have equal potential for eliciting complex responses and represent the maturation of children's literature depicting Blacks. *Daddy, Daddy, Be There* captures joyful and bittersweet moments of childhood: a child who patiently waits for a father to return home from work; a child, whose parents are divorced, waits for the non-custodial parent's visit; or the child who cowers as she waits for Daddy to cease arguing with Momma. *Her Stories* entertains and advances themes about gender in a new way. Leo and Diane Dillon's illustrations are simply breathtaking. Walter Dean Myers alters traditional narrative structure in the *Glory Field*. Although gays and lesbians are not yet central characters in literature portraying Blacks, Jacqueline Woodson's groundbreaking book, *From the Notebooks of Melanin Sun* (featuring the curiously named character Melanin Sun), challenges our views of what constitutes a family and what counts as love. Rita Williams-Garcia's ability to create complex characters and capture the rhythms and languages of urban teenagers makes her one of the best and freshest voices in children's literature. *Like Sisters on the Home Front* has been heralded as a "truly outstanding" book for older readers and a good candidate for a Newbery Award by the interim editors of the *Horn Book Magazine*.[7]

Several questions were developed in order to ascertain support for the assertions that a renaissance is in development and that an aesthetic revolution emerged unfettered by restraints of the past. Among the questions were the following. What is the history of children's literature depicting Blacks? Are specific trends and themes evident in contemporary literature? Can one identify exemplary texts? Does a "Black experience" exist which is apparent in the literatures emanating from Africa, the United States, the Caribbean, and other areas of the world where the African diaspora is found? If so, are there recurring themes which concentrate on identity, gender, class, religion, sexual preference, religion, geographical region, language, or other markers of identity? In short, does the "politics of identity" infect the literature? What is the status of problematic texts? Finally, how might teachers, librarians, parents, or others share the literature in a manner which may elicit extended and/or complex responses and critical assessments of texts?

A vast amount of literature and critical studies was read in order to generate some answers to the aforementioned questions. The conclusions drawn in each section are not offered as gospel; rather, they represent one perspective influenced by disparate factors such as literary quality, appeal for children, socio-cultural concerns, and the multiple functions of literature.

HISTORICAL OVERVIEW[8]

Early Pioneers

Evidence for the existence of this new period abounds in the work of pioneering and contemporary librarians, critics, and scholars. Virginia Lacy, Charlemae Rollins, Augusta Baker, Henrietta Smith, and Elinor Sinnette, and more recently, Rudine Sims Bishop, Daphne Muse, James Frasier, Donnarae McCann, Opal Moore, and Diane Johnson-Feelings documented the status of literature featuring Blacks as well as the literary merit of the works. Their efforts and those of others elevated the status of the literature and laid the foundation for its recognition and growing readership. Major, historic touchstones are briefly reviewed in the next section.

Children's literature depicting Blacks has existed for well over 150 years. However, most of that literature featured stereotypes. A different kind of literature emerged in the early 1900s as individuals intimately familiar with elements of Black cultures created works. For instance, Mary White Ovington's *Hazel* (1903) and *Zeke* (1931) challenged prevailing images in books such as *The Story of Little Black Sambo* (Bannerman, 1899; 1923). Later, W. E. B. Du Bois, Jessie Fauset, and Augustus Dill published *The Brownies' Book* (1920–21), a literary magazine for the "children of the sun" noted for its photographs, literature, and columns.

A substantial, critically praised body of literature resulted from the combined and separate efforts of Langston Hughes and Arna Bontemps. Hughes and Bontemps wrote *Popo and Fifina: Children of Haiti* (1932), which was subsequently published in several languages. Bontemps received a Newbery Honor Medal in 1949 for *Story of the Negro*. The 1940s saw the emergence of novelists Lorenzo Graham and Jessie Jackson and biographer Shirley Graham DuBois. Many of the aforementioned writers continued producing during the 1950s and 1960s.

Many of the books written by these individuals are out-of-print. A few have received renewed attention in the 1980s and 1990s. For example, Diane Johnson-Feelings (1995) edited a new volume of selections from *The Brownies' Book*. Her resurrection of this historic gem helps fill a void left by the demise of *Ebony, Jr.* Arna Bontemps' best work, *Lonesome Boy* (1955; 1988) reappeared briefly during this period.

One might argue that the brightest light among these pioneers was Langston Hughes. A veritable cottage industry exists to honor his life.[9] A few of his children's books appear with new illustrations or original ones.

New poetry volumes for children were republished or newly published: *The Dreamkeeper* (1932; 1994) with new illustrations by Brian Pinkney, *The Block* (1995) with six panel collages of Romaire Bearden, and *Black Misery* (1969; 1994). Other work published includes *The Sweet and Sour Animal Book* (1994), an ABC volume.

The historic value of this literature is unquestioned. A new generation of readers will determine if the works merit acclaim and continued readership. Some scholars argue that a few of the books earned recognition as classics. Muse, for example, argues that nearly a score of books are legitimate classics.[10] Among the books for the period covering the 1930s through the 1990s that she designates as classics are books such as *The Dreamkeeper and Other Poems* (Hughes, 1932; 1994), *M. C. Higgins, the Great* (Hamilton, 1974), *Roll of Thunder, Hear My Cry* (1975), and *Scorpions* (Myers, 1988). Muse designated 13 books—for instance, *Tar Beach* (Ringgold, 1990) and *Brown Honey in Broomwheat Tea* (Thomas, 1993)—as likely classics.

Contemporary History

The 1960s through the 1990s mark a turning point for children's literature portraying Blacks. Virginia Hamilton's *Zeely* (1967) is viewed by many as the beginning of the ongoing renaissance. Since *Zeely*'s publication, Hamilton has produced more than 30 books in every genre except poetry. She has set a standard of excellence—Newbery Medal and Honor Medals, Edgar Allan Poe Award, National Book Award, Hans Christian Andersen Award, Boston Globe-Horn Book Awards, and MacArthur Genius Award—that is difficult for most authors to achieve. She has continued this tradition of excellence by being awarded with the Coretta Scott King Award for *Her Stories* in 1996.

Several authors create books that receive equal critical acclaim. Many of those who launched careers around the same time as Hamilton—Walter D. Myers, Mildred Taylor, Eloise Greenfield, Lucille Clifton, Tom Feelings, and John Steptoe (who died in 1989), for example—capture the multifaceted complexity of Black lives. Their continuous output ensures the survival of children's literature featuring Blacks. One might regard these writers as the first generation of the renaissance.

A second generation is represented by authors such as Sharon Bell Mathis, Candy Dawson Boyd, the late Alice Childress, Rosa Guy, James Haskins, Patricia McKissack, and June Jordan. Hallmarks of their work include linguistic variation, complex characters, varied settings, and reinterpretations of universal themes through Black experiences. Their productivity, too, cements the continued existence of literature depicting Blacks. Parents, librarians, teachers, critics, scholars, and booksellers who have expressed doubts about whether the literature would continue to exist should have some of their fears allayed.

The longevity and success of the first and second generation of writers enabled the emergence of a third generation which exhibits a certain amount of literary bravura. Among this group are Angela Johnson, Christopher Curtis—whose novel, *The Watsons Go to Birmingham—1963* (1995), is a 1996 Newbery Honor winner—Jacqueline Woodson, Elizabeth Fitzgerald Howard, Joyce Hansen, Eleanora Tate, Joyce Carol Thomas, Faith Ringgold, Gloria Pinkney, Brian Pinkney, Andrea Davis-Pinkney, Rita Williams-Garcia, and many others. These authors embrace traditional and controversial themes and characters.

Nowadays, one can look forward to the consistent publication of books written by members of the three generations. Occasionally, the number of books published, in a given year, hovers around fifty.[11] Demands for the literature spark intermittent periods when the number of books published ranges from 50 to 200 or so. Despite the fluctuations in numbers, several trends are discernible because a relatively stable number of books is published. Changes in genre, the appearance of new artistic talent, and thought-provoking, if not controversial, topics signal a certain amount of robust longevity. These trends and others are discussed next.

CONTEMPORARY TRENDS AND THEMES

Eight trends are examined in this section. Among those discussed are the growing ranks of writers and illustrators, artistic risks, controversial content, revival of poetry, expansion of folk tales, growth and improved quality of nonfiction, technical proficiency and individuality in illustrations, and the affirmation of children's interests as evident in the expansion of series fiction.

Authors and Illustrators

The sheer abundance of talent characterizes the first trend. At least 50 Blacks actively engage in editing, writing, or illustrating books. Consider the various members of the Pinkney family—Jerry, Gloria, Brian, and Andrea Davis-Pinkney. According to Sims Bishop, they are unique, representing two generations and several familial relationships.[12] Jerry and Brian each have won awards for their illustrations. For example, *John Henry* (Lester, 1994) received a 1995 Caldecott Honor Medal for Jerry; Brian won a 1996 Caldecott Honor Medal for *The Faithful Friend* (San Souci, 1995). Both men illustrated books authored by their wives, for instance, *Back Home* (1992) and *The Sunday Outing* (1994), written by Gloria and illustrated by Jerry, and *Alvin Ailey* (1993), a collaborative effort between Brian and Andrea.

The Pinkneys have established reputations and are more than likely to find outlets for their work. Other writers and artists enter the field in a serendipitous manner. A case in point is new author Christopher Paul Curtis.[13] A former autoworker, Curtis submitted a manuscript to a multicultural children's fiction contest sponsored by Little, Brown; he also submitted the same manuscript to Delacorte's young adult, contemporary fiction contest. The manuscript, a novel, was rejected by Little, Brown, but accepted by Delacorte—but not for the young adult contest. That manuscript became *The Watsons Go to Birmingham—1963*, a 1996 Newbery Honor Book.

The novel chronicles an aspect of life for many Blacks that has assumed almost mythic qualities: going South for vacations, funerals, reunions, or any other reason monumental or minor. Because the destination is Birmingham in 1963, the book captures the frightening period when four Black girls died in the White supremacists' bombing of a Black church. Curtis's novel provides a poignant reminder that racial violence of the past can reassert itself, as evident in the burnings of more than thirty Southern Black churches since 1994.

Every author and illustrator does not live up to the standards set by the Pinkneys or Christopher Curtis. Several demonstrate improved craftsmanship with each new book. The fact that some writers and artists need time to develop should not necessarily prevent publication of their works. A perceived "blockbuster" effect may contribute to the urgency for books that generate exceptional sales and "buzz," as in the case of the Goosebumps series. What is most important is that the authors and artists have more than one opportunity to prove themselves or garner an audience. Given the fluctuating status of literature depicting Blacks, second chances are important. Some companies are willing to nurture writers. For example, Orchard Books editors nurtured and guided Angela Johnson. They allowed her gradual development and she acquired an audience for her picture books and novels.

The freedom acquired from signing book contracts or a growing readership may enable the author or artist to take greater artistic risks. A second trend is a willingness to expand artistic limits. Virginia Hamilton exemplifies the writer willing to explore controversial topics, such as heavy metal rock music and drugs, mental illness, the homeless, and biracial and multiracial identity in novels such as *White Romance* (1989), *Arilla Sundown* (1976), and *Plain City* (1993).

New challenges can involve switching audience and format, as in the case of Angela Johnson. Beginning with *Tell Me A Story, Mama* (1989), the first of seven picture books, Johnson crafted gentle family stories highlighted by the soft, impressionistic paintings of David Soman. Johnson's young adult novel, *Toning the Sweep* (1993), takes place in the Southwest, a less common region for literature depicting Blacks. The intergenerational quest for understanding and connectedness depicted in the novel is a familiar one; yet, Johnson infuses the tale with a fresh voice. Johnson's latest novel, *Humming Whispers* (1995), tackles the sensitive topic of schizophrenia and its effects upon a family. *Humming Whispers*, too, received excellent reviews among critics.

Controversial Content

Closely related to artistic risks is the third trend, a willingness to create plots involving controversial topics such as abortion, gangs, drugs, and other societal problems. The authors are willing to depict characters in all their "beautiful-ugly selves." Pat solutions, moral platitudes, and cliches are missing. The books' languages capture the rhythm of the streets—"New Jacks and Jills" live their lives to a hip-hop beat.

Rita Williams-Garcia is a case in point; her honesty is refreshing. Williams-Garcia improves with each book; justifiably, she is regarded as an exceptional talent and new voice. *Blue Tights* (1989), her first novel, explored intragroup color differences, budding sexuality, and mother-daughter conflicts. Joyce, the protagonist, hungers for love and acceptance; but her search for love does not end in pregnancy. Instead, she finds herself and freedom in dance. In contrast, Denzel in *Fast Talk on a Slow Track* (1991) is a "buppie" who has material goods galore, self-confidence, a loving, prosperous family, and a strong sense of identity. His world crashes when he washes out of a special program at Princeton. Additional demoralization awaits. He must work at a summer job with people whom he considers his intellectual, economic, and social inferiors.

Williams-Garcia's *Like Sisters on the Home Front* (1995) is an exceptional novel which takes one slice of urban life and presents it realistically without succumbing to relentless pathology. Gayle, the main character, is womanish, brash, immature, funny, and a premature mother at age fourteen. These attributes alone would have filled one novel. Williams-Garcia places Gayle in the company of her upstanding, upper-middle-class relatives in the South. The resulting dialogue and characterizations reveal some of the multifaceted complexities of becoming a Black girl or woman. At the 1996 International Reading Association annual meeting in New Orleans, Williams-Garcia acknowledged the fact that her books might engender controversy and would not likely receive major awards. However, she felt a need to continue to write her stories because of her desire to write the stories of urban Blacks situated in a particular cultural milieu.

Changes in Genre

A fourth trend is the revival of poetry. Eloise Greenfield was responsible for most of the poetry in the 1990s with volumes such as *Nathaniel Talking* (1987) and *Night on Neighborhood Street* (1991). Anthologies with lavish illustrations introduced young readers to a wide selection of poetry. In some instances, the illustrations are as important as the poetry in several of these volumes. These include *Soul Looks Back in Wonder* (Feelings, 1994), *Pass It On* (Hudson, 1993), one collection edited by Dorothy and Michael Strickland, *Families* (1994), and a volume edited by Michael Strickland, *Poems That Sing to You* (1993). The Stricklands are a mother and son team. Writers typically associated with novels or folktales gave full reign to their poetic voices. Joyce Carol Thomas's *Brown Honey in Broomwheat Tea* (1993) and Ashley Bryan's *Sing to the Sun* (1992) signalled their emergence as published poets. Publishers experimented with using the picture book format in order to market some inspired pairings of "adult" poets and artists (Maya Angelou and Jean Michel Basqiuat, Ntozake Shange and Romaire Bearden, and Langston Hughes and Romaire Bearden) to children. The continued interest in Langston Hughes encouraged republication of his work or publication of manuscripts housed in archives.

Folktale collections or individually illustrated tales constitute the fifth trend. Robert San Souci established himself as an adept and entertaining reteller with *The Talking Eggs* (1985), *Sukey and the Mermaid* (1992), and the 1996 Caldecott Honor winner, *The Faithful Friend* (1995). James Haskins creates chills and thrills with *The Headless Haunt* (1994). Some West African tales are familiar; tales from East Africa may be less so. Two collections, *Fire On The Mountain* (Courlander & Leslau, 1950, 1995) and *Tales From the African Plains* (Gatti, 1995) will acquaint readers with Ethiopian, Eritrean, Somalian, and Kenyan tales. Walter D. Myers' *The Dragon Takes a Wife* (1972; 1995) was re-issued. Its hipster language ages well and the new illustrations add another level of interest.

Virginia Hamilton's *Her Stories*, illustrated by Leo and Diane Dillon, received the 1996 Coretta Scott King Award for fiction. Hamilton retells stories created and passed on by women. The decision to focus on girls and women may cause the reader to think about gender issues in a new way. For example, how are the tales different from those created by men? Will the stories feature tall, dark, and handsome princes who rescue docile heroines? Some of the tales have romantic overtones, but historic and cultural conditions mitigate against any overwhelming preponderance of romance. This is Hamilton's sixth folktale collection. The volume received popular and critical acceptance comparable to that of her *The People Could Fly* (1986).

A sixth trend parallels the general improvement in quality and quantity of nonfiction. Biographies, autobiographies, and single topic studies seemingly abound. Patricia and Frederick McKissack, James Haskins, and Clinton Cox write about topics as diverse as "Buffalo Soldiers," Negro baseball leagues, and dance, and traditional biographical subjects, for example, Sojourner Truth. Rather than present individuals, groups, or historical events as footnotes or as only peripherally important, the authors often place them near or at the heart of events. For instance, books about the wars on the plains during the 1870s and 1880s feature historic figures such as General George Custer and Sitting Bull. Cox's (1993) *The Forgotten Heroes* documents the extensive participation and centrality of Black soldiers, or as they were referred to by Indians, the Buffalo Soldiers. Ironic aspects of the wars are fully discussed, such as the disenfranchisement of Buffalo Soldiers and their families while they, in turn, enforced government policies that placed Indians on reservations.

Artists and their work achieved greater prominence, which denotes a seventh trend. Styles ranging from realism to impressionism to collage to eclecticism are found. Vibrant color, for instance, in Ashley Bryan's work, is one hallmark. Attention to detail is another. Of special note is the work of Leo and Diane Dillon, the 1996 U.S. nominees for the Hans Christian Andersen Award. Consider the illustrations in *Pish, Posh Said Hieronymous Bosch* (Willard, 1991) and *Her Stories* (Hamilton, 1995). Each combines elements of fantasy and realism in a thought-provoking manner. Biographies of artists Faith Ringgold, Horace Pippin, and Willie Johnson are available for children. Readers can acquire some basic information about art, artistic styles, and the creative catalysts for individuals who pursued their artistic careers despite racial, gender, and economic strictures.

Children's Interests

A final trend speaks to affirming children's reading interests. Many children between the ages of 7 and 12 are avid readers of series fiction. A decided lack in Black children's literature had been the absence of series fiction. Now, several series provide children with likeable characters, action, humor, occasional moments of poignancy and historical knowledge, and quick reads. Among the offerings are two historical series featuring girls, Connie Porter's *Addy*, a part of the American Girls collection, and Michelle Green's *Willie Pearl*. Several contemporary series portray characters between the ages of 10 and 18: Jeanne Betancourt's *Pony Pals*, an interracial group of girls who own and love horses; Sandra Draper's *Ziggy and the Black Dinosaurs* (1995), Black boys; Teresa Reed's Magic Attic volumes featuring Keisha and her group of interracial friends; Debbie Chocolate's N.E.A.T.E. books, another interracial group focusing on junior high students; and Walter D. Myers, *18 Pine Street*, set in an interracial high school.

Other trends will emerge in the future and some of the aforementioned ones may lessen in importance or disappear. The fact that trends are discernible suggests that literature featuring Blacks has become institutionalized and the year-to-year struggles to exist may no longer dominate.[14] Cautious optimism, however, is tempered by past experiences. Some of the themes that emerged as components of a major trend are assessed next.

EXEMPLARY WORKS

Any efforts to list exemplary works may convey the impression that only the books listed are examples of "the best." A conclusion of this sort is not intended. Numerous factors may result in some books being categorized as exceptional and becoming parts of canons, appearing on recommended reading lists, or capturing devoted readers. Explicit reasons for selecting the books included in this section are based in part on traditional literary criteria such as characterization and style, recognition of the writer's or artist's growing talent, omission of gratuitous stereotypes, and the ability of the work to evoke myriad responses such as laughter, awe, anger, or disbelief. The annotations in the next section are not exhaustive; many worthy books exist. Several reference guides have been published over the past five years that provide recommended reading lists categorized by theme or topic, genre or format, and age or grade level. Among these are *The Black Experience in Children's Books*, which was published under the auspices of the New York Public Library, *The Multicolored Mirror* (Moore-Kruse), *Venture in Cultures: A Resource Book of Multicultural Materials and Programs* (Hayden), *Black Authors and Illustrators of Children's Books* (Rollock), *The Coretta Scott King Awards Books From Vision to Reality* (Smith), *Kaleidoscope* (Sims Bishop), and *The Multicultural Catalogue* (Muse, in press).

Discussing the works by genre may serve as a useful method for identifying exemplary books. The breadth of genre and the listing of authors may prompt exploration of other works by a particular writer or on a specific theme.

The resurgence of poetry is a hopeful sign that the oft-ignored genre will garner new readers. Classics such as *The Dreamkeeper* (Hughes) reveal a vitality that has withstood changing tastes and the general neglect of the genre. Two other classics, *Knoxville, Tennessee* (Giovanni) and *Honey, I Love* (Greenfield) debuted as picture books.

Brown Honey in Broomwheat Tea (1993) represented novelist Joyce Carol Thomas's entry into the genre. The poems, mainly lyric, combine to tell a story about one family and its interactions. Clearly, the family is loving and untroubled by internal dysfunction or societal pathologies. Thomas does include some poetic images which suggest that the wider world may not offer the comfort and love found within the family. The gentle, meditative, sometimes joyful tone of the poetry is echoed in Floyd Cooper's illustrations.

Folktales retain their popularity. *The Faithful Friend* (San Souci), *The Headless Haunt* (Haskins), and *Her Stories* (Hamilton) are welcome alternatives to Anansi and Brer Rabbit tales. Martiniqué is the setting for *The Faithful Friend*. San Souci establishes a sense of place with a mixture of Creole and French phrases and descriptions of Caribbean foods, and characters' names, for instance. The multiple themes of love and devotion between friends and paramours, the greed and evilness of some, and the power of truth and kindness to ward off evil are vividly presented. San Souci does not resort to distortions of Vodun or Voodoo to convey magic. Rather, he uses time-honored agents or objects of malice such as witch-like women, poisonous snakes, and deadly food. Brian Pinkney's illustrations, arguably his best to date, call forth memories of pastels found in flowers, water, sky, and painted houses in the Caribbean.

Ghost stories are a folkloric tradition; in these the haunt or "haint" is an apparition. The tales collected by Haskin in *The Headless Haunt* can inspire fright. The short tales lend themselves to oral storytelling, creative dramatics, or silent reading. Storytellers, experienced or novice, can create unique renditions by adopting varying linguistic nuances to enhance fright appeal.

Virginia Hamilton placed her creative stamp on folktales with *The People Could Fly* (1986). Subsequent collections combined stories of clever animals; resourceful, brave individuals; creation myths; and tales about "the dark way." *Her Stories* (1995) reveals Hamilton's continuing ability to take artistic risks. The book's dedication celebrates women—some unsung and unknown, others immortalized in tales passed down through the generations:

> To our mothers and grandmothers, aunts and great-aunts. To
> all the women who stood before us, telling us about where
> they came from, what they saw, did, and imagined. They let
> us know they stood for us. Talking, they combed our hair,
> rocked us to sleep, sang to us, told us tales of then and now—
> and tomorrow. They worried about us. They hoped for us and
> showed us the way. They cared. (Dedication, unpaged)

These are more than survival or perseverance tales. They are the embodiment of the indomitable spirits of women who were not and will not be moved (much in the manner of an old Negro spiritual). Moments of levity are also a feature of a few of the tales. Hamilton divides the volume into 5 sections: "Her Animal Tales," "Her Fairy Tales," "Her Supernaturals," "Her Folkways and Legends," and "Her True Tales."

Another hallmark of Hamilton's creativity is her ability to connote and maintain a sense of orality in written language. She reinterprets the combination of European languages, retained remnants of West African languages, and the resulting patois and creoles known as Black English vernacular. Hamilton does not resort to using the "plantation" dialects evident in other collections.

Even though the tales stand on their own merit, they are raised another creative notch by Leo and Diane Dillon's illustrations. The illustrations are notable for the technical mastery of the Dillons and for the moods evoked through bold images of haughtiness, innocence and self-love; a few, however, are frightening.

Recently, a graduate student shared with the members of a class the kinds of books her daughter selected. The pre-teen gravitated toward books with cover illustrations of girls who resembled her: brown-skinned, more pecan than walnut; thick, natural hair in braids or pony-tails; and happy demeanors. It is not unusual to note the looks of awe and enchantment on the faces of Black children and others as they look at illustrations from the Pinkneys, Tom Feelings, James Ransome, Meloyde Rosales, Floyd Cooper, Ashley Bryan, and others. Such responses are understandable if one notes the historic denigration of Blacks in illustrations, popular culture items, movie or television characters, household goods, stationery, and other forms upon which an image could have been imprinted. Variations of stereotypes or invisibility did not allow Black children to see realistic images of themselves on a frequent basis. Now authentic, realistic, and multiple images exist. Only infrequently do stereotypic images of another era slip through. Sims Bishop's evaluation (in this volume) of *Secret Valentine* (Stock, 1991), *Amazing Grace* (Hoffman, 1993), and *Tar Beach* (1990) delineates the visual differences between stereotypes and realistic, or probable, images.

Saturday at the New You (Barber, 1994) is a good example of artistic sensibility and individuality. Text and illustrations meld in a pleasing form. On some level, visits to beauty salons or hairdressers have the same elements: the feeling of community, the beauty rituals, and the gossiping. Barber captures some of the distinguishing characteristics of Black salons, such as the particular hairstyling techniques associated with some hair textures. Barber's illustrations are also appealing because they lack the "picture-perfect" style of some illustrations. For example, the perspective is a bit off-center. The characters resemble individuals you might encounter sitting next to you rather than idealized, model types. Barber portrays several common images: the young, obstinate child about to enter an inner sanctum of femaleness; women engaged in talk; and the heads under the dryer reflecting various states of relaxation.

Other picture book writers capture snippets of Black life; combined they offer some glimpses of Black life. For example, the experiences of family members temporarily separated by immigration are captured in *The Tangerine Tree* (Hanson, 1995). Fun in one's neighborhood is one focus of *Jamal's Busy Day* (1991). Worry about a parent's illiteracy in *Papa's Stories* (Johnson, 1994) or a mother's new job in *You're Still My Nikki* (Eisenberg, 1992) are examples of more serious concerns found in some books. Overall, a growing assortment of books is available, but one area is lacking. More picture books with humor—rollicking, slap-stick, subtle, corny, or sophisticated—are needed. Contemporary settings, children with foibles and virtues, and minimal or no didacticism and moralizing, all evident in *The Math Curse* (Scieska, 1994) or Paula Danziger's Amber Brown series, would provide the right touch of levity.

Mildred Taylor's eight works of historical fiction, from *Song of the Trees* (1975) to *The Well* (1995), have set standards for other writers along with educating and entertaining readers. While slavery remains a perennial topic, some authors manage to impart new perspectives or interpretations. *Christmas in the Big House, Christmas in the Quarters* (McKissack and McKissack,

1994) exposes many of the complexities and contradictions in the "peculiar institution." Juxtaposing the life of slaves and the pampered, indolent existence of owners during the holiday season enables the reader to understand some of the moral, political, *and* economic dilemmas. John Thompson's illustrations can have an unintentional effect. The pristine, portrait-like images belie the experiences and emotions depicted in the text. There is a gentle quality to the illustrations which may suggest that slavery was not so bad. Perhaps the visual and textual images in other books such as *The Middle Passage* (Feelings, 1995) or *To Be A Slave* (Lester, 1968) are so powerful in their impact and pervasiveness that others pale. Nevertheless, the McKissacks' book provokes thought and the extensive bibliography encourages further reading.

Another novel tackling slavery is Mildred P. Walter's *Second Daughter* (1996). The Revolutionary War era is the setting for this novel which weaves fact and fiction. The fact emanates from a 1791 court case, *Brom & Bett v. Ashley*; the fiction results from Walter's imagined life for the two sisters, Bett and Arssa, who are caught up in the fervor of the time period. Their enslavement serves to underscore the contradiction of those who fought for the end of English domination and tyranny while enslaving Africans and their descendants.

The Righteous Revenge of Artemis Bonner (Myers, 1992) parodies "the West," our conceptions of Indians, the lawlessness of western states, and the "high falutin" moral indignation and righteousness of a young man on the verge of adulthood. Joyce Carol Thomas focuses on life in the West and Southwest in novels such as *Marked by Fire* (Thomas, 1987). Books set in the West or Southwest serve to entertain and educate. They enable the reader to discover some experiences of Blacks in places other than "the South" or urban areas.

Science fiction and fantasy are not extensive in literature written by Blacks. Of course, fantasy and science fiction have roots in folklore, which is well-represented. But a large body of work does not exist. Virginia Hamilton's Justice trilogy—*Justice and Her Brothers* (1978; 1989), *Dustland* (1980; 1989), and *The Gathering* (1981; 1989)—are major examples. The books explore primordial, emotional, and psychic connections between twins; psychic mind melding; and traditional science fiction and fantasy themes such as the nature of goodness and evil as well as the interactions of family members. Myers contributed two books, *The Legend of Tarik* (1991) and *Shadow of the Red Moon* (1995). *The Legend of Tarik*, set in Africa and Spain during a time reminiscent of the Moorish period, possesses an epic quality.

In contrast to the dearth of science fiction and fantasy, realistic fiction abounds. Mysteries, while few in number, may herald a new direction in the literature. Foremost are the three books which comprise the Imamu

Jones series written by Rosa Guy. The novels, *The Disappearance* (1979; 1989), *New Guys Around the Block* (1983), *And I Heard A Bird Sing* (1987), combine intrigue and some social problems. A more recent whodunit is *Where Do I Go From Here?* (Wesley, 1993). Nia is a working-class student enrolled in a private boarding school. She struggles to succeed, not academically—which she does—but socially and emotionally. Some balance comes in the form of her friend Marcus, who mysteriously disappears. W. D. Myers' series, Smiffy Blue: Ace Crime Detective, debuted with *The Case of the Missing Ruby and Other Stories* (1996). The humorous mystery series is intended for readers aged 8 to 11.

Several novels illustrate the growing literary excellence of Black literature. *For the Life of Laetitia* (Hodge, 1993) details mother-daughter and father-daughter conflicts, post-colonial tensions among different racial groups, and the painful pleasure of school days. Jacqueline Woodson's "Maizon" books dissect the nature of friendship, family, and community with a gentle, yet piercing style. Even a despicable subject such as incest retains its horrifying nature in non-sensational fashion in Woodson's *I Hadn't Meant to Tell You This* (1994). The book presents one of the most bittersweet interracial friendships since Taylor's *The Mississippi Bridge* (1990) and *The Road to Memphis* (1990). Eleanora Tate's *Front Porch Stories* (1993) and *Blessing in Disguise* (1994) portray nearly perfect and not so perfect fathers. Veteran novelists W. D. Myers and Virginia Hamilton continue to push themselves in novels such as *Plain City* (1993) and *Somewhere in Darkness* (1992). These and other works document the growing artistic excellence and the willingness to take artistic risks in terms of themes, characters, and style.

The days when Black history focused primarily on great men and women are a part of the recent past. Individuals such as Martin Luther King, Jr., Harriet Tubman, and Rosa Parks remain staples in biography series. One variation in autobiographical writing is a statement of wisdom and advice for youth written by Rosa Parks with Gregory J. Reed, titled *Dear Mrs. Parks: A Dialogue With Today's Youth* (1996). One intent of Mrs. Parks is to inspire youth to live full and honorable lives. Other individuals and topics earned attention as well. For example, James Haskins is a veritable one-person nonfiction industry. He is the author of more than 80 books for children and adults. Two of his works, which illustrate his attention to detail and his ability to tell an historic story, are *Black Inventors and Their Inventions* (1991) and *Black Eagles: African Americans in Aviation* (1995).

Military history comes to life through Clinton Cox's pen. Two volumes, *Undying Glory* (1992) and *The Forgotten Heroes* (1994), chronicle the role of Black soldiers in the Civil War and the "Indian Wars," respectively. The relationships between Blacks and Native Americans from slaveholders to "maroon" insurgents, intermarriage, to the conflicted heroism of Buffalo soldiers illustrate the ways in which two oppressed groups coalesce with and oppose each other. Cox's sensitive yet candid presentation documents the ways in which ordinary individuals are a significant part of history. Few social studies texts for children will provide as thorough an analysis.

Artist Jacob Lawrence's monumental series of paintings, "The Great Migration," toured the country in 1995 and 1996. This represented the first time the scores of paintings have been shown together since the 1940s. Prior to the mounting of the exhibit, a children's book, *The Great Migration* (1993), enabled readers to experience, visually, one of the greatest migrations in U. S. history. Approximately 5 million Blacks left the South for the Northeast, Midwest, Southwest, and West. They left for a multitude of reasons, including escape from political and economic oppression and to seek education, better housing, and those intangibles of opportunities and freedom. Lawrence's paintings give voice to this often overlooked exodus. Similarly, his *Harriet and The Promised Land* (1993) captures the proud, defiant, and courageous behavior of Harriet Tubman.

The preceding discussion of books, while selective, documents growing numbers of authors and illustrators. At least 50 authors and illustrators easily come to mind. Rollock's (1992) reference work, *Black Writers and Illustrators of Children's Books*, allows for a more systematic identification of authors and illustrators. Additionally, the books noted offer an understanding of some of the themes which captivate and illustrate the expansiveness of genre.

RECURRING THEMES

One idea debated periodically is whether being a Black is an experience unique in human history. In terms of literary exploration of this idea, one might phrase the ideas in questions such as these: Are there universal institutions, cultural mores, beliefs, and practices, characters or archetypes, and experiences perceptible in literature written about Blacks? Or, are the aforementioned unique to the extent that connections with other groups are unlikely? Many authors explore these ideas in simple and complex fashion.

Universal themes—for example, meeting a new baby-sitter, a mother returning to work or school, or a father telling stories to his children—are fairly typical now. Other themes acquire a unique cast because they reflect the experiences of Blacks in a range of geographic locations and contexts. For example, intragroup color differences or the way in which one self-identifies are important themes in novels such as *For the Life of Laetitia* (Hodge, 1993), *Plain City* (Hamilton, 1993), and *From the Notebooks of Melanin Sun* (Woodson, 1995).

Some artistic tension is evident in the works of the authors. Few of the books (some picture books and some folktales are notable exceptions) are universal to such an extent that they are race neutral or devoid of the aspects of culture identified with Blacks. Consider books such as *You're My Nikki* (Eisenberg, 1992), and *The Leaving Morning* (Johnson, 1992), which could portray any group in any geographic locale. Many books, even series fiction, include some historical content. Several themes focus on historic conditions or events and their effects on current life. These include the impact of slavery, *Christmas in the Big House, Christmas in the Quarters* (McKissack and McKissack, 1994); struggles for justice and equality, *Frederick Douglass in His Own Words* (Meltzer, 1995); effects of and overcoming racism, discrimination, and bigotry, *Children of Fire* (Robinet, 1991); the ability of Blacks to persevere despite the onslaught of opposition from a variety of sources, *Hold Fast to Dreams* (Davis-Pinkney, 1995); the importance of education to individual and group advancement, *The Girl on the Outside* (Walter, 1992); discovering and passing on knowledge about Blacks' contributions to U.S. history and culture, *Mississippi Challenge* (Walter, 1992); and preserving and honoring Black history and culture, *Ajeemah and His Son* (Berry, 1993).

Another major thematic emphasis is family. Family configurations vary from traditional nuclear ones, *Front Porch Stories* (Tate, 1992); to extended families, *Tanya's Reunion* (Flournoy, 1995); single-parent homes, *Definitely Cool* (Wilkinson, 1993) or *I Hadn't Meant to Tell You This* (Woodson, 1994). Family members face a multitude of joys, disappointments, and commonplace activities. Consider picture books that explore many of the internal dilemmas faced by young children: Jojo in *Jojo's Flying Sticks* (Pinkney, 1995) must overcome her fear of a specific move in Karate class as well as the monstrous images created by the tree near her bedroom window. Annie in *Annie's Gifts* (Medearis, 1994) bemoans her lack of talent and creativity but discovers her gifts through trial and error. Many grandmothers find themselves rearing grandchildren for a multitude of reasons. The *Glass Bottle Tree* (Coleman, 1995) captures the uncertainty that results when social service agencies determine the fitness of a grandparent.

Older children face familial anxieties as well. Darnell in *Darnell Rock Reporting* (Myers, 1994) is not unlike many Black boys who are not challenged academically and end up bored and in minor trouble with teachers, parents, and principals. Novels such as *Somewhere in Darkness* (Myers, 1992), *A Blessing in Disguise* (Tate, 1995), and *Oren Bell* (Burgess, 1991) unravel the tangled causes of emotional pain inflicted by loved ones.

Beauty, ideal and otherwise, remains a thematic emphasis. Some Black girls seem to enjoy circumstances in which their beauty is a non-issue because family and community members accept and celebrate their appearance. Some authors make explicit comments, for instance, *Bright Eyes, Brown Skin* (Hudson and Ford, 1990) and *The Enchanted Hair Tale* (Deveaux, 1987). Others omit specific references but the illustrations convey a sense of beauty not based on stereotypic, European standards such as the blue-eyed blonde with long, flowing tresses, and thin lips and nose. For example, Jamaica in *Jamaica's Blue Marker* (Havill, 1995) has soft, thick, luxuriant crinkly hair. Her skin is a warm pecan brown. Keep in mind, however, that some Blacks possess physical traits which fit the stereotype. *The Aunt in Our House* (Johnson, 1996) depicts the varied shadings, hair textures, and physical features found in an increasing number of biracial families. Permed or "relaxed" hair, dreadlocks, and braids common among Black girls suggest that the illustrators are familiar with hair styles and issues among members of the group. *Brown Honey in Broomwheat Tea* (Thomas, 1993) deftly uses metaphors in much the same way as poet Langston Hughes did to describe the beauty of Blacks' physical features.

Novelists, in contrast, usually insert some discussion about intragroup beauty squabbles. Buhlaire in *Plain City* (Hamilton, 1993) stands out because of her fair skin coloring and carrot red dreadlocks. *The Shimmershine Queens* (Yarbrough, 1989) and *Thank You Dr. Martin Luther King, Jr!* (Tate, 1990) painfully chronicle the hurt endured by a significant number of dark-skinned girls. Causes of the intragroup color differences are presented in subtle and sometimes overt fashion. Boys are not as affected by the beauty standards that can inflict such pain on girls. Skin color, hair texture, and eye color do not seem to determine boys' desirability to the same extent as for girls.

Candid and loving portrayals of the passionate and intricate friendships among Black girls are found. The label, sister-friend, is often evoked to describe the bond. Sisterhood among friends, and increasingly brotherhood among boys has emerged as a major theme. *Hold Fast to Dreams* (Davis-Pinkney, 1995) and *Like Sisters on the Homefront* (Williams-Garcia, 1995) explore the depth of the friendship bond. Dee's lifeline, in *Hold Fast to Dreams*, after her family moves from Baltimore to an all-white town, is her girlfriend Lorelle. Gayle's "sisters on the homefront" remain in New York as she heads for re-education in the family homestead in Georgia. Davis Pinkney and Williams-Garcia, to their credit, recognize the tenuous nature of adolescent friendships, too. Dee and Gayle change and grow and their previous friendships are altered in the process.

Walter Dean Myers depicts male bonding with a gentle touch shaped by humor and a notable lack of chest-thumping machismo. This does not mean, however, that "in-your-face" posturing is lacking; his earlier novels featured many aspects of male bravura. A wonderful sensitivity emanates from his later work. For example, Jimmy and his father Crab, in *Somewhere in Darkness* (1992), struggle to establish a fragile father-son connection. *The Righteous Revenge of Artemis Bonner* (1992) and *Scorpions* (1988) depict interracial friendships realistically without overt, didactic messages. Sandra Draper's *Ziggy and the Black Dinosaurs* (1994) and *Tears of a Tiger* (1995) portray multifaceted male friendships, too.

Occasionally, a novel encapsulates several overlapping themes. Myers' *The Glory Field* (1994) is an example. The novel contains interrelated themes such as recognizing and drawing upon the strengths of Black families, accepting familial love and care, falling in love, ameliorating the consequences of social problems such as drug addiction, completing everyday tasks and rituals, and surviving extraordinary events that create unlikely heroes and heroines. This multigenerational saga is a break-through novel because of the thematic complexity and the atypical narrative structure.

Physical or mental illness as thematic foci are not unusual, but Johnson's *Humming Whispers* (1995) gently conveys, especially well, the psychic horrors of schizophrenia. The minimalist text and vivid imagery enlighten the reader in a subtle yet intense manner. The reader waits for Nicole's next psychotic break, but is just as startled as her sister Sophy, their Aunt Shirley, and Nicole's boyfriend Reuben when it is manifested. The setting, Cleveland, Ohio, is a welcome change of location from novels set on the East Coast or in the South. Burgess explores psychic abilities and genius in two mysteries, *Oren Bell* (Burgess, 1991) and *The Fred Field* (Burgess, 1995). These books insert race in an understated form. Interracial friendships grow out of natural attractions rather than racial characteristics. Similarly, racism, prejudice, or bigotry are tangential to other concerns, such as homeless children or caring for the elderly.

Clearly, the themes addressed in picture books, novels, and poetry reflect everyday, historic, universal and/or culturally specific interactions, behaviors, beliefs, and foibles. A "quieter," subtle tone characterizes many of the novels of the 1990s. It seems as if the authors write in a semi-autobiographical, introspective, or confessional style. The urgency of race and racism reflected in the naturalistic novels of Mildred Taylor seems to have lessened in intensity. Other issues, for instance, gender, class, and to a lesser extent, sexual preference, are gaining in popularity.

Some view these as "extra-literary" issues which threaten to overshadow literary concerns such as quality of writing. For instance, the March/April 1995 issue of *The Horn Book Magazine* featured some of the conservative, moderate, and radical stances in support of and opposition to multiculturalism. Similarly, *The New Advocate*, throughout 1995, handled the hot topic, political correctness. Examples of the most visceral responses to extraliterary issues were evoked when the interim editors of *The Horn Book Magazine* suggested in the January/February 1996 issue that the Newbery Committee needed to consider a broader array of literature, especially the exceptional work of Judith Ortiz Cofer, Christopher Curtis, Angela Johnson, and Rita Williams-Garcia. The editors noted the urgency of the issue, given the fact that a person of color, Mildred Taylor, last won the Newbery Medal in 1976 despite the considerable talents of the identified authors.

LITERARY OR EXTRA-LITERARY CONCERNS

Multiple Identities: Gender, Age, and Class

Essays about the effects of politics or social-cultural issues in a writer's or illustrator's aesthetic philosophy appear infrequently. For example, Virginia Hamilton wrote about "liberation literature"; Walter D. Myers discussed the "revolutionary" intentions of writers in the 1960s and 1970s; and Tom Feelings' statements about improvisation in Black art apply to children's literature and art as well.[15] These artistic statements concentrate on race. Authors and illustrators do not necessarily consider other issues—class and gender, for example—less important. Generally, the issues are welded with notions about race.

Artistic statements that incorporate commentary about "extra-literary" perspectives have become more evident. Faith Ringgold (Ringgold et al., 1995) links concerns about gender, age, and race to her development as an artist:

> Looking back at the 1930s, people didn't ask little girls what they wanted to be when they grew up. It was kind of assumed that you were going to be a wife and mommy, you know? Now my mother wanted us to be somebody out there in the world. So what we knew and what we were trained to think about was that we were going to college. That was definite. But it wasn't said what we were going to be. My family had no idea I would be an artist. (Ringgold et al., 1996, p. 8)

Ms. Ringgold's family supported her artistic endeavors, especially her mother who was instrumental in providing help with her story quilts. Encouragement, however, was not forthcoming from some of her art professors. Ringgold related the story of one professor who told her that she lacked the necessary "indications" for an artist:

> I had a professor at the City College of New York, where I graduated with a degree in art, who never once told me that he didn't like my drawings. At the end of the semester, we had a series of four drawings to do as a test. One of them had to do with mountains. Now, I was born and raised in New York City and in the summers we went to the seashore, so the mountains I don't know about, okay? So I did these mountains and I gave them to him and he said, "What are *these*?" And I said, "Those are mountains." So he said, "Write it on there." I said, "Does this mean you don't think I can draw? I plan to be an artist." He said, "Well, I don't see any indications that you can." So when he said, "You can't be an artist, you can't draw," I said, "Oh, yes, I can. I *definitely* can." I mean, I wasn't sure whether I could, but now I can—just 'cause you say I can't. (Ringgold et al., 1996, p. 8)

The independent and defiant spirit as well as the belief in her abilities and the desire to dream evident in the quotations are qualities infused throughout *Tar Beach* (1990), Ringgold's first picture book for children and her latest, *My Dream of Martin Luther King* (1995). Cassie, in *Tar Beach*, dreams about "flying" and shares her hopes; but she is also aware of racism and its effects.

Multiple Identities: Race, Gender, Class, and Sexual Preference

Jacqueline Woodson spoke about writing as saving her life and allowing her to become visible (ALAN Workshop, November 1995). Her voice could have remained muted if four essential and interconnected elements of her identity—gender, class, race, and sexual orientation—were denied expression or if she were forced to choose one rather than others. She discusses the fluidity of identities in the following manner:

> It's hard for me to talk about myself in the context of gayness without talking about the part of me that is black, because all of this continues to be threatened by people who believe that no part of me should be in the world. As a writer who is black and gay but neither a black writer nor a gay writer, I do not feel as though I have a responsibility to only these two communities but a responsibility to write beyond the systems of oppression in *all* communities. As people who exist on the margins, we do have a different view of the world, and it is our responsibility to refocus. In the course of refocusing, we may help a child who is coming out or struggling with abuse or with family or with health to acquire a clearer vision of the world and thereby grow up stronger. (Woodson, 1995; pp. 712–713)

Woodson's novel, *From the Notebooks of Melanin Sun* (1995), received glowing critical reviews and augments the small body of literature featuring lesbians. Earlier books, *Ruby* (Guy, 1976; 1983) and *The Dear One* (Woodson, 1993) generated controversy, readers, and fairly good reviews, too. Whether this signals the beginning of more books featuring Black gays and lesbians is uncertain. It is certain, however, that the books have and will garner some readers.

Class Notions

Class consciousness among characters arises more frequently than some other issues. Characters are aware of their financial straits or advantages. Older novels portray class struggles. For instance, T. J. in *Roll of Thunder, Hear My Cry* (Taylor, 1976) resents and admires the Logan's land-owning status. A record contract for his mother is M. C.'s dream in *M.C. Higgins, The Great* (Hamilton, 1974). Current works, even series fiction, bring class skirmishes to the fore. For example, Willie Pearl is working class and her best friend Ella Mae is middle class in the Willie Pearl series. Willie Pearl wishes she had Ella Mae's affluence but she values her family's work ethic. The extent to which a family will go to extremes to maintain a false notion of its upper-middle-class status is evident in Wilson's *Rich Girl, Poor Girl* (1992).

Language

Linguistic diversity of several types is evident in the literature. One form adopts vernacular language to suggest region. For example, Taylor's *The Well* (1995) provides excellent examples of Southern dialects, Black and White, rich, middle class, working class, and poor, male and female, young and old. Another type of language diversity is found in the works of Joyce Hansen, for example, *Yellow Bird and Me* (1991), and Rita Williams-Garcia. Both capture the argot of teenagers. Williams-Garcia's deft handling of hip-hop "voice" is evident throughout *Like Sisters on the Homefront*. A third discernible use of language is apparent in the patois and creoles found in the works of Lynn Joseph and James Berry. Joseph's folktale collections, *A Wave in Her Pocket* (1991) and *The Mermaid's Twin Sister* (1994), and picture books, *Jasmine's Parlour Day* (1995) and *An Island Christmas* (1994), contain examples of Trinidadian language styles. James Berry, too, captures linguistic rhythms of the Caribbean. *A Thief in the Village* (1987) and *The Future-Telling Lady and Other Stories* (1993) feature the lilting sounds of Jamaican dialects. Virginia Hamilton presents another kind of language facility. Her command of dialects is exceptional and varied: West Indian forms in *Junius Over Far* (1985), Black rural in *Willie Bea and the Time the Martians Landed* (1983; 1989), and linguistic interpretations in *Cousins* (1990), *Her Stories* (1995), and *Jaguarundi* (1994). Her books are notable because she conveys linguistic differences, cadences, and orality without resorting to orthographic representations such as *gwine* or *gon'*.

Aging Gracefully

Multifaceted portrayals of the elderly are found in picture books, novels, and poetry. Vibrant, active elderly are depicted in *When I Was Little* (Igus, 1993), *What Kind of Baby-sitter Is This?* (Johnson, 1991), and *Humming Whispers* (Johnson, 1995). The bequeathing of historic or family memories is one function the elderly serve in some books. In *Fallen Secrets* (Boyd, 1994), Grandmother uses her acting talents and knowledge of Black history to help her granddaughters grow into womanhood despite the pitfalls of unreasonable beauty standards and self-doubts. Coincidentally, Grandmother plays the same role in the *18 Pine Street* series; she, too, is an actress who is a font of knowledge as she steers her granddaughters through adulthood. Infirmed elderly also figure in the literature. The loss of memories and physical abilities are sensitively depicted in *William and the Good*

Old Days (Greenfield, 1994) and *Cousins* (Hamilton, 1990). A curious portrait of an elderly woman dominates *The Glass Bottle Tree* (Coleman, 1995). The unnamed Grandmother communicates with her granddaughter through spirits, vibes, modeling of behaviors, and the sharing of skills such as gardening. Speech does not seem to exist between the two. Despite the lack of dialogue, the reader can sense that meaningful communication takes place between the two.

Sacred Matters

Religion is not a prominent issue in the literature. Certain novels, such as *Like Sisters on the Homefront*, present characters with overt religious or spiritual beliefs, but only a few books were written with religion or religious values as the sole theme. Some notable exceptions are the four picture books written by former NFL athlete Shaun Gayle, the volumes of Black spirituals illustrated by Ashley Bryan, James Berry's retelling of Jesus' birth, *Celebration Song* (1994) set in the Caribbean, and *Baby Jesus Like My Brother* (Brown, 1995). Gayle's books are "race neutral" in content but feature a multiracial cast of characters. More books can be expected, especially from independent presses such as Derek-Winston.

Special Needs

People with disabilities appear infrequently in the literature. *Willy's Summer Dream* (Brown, 1989) is, however, an example that does feature the disabled. Brown discussed her attempts to share the feelings of those labeled "different."

> Specifically regarding *Willy's Summer Dream*, I try to tell the narrative from the point of view of the world. The reader feels Willy's anguish and frustration at being labeled, and the social isolation at being "different." Young people could identify with awkwardness and trauma of passing through such a period and would share the joy of Willy's small success. It helps to point direction and offer hope. (Rollock, 1992, p. 26)

One focus of the novel is Willy's infatuation with his tutor and his attempts to date her. In a subtle fashion, the "romance" helps the reader to perceive the complex emotions of those labeled special needs. Hamilton's *A Little Love* (1984) explores romance, schooling, developing a sense of belonging, and the search for familial identity and connections in a sensitive manner, too.

Few writers or artists publish aesthetic manifestoes or treatises in which they argue for examination of their art or writing solely on the basis of extra-literary concerns. Those who have published commentary sometimes acknowledge the effects of gender, class, language, or other aspects of difference. Yet, they also exhort readers to understand and respond to the works as creative products. No suggestion is made that social-cultural or economic issues remain tangential. Rather, books alone cannot substitute for integral changes in institutions and behaviors despite the ability of some books to serve as catalysts for change.

PROBLEMATIC TEXTS AND LITERARY DISAGREEMENTS

Stereotypic texts dominated in the years prior to the mid-1960s. A few of these remain in circulation and garner a few readers in each generation, for example, *Epaminondas* (Bryant, 1907; 1938) and *The Story of Little Black Sambo* (Bannerman, 1899; 1923). Their pervasiveness decreased as societal attitudes towards Blacks changed, or at least the public expression of prejudice became less tolerated, and a body of literature emerged that offered different literary and artistic engagements. Despite criticism, the books remain popular; *The Story of Little Black Sambo* is a staple and readily available from the publisher. The debates should emerge anew with the publication of Julius Lester's (1996) retelling of *The Story of Little Black Sambo*, with illustrations by Jerry Pinkney, titled *Sam and the Tigers*. Lester, Pinkney, and the publishers, Dial Books, acknowledge the controversial nature of the text. Lester and Pinkney shared their reactions upon hearing or reading *The Story of Little Black Sambo*. Both noted their enjoyment of the text; but the derogatory illustrations affected them as well. Lester recounted his feelings then and now:

> Last year Julius Lester read *Little Black Sambo* with Helen Bannerman's illustrations for the first time since childhood. "My memory of reading the story [as a child] is very vivid, particularly the conflicting emotions," Mr. Lester says. "I liked the story, but the drawings and the names left me feeling deeply hurt and shamed, as if I as a black child was being ridiculed. I was left not knowing what I felt. Rereading the book, I found the story to be absolutely wonderful—except for the names of the characters: Black Sambo, Black Mumbo, Black Jumbo. Whatever Bannerman's intentions, the names had come to have racist associations. I began wondering if it would be possible to do a new version of *Little Black Sambo*." (Publisher's catalogue, 1996, p. 28)

Pinkney's recollections are eerily similar:

> Jerry Pinkney also liked the story as a child and remembers singular pleasure in "claiming a child of color as a hero in a children's book. I fondly recall a brave boy, the color of his new clothing, and the menacing, foolish tigers." However, recently when he examined at least twenty-five versions of the tale, he found that the characters were often depicted in an "outright vicious" manner. Consequently, Mr. Pinkney

discovered he "had a strong need to retrieve" the tale in a way
that would eliminate the racist elements and shed light on
what for him was a delightful and humorous fantasy. (Publishers catalogue, 1996, p. 28)

The preview of the text and illustrations suggests that Lester and Pinkney
intend to entertain but not with vicious stereotypes. Further, Lester adopts
the vernacular language used in his three volumes of Uncle Remus tales.

The collaboration between Lester and Pinkney, undoubtedly, will send
some scurrying for the "original" versions. Others will question the need
for resurrecting a tale with a tangled socio-cultural history. A few will celebrate the appropriation of a stereotype and its reinterpretation. The book
will capture some readers; more than likely, Bannerman's version will sell
in greater numbers. The ensuing debates should be intense. Rudine Sims
Bishop's chapter in this volume delineates the reasons why some texts may
engender criticism.

Two major issues are authenticity and authorship.[16] Because so few
books were published in the past, became a part of curricula or canons, or
acquired visibility, many individuals exhibited a measure of protectiveness
about the images of Blacks. The caution is certainly understandable, but
care needs to be taken in order to prevent the dominance of monolithic
stories. Although Blacks share multitudes of experiences, many factors—
for example, gender, language, class, and geographic location—can add de-
grees of difference. Further, the multiplicity of stories and stylistic voices
can encourage readers to recognize the diversity among Blacks.

Questions about authorship may prove more divisive. A few suggest
that a critical cabal exists which prevents White authors or, at the very
least, discourages White authors from writing about Blacks or other similarly situated groups.[17] A perusal of publishers' catalogues offers conclu-
sive evidence that White writers are not the "victims" of wholesale discrimination. Rather, Black writers and artists are not often afforded the
opportunity to exist solely as writer or artist. Black is always a marker of
identity. Of course, some would not have it otherwise; yet many cannot
exercise choice in the matter. The next section demonstrates how a theme,
acquiring an identity as a Black, can be artistically examined while important extra-literary aspects are addressed.

BECOMING A BLACK

Growing up and acquiring an identity as a Black child can be problematic
as well as pleasurable. In many ways, whether the Black child grows up in
New York, Brixton, England, Waycross, Georgia, Kingston, Jamaica, or
Soweto, South Africa, the experiences are parallel and different. At the
core, growing up Black encompasses universal experiences such as learn-

ing to walk and talk, going to school, learning etiquette, and so on. Growing up Black also means learning that you may experience rejection because of your color, circumscribed mobility, racially motivated violence, and segregation.

The process is complicated by the melding of several other identities with the racial identity: male/female, child/adult, Southerner/West Indian, born-again Christian/Bahai, meat-eater/vegetarian, and so forth. Biracial or multiracial individuals demand inclusion, too. Many resent being forced to identify as Black because of one parent's heritage, laws, or customs. Some, however, choose to label themselves as Black. Few picture books or novels examined their lives and dilemmas. For a number of years, Arnold Adoff created stories in which biracial identity was neither tragic nor special in books such as *Hard to Be Six* (1991). Often, his was the lone voices at times. Each aspect of identity can combine with or separate from other attributes and push to the forefront or recede into the background. For many, however, race remains the most salient aspect of their identity.

Poets and musicians seem uniquely qualified to capture the essence of what it means to be a Black. Think about the sparse, elegant phrasing of Miles Davis in "Kind of Blue," the pulsating reggae of Bob Marley, the pure holiness of Mahalia Jackson, or the bawdiness of Howlin' Wolf. New Jacks and New Jills, for example, Boyz to Men and Mary J. Blige, are no less influential as they emerge as the bards for a new generation.

Nikki Giovanni (1996) edited a volume of poetry, *Shimmy Shimmy Shimmy Like My Sister Kate* which helps preserve the voices of poets who participated in or were influenced by the Harlem Renaissance, a literary and artistic movement among Blacks lasting from approximately 1917 to 1935.[18] Poems such as "We Wear the Mask," "A Negro Love Song," "If We Must Die," "The Negro Speaks of Rivers," "A Black Man Talks of Reaping," "Yet Do I Marvel," "No Images," "For My People," "Nikki-Rosa," and "it's not so good to be born a girl/sometimes" offer readers an opportunity to glimpse some of the myriad ways of becoming a Black.

One might well argue that music and poetry reveal the soul of a people. Picture books, chapter books, and novels can offer insights as well. Several board books are especially appropriate for enabling young children to see images of children who look like themselves. For example, Angela Johnson's series of board books about Joshua feature a family of varying color hues and hair textures. These books, in addition to entertaining and educating readers, may help mitigate against children accepting negative conceptions of their physical features. Similarly, board books written by Eloise Greenfield depict young children engaged in universal activities such as playing with toys or making music. These, too, may encourage children to view themselves as "normal," and not as some kind of exotic or invisible humans.

Several recent picture books document daily life, ranging from mundane activities to rituals centered on sharing family and group history. In *Dinner at Aunt Connie's House* (Ringgold, 1993), Lonnie is adopted. His green eyes and red hair set him apart. He is a loved and welcomed member of the family who participates in an annual family dinner. A favored niece in *Uncle Jed's Barbershop* (Mitchell, 1993) recalls the sacrifices and steadfastness of an uncle whose dreams are deferred as he helps family and community members. Greenfield captures the closeness of grandson and grandmother in *William and the Good Old Days* (1994). William hangs out at his grandmother's diner. Her wisdom, served up in small doses along with helpings of food, encourages William to show courtesy, self-love, and respect for family and community. Jasmine looks forward to heading to the town and sharing food and drink, greeting friends, and frolicking in *Jasmine's Parlour Day* (1994). A son's love for his mother is the central focus of *Jonathan and His Mommy* (Smalls-Hector, 1992). An elderly baby-sitter in *Red Dancing Shoes* (Lewis-Patrick, 1993) urges her charges to experience the joys of dancing. These books, more often than not, portray racial identity in a matter-of-fact manner, as a wonderful given.

A few chapter books and novels intended for primary and middle grade readers concentrate on children struggling to break away from and returning to the comfort of family as they seek their places in life. For instance, *Mariah Keeps Cool* (Walter, 1990) and *Mariah Loves Rock* (Walter, 1992) contain light-hearted vignettes about a middle-class girl's adventures and misadventures. In a comparable fashion, Greenfield's (1992) *Koya Delaney and the Good Girl Blues* chronicles the emerging adolescence of a character unencumbered by racism or prejudice. Boys are the featured characters in the Julian series written by Ann Cameron. Julian, a likeable character between the ages of 8 and 10, is big brother, joker, and adventurer.

Novels such as *Trouble's Child* (Walter, 1985) and *When the Nightingale Sings* (Thomas, 1992), which are set in conservative, insular communities, illuminate the strictures placed on some girls and women who display a streak of independence, talent, and intelligence. In some ways, Marigold in *When the Nightingale Sings* and Martha in *Trouble's Child* are talented outsiders. Marigold possesses the voice of an angel in this novel with a Cinderella motif. She perseveres and wins the heart of the choir director after her magnificent performance in a gospel music festival. Martha has healing hands and skills in using herbs and roots to treat various illnesses. Martha desires to leave her island home and acquire "book knowledge" beyond the limited amount available to her on the island. The intellectual guidance of a young researcher helps spur her need to explore the wider world. Both girls accept their special gifts and the cultural traditions which they must help sustain because community members have imbued them with a sense of belonging, heritage, and identity. Yet, they also crave a space for their individual dreams.

Intelligent, gifted day-dreamers with visions of dragons rather than geometric theorems filling their heads are likely to find school boring on occasion. Jimmy, the sensitive teenager in *Somewhere in the Darkness* (Myers, 1992) embodies these traits and more. He is at loose ends and about to embark on the emotional journey of his life when his father walks away from the hospital and prison and takes custody of him. Not unexpectedly, Jimmy is distant, confused, and angry. He knows that he does not want to be like his father but he is attracted by the chance to discover a part of himself.

In a comparable way, Justin, the central character in *Justin and the Best Biscuits in the World* (Walter, 1985) struggles to become a "man" in a family of girls and women. He retains old-fashioned notions about men's and women's work. The gentle guidance of his grandfather during a summer on the ranch gradually replaces Justin's antiquated notions. Real men and boys, he learns, know how to cook, clean, wash, and perform chores around the ranch. These tasks are not gender-based but reflective of an individual who knows how to take care of himself. Equally important, Justin acquires a sense of his heritage and identity in family stories about living in the Southwest and facing racism and less than hospitable weather and land conditions. He also understands that men exhibit many characteristics, from the gentle to the brusque.

For those boys and girls who desire "role models" or models of behavior, the literature offers numerous variations on acquiring an identity as a Black. Becoming a Black, however, is not a paint-by-number process, although some shared experiences, beliefs, knowledge, and behaviors are possible. The body of literature that exists today dispels notions about monolithic hordes of Blacks who are the same in all aspects. Some responsibility for the recognition of diversity can be linked directly to the expanding number of Black authors and non-Black authors (who have extensive experiences with and/or knowledge about the groups) who have elected to tell untold stories. These untold stories reveal not dysfunction but rather normalcy in restricted circumstances.

Author Elizabeth Fitzgerald Howard (1996) captures the normalcy in her picture book, *What's in Aunt Mary's Room?* Aunt Mary's room contains treasures such as the family Bible that documents the family heritage. Howard wrote about some of her literary goals and her desire to help

> . . . present-day children, black and white, to know that blacks have been a part of all of this country's growth since the beginning. And that there were black grocers and doctors and postmen and teachers and porters and lawyers who celebrated holidays and sat in the balcony at the opera and went to church and sent their children to college—and hoped that the American dream included them. And lived as though it did, in spite of everything that might or might not have gone wrong. (Rollock, 1992; p. 99)

Essentially, then, becoming a Black means becoming a human being shaped by particular historical and cultural conditions.

STRATEGIES FOR SHARING THE LITERATURE

Given the fluctuating availability and quantity of literature, expansiveness of genre, and the improving quality, how might children engage with texts in meaningful ways? Engagement can assume many forms. Activities described in the next section may encourage children to respond to texts in many ways.

One essential strategy for eliciting meaningful engagement with children's literature featuring Blacks is simply to share the literature. This action alone might create significant demand for the literature. My travels throughout the country to talk with teachers and parents about the literature suggest that many are unaware of its existence or acquainted with only a few books. Children, too, are not likely to have an extensive amount of information about the literature unless they routinely purchase the books, are given books by adults, or find themselves enrolled in classes where the literature is a part of the curriculum. Creating literature centers or displays featuring a single author, poet, or illustrator or several are effective methods for generating interest. Daily read alouds can introduce children to the books.

Art offers many possibilities for thinking, talking, writing, enjoying, and inspiring. A single artist, for example, Jerry Pinkney, might become the focal point. A teacher might pose a question such as the following: "Let's look at the following books: *Back Home* (Pinkney, 1992), *Mirandy and Brother Wind* (McKissack, 1988), and *John Henry* (Lester, 1995). Think about the illustrations. Write down some thoughts about the pictures. For example, does the style remain the same? Are the same colors used in each book? What kinds of feelings do you have as you look at the pictures? Can you determine the artist's attitudes about the people included in the illustrations? Can you detect changes in the artist's style over the years?"

Another approach one might take is to create an art center with books illustrated by major artists—Leo and Diane Dillon, Brian Pinkney, Ashley Bryan, Floyd Cooper, Tom Feelings, Faith Ringgold, James Ransome, and others. Biographical and artistic information about the artists such as biographies, for example, *Faith Ringgold* (Turner, 1993) and *Li'l Sis and Uncle Willie* (Everett, 1991), were written for children, some as components of art exhibits. Pat Cummings edited two volumes, *Talking With Artists* (1992) and *Talking With Artists, II* (1995), which present glimpses of the artists' lives, the reasons why art was chosen as a vocation or avocation, examples of their work as a child, and some commentary about the artists' philosophies. Each book is written in a chatty style, which makes the subject matter less intimidating. Discussion and writing can occur after students have been immersed in the artists' work. Tasks and questions such as the following are appropriate: Discuss the elements of the artist's work that appeal to you. Identify the ways in which the artist's interpretation of the text causes you to react in specific ways. After examining the work of a sampling of artists, can you argue that a "Black" artistic style or styles exist?

A final project might involve comparing and contrasting the manner in which artists interpret the same or different aspects of the same experience. For instance, *The Middle Passage* (Feelings, 1995), *Aunt Clara and the Freedom Quilt* (Hoskins, 1994), *The Door of No Return* (Barboza, 1992), and *Christmas in the Big House, Christmas in the Quarters* (McKissack and McKissack, 1994) depict slavery and offer substantial differences in artistic interpretation.

Oratorical contests are a feature of youth programs, some religious denominations, and organizations such as the NAACP's ACTSO program. Langston Hughes' poetry and Martin Luther King, Jr.'s "I Have a Dream" speech are perennial favorites. Now, other equally compelling speeches—replete with passion and unswerving commitment to justice and equality—are possible alternatives. Consider the volume, *Frederick Douglass in His Own Word*s (Meltzer, 1995), a chronological presentation of some of Douglass's speeches and articles. Douglass's contemporaries viewed him as a magnificent orator. His visage, framed by a cottony mane of hair, added to the effect. More important, his work symbolized the unfettered intelligence of Blacks and the desire for liberation and justice.

Douglass's speeches are excellent examples of the power of oratory, which is decidedly missing from today's political polemics. For example, the speech, "Do People of Color All Think Alike?" (p. 51) is a short paragraph questioning the idea of monolithic opinions among Blacks. A teacher might share articles or quotations from individuals who argue that conservative Black voices are silenced. Having students read this brief missive along with speeches by Booker T. Washington, founder of Tuskegee Institute, might enable students to debate competing political ideas and understand that varying political stances have always existed among Blacks and always will.

In a parallel fashion, a teacher might pose a question about the relevance of specific political movements, for example, feminism, for Blacks. Douglass's speech, "The Rights of Women" (pp. 41–43); excerpts from Anna J. Cooper's *A Voice From the South* (1898; 1988)—regarded by some as the foundational intellectual work of a Black feminist; quotations from W. E. B. Du Bois, another intellectual revered for his stances on women's rights; and Sojourner's Truth powerful plea, "Ain't I a Woman," offer variance in oratorical style and argument that should spark extensive and intensive debate and discussion.

The literature offers untold opportunities to entertain, inspire, challenge, and inform readers. Special training is not required before it can be approached. This is not to suggest that some background knowledge is not necessary for understanding some of the information. The primary prerequisites, however, are intellectual openness and curiosity.

SUMMARY AND FINAL THOUGHTS

Cautious optimism is warranted. The common stereotypes delineated by Dorothy Broderick in the 1970s remain in the background and rarely surface.[19] Now, the "culturally conscious" literature, delineated by Rudine Sims Bishop in *Shadow and Substance* (1982), dominates. The precarious status of the literature seems a part of the past. One can usually expect certain authors—Hamilton, Myers, Taylor, and a few others—to publish at least one book every year or so. They have a devoted following and can be assured of having a continued readership. Additionally, illustrators such as Jerry and Brian Pinkney are in demand as well. Equally important, the literature is becoming institutionalized. For example, most of the major reading programs include a representative sampling of literature featuring Blacks. Authors and illustrators routinely appear on the programs of the national conferences of such groups as the International Reading Association and the National Council of Teachers of English. The number of book signings increases as well. For instance, enthusiastic crowds greeted Connie Porter, the author of Pleasant Company's Addy series, throughout the country. Another example of the growing acceptance of the literature is the recognition accorded by awards committees such as the Newbery, Caldecott, *Boston Globe-Horn Book Magazine*, and Hans Christian Andersen. Artistic risks are apparent as well as authors tackle controversial topics and modify narrative structure. There is a willingness to buck trends and shatter expectations. Changes in geographic locations, for example, from urban enclaves to the Southwest, encourage readers to understand that Blacks are found throughout the country. Finally, the fact that many of the books are good sellers or best sellers helps shatter the perception that a market for the books is limited.

Although considerable advances are evident, monitoring, cajoling, encouraging, and purchasing are required in order to sustain the advances. Adults have to display a willingness to select books featuring Blacks even though they do not live near or know any Blacks. If Black children can develop an intellectual openness that allows them to read the Goosebumps series, then other children can read the Ziggy series and other works. Adults should help them in this effort.

The next phase of the literature that deserves extensive attention is criticism. The desire to celebrate any book, because so few were published in the past, is leveling off. Critics and readers are beginning to demand literature that is not didactic or idealized. Several authors are in the vanguard of creating literature that meets or exceeds standards of literary excellence, and thoughtful criticism can help to nurture others. Scholars such as Rudine Sims Bishop, with her critical studies on African-American children's literature and critical biography of Walter Dean Myers, and Diane Johnson-Feelings, with her critical history of African-American children's literature and *The Brownies' Book*, lead the way.

NOTES

1. Naming a group, cultural process or product, cultural movement, or institution can result in confusion. Deciding on a title for this chapter illustrates the difficulty inherent in creating a name for something that is precious and controversial. I suspect that some will argue that the label given this chapter is too exclusive or not inclusive enough. For example, a few individuals will argue that Blacks are an African people and the literature should begin with examples from African literature. Keep in mind, Africa contains more than 45 countries and each does not possess a body of written children's literature. Blacks are part of the African diaspora, true enough, but those who live in the Caribbean or are of Caribbean descent may identify as a Jamaican, Anguillan, Trinidadian, or Bajan. Others, who are descendants of those from French- or Spanish-speaking countries in the Caribbean, and Central and South America, will exhibit a certain amount of petulance if their voices are excluded. Finally, there are those who self-identify as biracial, tri-racial, or multiracial. Where do they fit? Is Black sufficient to describe their status? Maybe, occasionally, or not at all, but discussion will continue. "Children's Literature Depicting Blacks" will have to suffice as the title and its inclusiveness inferred. After all, poets such as Langston Hughes note that black ranges from ivory to mahogany and everything in between.

2. Tom Feelings' *Middle Passage: Black Cargo, White Ships* should not be confused with the adult novel, *Middle Passage* (1990) written by Charles Johnson. Feelings' book is a volume of paintings with a foreword written by historian John Henrik Clarke. Both, however, focus on the capture, enslavement, and sale of Africans in the "New World."

3. Feelings, T. (1985). Illustration is my form, the Black experience my story and content. *The Advocate*, 4(2), 73–82.

4. Ibid., p. 79.

5. Lee, S. (1996, Spring). Can educators communicate with the religious right? The nature of the dialogue. *The New Advocate*, 9(2), 123–134. Lee writes about the dilemmas faced by a professor with religious convictions who is uncritically lumped with and vilified as a fundamentalist Christian. She also attempts to explain the behavior of some conservative Christians who are regarded as censorious.

6. Two early volumes, MacCann, D. and Woodard, G. (Eds.). (1972). *The Black American in Books for Children: Readings in Racism*. Metuchen, NJ: Scarecrow Press, and MacCann, D. and Woodard, G. (Eds.). (1977). *Cultural Conformity in Books for Children: Further Readings in Racism*. Metuchen, NJ: Scarecrow Press, include discussions of controversial texts such as *Sounder* and *The Slave Dancer*. Considerable debates about Pleasant Company's Addy series appeared in newspapers such as the *New York Times*, the *Chicago Tribune*, and others throughout the nation.

7. Parravano, M. V. and Adams, L. (1996, January/February). A wider vision for the Newbery. *The Horn Book Magazine, 72*(1), 4–5.

8. An expanded discussion of the historical development of the literature appears in the earlier volume, Harris, V. J. (Ed.). (1992). *Teaching Multicultural Literature in Grades K–8*. Norwood, MA: Christopher-Gordon Publishers, Inc. Rudine Sims Bishop apprised me of an error which appears in this volume. *Little Brown Baby*, a collection of Paul Laurence Dunbar's poetry for children, was first published in the 1940s and not in the early 1900s as indicated in the chapter I wrote. The "first" book written by a Black depicting Blacks, then, remains a matter of debate. Diane Johnson-Feelings' volume, (1991). *Telling Tales: The Power and Pedagogy of African American Literature for Youth*. Westport, CT: Greenwood Press, is an exceptional scholarly work which analyzes the history of the literature.

9. Some of the books which are a part of the new Hughes canon include Harper, D. S. (1994). *The Return of Simple*. NY: Hill & Wang; Harper, D. S. (1995). *Not So Simple: The Simple Stories by Langston Hughes*. Columbus, MO: University of Columbia Press. Arnold Rampersad was awarded the Pulitzer Prize for his biographies of Langston Hughes: (1986). *The Life of Langston Hughes*. Volume 1, New York: Oxford Press, and (1988). *The Life of Langston Hughes*. Volume 2, New York: Oxford Press.

10. Muse, D. (December 1993/January 1994). Black American classics in fiction and poetry for young readers. *American Visions, 8*, pp. 33–37.

11. Davis, M. (1996, April). Black literary renaissance. *Emerge Magazine, 7*(6), 50–57.

12. Sims Bishop, R. (1996, January/February). The Pinkney family: In the tradition. *The Horn Book Magazine 72*(1), 42–49.

13. Frederick, H. V. (1995, December 18). Flying starts. *Publishers Weekly, 242*(51), 28–29.

14. Muse, op. cit., pp. 20–21.

15. Feelings, op. cit., pp. 73–82.

16. Debates about the portrayal of Blacks in literature are numerous and historic. See Brown, S. (1933). Negro character as seen by white authors. *Journal of Negro Education, 2*, 179–203; Clifton, L. (1981). Writing for Black children. *The Advocate, 1*, 32–37; Sims, R. (1984). A ques-

tion of perspective. *The Advocate, 3,* 145–155; and Howard, E. (1991). Authentic multicultural literature for children: An author's perspective. In Lindgren, M. (Ed.). *The Multicolored Mirror: Cultural Substance in Literature for Children and Young Adults,* pp. 91–100. Fort Atkinson, WI: Highsmith Press. Several have written from the perspectives of White authors: Hurmece, B. (1984). A question of perspective, *The Advocate, 3,* 20, 23.

17. Rochman, H. (1993). *Against Borders.* Chicago: American Library Association and Lasky, To Stingo With Love: An Author's Perspective on Writing Outside One's Culture. *The New Advocate, 9,* 1–7, suggest that individuals who argue for or impose notions of political correctness prevent others, usually Whites, from writing about other races or cultures and individuals associated with them.

18. The specific dates for the Harlem Renaissance may vary in some critical studies. Generally, scholars place the beginning sometime after World War I and the ending sometime prior to World War II.

19. Broderick, D. (1973). *Image of the Black in Children's Literature.* New York: R. R. Bowker.

WORKS CITED

Adoff, A. (1991). *Hard to be six.* New York: Lothrop, Lee & Shepard.

Bannerman, H. (1899; 1923). *The story of Little Black Sambo.* New York: Harper & Row.

Barber, B. (1994). *Saturday at the New You.* New York: Lee & Low.

Barboza, S. (1994). *The door of no return.* New York: Cobblehill Books.

Berry, J. (1987). *A thief in the village.* New York: Orchard.

Berry, J. (1993). *Ajeemah and his son.* New York: HarperCollins.

Berry, J. (1993). *The future-telling lady and other stories.* New York: HarperCollins.

Berry, J. (1994). *Celebration song.* New York: Simon & Schuster.

Betancourt, J. (1995). *A pony in trouble.* New York: Scholastic.

Bontemps, A. (1948). *Story of the Negro.* New York: Knopf.

Bontemps, A. (1955). *Lonesome boy.* Boston: Houghton Mifflin.

Bontemps, A. and Hughes, L. (1932). *Popo and Fifina: Children of Haiti.* New York: Macmillan.

Boyd, C. D. (1994). *Fall secrets.* New York: Puffin Books.

Boyd, C. D. (1995). *Daddy, Daddy be there.* New York: Philomel.

Broderick, D. (1973). *The image of the Black in children's literature.* New York: R.R. Bowker.

Brown, K. (1989). *Willy's summer dream.* New York: Gulliver/Harcourt.

Brown, M. (1995). *Baby Jesus like my brother.* Orange, NJ: Just Us Books.

Bryan, A. (1992). *Sing to the sun.* New York: HarperCollins.

Bryant, S. (1907; 1938). *Epaminondas.* Boston: Houghton Mifflin.

Burgess, B. (1991). *Oren Bell.* New York: Delacorte.

Burgess, B. (1995). *The Fred field.* New York: Delacorte.

Coleman, E. (1995). *The glass bottle tree.* New York: Orchard Books.

Cooper, A. J. (1892; 1988). *A voice from the South*. New York: Oxford Press.

Courlander, H. and Leslau, W. (1950; 1995). *Fire on the mountain*. New York: Henry Holt.

Cox, C. (1991). *Undying glory*. New York: Scholastic.

Cox, C. (1993). *The forgotten heroes*. New York: Scholastic.

Cummings, P. (Ed.). (1992). *Talking with artists*. Vol. I. New York: Bradbury.

Cummings, P. (1995). *Talking with artists*. Vol. II. New York: Bradbury.

Curtis, C. (1995). *The Watsons go to Birmingham–1963*. New York: Delacorte.

Davis-Pinkey, A. (1993). *Alvin Ailey*. New York: Hyperion Books for Children.

Davis-Pinkey, A. (1994). *Hold fast to dreams*. New York: Morrow.

Draper, S. (1995). *The tears of a tiger*. New York: Atheneum/Macmillan.

Draper, S. (1995). *Ziggy and the black dinosaurs*. Orange, NJ: Just Us Books.

Eisenberg, P. (1992). *You're my Nikki*. New York: Dial Books.

Everett, G. (1991). *Li'l Sis and Uncle Willie*. Washington, DC: National Museum of American Art/Rizzoli.

Feelings, T. (1993). *Soul looks back in wonder*. New York: Dial Books.

Feelings, T. (1995). *The middle passage*. New York: Dial Books.

Flournoy, V. (1995). *Tanya's reunion*. New York: Dial Books.

Fox, P. (1973; 1984). *The slave dancer*. New York: Laurel Leaf.

Gatti, A. (1999). *Tales from the African Plains*. New York: Dutton.

Giovanni, N. (1994). *Knoxville, Tennessee*. New York: Scholastic.

Giovanni, N. (1996). *Shimmy Shimmy Shimmy Like My Sister Kate*. New York: Henry Holt.

Green, M. (1990). *Willie Pearl*. Temple Hills, MD: Ruth Williams & Co.

Greenfield, E. (1988). *Nathaniel talking*. New York: Black Butterfly Children's Books.

Greenfield, E. (1991). *Night on neighborhood street*. New York: Dial Books.

Greenfield, E. (1992). *Koya Delaney and the good girl blues*. New York: Scholastic.

Greenfield, E. (1994). *William and the good old days*. New York: HarperCollins.

Greenfield, E. (1995). *Honey, I love*. New York: HarperCollins.

Guy, R. (1976; 1983). *Ruby*. New York: Bantam.

Guy, R. (1979; 1985). *The disappearance*. New York: Dell.

Guy, R. (1987). *And I heard a bird sing*. New York: Delacorte.

Guy, R. (1983). *New guys around the block*. New York: Delacorte.

Hamilton, V. (1967). *Zeely*. New York: Macmillan.

Hamilton, V. (1974). *M. C. Higgins, the Great*. New York: Macmillan.

Hamilton, V. (1976). *Arilla Sundown*. New York: Greenwillow.

Hamilton, V. (1978; 1989). *Justice and her brothers*. Odyssey/Harcourt Brace Jovanovich.

Hamilton, V. (1980; 1989). *Dustland*. Odyssey/Harcourt Brace Jovanovich.

Hamilton, V. (1981; 1989). *The gathering*. Odyssey/Harcourt Brace Jovanovich.

Hamilton, V. (1983; 1989). *Willie Bea and the time the Martians landed*. New York: Aladdin Books.

Hamilton, V. (1984). *A little love*. New York: Philomel.

Hamilton, V. (1985). *Junius over far*. New York: HarperCollins.

Hamilton, V. (1986). *The people could fly*. New York: Knopf.

Hamilton, V. (1990). *Cousins*. New York: Apple Paperbacks/Scholastic.

Hamilton, V. (1993). *Plain City*. New York: Blue Sky Press.

Hamilton, V. (1994). *Jaguarundi*. New York: Blue Sky Press.

Hamilton, V. (1995). *Her stories*. New York: Blue Sky Press.

Hansen, J. (1991). *Yellow bird and me*. New York: Clarion.

Hanson, R. (1995). *The tangerine tree*. New York: Clarion Books.

Haskins, J. (1991). *Outward dreams: Black inventors and their inventions*.

Haskins, J. (1994). *The headless haunt*. New York: HarperCollins.

Haskins, J. (1994). *The Scottsboro Boys*. New York: Henry Holt.

Haskins, J. (1995). *Black eagles: African Americans in aviation*. New York: Scholastic.

Havill, J. (1995). *Jamaica's blue marker*. New York: Houghton Mifflin.

Hodge, M. (1993). *For the life of Laetitia*. New York: Farrar Straus & Giroux.

Hoffman, M. (1993). *Amazing Grace*. New York: Dial Books.

Hopkinson, D. (1993). *Sweet Clara and the freedom quilt*. New York: Knopf.

Howard, E. F. (1996). *What's in Aunt Mary's room?* New York: Clarion Books.

Hudson, C. and Ford, B. (1990). *Bright eyes, brown skin*. Orange, NJ: Just Us Books.

Hudson, W. (1991). *Jamal's busy day*. Orange, NJ: Just Us Books.

Hudson, W. (1994). *Pass it on*. New York: Scholastic.

Hughes, L. (1969; 1994). *Black misery*. New York: Oxford Press.

Hughes, L. (1994). *The dreamkeeper*. New York: Knopf.

Hughes, L. (1994). *The sweet and sour animal book*. New York: Oxford Press.

Hughes, L. (1995). *The block*. New York: The Metropolitan Museum of Art.

Igus, T. (1993). *When I was little*. Orange, NJ: Just Us Books.

Igus, T. (1996). *Two Mrs. Gibsons*. San Francisco: Children's Book Press.

Johnson, A. (1989). *Tell me a story, Mama*. New York: Orchard Books.

Johnson, A. (1992). *The leaving morning*. New York: Orchard Books.

Johnson, A. *Toning the sweep*. New York: Orchard Books.

Johnson, A. *Humming whispers*. New York: Orchard Books.

Johnson, A. *The aunt in our house*. New York: Orchard Books.

Johnson, C. (1990). *The Middle Passage*. New York: Atheneum.

Johnson, D. (1991). *What kind of baby-sitter is this?* New York: Macmillan.

Johnson, D. (1994). *Papa's stories*. New York: Macmillan.

Joseph, L. (1991). *A wave in her pocket*. New York: Clarion Books.

Joseph, L. (1992). *An island Christmas*. New York: Clarion Books.

Joseph, L. (1994). *Jasmine's parlour day*. New York: Lothrop, Lee & Shepard.

Joseph, L. (1994). *The mermaid's twin sister*. New York: Clarion Books.

Lawrence, J. (1993). *Harriet and the promised land*. New York: Simon & Schuster.

Lawrence, J. (1993). *The great migration*. New York: HarperCollins.

Lester, J. (1968). *To be a slave*. New York: Dial/Scholastic Paperbacks.

Lester, J. (1994). *John Henry*. New York: Dial Books.

Lewis-Patrick, S. (1993). *Red dancing shoes*. New York: Tambourine Books.

McKissack, P. (1988). *Mirandy and Brother Wind*. New York: Knopf.

McKissack, P. and McKissack, F. (1994). *Christmas in the big house, Christmas in the quarters*. New York: Scholastic.

Medearis, A. (1994). *Annie's gifts*. Orange, NJ: Just Us Books.

Meltzer, M. (Ed.). (1995). *Frederick Douglass in his own words*. New York: Harcourt Brace.

Mitchell, M. K. (1993). *Uncle Jed's barbershop*. New York: Simon & Schuster.

Morrison, T. (1988). *Beloved*. New York: Plume Contemporary Fiction.

Myers, W. D. (1988). *Scorpions*. New York: Harper & Row.

Myers, W. D. (1992). *The righteous revenge of Artemis Bonner*. New York: HarperCollins.

Myers, W. D. (1992). *Somewhere in darkness*. New York: Scholastic.

Myers, W. D. (1994). *Darnell Rock reporting*. New York: Delacorte Press.

Myers, W. D. (1994). *The glory field*. New York: Scholastic.

Myers, W. D. (1995). *The dragon takes a wife*. New York: Scholastic.

Myers, W. D. (1995). *Shadow of the red moon*. New York: Scholastic.

Myers, W. D. (1996). *The case of the missing ruby and other stories*. New York: Scholastic.

Myers, W. D. (1991). *The legend of Tarik*. New York: Scholastic/Point.

Ovington, M. (1903). *Hazel*. Freeport, NJ: Books for Libraries.

Ovington, M. (1931). *Zeke*. New York: Harcourt Brace.

Parks, R. and Reed, G. (1996). *Dear Mrs. Parks*. New York: Lee & Low Books.

Pinkney, B. (1995). *Jojo's flying sticks*. New York: Simon & Schuster.

Pinkney, G. (1992). *Back home*. New York: Dial Books.

Pinkney, G. (1994). *Sunday outing*. New York: Dial Books.

Porter, C. (1993). *Meet Addy*. Middleton, WI: Pleasant Company.

Ringgold, F. (1990). *Tar beach*. New York: Crown Books.

Ringgold, F. (1993). *Dinner at Aunt Connie's house*. New York: Hyperion.

Ringgold, F. (1995). *My dream of Martin Luther King*. New York: Crown Books.

Ringgold, F., Freeman, L., and Roucher, N. (1995). *Talking to Faith Ringgold*. New York: Crown Books.

Robinet, H. (1991). *Children of fire*. New York: Atheneum.

Rollock, B. (1992). *Black authors and illustrators of books for children*. Revised ed. New York: Garland

San Souci, R. (1985). *Talking eggs*. New York: Dial Books.

San Souci, R. (1992). *Sukey and the mermaid*. New York: Four Winds/ Macmillan.

San Souci, R. (1995). *The faithful friend*. New York: Simon & Schuster.

Scieska, J. (1994). *The math curse*. New York: Viking.

Sims-Bishop, R. (1982). *Shadow and substance*. Urbana, IL: National Council of Teachers of English.

Sims, R. (1992). *Shadow and substance*. Urbana, IL: National Council of Teachers of English.

Smalls-Hector, I. (1992). *Jonathan and his mommy*. New York: Little, Brown & Co.

Stock, C. (1991). *Secret Valentine*. New York: Bradbury.

Stowe, H. (1988). *Uncle Tom's cabin*. New York: Signet Classic.

Strickland, D. and Strickland, M. (1994). *Families: Poems celebrating the African American experience.* Honesdale, PA: Wordsong/Boyds Mill Press.

Strickland, M. (1993). *Poems that sing to you.* Honesdale, PA : Wordsong/ Boyds Mill Press.

Tate, E. (1990). *Thank you Dr. Martin Luther King, Jr.!* New York: Franklin Watts.

Tate, E. (1992). *Front porch stories at the One-Room School.* New York: Bantam.

Tate, E. (1995). *A blessing in disguise.* New York: Delacorte.

Taylor, M. (1975). *Roll of thunder, hear my cry.* New York: Dial Books.

Taylor, M. (1975; 1988). *Song of the trees.* New York: Bantam Books.

Taylor, M. (1990). *The Mississippi bridge.* New York: Dial Books.

Taylor, M. (1990). *The road to Memphis.* New York: Dial Books.

Taylor, M. (1995). *The well.* New York: Dial Books.

Thomas, J. (1987). *Marked by fire.* New York: Avon.

Thomas, J. (1992). *When the nightingale sings.* New York: HarperCollins.

Thomas, J. (1993). *Brown honey in broomwheat tea.* New York: HarperCollins.

Turner, A. (1993). *Faith Ringgold.* New York: Crown Books.

Walter, M. P. (1985). *Justin and the best biscuits.* New York: Lothrop.

Walter, M. P. (1985). *Trouble's child.* New York: Lothrop.

Walter, M. P. (1988). *Mariah loves rock.* New York: Simon & Schuster.

Walter, M. P. (1990). *Mariah keeps cool.* New York: Simon & Schuster.

Walter, M. P. (1992). *The girl on the outside.* New York: Scholastic/Point.

Walter, M. P. (1992). *Mississippi challenge.* New York: Simon & Schuster.

Walter, M. P. (1996). *Second daughter.* New York: Scholastic.

Wesley, V. W. (1993). *Where do I go from here?* New York: Scholastic.

Wilkinson, B. (1993). *Definitely cool.* New York: Scholastic.

Willard, N. (1991). *Pish, posh, said Hieronymous Bosch.* New York: Harcourt Brace Jovanovich.

Williams-Garcia, R. (1989). *Blue tights.* New York: Bantam Starfire Book.

Williams-Garcia, R. (1991). *Fast talk on a slow track.* New York: Lodestar.

Williams-Garcia, R. (1995). *Like sisters on the homefront.* New York: Lodestar.

Wilson, H. (1983). *Our Nig.* New York: Vintage.

Wilson, J. (1992). *Poor girl, rich girl.* New York: Scholastic.

Woodson, J. (1993). *The dear one.* New York: Laurel Leaf.

Woodson, J. (1994). *I hadn't meant to tell you this.* New York: Delacorte Press.

Woodson, J. (1995). *From the notebooks of Melanin Sun.* New York: Blue Sky Press.

Woodson, J. (1995 Nov/Dec). A sign of having been here. *The Horn Book Magazine, 71*, 711–715.

Yarbrough, C. (1989). *The shimmershine queens.* New York: G. Putnam's Sons.

Yates, E. (1950). *Amos Fortune, free man.* New York: E. P. Dutton.

Chapter 3 _____

We Have Stories to Tell:
Puerto Ricans in Children's Books

Sonia Nieto

ଞ୍ଚ ଞ୍ଚ ଞ୍ଚ ଞ୍ଚ ଞ୍ଚ

As a child growing up in New York City, I remember taking the long walk to the Brooklyn Public Library in our neighborhood once a month with my mother and sister. In what I am now certain is a building much less imposing than I thought it was at the time, I would search the stacks, looking for the six perfect books, the maximum allowed. After carefully selecting the books, I would clutch them eagerly, anxious to get home and get lost in stories for the next few days.

Reading was an important part of my youth, but somehow it was separated from the rest of my life. There was, in fact, a deep chasm that I could not reconcile between stories at home and books from the library. Little could I imagine when I was a child that there could be books whose pages told stories about children like me, children who spoke Spanish at home, whose parents came from faraway places, and who lived in communities that did not look at all like the ones in the books. No babbling brooks or trees or cows or horses here; no lawns, even. The thought that anybody would write stories whose names sounded like ours (Sonia, Lydia, Milagros, Ricardo), whose parents' voices were thick with accents when they spoke English, and whose concerns centered around our songs and poems and folktales or just our everyday lives—was inconceivable to me.

Yes, we told stories at home and they were, of course, in Spanish. I can remember listening to "Juan Bobo" stories, or sitting around the kitchen table as the adults told the children hilarious tales about "jíbaros," or peasants newly arrived from Puerto Rico, who got into comical jams but in the end used their considerable wits to get out of them. I can remember my mother telling us riddles she had learned as a girl and we children trying to guess what she was describing, or my aunt recounting scary stories at night in the dark. These were fun, but library books, well, they were something

59

else. They told us "real" stories because they were written down by important people who wrote in English and described other worlds. Naturally, I reached these conclusions for a very good reason: I never saw Puerto Ricans in children's books as protagonists, authors, or illustrators.

Over the years, I have come to believe that these walls between home and "real" stories, that is, stories found in libraries, need not be erected. All children have the right to see themselves, their families, and their communities in the books they read, just as they have the right to see people, events, and circumstances with which they are totally unfamiliar. Stories, in short, should reflect both our world and the worlds beyond our reach because learning takes place in the space created by them. We all have stories to tell, no matter what language they are in or what experiences they recount. All children need to know this.

This chapter will focus on Puerto Ricans, the second largest Latino group in the United States, and how they are reflected in children's books. I will briefly describe the history of Puerto Ricans in the United States in order to provide the necessary context for understanding their experiences here. I will also analyze a number of themes in recent children's literature about Puerto Ricans and suggest criteria for selecting books as well as strategies for using them in the curriculum.

WHO ARE THE PUERTO RICANS?

The Latino population in the United States is highly diverse, growing dramatically, and on the road to becoming the nation's largest minority.[1] As of 1994, it was estimated that there were over 26,600,000 Latinos living in the United States, constituting over 10 percent of the total U.S. population, more than a 40 percent increase since the 1980 census.[2] Mexican Americans, Puerto Ricans, and Cubans are the largest groups, and they are joined by Central Americans, South Americans, and Spanish-speaking Caribbeans to make up what is known as the Latino or Hispanic community. Latinos live in every major metropolitan area in every state and in many rural and suburban areas. Although the majority live in three regional areas (the Southwest, the Northeast, and Florida), no area in the United States has remained untouched by the Latino presence.[3]

A number of issues emerge from the contradiction between the dramatic growth of Latinos in the United States and their invisibility in popular children's literature. First, their lack of representation jeopardizes all youngsters because both Latinos and non-Latinos are often left with little but misinformation or stereotypes about the entire group. Furthermore, Latinos are frequently perceived as a monolithic group, as if differences in national origin, geography, native language, race, class, place of birth, and length of residence in the United States, among others, did not exist. The feeling that "if you've seen one Latino, you've seen them all" is perpetuated in children's literature when these important inter-ethnic differences are not acknowledged.[4] Each Latino group presents a unique case and teachers and schools need to be aware of this in order to select literature that best reflects their experiences.

Although *Latino(a)* or *Hispanic* are useful in expressing the deep connections among those in the Americas who are descendants of native inhabitants, Spanish and other European colonizers, and enslaved Africans, or any combination of these groups, these terms sometimes hide more than they reveal. While they may convey the powerful legacy that extends from the southernmost tip of Latin America to the Spanish-speaking Caribbean to what is now the Southwest United States, such broad categories are not very useful in describing specific national origin groups. Puerto Ricans differ from other Latinos in the United States in very specific and unique ways. They are the poorest Latino subgroup, for example, and Puerto Rican children specifically have one of the highest poverty rates in the country. In addition, the dropout rate of Puerto Rican youngsters is extremely high, and has posed a continuing dilemma for the community.[5]

Nevertheless, although these are certainly difficult and trying situations, Puerto Ricans are not simply victims: they also have unique strengths, including a very high rate of bilingualism, strong family and community values, and a history of community activism and determined resilience in the face of adversity. Teachers, librarians, and others who select children's literature need to be familiar with Puerto Rican history and culture in order to make informed choices about the books they select and their outreach efforts to the community.[6] I will concentrate on just some aspects of the Puerto Rican experience, but urge readers to consult other resources to develop a better understanding of the history and culture of the Puerto Rican people both on the island and in the United States itself.[7]

Puerto Ricans in the United States

Puerto Ricans living in the United States number over 2,776,000, approximately two-fifths of the Puerto Rican people, and represent one of the most dramatic diasporas of any people in the world.[8] With a five-hundred-year history of colonialism, first under Spain and after 1898 under the United States, Puerto Rico was one of the spoils of the Spanish-American War. Although it was ceded to the United States by Spain through the Treaty of Paris, the Puerto Rican people were neither consulted about their fate after the war, nor about the U.S. citizenship that was unilaterally imposed on them in 1917. Because of their colonial status, since 1898, Puerto Ricans both in Puerto Rico and in the United States have been, according to sociologist Clara Rodríguez, "born in the U.S.A." regardless of their actual birthplace.[9] The Puerto Rican experience in the United States is impossible to understand without an appreciation of this fact. It explains why so many Puerto Ricans live here, as well as some of the great differences between their migration experience as compared with that of other Latinos and immigrants in general. Because of their citizenship, for example, Puerto Ricans are free to travel to and from the United States and have done so in large numbers since the early 1900s. Virtually no Puerto Rican has remained unaffected by the migration experience: at least one-third of the population has at one time or another lived in the continental United States.[10]

The reasons for migration have been many, but center on economic issues. Overpopulation of the island was often given as the primary reason during the early migration, but more recent explanations focus on the dramatic structural changes that took place in Puerto Rico as a result of U.S. control that virtually destroyed traditional patterns of individual land ownership, consolidating the domination of large corporations from the United States.[11] These changes meant an increase in unemployment and the growth of a marginal work force. The possibility of jobs in the United States has been and continues to be the single most important factor promoting migration.

The movement of Puerto Ricans to the continental United States is generally referred to as a *migration* rather than *immigration* because it takes place within a politically related area, although in recent years it has also been called "[im]migration" due to its complicated nature (Márquez, 1995). Whatever it is called, the movement of Puerto Ricans to the United States has been unique for a number of reasons. For one, Puerto Ricans represent the first group of newcomers to arrive as citizens. Also, the major Puerto Rican migration, which began in the 1940s, occurred at a time when a strong back was less important than technical and professional skills, and this has had a detrimental effect on the economic advancement of the entire group. That is, the low-skill but relatively good-paying and secure jobs available to earlier immigrants no longer exist to the same degree. Furthermore, "jet-age migration" also meant that travel back and forth has been quite easy and inexpensive. Thus, the migration has been characterized as a "revolving door,"[12] or "a process of Puerto Rican commuting,"[13] resulting in a linguistic and cultural continuity unavailable to earlier immigrants.[14] This has meant that Puerto Ricans have resisted to a great extent the pressure of assimilation that characterized the predominant experience of European immigrants.

There are numerous examples of cultural maintenance, including an extremely high rate of bilingualism, a proliferation of Spanish-language radio and television programs, bilingual literature, as well as *bodegas* (grocery stores catering to Latinos) and *salsa* (Caribbean music). Rather than a "single life-transforming experience," migration has in reality become a way of life.[15] Puerto Ricans currently reside in every state, but are concentrated in urban areas in the Northeast, including New York City (where about one million Puerto Ricans live) and the New England and mid-Atlantic states.[16]

Some Puerto Rican Cultural Values

This brief history points out some key differences that characterize the Puerto Rican community. A number of cultural values connected to this history are also necessary to keep in mind. First, however, a note of caution is in order. Culture is learned behavior and, as such, responds to many changes in society; thus it is ever-changing rather than fixed. Accordingly, there is no one "typical" Puerto Rican person or family, and searching for the "essential" or "pure" Puerto Rican culture is both a futile and, in the end, impossible exercise. Puerto Ricans differ among one another in social class, place of residence, family structure, educational background, racial characteristics, length of time in the United States, and many other variables. Furthermore, Puerto Rican culture, as all cultures, is in a constant state of flux. In spite of vast differences, however, there are a number of overarching values reflective of a majority of Puerto Ricans.

Because of its role in providing needed support for all members, the *family* is crucial in understanding the Puerto Rican experience. Although less so today than in previous times, it is still true that Puerto Rican families have extended and close networks. This means, among other things, that grandparents, other family members, and even unrelated individuals can be found living in the same home. More important, it also means that the connections among family members, including those referred to as *como familia* (close friends who for all intents and purposes serve the same role as family, especially kinship relations such as godparents) help explain a number of related values. The value of *responsibility for others within the family* (and *family* is often expansively defined), for instance, can help explain the practice of placing family rather than individual interests first. It is no coincidence that sayings such as the widely known "Mi casa es tu casa" or the less well-known "Donde comen dos, comen tres" (where two eat, three can eat) come from and reflect this particular value in Latino culture.

Other related strengths of the Puerto Rican community are its conception of *community responsibility* and its *resilience*. The history of Puerto Ricans in the United States is replete with examples of home-grown organizations that developed as a response to community problems, including such disparate groups as the early Puerto Rican Merchants Association, ASPIRA (an agency promoting youth education and leadership), and the National Congress for Puerto Rican Rights.[17] Values of family, collective responsibility, and sacrifice for children and community are important to keep in mind in the discussion of the depiction of Puerto Ricans in children's books.

Puerto Rican culture is also characterized by differences in roles and expectations of males and females. In general, females are more protected and are encouraged to stay closer to home than are males, who are given a wider freedom of movement. Girls are expected to help out more with household chores, at a young age, including cooking, whereas boys usually are not. Furthermore, girls are expected to be modest and chaste while boys are not.

These generalizations, however, do not take into account a number of factors. Gender is always a complicated issue that is too easily dichotomized to characterize entire cultures as more or less sexist, generally using United States dominant culture as the yardstick. Although it is true that Puerto Rican culture is sexist (as are most cultures, including United States mainstream culture), a simple characterization such as this does little to explain how gender roles and expectations are evident in everyday life. Such simplistic characterizations fail to account for women's historic resistance to, and victories against, exploitation. For example, women have played a central role in every liberation struggle of the Puerto Rican people, from "El Grito de Lares" (a revolutionary movement against Spain when the First Republic of Puerto Rico was proclaimed for one day in September, 1868), to twentieth-century social, political, and even armed actions against the colonial policies of the United States. In all of these, women have been in the vanguard, laying to rest the stereotype of the passive Puerto Rican woman. Women have also been well-known artists, activists for social justice, and politicians. For instance, at a time when few American women were political leaders, Felisa Rincón de Gautier became a legend as the mayor of San Juan, the capital of Puerto Rico, from 1944 to 1968.[18]

Another problem with simplistic characterizations of gender is that they treat culture as if it were static and finished rather than dynamic and everchanging. Although gender roles and expectations may describe a culture as it is idealized and imagined, they do not describe the culture that is lived every day by Puerto Ricans of diverse ages, backgrounds, experiences, social classes, and geographic locations. In any discussion of Puerto Rican children's literature these are important issues to keep in mind because there is a tendency, especially among those not intimately connected with the culture, to present males and females in stereotypical roles that do not adequately portray the tremendous complexities and contradictions in their lives.

In conclusion, Puerto Rican cultural values differ in general from United States mainstream values in a number of ways, and these differences need to be reflected in children's books that focus on Puerto Ricans. Furthermore, the number of Puerto Ricans living in the United States has increased dramatically throughout the century and represents a sizable proportion of the population of many cities and towns in the Northeast. Yet, in spite of the fact that so many Puerto Rican youngsters are found in U.S. schools, the curriculum has changed relatively little to accommodate them. Even bilingual programs are generally only a transition to all-English classes,[19] and children's literature that focuses on the experiences of this population, whether in English or Spanish, is often hard to find.

PUERTO RICAN CHILDREN'S LITERATURE IN THE UNITED STATES

Very little research has been done on Puerto Rican children's literature in the United States. One of the few studies, probably the first, was a 1972 study by the Council on Interracial Books for Children (CIBC). In a special issue on Puerto Rican themes in children's books, to their surprise the CIBC discovered that one hundred books with what could loosely be termed "Puerto Rican themes" had been published since the 1940s.[20] That is, all concerned the Puerto Rican experience either on the island or in the United States, and had one or more protagonists who were Puerto Rican. In spite of the rather large number of books they found, the CIBC concluded that the vast majority, written almost exclusively by non-Puerto Ricans, were pervaded by racism, sexism, and an ethnocentric colonialism. Specifically, they said, "Far from finding the books accurate and authentic, the reviewers discovered extraordinary distortions and misconceptions ranging all the way from simple misuse of Spanish to the grossest insensitivities and outright blunders, including editorial errors that in 'non-minority' books would never be tolerated."[21]

Ten years after the special issue on Puerto Ricans first appeared, the CIBC asked me to do a follow-up to determine whether newer books were less biased and more accurate than those published prior to 1972.[22] In my review, I found that fifty-six titles, including fiction and nonfiction, had been published in the ten-year period from 1973 to 1983. Although a small number of books reflected a more comprehensive understanding of Puerto Rican reality, the majority were still assimilationist and stereotypical, reflecting conventional assumptions of inferiority. The fact that more of these books were written and illustrated by Puerto Ricans had a decidedly positive effect on their quality and accuracy because a larger number of books were being written by authors who had direct knowledge and experience in the Puerto Rican community. Although one does not have to be Puerto Rican to write good children's literature with Puerto Rican themes, as is evident from the list of recommended books at the end of this chapter, it is nevertheless true that real-life experiences in the culture usually help to make books more believable and less stereotypical than those of authors who have not had similar experiences. Until recently, a majority of children's books with Puerto Rican themes were written by those with a limited awareness and experience with Puerto Rico and Puerto Ricans.

How the situation has changed in the past dozen years or so is the subject of the remainder of this chapter. Given the tremendous demographic changes in our society, one would suspect that the situation has improved, if not dramatically, as least considerably, and that the negative messages about Puerto Ricans found in earlier books would be far less apparent today. In some ways, this optimism is warranted because more sensitive images can be found in many of the newer books. Nevertheless, the situation is little changed: There is still a small number of books being published and there are still negative messages still being perpetuated in some of them. In what follows, I will explore how images of Puerto Ricans in children's books have changed since 1983.

THEMES IN CHILDREN'S BOOKS WITH PUERTO RICANS

I began this review by trying to locate all the children's books published in the United States since 1983 that could be said to deal in any way with Puerto Ricans. I have generally included only works of fiction, although there are some exceptions (that is, I have included biographies, as there have been precious few of these in the past, and such books as *How My Family Lives in America* by Susan Kuklin, although it is a photo essay, because it is one of the few books that has a cross-cultural perspective). I included Puerto Rican and non-Puerto Rican authors, and considered books for all ages from pre-school through young adult. I even included books that *appeared* to be about Puerto Ricans, even if they did not specifically identify the characters as such (for example, *Abuela*, by Arthur Dorros, an enchanting story about a girl and her grandmother, gives clues that could make the protagonists Puerto Ricans, Dominicans, Cubans, or Central Americans); or *Hispanic, Female, and Young*, edited by Phyllis Tashlik, and José-Luis Orozco's *De colores and Other Latin-American Folk Songs for Children* because they include Puerto Ricans within the larger framework of Latinos. As I read these books, three recurring and sometimes contradictory themes became apparent:

- The continuing invisibility of Puerto Ricans in the field of children's literature;
- The absence, neglect, or stereotyping of the family and family life in some books, including a reluctance to include only superficial aspects of the culture; and
- The emergence of an incipient children's literature that is beginning to illuminate the Puerto Rican experience in more depth.

Each of these three themes will be discussed briefly.

Invisibility

By 1995, the Puerto Rican presence in children's literature in the United States was still largely invisible. Although the number of Puerto Ricans residing in the United States has more than doubled to over two million during the past three decades, it is hard to know it by their presence in children's books. Just forty-five books published or reissued since 1983 were located. (See the complete listing of books at the end of this chapter). Even this number is misleading because almost a fifth are books that were published previously and have been either released in a new edition or reissued by another publisher. If we consider the fact that over 40,000 children's books have been published during the same time period, this number is about a tenth of one percent. Although the one hundred books found in 1972 and the fifty-six books published from 1973 to 1983 also included nonfiction titles, and I have included primarily works of fiction among those published from 1983 to 1994, by any measure this number hardly represents tremendous progress.

What accounts for the continuing invisibility of Puerto Ricans in children's books? One explanation is the political mood of the country, especially during the 1980s, and how it was reflected even in publishing policies and practices. The 1980s were among the most politically conservative in U.S. history. Ample evidence of this conservatism can be found in the loss of many of the gains made during the civil rights movement (including civil rights legislation, affirmative action, desegregation, bilingual and multicultural education, and programs such as Chapter 1 and Head Start). The publishing industry has echoed this trend. Whereas Puerto Rican themes might have been more fashionable in the early 1970s (twenty books were published in 1973, the year when more books about Puerto Ricans were published than ever before or since), this was not the case in the 1980s. There were times in the decade of the 1980s when *no* books were published (1983 through 1985). A change in this trend began in the late 1980s and is continuing today: five books were published or reissued in 1988, 1990, and 1991, six in 1992, and seven, the largest number in two decades, were published in 1993. In 1994, four books were published. A progress of sorts, these numbers represent a renewed and emerging interest on the part of publishers in the 1990s to locate and print a more multicultural literature and they give cause for some hope. Renewed interest is apparent also at national conferences and meetings, and in their brochures, publishing companies are making it clear that they are on the lookout for authors who represent those communities whose voices have been largely silent in children's literature. Given the huge political changes forecast for the second half of the 1990s, during which time the conservative agenda is again expected to be in full swing, it is unclear whether the trend to locate and publish more multicultural literature will continue or come to an abrupt halt.

While the percentage of books written and illustrated by Puerto Ricans or other Latinos is now greater than ever before, probably not coincidentally, the most blatant of the negative stereotypes found in previously published books have decreased. Although there is still an unacceptably low number of Latino, and specifically Puerto Rican, authors writing children's books, there has been a significant change in the past several years. Of the forty-five books reviewed, thirty were written or co-written, edited, and/or illustrated by Latinos, most of whom are Puerto Ricans. This is a striking difference from 1973, when only five Puerto Ricans were among the authors of the 100 books, and 1983, when there were just twelve Latinos or Puerto Ricans among the authors and illustrators. Even in 1992, when this chapter was first written, only eleven Puerto Rican or Latino authors were identified. Anthologies published during the past decade have also included more Puerto Rican authors. Although these numbers are a hopeful sign, the overall number of books is still disappointingly low. They also hide the fact that a few authors (notably Nicholasa Mohr and Lulu Delacre) are responsible for multiple titles.

Why are there then so few Puerto Rican authors? Although more Puerto Ricans are writing for children than ever before, the argument might be made that there are simply fewer Puerto Rican writers, or that what they do write is not necessarily good literature. The history of Puerto Rican literature, whether in Puerto Rico or in the United States, belies this claim. Numerous anthologies of adult Puerto Rican literature have been published. Some have focused on the Puerto Rican experience in the United States and on literature written in English. These anthologies point to a rich and varied literature that creatively, poignantly, and sometimes tragically describes the many facets of the Puerto Rican reality.[23] The claim that there are no legitimate literary voices within our ranks simply cannot be sustained.

In the past, the majority of books with Puerto Rican themes tended to focus on young adult rather than on younger readers, although there has been a dramatic shift: a majority of the books published since 1983 are now suitable for younger readers, including preschool children. It was true in the past that few Puerto Rican authors wrote for young children, and there were a number of explanations for this. One was the perceived market for such literature. Moreover, publishers did not necessarily feel pressure from the Puerto Rican community to produce books for young children. This is changing, however, as parents and other activists are making increased demands on publishers for this literature. Schools too have begun to press for more diversity in the children's books they use in their libraries and, increasingly, in their literature-based reading and language arts programs.

The result has been to send publishers scrambling in the search for Latino authors.

It is also evident that Latino children's literature has differed from other U.S. children's literature in that it has not been limited to the traditional children's themes found in mainstream literature. Latino children's literature has revolved around folklore, legends, riddles, games, poetry, and stories in the oral tradition rather than on the childhood or adolescent experience as interpreted in the U.S. context. By 1994, more of these traditional genres were evident in children's literature published in the United States than ever before (see the list of recommended books in Puerto Rican literature at the end of this chapter for many examples).

Furthermore, because children's stories have tended to be family or community stories, Puerto Rican children's literature has often been a variation on adult literature. The fact that some of this literature is marketed in the "young adult" category here in the United States although it may have originally been written and intended for adults is revealing. *Cuentos*, a bilingual collection of Puerto Rican short stories by a superb group of Puerto Rican authors, is a good example. Some of the stories are appropriate for young adults because of their style and level, not because they deal specifically with issues of relevance to young adults. Some of the stories written by Nicholasa Mohr, notably *El Bronx Remembered* and *In Nueva York*, originally intended for adults, have consistently been marketed for young adult readers. The same is true of *Silent Dancing*, a collection of autobiographical essays that can be appreciated by only the most sophisticated young adults. The "young adult" classification of these books does not necessarily mean that the themes, language, or content were intended for young people.

Absence and Disparagement of the Puerto Rican Family and a Recurrent Use of Stereotypes

Although the Puerto Rican family and family traditions are more salient in newer books than ever before, a few books, primarily but not exclusively those written by non-Latinos, continue to demean or exclude the family and to repeat worn stereotypes. The absence of the family as a central concern may be true of children's books in general, but given the great importance of the family in Puerto Rican culture, it is an especially troubling oversight in these books.

The characters, story line, and setting of *Secret City, U.S.A.*, by Felice Holman, provide a graphic example of this invisibility. It should be said that the author has never claimed that the main characters are Puerto Rican, and indeed it is unclear whether they are or not: their country of origin is never specifically mentioned, Spanish is never used, and most characters have nicknames that belie a Spanish language heritage. Nevertheless, there are hints of their Latino heritage throughout the book: the main character, Benno, and his best friend Moon come from what the author calls the "islands" and Jojo, Benno's grandfather, speaks in a "musical language"; Benno's cousins, who have recently come from "the islands," have Spanish names (Juan and Paco); Jojo's name used to be José, but he changed it; there is a Tío Chico; and the story takes place in New York, where about half of the two million Latinos are Puerto Rican. One could even say that the very fact that no mention is made of their ethnicity could be taken as a slight: while the protagonists' ethnicity may not be important to the author, it certainly would be to Latinos in general. No matter the ethnicity of the characters, however, the same disservice is done whether they are Dominican, Cuban, or South American.

Except for Juan and Paco, Tío Chico, and Jojo, the families of the main characters are barely mentioned. Benno's family is generally mentioned only in superficial and unflattering ways and the majority of references made to family and community are highly negative. In one scene, the people in the neighborhood are described: "At the sides of the stoops, the men, out of work or on welfare, stand in little groups nodding at each other or punching each other out . . . At the corners, knots of teenage kids or older boys play cards, smoke, deal in drugs or stolen objects. It's the commerce of the slums" (p. 23). Further on, the building is likewise characterized: "Smells that issue from the open doorways are those of too many people closed up together for the winter with bad plumbing and often not much cleaning. All the cooking odors still linger and have turned to garbage stinks" (p. 23). The neighborhood is described, in Benno's words, in equally negative terms: "There, the people scream obscenities at each other; do rotten stuff; try to kill each other" (p. 115). Hardly anywhere in the story is there a positive comment about the people, their homes, or the community in which they live. Negative portrayals center on drug addicts, the lack of cleanliness in the homes, and even "cooking odors," a characterization of Latino food that only an outsider would make.

In the midst of these overwhelmingly damaging images of people and community appears the most positive adult character in the book: Marie Lorry, a White woman, a "nice and pretty lady" who is a social worker at a local hospital and the only supportive adult. Her influence on him is more powerful than that of anybody else: "There has never been another adult in his life with whom he has exchanged so much conversation, except Jojo. There has never been a person who has taken such close notice of what he has done . . ." (p. 163) In the final scene, Marie's boyfriend Pete, a reporter for a local newspaper, characterizes Benno and his friends as "otherwise uncared for and sleeping on city streets" (p. 184), this in spite of the fact that both Benno and Moon live with their families. Because of the stories Pete writes about their "Secret City," an abandoned neighborhood they have begun to refurbish, a private citizen's commission of "outstanding, able, generous people" is formed. It is probably safe to assume that the saviors of these homeless waifs are primarily wealthy and White.

One searches in vain within the pages of this book for strong Latino adults. The curious absence of any reference to family in *Secret City* represents such an extreme example of the denial of the importance of the Latino family that it is both far-fetched and unbelievable. Not only are the families of the children in this story unresponsive, but the only support and love they can find is from communities outside their own. It is true that many Puerto Rican families live in dire poverty and have to contend with unresponsive agencies, crime, drugs, racism, and other negative situations. It is also true that some of these families are dysfunctional, abusive, and neglectful, as are some families of all ethnic groups. However, to imply that the majority of Latino families are like this, as this book would suggest, results in a story line that is patronizing and harmful.

Holman's books often portray alienated youth who confront an uncaring world, and this is an important issue. Furthermore, the theme of homelessness, particularly among children, is a crucial one that needs to be addressed by all communities. However, in misrepresenting Latino families to such a degree, the author has missed a golden opportunity to present the issue with the validity it deserves. Images such as these are dangerous because they perpetuate the image of Puerto Rican families as monolithic, particularly in their relationships with their children, and characterize them as uncaring and dismissive in the aggregate. This represents a rigidly limited, and therefore incomplete and misleading, perspective of the Puerto Rican community. Blanca Vázquez, writing about the images of Puerto Ricans in films, could just as easily have been referring to children's books:

> What was missing from all of those screen images of Puerto Ricans? *Mi abuela,* my sisters, my mother, my father, friends and neighbors. My mother was a sewing machine operator who worked 8 to 5, was never sick or late for work, and came home to raise four girls. My father worked six days a week driving a cab on the night shifts of New York. I'm not seeking to make icons of them (or saying that growing up in a working class Puerto Rican family didn't have its own internal contradictions and history of internalized structures of oppression), but my parents were more typical of Puerto Ricans in the city than the juvenile delinquents and prostitutes on the screen.[24]

Whereas *Secret City* represents an extreme case of the invisibility and inaccurate portrayal of the Puerto Rican family, other books are more subtle in their characterizations. One of the ways in which this is done is through a reluctance to include any but the most superficial aspects of the family culture in the stories. This may be an overreaction on the part of writers to past criticisms about stereotyping and racism, but it also reflects the authors' ignorance of the Puerto Rican experience and uneasiness in dealing with it. The story *Somewhere Green* by Karin Mango includes a Puerto Rican, Angel Rivera, who is the boyfriend of Bryan, the protagonist. Some of the authors' characterizations reveal her lack of in-depth experience with the Puerto Rican community. For example, Angel makes some highly unlikely utterances ("Why didn't you tell me, Bryan? It's terrific fun" [p. 64]; and the reference to Bryan and her brother and sister as "lucky devils" [p. 87]). These are not believable as renditions of the day-to-day language of a New York Puerto Rican youth.

The depiction of Angel's mother is equally superficial and displays an ignorance of the community and a demeaning use of the Spanish language. Mrs. Rivera, in describing the protagonist's father, says, "Ah, sí. Tall, blond señor" (p. 93). Using Spanish as a prop with which to identify characters' ethnicity has been a common ploy in children's books. Much less common now than in previous books, it still tends to result in a degrading use of the language. It also results in misspellings, misplaced accents, and faulty constructions. ("Erés tan bonita," Angel tells Bryan, adding an accent where none is needed). In *Juan Bobo and the Pig* by Jan Mike, one can find a grammatical mistake ("Bueno, mi hermanos!" rather than "mis hermanos") as well as stilted Spanish used as a prop ("Let him be, mi hermano").

This criticism is not meant to suggest that Spanish should not be used. On the contrary, code-switching, or using a mixture of Spanish and English, is very common in both the daily speech and written literature among Puerto Ricans and other Latinos. This strategy has been used successfully in many of the books in the annotated lists at the end of this chapter, including *My Name Is María Isabel* by Alma Flor Ada, and *Abuela* by Arthur Dorros (in most of these books, a glossary of Spanish words is included). Nevertheless, when those unfamiliar with the language attempt to incorporate it without a knowledge of the most rudimentary rules of spelling, vocabulary, or usage, the result is often ludicrous and insulting because the language becomes stilted, unconvincing, and simply incorrect.

The use of English among Puerto Rican characters in a few of the books is also stilted and contrived. This is directly related to some authors' ignorance of the way their characters would actually use language. The dialogue in *Secret City* is probably the most annoying in this regard: "Whady'a want? Ya want yer mama and papa don't care whatcha do?" (p. 35); or "How come is that?" (p. 17) are typical constructions used. This less-than-credible language use is in stark contrast to the dialogue of urban teen-agers used by Walter Dean Myers in *Scorpions*. Set in Harlem, this powerful story is about the friendship between Jamal, an African American boy, and Tito, who is Puerto Rican, and the very real dangers young men face with gangs, guns, and violence in urban communities. Myers uses dialogue in natural and believable ways and demonstrates a real understanding of the Puerto

Rican family. For instance, in explaining to Jamal what Puerto Rican grandmothers are like, Tito says, " . . . your grandmother is suppose to take care of you. She said in Puerto Rico everybody treats their grandparents like they were the real mother in the house. She said that your family is more important in Puerto Rico than here" (p. 33). Although both grandmothers and grandfathers are viewed very positively in Latino culture, Myers has captured the special reverence Puerto Ricans feel for grandmothers in this short segment (a look at the proliferation of stories with Latina grandmothers as protagonists is ample indication of their important place in the family). *Scorpions* is a good example of children's literature that, while not focusing centrally on the Puerto Rican experience, treats it with respect. There are no cases of misspelled words or trite expressions here.

Illustrations also help perpetuate incomplete or inaccurate images. Even when the text is good, the illustrations may fall into facile stereotypes. The poetic story *Flamboyán* by Arnold Adoff, with its beautiful descriptions of the girl named for the flame tree and the island of Culebra, is an example. The illustrations are vivid and breathtakingly beautiful, but they are also inauthentic. Some are more evocative of Mexican motifs than of the Caribbean, and scenes of women carrying baskets on their heads are more typical of other Caribbean countries than of Puerto Rico. The same can be said of *The Tiger and the Rabbit*, a Puerto Rican folktale illustrated by Francisco Mora, a Mexican artist. Although the illustrations are soft and lovely, they are also sometimes inaccurate, as when a farmer is shown wearing a Mexican sombrero and a *serape*.

Stereotypical or incomplete characterizations of Puerto Ricans are not made only by non-Latinos. *Where Angels Glide at Dawn,* an anthology of stories most of which were originally written in Spanish and translated into English, is an uneven attempt to provide a range of Latino voices about the Latino experience. One of the few stories about a Puerto Rican family, "Fairy Tale" by Barbara Mujica, repeats some of the same limiting stereotypes. The main character is Monica, a fifteen-year-old Puerto Rican girl living in New York who yearns to go to college. Her mother, Angela, wants her to go to vocational school instead: "Why should the girl be sitting in a classroom when she could be out earning money? It didn't make sense to her" (p. 79). Monica tries to do her studying before her mother gets home because "Angela would make a fuss if she caught Monica studying" (p. 78). It is true, but was especially so in the past, that when family resources were limited the education of males took precedence over that of females. Nevertheless, the situation described in this story, while a remote possibility, contradicts the tremendously optimistic educational aspirations of Puerto Rican parents who believe that education is the one sure way out of poverty. Some parents might urge their children to go to vocational school because they see it as the only realistic alternative to college, but one would be hard-pressed to find a Puerto Rican parent upset at the sight of her daughter doing homework.

An Incipient Puerto Rican Children's Literature

The search for an authentic literature is not the search for an upbeat, consistently positive, sentimental, romanticized, or idealized reality. Rather, it is the search for a more balanced, complete, accurate, and realistic literature that asks even young readers to grapple with sometimes thorny issues. It is literature that is neither sanguinely positive nor destructively negative, but one that attempts to reflect the range of issues and possibilities within the community's experience. This brings us to the third, and by far most promising trend in newer books: a slowly emerging children's literature that is beginning to reflect the Puerto Rican community in more depth.

In order to describe the emerging literature, I will first define what I believe are its central tenets. Although I have chosen to focus on books published in the United States, most of which have been written in English, this is not meant to overlook Puerto Rican children's books published in Puerto Rico (for example, the highly acclaimed Puerto Rican author of adult literature, Rosario Ferré, has also written or retold a delightful collection of six stories, including legends and folktales, titled *La mona que le pisaron la cola*, Ediciones Huracán, Río Piedras, Puerto Rico, 1981). Rather, it is to stress the necessity of making this literature accessible to all young people in the United States, regardless of their ethnicity or native language. A multicultural perspective is important for all children because it works against the tendency to ghettoize literature so that only Puerto Rican children read Puerto Rican authors, only African American children read African American authors, and so on. Consequently, although I focus on books in English, I will indicate when such books are bilingual or available also in Spanish.

First, Puerto Rican children's literature is usually, although not always, written by Puerto Rican authors. It is my hope that my decision to include three lists (see end of chapter) will help readers select excellent Puerto Rican children's literature as well as other appropriate books that include Puerto Ricans. The lists that I have included are first, the entire list of books reviewed for this study; second, the Puerto Rican children's literature that I especially recommend; and third, a list of other books from the complete list that include Puerto Rican and/or other Latino characters (along with biographies, which are strictly speaking not included in "literature"), most of which are written by non-Latinos. I have chosen to include this list because it is important, even necessary, to acknowledge non-Puerto Rican authors who write about Puerto Ricans with awareness, knowledge, and respect. Walter Dean Myers has done this consistently and convincingly.

Arnold Adoff's *Flamboyan* and José Luis Orozco's *De colores*, among others, are examples of books that include Puerto Rican characters in this way. It is also conceivable that in the future, more authors of non-Puerto Rican background may be able to write what can be described as Puerto Rican children's literature: stories and other literary genres that capture the mood and texture of the lives of Puerto Ricans in realistic and believable ways. For this to occur, they will have had to have a close and enduring relationship with at least part of the Puerto Rican experience, either in Puerto Rico or in Puerto Rican communities in the United States. Given the increasing interdependence of communities and the growing awareness of multiculturalism in our society, this is certainly possible.

Thus, in spite of the assertion that in most cases Puerto Rican children's literature is literature written by Puerto Ricans, books by non-Puerto Ricans of the Puerto Rican experience can serve an important role in multicultural children's literature. Unless more authors provide the perspective of meaningful and respectful outsiders, we are left with only insiders' lived realities, and this can sometimes result in romantic or one-sided views. Thus, both are necessary and important.

Second, Puerto Rican children's literature is founded on the tenets of adult Puerto Rican literature. That is, it is quintessential good literature that, although emanating from a specific experience, has universal applications. Its particularity does not necessarily make it provincial; its messages can be meaningful for all readers. Written in English or Spanish or a combination of both, from the island perspective or that of the United States, Puerto Rican children's literature attempts to place before all readers, not only those of Puerto Rican background, an experience that is realistic and free from sentimentality. In Lulu Delacre's book, for instance, non-Puerto Rican children learn something of Puerto Rican culture in a way that is fun and entertaining. Her latest book, *Vejigante/Masquerader*, is a beautifully told and illustrated book that tells the story about *carnaval* in Ponce, but more importantly touches on issues of family responsibility and caring. At the end of this chapter, there is an annotated list that includes those books that I would classify under the category of Puerto Rican children's literature as well as other highly recommended books written by non-Puerto Ricans.

Third, Puerto Rican children's literature depicts multiple realities based on a panorama of experiences within the diversity of the community itself. Not afraid to confront sometimes painful realities, it is also not averse to celebrating the small triumphs that individuals and the community can achieve in spite of overwhelming odds. Whether it is an urban experience, such as that chronicled by Piri Thomas in the recently reissued gem of a collection, *Stories from El Barrio*, or set in Puerto Rico, as is Felix Pitre's *Juan Bobo and the Pig*, or both as in Judith Ortiz Cofer's *Silent Dancing*,

the literature speaks of a variety of experiences, many of which are unknown to even some Puerto Ricans. Good literature should not simply rep-
licate our lives; it should challenge us to expand our experiences and shed
our preconceptions. In this regard, good Puerto Rican children's literature
is not squeamish about posing difficult dilemmas. Fernando Pico's inspiring story, *The Red Comb*, one of the few books that concerns the African
heritage of the island, focuses on how a community pulls together to help a
runaway slave in 19th-century Puerto Rico. The author is not afraid, however, to bring up the issue of collusion with slavery, even among the mixed-
race population. In *Going Home*, Nicholasa Mohr confronts the generation
gap, the tendency among many Puerto Rican parents to be overprotective,
the sometimes unreasonable rules of conduct for females within the family,
first love, the difficulty of adjusting to the island when one is confronted
with its less-than-sentimental realities, and the pain of being rejected within
both the United States and Puerto Rico—and all of this in less than two
hundred pages. In the process, both positive and negative portraits of particular characters emerge.

Some Persistent Dilemmas

An incipient literature of this type is not without its problems. The books
included at the end of this chapter are not of equal quality. Some are better
written and developed than others. Some, such as *Sing, Little Sack!*, may
be far-fetched and highly unlikely stories, but are rescued by an engaging
protagonist and sense of humor. Some, such as Lulu Delacre's books, have
lovely and evocative illustrations; the illustrations in others, such as *Atariba
and Niguayona* and *My Aunt Otilia's Spirits*, may appear to be bizarre (although I have found that children are generally enchanted by them). The
list of recommended books includes those whose positive qualities outnumber their negative ones. I have included them precisely because there are so
few books at all concerning Puerto Ricans.

Ironically, two other dilemmas with the literature written in the past
dozen years or so are probably a direct response to some of the criticisms
made about books with Puerto Rican themes written prior to the 1970s
(CIBC, 1972). First, the literature was roundly criticized because it focused
so much on "true-life" stories set in urban settings. These stories usually
provided simplistic solutions to the very complex problems faced by Puerto
Rican youngsters. For young readers, books generally resolved protagonists'
nostalgia for Puerto Rico by presenting the inevitable, and always magical,
first encounter with snow. It also meant that their major problem, learning
English, was always successfully confronted, and once it was, all other problems disappeared. For older readers, the focus was on gangs, crime, and
welfare, and because these themes predominated, negative stereotypes about

Puerto Ricans were reinforced. Little attention was paid to fantasy, folktales, or the native culture of Puerto Ricans. In addition, few books were available for young readers.

Most of the recent books with Puerto Rican themes are now targeted for young readers, and little is now available for older children. This leaves young adults with few resources other than a small number of "coming of age" books that are being published. Furthermore, many of the books are folktales (at least eleven in the past ten years), and the day-to-day lives of children are rarely addressed. Although folktales and fairytales are a welcome relief from the tedious and simplistic urban stories of the past, they are not the full extent of Puerto Rican literature. Somehow, a balance between traditional and realistic stories needs to be found.

The intolerably low number of books with Puerto Rican themes written in the past dozen years gives little cause for celebration but some reason for hope. A larger percentage of books are being written by Puerto Ricans than ever, but a handful of stories does not constitute a true Puerto Rican children's literature. When we have dozens of books from which to choose, books in English and Spanish and every combination in between, in every conceivable genre and by a great variety of authors who reflect the many Puerto Rican experiences whether in Puerto Rico, New York, Massachusetts, and even Hawaii—where a Puerto Rican community was established at the beginning of the twentieth century—only then can we feel that children's literature is becoming representative of the many communities that make up the Puerto Rican collectivity. Until then, however, this small number of books is an important beginning that points to a more promising future than at any time in the past.

CRITERIA FOR SELECTING PUERTO RICAN CHILDREN'S LITERATURE

Good Puerto Rican children's literature must be well-written, engaging, believable, and creative. In short, it must be excellent literature, measured by the same rigorous standards as any other excellent children's literature. It must be something more as well: a literature that honestly reflects Puerto Rican experiences. Criteria applied to all literature (story-line, characterization, quality of writing, creativity) must take their place alongside criteria specific to the Puerto Rican experience. Questions concerning books with Puerto Rican themes that might be helpful to teachers and librarians in making selections are:

- How are Puerto Ricans depicted? Are they presented as complex individuals rather than as simple stereotypes? Are they only secondary figures?

- Is the family depicted? How? Who is missing and who is included?

- Who are the heroes of the story? What do they accomplish?

- How do the characters resolve the dilemma they face in the story? What is the role of the family and close friends? Are non-Puerto Ricans always the saviors?

- Is Spanish used in the story? Is it accurate and natural?

- Who wrote the story? Who did the illustrations? What does the book jacket say about their familiarity with Puerto Ricans? Have they had a sustained experience in the Puerto Rican community?

- Is the diversity of the Puerto Rican community (racial, social class, urban, rural) evident?

If children's literature is to have an impact in schools, it cannot be separated from the rest of the curriculum. Teachers can help make a multicultural children's literature part and parcel of what and how children learn. For instance, *Felita* would be a natural to include in a unit on families in the elementary grades. A discussion of the issue of racism and discrimination can be introduced even with young children by talking about why Felita's family made the decision to move back to their old neighborhood. *Going Home* can be included in the study of immigration, exploring differences between Puerto Rican migration and the immigration of other groups. When studying bodies of water, children can read "How the water of the bay turned silver: A story about Puerto Rico" by Franklyn Varela-Pérez (in *Kikiriki*), or *How the Sea Began: A Taíno Myth* by George Crespo. Using the story *Vejigante/Masquerader* can be a powerful way to shatter gender stereotypes, for in this story Ramón does errands for his mother and neighbors and sews his own costume for Carnival.

For older students, a unit on identity can include Ortiz Cofer's *Silent Dancing*, which examines the identity of a young girl whose family moves back and forth between Puerto Rico and the United States. Most children have moved from at least one home to another, so whether they are Puerto Rican or not, they can write about how it feels to be "the new kid on the block." "La Peseta," a story-poem in *Stories from El Barrio*, can serve as the stimulus for student writing about a time when they lied to their parents, what happened as a result, and how they felt about it.

Multicultural understanding can be introduced in ways both simple and elaborate. Simply asking young children what they like about their names after reading *My Name is María Isabel* can help them understand why it is important to learn to say others' names correctly. *My Aunt Otilia's Spirits* can be integrated with a multicultural understanding of Halloween by providing examples of how scary stories are part of many cultures. And the new versions of the stories of Juan Bobo, the older version of *Perez and*

Martina, and the recent collection of *Fairy Tales of Puerto Rico* by David García can all be part of a unit on folktales from around the world.

Using a multicultural children's literature helps readers understand that everyone has a story to tell. Until recently, most children's stories in the United States have reflected a very limited range of realities. Using Puerto Rican children's literature can result in Puerto Rican children developing a healthy respect for their community and non-Puerto Rican children learning to understand the importance of different experiences on people's lives. At the same time, they can learn that ethnicity is only one difference, and that the unique character of every individual needs to be respected and affirmed. For example, Nicholasa Mohr's *All for the Better: A Story of El Barrio* celebrates the life of Evelina Antonetty, a community organizer and activist from New York City, but also tells the universal story of how one person who strives for justice can make a difference in the lives of many others.

Exposing children to excellent literature can motivate them to seek all kinds of literature. For example, baseball enthusiasts reading one of the many biographies of Roberto Clemente may in the process also learn something of Puerto Rican culture and about the racism he had to endure. (Clemente is probably the most chronicled Puerto Rican in biographies for young people, and this is unfortunate because there are so many others in fields as diverse as the arts, politics, and community activism that could be written about as well.) Using literature as a springboard for other activities is an added benefit. After reading Lulu Delacre's *Arroz con leche* or *Las navidades*, teachers can ask students to collect riddles, rhymes, and other kinds of oral literature from their families and other community residents. Using Taíno legends as a basis, students can be motivated to write their own legends.

As children learn to interact with and respond to all literature with a more open and flexible outlook, they can learn to be critical and questioning of what they read. The purpose of using Puerto Rican literature is not to romanticize or uncritically accept the experience it may depict, but to develop the tools to critique both it and the printed word in general. Literature can become what Paulo Freire has called "problem-posing education," where students learn to critically analyze what they read.[25] For instance, younger students might be asked to talk about how they and their families are different from their friends after reading Susan Kuklin's *How My Family Lives in America*. *The Red Comb* might engage young readers in discussing the morality of slave-catchers or exploring the African heritage in Puerto Rico. Using *The Song of el Coquí and Other Stories from Puerto Rico* by Nicholasa Mohr and Antonio Martorell can extend the theme of Puerto Rico's cultural and racial identity by having students reflect on stories that focus on the Taíno, African, and Spanish heritages. Older students might write about how they have felt when somebody tries to change something about them after reading Alma Flor Ada's *My Name is María Isabel*, about a young girl who resolves the dilemma of being called "Mary" by her teacher. *Nilda* can lead to important discussions about girls' complex relationships with their mothers, or about confronting the death of beloved family members, in this case, a grandmother.

CONCLUSION

Seeing themselves in books is an everyday experience for children from the majority culture, but this is not usually the case for Puerto Rican youngsters. Because children's literature in the United States has yet to catch up with the dramatic demographic changes in society or with growing sensibilities toward diversity, many youngsters develop the impression that books are not about them, their families, or communities. Publishers, teachers, and schools have a responsibility to make it possible for all children to see themselves and their experiences in the books they read. Equally important, children need to see the experiences of others different from themselves in books.

Puerto Rican children's literature is still woefully underrepresented in mainstream children's literature. Rather than simply negative images, there are almost no images of Puerto Ricans in children's books. Of those books that are published, a few are still full of stereotypical and unconvincing story lines, characters, and situations. Nevertheless a vibrant, but as yet incipient and tentative, Puerto Rican children's literature is developing. Written by writers who represent a range of experiences, viewpoints, and aesthetics, this literature is demanding a space for the voices of those who have until now remained relatively silent. They are demanding that the "mainstream" be widened to accommodate us all. They are beginning to let everybody know that we have stories to tell.

NOTES

1. U.S. Census Bureau, *March 1990 Survey of 56,400 Households*, Washington, D.C., 1990.

2. A recent estimation concluded that there were 26,646,000 Latinos in the United States, of which 2,776,000 were Puerto Rican. See Institute for Puerto Rican Policy (August, 1995), *IPR DATANOTE on the Puerto Rican Community*, 17.

3. Hispanic Community Mobilization for Dropout Prevention, *Facing the Facts: Hispanics in the United States, 1990*. Washington, D.C.: ASPIRA Institute for Policy Research, 1990.

4. Marín, Gerardo and Marín, Barbara Vanoss, "Methodological Fallacies When Studying Hispanics," *Applied Social Psychology*, 3 (1983), 99–117.

5. See, for example, Nieto (1995), Carrasquillo (1991), and Pérez (1991).

6. For information on how libraries can use Puerto Rican history, culture, and literature in their programming and outreach efforts, see Lori Mestre and Sonia Nieto (forthcoming). Puerto Rican children's literature and culture in the public library, *Multicultural Review*.

7. See, especially, Rodríguez, Clara (1991). *Puerto Ricans: Born in the U.S.A.*; Fitzpatrick, Joseph P. (1987). *Puerto Rican Americans: The meaning of migration to the mainland*; Sánchez Korrol, Virginia E. (1983). *From colonia to community: The history of Puerto Ricans in New York, 1917–1948*; Walsh, Catherine E. (1991). *Pedagogy and the struggle for voice: Issues of language, power, and schooling for Puerto Ricans*; Márquez, Roberto (1995). Sojourners, settlers, castaways, and creators: A recollection of Puerto Rico past and Puerto Ricans present, *Massachusetts Review*; and Nieto, Sonia (1995). A history of the education of Puerto Rican students in U.S. mainland schools: 'Losers,' 'Outsiders,' or 'Leaders'? In Banks, James A. and Banks, Cherry McGee (Eds.), *Handbook of research on multicultural education*. In addition, teacher resources include *Caribbean connections: Classroom resources for secondary schools*, a series of resources including one on Puerto Rico, edited by Deborah Menkart and Catherine A. Sunshine (available from Network of Educators on the Americas, 1118 22nd Street NW, Washington, D.C. 20037; and *Building bridges of learning and understanding: A collection of classroom activities on Puerto Rican culture* developed by Perez-Selles, Marla E. and Barra-Zuman, Nancy Carmen (Andover, MA.: The Network, 1990). See also the resource list and sample lessons included in Chapt. 11 of Banks, James A., *Teaching strategies for ethnic studies*, 6th ed. (Boston: Allyn & Bacon, 1996).

8. Institute for Puerto Rican Policy (1995, August).

9. Rodríguez, Clara. (1991). *Puerto Ricans: Born in the U.S.A.* Boulder, CO.: Westview Press.

10. Cafferty, Pastora San Juan and Rivera-Mártinez, Carmen. (1981). *The politics of language: The dilemma of bilingual education for Puerto Ricans*. Boulder, CO: Westview Press.

11. See, for example, Rodríguez, Clara (1991) and Sánchez Korrol, Virginia (1983).

12. Bonilla, Frank and Campos, Ricardo. (1981). A wealth of poor: Puerto Ricans in the new economic order. *Daedalus*, 110, 133–176.

13. Fitzpatrick, Joseph P. (1987). *Puerto Rican Americans: The meaning of migration to the mainland*. Englewood Cliffs, NJ: Prentice-Hall.

14. For more information on Puerto Rican migration, see the following: History Task Force (1982), *Sources for the study of Puerto Rican migration*; Sánchez Korrol, Virginia E. (1983), *From colonia to community*; and Rodríguez, Clara (1991), *Puerto Ricans: Born in the U.S.A.*

15. This was the term used by the History Task Force in describing the migration (1982).

16. Institute for Puerto Rican Policy (1995).

17. See Sánchez Korrol (1983); and Nieto (1995).

18. See, for example, Acosta-Belén, Edna (Ed.) (1986). *The Puerto Rican Woman: Perspectives on Culture, History, and Society*. 2nd ed.

19. Santiago-Santiago, Isaura (1986, November). *ASPIRA v. Board of Education* revisited. *American Journal of Education*, 95 (1), 149–199.

20. Council on Interracial Books for Children *Bulletin*, "Special Issue on Puerto Rican Materials," v. 4, n. 1 & 2, 1974.

21. *Ibid.*, p. 1.

22. Nieto, Sonia (1983). Puerto Ricans in children's literature and history texts: A ten-year update, *Bulletin* of the Council on Interracial Books for Children, 14, 1 & 2.

23. Examples of these anthologies and references include Flores, Juan (1993). *Divided borders: Essays on Puerto Rican identity*, Arte Público Press; and Rodríguez de Laguna, Asela (Ed.) (1987). *Images and identities: The Puerto Rican in two world contexts*. Transaction Publications.

24. Vázquez, Blanca (1990–91). Puerto Ricans and the media: A personal statement, *Centro Bulletin*, 3, 1, p. 7.

25. Freire, Paulo (1970). *Pedagogy of the oppressed*. New York: Seabury Press.

BOOKS REVIEWED

* means book is bilingual;
** means book is available in a Spanish version as well

Ada, Alma Flor. (1993). *My name is María Isabel*. Illustrated by K. Dyble Thompson. New York: Atheneum.

Adoff, Arnold. (1988). *Flamboyan*. New York: Harcourt Brace Jovanovich.

** Belpré, Pura. (1991). *Perez and Martina: A Puerto Rican folktale*. Illustrated by Carlos Sánchez. Revised edition. Viking (Also available in Spanish as *Perez y Martina*).

Bernier-Grand, Carmen T., reteller. (1994). *Juan Bobo: Four Folktales from Puerto Rico*. Pictures by Ernesto Ramos Nieves. New York: HarperCollins Publishers.

Bryant, Jennifer. (1991). *Ubel Velez: Lawyer*. Photographs by Pamela Brown. Frederick, MD.: Twenty-first Century Books (Series: *Working moms: A portrait of their lives*).

Carlson, Lori M. and Cynthia L. Ventura. (1990). *Where angels glide at dawn: New stories from Latin America*. New York: J.B. Lippincott.

Crespo, George. (1993). *How the sea began: A Taíno myth*. New York: Clarion.

* Delacre, Lulu. (1989). *Arroz con Leche: Popular songs and rhymes from Latin America*. New York: Scholastic.

* Delacre, Lulu. (1990). *Las navidades: Popular Christmas songs from Latin America*. New York: Scholastic.

* Delacre, Lulu. (1993). *Vejigante / Masquerader*. New York: Scholastic.

Dorros, Arthur. (1991). *Abuela*. Illustrated by Elisa Kleven. New York: Dutton.

* Fontánez, Edwin. (1994). *The vejigante and the folk festivals of Puerto Rico: A coloring book.* Washington, DC: Exit Studio (P.O. Box 6028, Washington, DC 20005).

García, David. (1992). *Fairy tales of Puerto Rico*. Designed and illustrated by Gus Anavitate. Santurce, Puerto Rico (Puerto Rico Almanacs, Inc., P.O. Box 9582, Santurce, P.R., 00908). (Elem.)

* García, Richard. (1987). *My Aunt Otilia's spirits*. Revised edition. San Francisco: Children's Book Press.

Holman, Felice. (1990). *Secret City, U.S.A.* New York: Charles Scribner's Sons.

Hurwitz, Johanna. (1990). *Class president*. New York: Morrow.

* Jaffe, Nina. (1993). *Sing, little sack! ¡Canta, saquito! A folktale from Puerto Rico*. Illustrated by Ray Cruz. New York: Bantam Little Rooster Book, from the *Bank Street Ready to Read Series*.

Kuklin, Susan. (1992). *How my family lives in America*. New York: Bradbury Press.

Mango, Karin N. (1987). *Somewhere green*. New York: Four Winds Press.

McConnie Zapater, Beatriz. (1992). *Three Kings' Day* (Part of the *Multicultural Celebrations* Series, Boston Children's Museum). Illustrated by Nayda Collazo Llorens. Modern Curriculum Press. (Elem.)

Mike, Jan. (1995). *Juan Bobo and the horse of seven colors*. Troll Associates. Illustrated by Charles Reasoner.

Mohr, Nicholasa. (1993). *All for the better: A story of El Barrio*. Illustrations by Rudy Gutierrez. Austin, TX: Raintree Steck-Vaughn Publishers.

Mohr, Nicholasa. (1986). *Going home*. New York: Dial.

Mohr, Nicholasa. (1988). *In Nueva York*. Revised edition. Houston, TX: Arte Público Press.

Mohr, Nicholasa. (1986). *Nilda*. Revised edition. Houston, TX: Arte Público Press.

Mohr, Nicholasa. (1986). *El Bronx remembered*. Revised edition. Houston, TX: Arte Público Press.

** Mohr, Nicholasa and Martorell, Antonio. (1995). *The song of el coquí and other tales of Puerto Rico*. New York: Viking.

Mora, Francisco X. (Illustrator). Book with no words; accompanied by an audiocassette and narrated by Anamarie García. (1991). *The tiger and the rabbit: A Puerto Rican folktale*. Chicago: Children's Press.

Myers, Walter Dean. (1988). *Scorpions*. New York: Harper & Row.

** Nodar, Carmen Santiago. (1992). *Abuelita's paradise*. Illustrated by Diane Paterson. New York: Albert Whitman & Co. (also available in Spanish as *El paraíso de Abuelita*).

* Orozco, José-Luis. (1994). *De colores and other Latin-American folk songs for children*. Illustrated by Elisa Kleven. Dutton children's books. (Preschool - Elem.)

Ortiz Cofer, Judith. (1990). *Silent dancing: A partial remembrance of a Puerto Rican childhood*. Houston, TX: Arte Público Press.

* Peña, Sylvia Cavazos. (1987). *Kikirikí: Stories and poems in English and

Spanish for children. Houston, TX: Arte Público Press.

* Peña, Sylvia Cavazos. (1986). *Tun-ta-ca-tún: More stories and poems in English and Spanish for children*. Houston, TX: Arte Público Press.

** Picó, Fernando. (1991). *The red comb*. Translated and adapted by Argentina Palacios. Illustrated by María Antonia Ordóñez. BridgeWater Books, Troll Associates. (Also available in Spanish as *La peineta colorada*, published by Huracán Press, Puerto Rico).

Pitre, Felix, reteller. (1993). *Juan Bobo and the pig*. Illustrated by Christy Hale. New York: Lodestar Books, Dutton.

** Pitre, Felix, reteller. (1995). *Paco and the witch: A Puerto Rican folktale*. Illustrated by Christy Hale. New York: Lodestar Books, Dutton, 1995.

* Rohmer, Harriet and Jesús Guerrero Rea. (1988). *Atariba y Niguayona*. Revised edition. San Francisco: Children's Book Press.

Sabin, Louis. (1992). *Roberto Clemente: Young baseball hero*. Illustrated by Marie DeJohn. Mahwah, NJ: Troll Associates.

Stefoff, Rebecca. (1994). *Raul Julia*. Hispanics of Achievement Series. NY: Chelsea House.

Tashlik, Phyllis, ed. (1994). *Hispanic, female, and young: An anthology*. Piñata Books, a division of Arte Público Press.

Thomas, Piri. (1992). *Stories from El Barrio*. Reissue. New York: Knopf Books.

* Wagenheim, Kal. (1987). *Cuentos: An anthology of short stories from Puerto Rico*. Reissue. Schocken.

Walker, Paul Robert. (1988). *Pride of Puerto Rico: The life of Roberto Clemente*. San Diego, CA: Harcourt Brace Jovanovich.

West, Alan. (1993). *Roberto Clemente: Baseball legend*. Brookfield, CT: Hispanic Heritage. With previously published photos. (Elem.)

ANNOTATIONS OF RECOMMENDED CHILDREN'S PUERTO RICAN LITERATURE

Ada, Alma Flor. (1993). *My name is María Isabel*. Illustrated by K. Dyble Thompson. New York: Atheneum. (Elem.)

When her 3rd grade teacher begins to call her "Mary" to differentiate her from the other two Marías in the class, María Isabel Salazar López becomes upset and distracted. María Isabel gets the chance to write down how proud she feels of her name when the students are asked to write an essay for the new year on "My Greatest Wish." With many references to Puerto Rican culture, this is a heartwarming and affirming story.

** Belpré, Pura. (1991). *Perez and Martina: A Puerto Rican folktale*. (Also available in Spanish as *Pérez y Martina*). Illustrated by Carlos Sánchez. New York: Viking Penguin. First published in 1932 by Frederick Warne & Co., Inc., and renewed by Pura Belpré White, 1960. (Elem.)

A traditional Puerto Rican folktale with origins in Spain, this is the story of Martina, a Spanish cockroach, whose many suitors woo her with a variety of sounds. She finally settles on Pérez the Mouse, but

Señor Pérez meets an untimely demise due to his inquisitive nature when he falls into a rice pudding that Martina is cooking for him as a Christmas surprise.

Bernier-Grand, Carmen T., reteller. (1994). *Juan Bobo: Four folktales from Puerto Rico*. Pictures by Ernesto Ramos Nieves. New York: HarperCollins Publishers. (Pre-school - Elem.)

A delightful retelling of four of the best-known Juan Bobo stories, this "I can read book" loses none of the charm of the originals in spite of the simple language used to make it possible for young children to read by themselves. The illustrations are glorious and colorful and capture the feeling of the island countryside.

Crespo, George. (1993). *How the sea began: A Taíno myth*. New York: Clarion Books. (Elem.)

The retelling of a creation myth of the Taíno people (the original inhabits of Puerto Rico when it was explored by Columbus in 1493) as collected by Fray Ramón Pané almost 500 years ago. The illustrations, which are vivid and beautiful, were painted in oils on rag paper and are a fitting accompaniment to the story.

* Delacre, Lulu. (1989). *Arroz con leche: Popular songs and rhymes from Latin America*. New York: Scholastic. (Preschool - Elem.)

Twelve of the best-known children's songs and rhymes from the Spanish-speaking world are included in this lovely book, written in the original Spanish and in English translations with accompanying music at the end. Beautifully illustrated with scenes evocative of Puerto Rico, Mexico, and Latin America, this book is especially recommended for use with young children, but can also be used with older elementary grades to teach actual songs and games played by children in Latin America.

* Delacre, Lulu. (1990). *Las navidades: Popular Christmas songs from Latin America*. New York: Scholastic. (Preschool - Elem.)

By the same author, this beautiful book illustrates twelve Christmas songs from Spanish-speaking countries. Descriptions of the traditions associated with each are also included, and the country of origin of each scene is identified. Events are arranged chronologically, starting with Christmas Eve and finishing on the Epiphany (Three Kings' Day), and musical scores are included at the end.

* Delacre, Lulu. (1993). *Vejigante / Masquerader*. New York: Scholastic. (Elem.)

Ramón works hard to earn money to make himself a beautiful *vejigante* (masquerader) costume for the annual Carnival celebration in the city of Ponce. The story of how he makes his dream come true touches on family ties, the importance of cultural symbols, and community solidarity. Exquisitely illustrated, the book includes historical references, directions for making *vejigante* masks, and a glossary and bibliography.

* Fontánez, Edwin. (1994). *The vejigante and the folk festivals of Puerto Rico:A coloring book.* Washington, DC: Exit Studio (P.O. Box 6028, Washington, DC 20005) (Elem.)

    A lavishly illustrated bilingual coloring book written and published by an artist who has done many art workshops with children. The book includes information about several of the folk festivals of Puerto Rico and is accompanied by a video, *The Legend of the Vejigante*, in which instructions for making the masks are included.

García, David. (1992). *Fairy tales of Puerto Rico.* Designed and illustrated by Gus Anavitate. Santurce, Puerto Rico (Puerto Rico Almanacs, Inc., P.O. Box 9582, Santurce, P.R., 00908). (Elem.)

    These three folk tales, ranging in time from "long, long ago" to eighteenth-century colonial Puerto Rico, have a magical quality about them. One explains how the *coquí* got his song; another focuses on the story behind *la piedra del perro*, a stone in the shape of a dog that can be seen near the Castillo San Jerónimo, a colonial fortress in Puerto Rico; and the third explains the legend of the Cristo Chapel in Old San Juan. It is unfortunate that there are no female characters in any of the stories.

* García, Richard. (1987). *My Aunt Otilia's spirits* (Revised edition). San Francisco: Children's Book Press. (Elem.)

    In this funny and scary story, a young boy recollects his Aunt Otilia's visits to New York from Puerto Rico and the magical goings-on associated with her spirits.

* Jaffe, Nina. (1993). *Sing Little Sack! ¡Canta, Saquito! A Folktale from Puerto Rico.* Illustrated by Ray Cruz. New York: Bantam Books. (Preschool - Elem.)

    Part of the Bank Street "Ready-to-read" collection, this folktale is about Marisol, a little girl who is kidnapped by a strange little man who hides her in a sack and makes her sing, tricking audiences into thinking the bag itself is singing, and her subsequent rescue by her mother.

Martel, Cruz. (1976). *Yagua days.* New York: Dial Books. (Preschool - Elem.)

    This delightful story depicts a young boy's first visit to Puerto Rico and his experiences there, including *yagua days*, those days after rainstorms when the children use yagua leaves as sleds to slide down the hills. Although the book is no longer in print, it can still be found in some libraries.

McConnie Zapater, Beatriz. (1992). *Three Kings' Day* (Part of the *Multicultural Celebrations* Series, Boston Children's Museum). Illustrated by Nayda Collazo Llorens. New York: Modern Curriculum Press. (Elem.)

    Written in English with some Spanish words, this story focuses on Melinda, a Puerto Rican girl who lives in the United States with her mother and two brothers, and how they celebrate Three Kings' Day on January 6. The text is accompanied by colorful illustrations and a few small photographs that depict such holiday customs as making *pasteles* and preparing the box with hay for the camels.

Mohr, Nicholasa. (1993). *All for the better: A story of El Barrio*. Illustrations by Rudy Gutierrez. Austin, TX: Raintree Steck-Vaughn Publishers. (Elem.)

    The biography of Evelina López Antonetty (1922–1984), a well-known community activist in New York who organized the United Bronx Parents in the 1960s to demand better educational opportunities for all children. The story of her young adolescence, from the time she arrived in New York's *El Barrio* (Spanish Harlem) at the age of eleven until she began her work as a community organizer at the age of 13, it makes the point that Evelina made life "all for the better" for many people in her community and beyond.

Mohr, Nicholasa. (1979). *Felita*. New York: Dial Press. (Elem.)

    Felita, a nine-year-old girl living in New York City, has a warm relationship with her family, especially with her beloved grandmother. In this story, her family's decision to move, and later to return to their own neighborhood, and the death of Felita's grandmother, is movingly told.

Mohr, Nicholasa. (1986). *Going home*. New York: Dial Press. (Upper Elem.)

    We meet Felita in this sequel at eleven, two years after her beloved Abuelita has died. Given the opportunity to go to Puerto Rico for the first time to spend the summer with her uncle, Felita faces discrimination for being a "Niuyorican," a Puerto Rican from New York. This story confronts some difficult issues, including discrimination against Puerto Ricans who do not speak Spanish and the limited roles and expectations of females, in an honest and believable way.

Mohr, Nicholasa. (1989). *El Bronx remembered*. (Reissue). Houston, TX: Arte Público Press. (Young Adult).

    Mohr's first collection of short stories originally published in 1973, these stories relate experiences of the early Puerto Rican community in the Bronx that range from comical to tragic.

Mohr, Nicholasa. (1991). *In Nueva York*. (Reissue). Houston, TX: Arte Público Press (Young Adult).

    An interconnected collection set in the Lower East Side of New York City, these stories revolve around the lives of Puerto Ricans trying to survive in New York City.

Mohr, Nicholasa. (1991). *Nilda*. (Reissue). Houston, TX: Arte Público Press. (Young Adult).

    A novel about a young girl's coming of age in New York City during the 1940s, this book confronts such delicate issues as discrimination from the general society, and the limited choices offered to women within the Puerto Rican community itself.

** Mohr, Nicholasa and Martorell, Antonio. (1995). *The song of el coquí and other tales of Puerto Rico*. New York: Viking. (Pre-school - Elem.; also available in Spanish as *La canción del coquí y otros cuentos de Puerto Rico*)

In this breathtakingly illustrated book, Nicholasa Mohr has teamed up with the well-known Puerto Rican artist Antonio Martorell to retell three tales of Puerto Rico that reflect the Taíno, African, and Spanish heritage of the country. Mohr and Martorell each contributed to the illustrations and the text, and the book concludes with some facts about the stories themselves.

** Nodar, Carmen Santiago. (1992). *Abuelita's paradise*. Illustrated by Diane Paterson. New York: Albert Whitman & Co. (Pre-school - Elem.; also available in Spanish as *El paraíso de Abuelita*.)

This is the story of Marita, a little girl who inherits her grandmother's rocking chair when she dies. As she rocks and leans on Abuelita's old faded blanket with the word "paraíso" (paradise) printed on it, she recalls the wonderful stories her grandmother used to tell of her youth in Puerto Rico. The story, which takes place in the United States, provides a good way to talk with young children about death, family stories, and cultural roots. The evocative illustrations add to the poignancy of the story.

Ortiz Cofer, Judith. (1990). *Silent dancing: A partial remembrance of a Puerto Rican childhood*. Houston, TX: Arte Público Press. (Young Adult).

A beautifully written and evocative autobiographical account of the author's childhood as the daughter of a military father, and her family's life shuttling between Puerto Rico and New Jersey.

** Picó, Fernando. (1991). *The red comb*. Illustrated by María Antonia Ordóñez. New York: Bridge Water Books, Troll Associates. (Elem.; also available in Spanish as *La peineta colorada*, published by Huracán Press, Puerto Rico; translated and adapted by Argentina Palacios.)

One of the very few books that focuses on Puerto Rico's African heritage, this is an inspiring story about two women, one young and the other old, who discover a runaway slave in 19th-century Puerto Rico. How they help her escape from the local slave catcher, himself of mixed race, and begin a new life of freedom brings up issues of solidarity, generosity, and caring. The text, written by a distinguished Puerto Rican historian, is based on characters and events drawn from historical documents. A sensitively written story of intergenerational friendship, it is accompanied by vivid and dramatic illustrations by a noted artist.

Pitre, Felix. (1993). *Juan Bobo and the pig* (retold by author). Illustrated by Christy Hale. New York: Dutton. (Preschool - Elem.)

A retelling of one of the famous stories of Juan Bobo, called "the folk hero of Puerto Rico," who reflects the humorous wisdom of the *jíbaros* (peasants). Juan Bobo dresses his pig up for church with his mother's dress and jewelry, hence the saying "como la puerca de Juan Bobo" (like Juan Bobo's pig) to refer to somebody who is overdressed and gaudy.

** Pitre, Felix, reteller. (1995). *Paco and the witch: A Puerto Rican folktale*. Illustrated by Christy Hale. New York: Lodestar Books, Dutton, 1995. (Elem.; also available in Spanish as *Paco y la bruja*.)

This story was originally included in Pura Belpré's collection of folktales, *The tiger and the rabbit* (1946). The Puerto Rican version of "Rumpelstiltskin," the story is retold here by Felix Pitre with many references to Puerto Rico's countryside, foods, and native animals, including the crab who ultimately tells Paco the name of the witch.

* Rohmer, Harriet and Jesús Guerrero Rea. (1988). *Atariba & Niguayona* (Revised edition). San Francisco: Children's Book Press. (Elem.)

Told in the tradition of a Puerto Rican legend, this bilingual story focuses on the friendship between two young Taínos, a boy and a girl, and the boy's commitment to help cure her when she gets sick.

Thomas, Piri. (1992). *Stories from El Barrio*. (Reissue). New York: Knopf Books. (Young Adult)

This wonderful collection of short stories from the author's memories of growing up in East Harlem is a treasure that has been reissued after many years. The eight stories cover a broad range of topics from getting a "konk" (a painful hair-straightening process), to meeting a new cousin from Puerto Rico. Many are funny, some are poignant, all are well written and rich with meaning.

* Wagenheim, Kal. (1987). *Cuentos: An anthology of short stories from Puerto Rico*. (Reissue). New York: Schocken. (Young Adult)

With English and Spanish on facing pages, this is an excellent collection of short stories, although not always appropriate for high school students. It includes some of the most notable Puerto Rican short story authors. Some of the stories are set in New York, and most focus on the political and cultural tensions of the Puerto Rican experience.

ANNOTATIONS OF OTHER BOOKS THAT INCLUDE PUERTO RICANS

Adoff, Arnold. (1988). *Flamboyan*. New York: Harcourt Brace Jovanovich.

Poetic prose about a young girl by the name of Flamboyàn (named after the tropical tree with fiery red blossoms) as she flies above her beautiful Caribbean island. The illustrations, although beautiful and vivid, seem more to reflect the scenes of other Caribbean islands and Central America.

Bryant, Jennifer. (1991). *Ubel Velez: Lawyer*. (Series: *Working moms: A portrait of their lives*.) Photographs by Pamela Brown. Twenty-first Century Books. (Elem.)

A photographic essay of a Puerto Rican lawyer in Delaware who juggles her law practice, where she represents the rights of immigrants, and her family life as a wife and mother of two teenage girls.

Dorros, Arthur. (1991). *Abuela*. Illustrated by Elisa Kleven. New York: Dutton Books. (Preschool - Elem.)

A nicely told and beautifully illustrated story of Rosalba and her loving and adventuresome grandmother who live in New York City, and the imaginary trip they take in the sky. The illustrations, a striking mixed-media collage with water color, pastels, ink, and cut paper, are reminiscent of Central American art. Spanish words are explained in context, and the author also includes a glossary.

Hurwitz, Johanna. (1990). *Class president*. New York: Morrow.
A fast-paced story of Julio Sánchez, a fifth grader who decides to run for class president even though one of his classmates is convinced he cannot win because he was born in Puerto Rico. Predictable, but affirming of Julio, his family, and heritage.

Kuklin, Susan. (1992). *How my family lives in America*. New York: Bradbury Press. (Preschool - Elem.)
A photo essay of three children reflecting their everyday lives and depicting in a way young children can understand how culture is naturally transmitted by families. The children are Eric, a Puerto Rican; April, a Chinese girl from Taiwan; and Sanu, whose father is Senegalese and mother is African American. The book concludes with a recipe from each family.

Mora, Francisco X. (Illustrator). Book with no words; accompanied by an audiocassette and narrated by Anamarie García. (1991). *The tiger and the rabbit: A Puerto Rican folktale*. Chicago: Children's Press.
A nice rendition of this Puerto Rican folktale, first published by Pura Belpré in her collection *The Tiger and the Rabbit* (1946). This version, however, loses some of the charm of the original narration and includes some inaccurate illustrations.

Myers, Walter Dean. (1988). *Scorpions*. New York: Harper & Row.
Set in Harlem, this is the story of Jamal, who is African American, and his best friend, Tito, who is Puerto Rican. Jamal feels responsible for taking over the leadership of the Scorpions after the arrest of his brother. Unfortunately, he soon finds out that guns can lead to tragedy. The story demonstrates awareness of and respect for Puerto Rican values and the community.

* Orozco, José-Luis. (1994). *De colores and other Latin-American folk songs for children*. Illustrated by Elisa Kleven. New York: Dutton children's books. (Preschool - Elem.)
In this gloriously illustrated collection of twenty-seven songs, the arranger has chosen well-known selections from all over Latin America that have special meaning for birthdays, holidays, and other occasions, as well as two pieces he wrote himself. The book offers lyrics, background notes and suggestions for sing-alongs, hand gestures, and games. In addition, the English translations are singable and thus appropriate for both Spanish and English classrooms. All the songs have been recorded by the artist and are available from Arcoiris Records (P.O. Box 7428, Berkeley, CA, 94707).

* Peña, Sylvia Cavazos. (1987). *Kikirikí: Stories and poems in English and Spanish for children*. Houston, TX: Arte Público Press. (Elem.)

A series of short stories, poems, and *adivinanzas* (riddles) originally published in 1981, this book includes some selections in Spanish and others in English. Written by Latinos, the selections are presented by grade level from kindergarten through sixth grade. This a particularly appropriate volume to use in bilingual classrooms.

* Peña, Sylvia Cavazos. (1986). *Tun-ta-ca-tún: More stories and poems in English and Spanish for children* (1986). Houston, TX: Arte Público Press. (Elem.)

This second anthology also realistically reflects the Latino experience in the countries of origin of the authors and as brought to the United States. Selections are in either English or Spanish and include stories by Puerto Rican authors Nicholasa Mohr and Franklyn Varela.

Sabin, Louis. (1992). *Roberto Clemente: Young baseball hero*. Illustrated by Marie DeJohn. New York: Troll Associates. (Elem.)

In this biography of the beloved Puerto Rican athlete who died at 38 on a mercy mission after the Nicaraguan earthquake, Clemente's youth, upbringing, and family are featured more than is his professional career in the Pittsburgh Pirates. Replete with examples of the dignity of his family and his cultural roots, the story is certain to appeal to a wide range of readers, not just baseball fans.

Stefoff, Rebecca. (1994). *Raul Julia*. Hispanics of Achievement Series. NY: Chelsea House. (Upper Elem. - Young Adult)

Because it provides little information on Julia's life aside from his acting career, this well-written biography (written before the actor's death in 1994) may not be appropriate for all readers. It might, however, be just what young people interested in the theater are looking for because it provides detailed information about Julia's acting career.

Tashlik, Phyllis, (Ed.) (1994). *Hispanic, female, and young: An anthology*. Houston, TX: Piñata Books, a division of Arte Público Press. (Young Adult)

This inspiring and poignant book documents the experiences, thoughts, and writings of *Las mujeres hispanas*, a group of eighth-grade Hispanic teenagers at Manhattan East, a public alternative school in El Barrio, New York City, while they took a course that focused on reading the work of Hispanic female authors and writing about their own experiences as Latinas. It includes works by Nicholasa Mohr, Judith Ortiz Cofer, Lorna Dee Cervantes, Roberta Fernández, and other Latina authors, as well as the students' poems and stories and interviews with a number of both well-known and local Latinas. The anthology contains nine chapters that concern themes important to the young women, including culture, family, and prejudice.

Walker, Paul Robert. (1988). *Pride of Puerto Rico: The life of Roberto Clemente*. San Diego: Harcourt Brace Jovanovich. (Young Adult)

Certain to delight baseball enthusiasts, this biography of the Puerto Rican right-fielder for the Pittsburgh Pirates offers insights into the life and values of Roberto Clemente. It discusses, for example, the many indignities he suffered because of his Spanish accent and dark skin, and also highlights his love for his family and generosity toward others.

West, Alan. (1993). *Roberto Clemente: Baseball legend*. Brookfield, CT: Hispanic Heritage. With previously published photos. (Elem.)
　　This story gives information on Puerto Rico's cultural and racial heritage, providing an important context for readers to understand Clemente's experiences with racism in the United States. The book, written by a Cuban American, also includes important dates in the baseball player's life, an index, and resources for further reading.

BIBLIOGRAPHY

Acosta-Belén, E., (Ed.) (1986) *The Puerto Rican woman: Perspectives on culture, history, and society*, 2nd ed. New York: Praeger.

Banks, James A. (1996). *Teaching strategies for ethnic studies*, 6th ed. Boston: Allyn & Bacon.

Bonilla, Frank and Campos, Ricardo. (1981). A wealth of poor: Puerto Ricans in the new economic order. *Daedalus*, 110, 133–176.

Cafferty, Pastora San Juan and Rivera-Martinez, Carmen. (1981). *The politics of language: The dilemma of bilingual education for Puerto Ricans*. Boulder, CO: Westview Press.

Carrasquillo, Angela L. (1992). *Hispanic children and youth in the United States: A resource guide*. New York: Garland.

Council on Interracial Books for Children (CIBC). (1972). *Bulletin*. Special issue on Puerto Rican materials, 4 (1 & 2).

Fitzpatrick, Joseph P. (1987). *Puerto Rican Americans: The meaning of migration to the mainland*. Englewood Cliffs, NJ: Prentice-Hall, Inc.

Flores, Juan. (1993). *Divided borders: Essays on Puerto Rican identity*. Houston, TX: Arte Público Press.

Freire, Paulo. (1970). *Pedagogy of the oppressed*. New York: Seabury Press.

History Task Force. (1982). *Sources for the study of Puerto Rican migration: 1879–1930*. New York: Centro de Estudios Puertorriqueños, Research Foundation of the City University of New York.

Institute for Puerto Rican Policy. (1995, August). *IPR DATANOTE on the Puerto Rican Community*, 17.

Márquez, Roberto. (1995). Sojourners, settlers, castaways, and creators: A recollection of Puerto Rico past and Puerto Ricans present. *Massachusetts Review*, 36 (1), 94–118.

Mestre, Lori and Nieto, Sonia. (forthcoming). Puerto Rican children's literature and culture in the public library, *Multicultural Review*.

Nieto, Sonia. (1995). A history of the education of Puerto Rican students in U.S. mainland schools: 'Losers,' 'outsiders,' or 'leaders'? In James A. Banks and Cherry McGee Banks (Eds.), *Handbook of research on multicultural education*. New York: Macmillan Publishing Co.

Nieto, Sonia. (1983). Children's literature on Puerto Rican themes, *Bulletin* of the Council on Interracial Books for Children, 14 (1 & 2), 10–16.

Nieto, Sonia. (1987). Self-affirmation or self-destruction? The image of Puerto Ricans in children's literature written in English. In Asela Rodríguez de Laguna (Ed.), *Images and identities: The Puerto Rican in two world contexts*. New Jersey: Transaction Books.

Pérez, Sonia. (1991). Hispanic child poverty: Signs of distress, signs of hope. *Agenda* (National Council of La Raza), 10 (2), 15–17.

Rodríguez, Clara E. (1991). *Puerto Ricans: Born in the U.S.A.* Boulder, CO: Westview Press.

Rodríguez de Laguna, Asela. (Ed.). (1987). *Images and identities: The Puerto Rican in two world contexts*. New Jersey: Transaction Books.

Sánchez Korrol, Virginia E. (1983). *From colonia to community: The history of Puerto Ricans in New York, 1917–1948*. Westport, CT: Greenwood Press.

Santiago-Santiago, Isaura. (1986, November). *ASPIRA v. Board of Education* revisited. *American Journal of Education*, 95 (1), 149–199.

Vázquez, Blanca. (1990–91, Winter). Puerto Ricans and the media: A personal statement, *Centro Bulletin*, 3 (1), 5–15.

Walsh, Catherine E. (1991). *Pedagogy and the struggle for voice: Issues of language, power, and schooling for Puerto Ricans*. New York: Bergin & Garvey.

Chapter 4 _____

Asian Pacific American Children's Literature: Expanding Perceptions About Who Americans Are

Sandra S. Yamate

୨୦ ୨୦ ୨୦ ୨୦ ୨୦

FOREIGNERS IN THEIR OWN COUNTRY

California judge Lance Ito has one of the most recognized faces in America. His fame is particularly interesting in that it is linked so intrinsically to his fundamentally American role as a trial judge. It is not a role commonly associated with Asian Pacific Americans. Ito's celebrity, however, also has served to remind Asian Pacific Americans and their fellow Americans about how America tends to view its Asian Pacific citizens.

Two well-publicized attacks that were leveled at Judge Ito's American-ness illustrate this point. Although the Judge was born and grew up in the United States, and is the third generation of his family to do so, Senator Alphonse D'Amato of New York nevertheless chose to attempt an impersonation of Ito by mimicking an Asian accent using Pidgin English.[1] Sadly, this U.S. Senator could not view Ito, who speaks accentless English, as simply another American but only as an Asian. D'Amato later apologized but the message was clear: regardless of Ito's status as a judge, to Americans like D'Amato, he was not one of them, not an American.

Then there was the publication of the book *O.J.'s Legal Pad* by Henry Beard and John Boswell, and illustrated by Ron Barrett, by Villard Books, a division of Random House. Purported to represent the doodles and random thoughts of O.J. Simpson during his trial proceedings, it featured cartoon depictions of Judge Ito as a Japanese kamikaze pilot and a World War II-era Japanese soldier with a bayonet. One cartoon pictured a U.S. bomber dropping an atomic bomb on the Judge's head. The caption read, "Ito, Ito, bag of Fritos/Hiroshima, nuke Judge Ito/Banzai, banzai, Nagasaki/Use his head for backyard hockey!"[2] The authors and illustrator were unable to distinguish between foreign nationals and Asian Pacific Americans and, instead, perpetuated the notion that anyone of Asian Pacific ancestry surely must be a foreigner.

This view of Asian Pacific Americans as foreigners in their own country is neither a new nor an isolated attitude. At its most benign, it results in an embarrassing faux pas, such as when Congressman Roscoe Bartlett of Maryland, lamenting that the majority of state scholarship recipients consisted of students with a disproportionately large number of "Oriental" and Indian names, complained to a group of state officials that people with Asian and East Indian surnames do not have "American names" and do not "represent the normal American."[3]

At its most inimical, however, it has resulted in murder and the abrogation of constitutionally protected civil rights and liberties. In 1980, Chinese American Vincent Chin encountered two out-of-work men who, angry about Japanese economic success, used baseball bats to beat him to death. In 1988, another Chinese American, Ming Hai "Jim" Loo, was killed by a group of men angered about the way the North Vietnamese treated American soldiers during the Vietnam War. And, in 1942, it resulted in the wholesale internment of almost 120,000 Americans of Japanese ancestry from the West Coast.

THE STATUS OF ASIAN PACIFIC AMERICAN CHILDREN'S LITERATURE

Children's literature has reinforced the perception of Asian Pacific Americans as foreigners, rather than fellow Americans, for generations of Americans. An abundance of Asian and Pacific Island fables (like *Taro Urashima*, *How Maui Harnessed the Sun*, and *Why Rat Comes First*), folk tales (*Lon Po Po*, *Little One-Inch*, and *The Blue Jackal*, to name a few) and psuedo-folk tales (such as *Five Chinese Brothers* and *Tikki Tikki Tembo*), coupled with an almost complete absence of authentic Asian Pacific American children's literature, has contributed and continues to contribute to the perpetuation of this and other serious misperceptions and misunderstandings about Asian Pacific Americans.

Asian Pacific Americans are a diverse group. They are comprised of over fifty different ethnic groups who share no common history, language, religion, or culture.[4] Some belong to families who have lived in the United States for five generations, no longer speaking any language but English, and having never known or lived in any culture that was not American. Others are recent arrivals, clinging to the familiar cultures and traditions of the past as they build new lives. Some came to the United States as sojourners, students, or workers whose intended temporary stay became permanent. Many came willingly, as immigrants searching for a better life, while others came as refugees, seeking escape and safety. In any event, the diversity of the Asian Pacific American community must be recognized, understood, and appreciated before addressing its presentation and representation in children's literature.

Although some segments of the Asian Pacific American community have over 150 years of history in the United States, the first hundred years or so were characterized by fluctuating levels of anti-Asian sentiment that fueled fears of the "Yellow Peril," resulted in laws such as the Chinese Exclusion Act, alien land laws, and the National Origins Act of 1924, and culminated in the internment of Japanese Americans during the Second World War. Indeed, prior to 1952, Asian immigrants were ineligible for U.S. citizenship. It took the civil rights movement of the 1960s to ignite pan-Asian American activism, beginning with the drive to promote Asian American studies on college campuses. Given the diversity of the community it tries to represent, and the history of that community, pan-Asian Americanism, later pan-Asian Pacific Americanism was, and in some quarters remains, a controversial concept.

It should not be surprising, therefore, to discover that by 1976, as pan-Asian Pacific Americanism began to take root, with growing numbers of pan-Asian and Pacific Islander organizations (as opposed to those with a single ethnic group as a base) being established, there at last would be enough community momentum for attention to turn to the status of Asian Pacific American children's literature and the persistently low number of such books being published. That year (1976), a committee of Asian American book reviewers undertook to identify and evaluate Asian American children's books.[5] In spite of the fact that approximately 4,500 new children's books are published each year in the United States, the committee found that only 66 children's books featured a child of Asian Pacific ancestry as a central character. They concluded that with one or two exceptions, the 66 books were "racist, sexist and elitist and that the image of Asian Americans they present is grossly misleading."[6]

Twenty years later, the number of Asian Pacific American children's books published each year has not increased significantly. In any given year, while four to five thousand new children's books are published, fewer than ten are by or about Asian Pacific Americans. That means that children of Asian Pacific ancestry are still more likely to find books featuring anthropomorphic animals and creatures of fantasy than people who look like them or their families. It also means that American children of all races and ethnic origins are being offered a disturbingly artificial view of the world in which they live, one that does not begin to reflect the diversity of the society in which they will be expected to live, work, play, and grow. Children are our hope for the future, yet they are handicapped when their books and educational materials persist in proffering a grossly distorted view of the diverse races and ethnic groups that comprise the United States.

If children see that most books that feature humans focus upon humans of European ancestry—that the hero or heroine who is most interesting, exciting, adventurous, . . . is usually of European ancestry; that European ancestry, values, traditions, and customs are celebrated and prized; that attention is lavished upon European history, arts, religions, and the like; while people of other races or ethnic origins are relegated to the role of a sidekick; or, are presented as two-dimensional characters; or, are the practitioners of strange (read not normal, foreign, less desirable, less correct, etc.) customs or habits; that traditions and cultures not of European origin are less appreciated, less desired, and less valued—then what kind of self-esteem can we anticipate from children who are not of European ancestry? What kind of tolerance, understanding, or respect for those children shall we expect from their European American peers?

While the number of Asian Pacific American children's books that are available remains disappointing, the depth and breadth of those books that are available are more promising. Twenty years ago, few Asian or Pacific Islander ethnic groups, other than Chinese or Japanese Americans, were featured in children's books. Now, we are seeing greater diversity in the Asian and Pacific Islander ethnic groups appearing in children's literature. As more groups, such as Korean Americans, Filipino Americans, and Indian Americans, become better established in the United States, each group is producing able and talented authors, interested in and enthusiastic about writing about their community. As the smaller and newer Asian Pacific ethnic communities adjust to life in America, they too will be producing more writers.

This is not to suggest that simply waiting until more Asian Pacific American writers emerge will lead to increased numbers of Asian Pacific American children's books being published. Nor is it meant to suggest that more writers of Asian Pacific ancestry will lead to the eventual and ultimate solution of any problems of inaccurate, misleading, offensive, or stereotypic portrayals of Asian Pacific Americans. Certainly, more writers who are familiar with the Asian Pacific American community, its history, politics, psychology, sociology, and culture are necessary, and groups such as the Asian American Writer's Workshop in New York, Asian American Renaissance in Minneapolis, DestinAsian and Riksha in Chicago, and others around the country have been working to address the need.

One such effort of note is *Children of Asian America*, a first of its kind anthology compiled on behalf of the Asian American Coalition, a grassroots coalition of Asian Pacific American community organizations. Frustrated by the difficulty of accessing authentic children's literature about Asian Pacific Americans, the leaders of the Coalition decided to commemorate their 12th anniversary by commissioning a collection of stories about their children's experiences, one from each of the Asian and Pacific Islander communities that participate in the Coalition. The result is a very special glimpse into Asian Pacific America. With a story from each of the Bangladeshi, Cambodian, Chinese, Filipino, Indian, Japanese, Korean, Laotian, Pakistani, Thai, and Vietnamese communities, as well as a poem celebrating the biracial Asian Pacific American child, and a gender-neutral, pan-Asian Pacific American story, the Asian American Coalition has presented a unique view of Asian Pacific American children that celebrates their diversity while embracing their American-ness.

But the writing of these stories is just one part of the solution. There is nothing to guarantee their publication and distribution. Polychrome Publishing, an independent press based in Chicago and the only company in the country dedicated to the publication of Asian Pacific American children's literature, is attempting to address the issue from another direction. Recognizing the dearth of authentic Asian Pacific American children's literature, in 1990 Polychrome began producing books to fill that void. While other publishers have their roots in other areas of publishing or education or library experience, Polychrome is unique because its origins come directly from within the grassroots Asian Pacific American community. Polychrome came into being in direct response to the Asian Pacific American community's frustration with the more common stereotypic, misleading, inaccurate, and non-substantive portrayals of Asian Pacific Americans and the issues of concern to them. Utilizing the editorial assistance of Asian Pacific American community leaders and others, Polychrome has been able to publish books that identify issues and articulate concerns that come from the heart of the Asian Pacific American community.

For example, contrary to *Tikki, Tikki, Tembo,* Asian and Pacific Islander names are neither funny nor unpronounceable, so Polychrome published *Ashok by Any Other Name.* And contrary to *Five Chinese Brothers,* Asian Pacific Americans don't all look alike, so Polychrome published *ONE small GIRL.* Nor are Asian and Pacific Islander foods especially strange or exotic, so *Char Siu Bao Boy* was published. Asian Pacific American homes and families are neither odd nor unnatural, as *Almond Cookies & Dragon Well Tea* showed, and Asian Pacific American adolescents have their share of problems and concerns just like their peers, as explored in *Stella: On the Edge of Popularity.* Nor do Asian Pacific Americans all excel in mathematics; indeed, such "positive" stereotypes are just as damaging as negative ones, so *Nene and the Horrible Math Monster* was published. And Asian Pacific American cultures integrate just as well as others into that which is American, as shown in *Thanksgiving at Obaachan's.*

The substantive issues addressed in Polychrome books can be disconcerting for readers expecting traditional and predictable fables and folk tales designed for commercial appeal, but in six short years, the company has shown that there is an appreciation and desire for stories that delve into experiences, feelings, and viewpoints common to children of Asian and Pacific Islander ancestry. Polychrome books may create controversy in that they do not necessarily conform to traditional commercial notions embraced by the publishing industry, but for many Asian Pacific American parents and their children, they are a refreshing, welcome, and long overdue addition to bookshelves.

Children's Book Press, a California-based company, has published a number of excellent Asian Pacific American (and other multicultural) children's books, some in bilingual editions. *Aekyung's Dream*, for instance, explores the difficulty that many Asian Pacific American immigrants face in reconciling themselves to cultural clash they encounter in the United States and developing and accepting a new sense of identity.

Several publishers based in Hawaii have produced some delightful children's books that focus upon the experiences of Hawaiian and Pacific Islander children, such as *Aunty Pua's Dilemma*, *Tutu and the Ti Plant*, and *Tutu and the Ulu Tree*, published by MnM; *I Visit My Tutu and Grandma*, from Press Pacifica; and *Whose Slippers Are Those?* from Bess Press.

Still, to improve the accuracy and authenticity of the portrayals of Asian Pacific Americans in children's literature and also increase the quantity that is available, requires acknowledgment, examination, and correction of the institutional barriers to multicultural children's books. These barriers include the book industry's traditional reviewing process; the monocultural criteria applied when evaluating books; ignorance about the distinction between that which is Asian or Pacific Islander and that which is Asian Pacific American; and misguided notions about who multicultural children's books are for and the market for such books.

THE REVIEWING PROCESS

A popular t-shirt reads, "So many books, so little time." Indeed, given the number of books published annually, it would be impossible to read each one. Reviews are necessary to help us sift through the hundreds of thousands of books published each year so that we can identify those that merit particular attention. While literary tastes are highly individual and one person's "must read" may be another's "waste of paper and ink," nevertheless, within the book industry there are certain review publications whose opinions are heavily relied upon by booksellers, librarians, educators, and parents when they are making purchasing decisions.

Within the industry, however, there is no uniform training or standards for book reviewers. Reviewers may be teachers, librarians, journalists, writers, or other industry insiders. Few, however, are qualified to review multicultural children's literature; while they may be knowledgeable about literature in general, it is rare for those reviewing for the industry giants and metropolitan dailies to have the multicultural background or the intimate knowledge of the multicultural community necessary to assess its literature. Nor can we presume that racial or ethnic diversity of reviewers alone is any guarantee that the criteria they apply in evaluating multicultural books incorporates any of the attitudes, values, or standards of any aspect of their community. Until the major review publications include reviews by people with insight into the communities that these multicultural books purport to reflect, they perpetuate an institutional racism that undermines the potential success of those books most deeply rooted in non-European-based cultures.

For example, when *Stella: On the Edge of Popularity* by Lauren Lee was published, *Publisher's Weekly,* one of the industry's heavyweight reviewers, described it as "uninspired" and commented that "there are few surprises here."[7] Uninspired? Few surprises? Perhaps, but interestingly, the same book led the *Korea Central Daily News,* a Korean American newspaper, to herald it as the book that "Korean American parents need to read to better understand their children."[8] According to *Asian Week,* a national Asian American newspaper, the book captured the conflict faced by many 1.5 generation (immigrants, usually from Korea, who come to the United States as young children and so receive part of their upbringing in Korea and the rest in the United States) and 2nd generation Korean Americans as they struggled to find a balance between Korean tradition and American lifestyle, particularly by Korean American girls.[9] And *Pan-Asian Panorama* said, ". . . many young Asian American girls will identify with her [Stella] as she struggles to balance family expectations, cultural values and peer pressure."[10] So who's right? *Publisher's Weekly*? The Asian American media? Both? Neither? Does it matter? Well, yes, it does. Consider all the teachers, librarians, and booksellers who may rely upon *Publisher's Weekly* but will never read the *Korea Central Daily News, Asian Week,* or *the Pan-Asian Panorama*. By relying upon *Publisher's Weekly*, they may choose not to purchase *Stella* for their library or classroom or to order it for their store, and thus will make it that much more difficult for Korean American and other girls to have access to a story that may instill greater self-esteem in Korean American readers and serve to educate others about the Korean American experience.

Again, this is not to imply that just because someone is of the same race as that purported to be represented in the book being reviewed, that that is a guarantee of the quality of the review. Particularly when dealing with the Asian Pacific American community, its diversity should be a reminder that the reviewer's race or ethnicity alone should not be the sole criteria in assessing the legitimacy of his or her opinion. For instance, *Thanksgiving at Obaachan's* by Janet Mitsui Brown was reviewed by a Chinese American librarian for *School Library Journal*.[11] The reviewer found it unexciting to say the least. That's not surprising. Mitsui Brown's book, a brief but intimate depiction of the relationship between an Issei (first generation American of Japanese ancestry, usually describing those immigrants who arrived from Japan between the late 1880s and 1924) grandmother and her granddaughter, is very much a Japanese American tale. In a simple story, she captured the feelings, attitudes, indeed, the very essence of a relationship to which many Japanese Americans can relate. Consequently, it has been a tremendously popular book among Japanese Americans, because "it speaks to a whole generation of Japanese Americans" and "has become the quintessential Sansei (third generation American of Japanese ancestry) story."[12] Unfortunately, the Chinese American reviewer may have missed the many nuances to which Japanese American readers are responding.

This issue is not unique to Asian Pacific American children's literature. Just Us Books, one of the pre-eminent publishers of Black and African American children's books, published a charming book to promote self-esteem, *Jamal's Busy Day*. The book has proven very popular among Blacks and African Americans. Still, its publisher vividly recalls the disappointment of discovering that the book's message of self-esteem escaped one major reviewer who criticized it for a lack of plot.

On the other hand, Allen Say's extraordinarily beautiful book, *Grandfather's Journey*, received universal acclaim from reviewers of all races. This is an exceptional book in which illustration, language, and story mesh seamlessly. As a story, however, the journey described is atypical of the experiences of many, possibly most, Japanese American families. While it is not necessary that a story be typical—after all, literature should encompass creativity, imagination, and individuality—one cannot help but wonder if stories presenting characters, values, or situations with which reviewers from other racial or ethnic or religious backgrounds may be unfamiliar must sacrifice some part of their integrity if they are to garner more favorable reviews.

Some might argue that if a book is not generic enough to communicate with and appeal to all people, then that may be a flaw in the book. That may be true. But it needs to be balanced against the recognition that the book that is less universal in appeal may be the book that allows a reader to experience a new way of looking at the world, to re-examine long (sometimes blindly) held values, to move beyond the superficial and discover a deeper understanding of other people as individuals, to accept and appreciate difference and diversity, and to truly incorporate tolerance for and understanding of diversity into the reader's soul.

MONOCULTURAL CRITERIA IN A MULTICULTURAL WORLD

Along with the growing demand for multicultural literature, there has been a rise in what have been called multicultural books with universal themes.

These are stories in which race or ethnicity play a marginal role. The issues confronted are "universal" ones to which almost any reader, regardless of his or her own ethnicity, can easily relate and identify. Race or ethnicity play little or no part in the story and it would be an easy matter to substitute another race or ethnicity with no damage to the tale. Among them have been some excellent Asian Pacific American examples, such as *Sachiko Means Happiness* by Kimiko Sakai, Allen Say's *The Lost Lake*, *Momo's Kitten* and *Umbrella* by the late Taro Yashima, and *First Snow* by Helen Coutant and Vo-Dinh.

Stories with universal themes play an integral role in reminding all of us of our common humanity. They reinforce the belief that regardless of skin color, hair color or texture, eye shape, language, or any other difference between people, at heart there are some things that we all desire, all value, all fear—in short, that we all share.

Important as universal themes are, there are some inherent differences among us that are linked to, among other things, race, ethnicity, culture, gender, religion, age, and socioeconomic status. Certainly, we are all equals, but it is neither unusual nor uncommon to discover feelings of greater or more intuitive understanding or shared or common experiences, perceptions, values, and attitudes arising from things such as race, ethnicity, culture, gender, and so on. The particular affinity that Japanese Americans have evidenced for Janet Mitsui Brown's *Thanksgiving at Obaachan's* is one example. Another is *Nene and the Horrible Math Monster* by Marie Villanueva. Nene is a Filipino American girl who is confronted by the model minority myth, the stereotype that suggests that everyone of Asian Pacific ancestry excels at mathematics. Rather than simply attack the stereotype by presenting Nene as an exception to the rule, Villanueva cleverly delves into some of the reasons the stereotype exists. Nene lacks an affinity for math; nevertheless, home tutoring, relentless self-discipline, and serious studying has allowed her to score highly on exams and on her homework. What the media often heralds as "amazing" and others tout as genetic is more often than not, as Nene shows, simply the result of hard work and discipline. While others may find the story hard to accept, for many Asian Pacific Americans, Nene's story, in portraying the sometimes unrealistic expectations of teachers, the familial pressures and support, and the self-demands, is almost autobiographical. As *Special Edition Press*, a Filipino American magazine, noted, this book is able "to dispel the racial stereotype that Asian kids are good at math and sciences and nothing else, a lingering drawback for those inclined to other liberal and creative pursuits."[13]

When children's literature begins to reflect some of these less universal themes and to incorporate commonalities based upon race, ethnicity, culture, and the like, a reviewer who does not share that commonality may not understand it and may not appreciate its appearance in literature. Still, as American society grows ever more diverse, and as historically marginalized segments of American society continue to grow, there is a greater likelihood that more books with a specific emphasis—racial, ethnic, cultural, and so on—will be written and should not be subjected to inappropriate bases of evaluation in favor of more monoculturally acceptable and understandable universal themes.

ASIAN PACIFIC *AMERICAN*

As discussed earlier, American society frequently fails to distinguish between Asian and Pacific Islanders and their fellow Americans of Asian Pacific American ancestry. Consequently, many Americans are content and more comfortable with the numerous fables and folk tales that show people of Asian and Pacific Islander ancestry living in foreign countries. *The Moon Lady* by Amy Tan and *Lon Po Po* by Ed Young, for instance, are charming folk tales, but while such fables and folk tales may serve to impart insight into a particular culture, they do little to explore Asian Pacific Americans as Americans. Why does that matter? Imagine, if you will, what American society would be like if Grimm's fairy tales, Aesop's fables, and Greek, Roman, and Norse mythology in a multitude of variations and re-tellings comprised the bulk of American children's literature. Imagine libraries without *Tom Sawyer, Huckleberry Finn,* the March sisters and Jo's Boys, *The Wonderful Wizard of Oz*, Nancy Drew, the Moffats, *Harriet the Spy*, the Ingalls of Little House fame, the American Girls, Meg and Charles Wallace Murray and Calvin O'Keefe, and all the other wonderful characters of European ancestry who have populated American children's literature. Imagine that and you'll begin to comprehend what the dearth of Asian Pacific American children's literature means. Fables and folk tales may entertain, but in view of the limited number of books featuring people of Asian and Pacific Islander ancestry as Americans, the abundance of fables and folk tales reinforces the notion of Asian Pacific Americans as foreigners. This results in readers developing a higher level of comfort and a greater degree of automatic acceptance for those stories that conform to their expectation that individuals of Asian and Pacific Islander ancestry are not Americans.

Collections of tales, such as *The Rainbow People* and *Tongues of Jade,* make a good start toward addressing these concerns but they still tend to rely upon perceptions of Asian Pacific Americans as "foreign," "exotic," and "unusual." *American Dragons* and *Growing Up Asian American* are much better collections that show the diversity of Asian Pacific Americans while still presenting them as Americans.

This attitude also explains the popularity and greater acceptance of stories about Asian and Pacific Islander experiences. Since the characters in these books are already understood to be foreigners, they can be permitted to articulate unfamiliar sentiments or philosophies, to live through exotic adventures, and to aspire to goals that Americans may take for granted.

Year of Impossible Goodbyes by Sook Nyul Choi and *Eighth Moon* by Sansan, as told to Bette Bao Lord, for example, are wonderful stories about life in Korea at the end of the Second World War and in China during the Cultural Revolution, respectively, and make compelling reading. Although written by authors who now make their home in the United States, neither, however, provides any insight into the Asian Pacific American experience. While both provide fascinating background into Asian history and introduce the reader to interesting heroines, the stories and the characters remain Asian, not Asian American.

MULTICULTURAL CHILDREN'S BOOKS ARE FOR EVERYONE

When it comes to multicultural children's books, a dangerous stereotype exists. This stereotype insists that multicultural books are only intended for the particular racial or ethnic group represented. Therefore, African American books are only for African Americans, Asian Pacific American books are only for Asian Pacific Americans, and so on. This has resulted in some rather skewed buying patterns. According to the proprietor of a well-known children's book fair company, when he visits primarily European American schools, the books purchased are almost entirely European American. In primarily African American schools, the purchases are almost entirely African American. He commented that it was sad that these students, who were growing up in racially homogenous neighborhoods, would have little or no exposure to the stories, cultures, or life experiences of other races or ethnic groups that comprise the world that these students would one day inherit.

Sadder still, by reinforcing the stereotype and offering only European American books to European Americans, and African American books to African Americans, this book fair proprietor is doing little to support a basic purpose of multicultural literature: to educate and inform those of other races and ethnicities about the experiences of others. Perpetuation of this stereotype has ramifications of particular concern to Asian Pacific Americans. The diversity of the Asian Pacific American community means that this stereotype reinforces the notion that a book about Chinese Americans is only for Chinese Americans, a book about Japanese Americans is only for Japanese Americans, one about Korean Americans is only for Korean Americans, etc. This makes for limited cross-cultural buying within the Asian Pacific American community and the perceived smaller market for such books makes for less incentive for publishers to produce Asian Pacific American children's books.

Certainly there are a few Asian Pacific American children's books that have a multicultural readership, such as *Grandfather's Journey* and *Dragonwings*, but this is more a testament to the respect and longevity of their authors, Allen Say and Laurence Yep, than a real exception to the trend. Too often these few stories become token samples rather than a means of introducing and stimulating greater interest in and acceptance of authentic Asian Pacific American children's literature.

RECURRING THEMES IN ASIAN PACIFIC AMERICAN LITERATURE

In spite of the diversity of the Asian Pacific American community, some themes do appear and re-appear, suggesting that there are some common issues within this community. Among the most common themes are: immigrant adjustment to life in the United States; Asian Pacific American history; the cross cultural conflict between traditional Asian and Pacific Islander culture and values and European American culture and values; sharing Asian Pacific American culture; and the search for or acceptance of an Asian Pacific American identity.

Immigrant Adjustment to Life in the United States

While adjustments are required of all immigrants, Asian Pacific American culture has made for some unique experiences for Asian and Pacific Islander immigrants seeking to adjust to life in the United States. While their European counterparts may at least share or recognize elements of American culture, immigrants from other parts of the world, especially Asia and the Pacific, may not find customs or religions or habits familiar. For the Asian Pacific American immigrant, this means trying to interpret and understand life in their new country with few common points of reference. A number of children's stories capture the confusion, bewilderment, and sometimes the terror, frustration, or exhilaration of the challenge of building a new life.

Some wonderful examples are *Angel Child, Dragon Child*, a picture book by Michele Surat, *Aekyung's Dream* by Min Paek, *Bamboo & Butterflies* by Joan D. Criddle, *Thief of Hearts* by Laurence Yep, and *Children of the River* by Linda Crew.

Asian Pacific American History

When it is mentioned at all in American textbooks, Asian Pacific American history rarely receives more than an isolated paragraph here or there. Indeed, the very rarity of mention might lead some to assume that there is little Asian Pacific American history. Small wonder, then, that so little of Asian Pacific American history is commonly known.

Despite the limited attention given to Asian Pacific American history in our schools, it has nevertheless proven a rich source of inspiration for writers. For instance, there are a number of exceptional stories about the Chinese immigrants of the nineteenth century, including *Dragon's Gate* by Laurence Yep, about Chinese workers on the Transcontinental railroad, and Ruthanne Lum McCunn's, *One Thousand Pieces of Gold,* about a Chinese American woman and the early Chinese miners, and the picture book, *Pie-Biter.*

The late Yoshiko Uchida wrote extensively about early Japanese American history, especially the Japanese American internment during the Second World War, including *Samurai of Gold Hill, Journey to Topaz, Journey Home*, and *The Invisible Thread*. More recently, *Blue Jay in the Desert* by Marlene Shigekawa explores and explains the history of the internment through the eyes of a child, while Allen Say's *Grandfather's Journey* describes the experiences of a Japanese sojourner.

Another book premised upon Japanese American history, *Baseball Saved Us,* is a disturbing book. At first glance, this story of a Japanese American boy who learns to play baseball while he and his family are interned seems quite poignant. But upon closer analysis, this book's message is more alarming. After the war, when the boy is subjected to taunts and racial epithets, the baseball skills he acquired allow him to climatically hit a home run and become a hero to those who had been jeering him. It's classic drama that masks some very negative messages. When the boy hits the home run, the racial name-calling changes to cheers; surely athletic prowess, or success by mainstream values as represented by the home run, is not a real solution to such racism. This book misses a prime opportunity to explore why racial epithets are dangerous and hurtful and what can be done in the face of such incidents. Further, the intimation that playing baseball and developing greater skills in the game was some sort of positive outcome of the internment is appalling. Certainly we might wish to remind children that good can often come out of bad, and the author does comment upon the family breakdowns resulting from the internment, but here, good intentions aside, it diminishes the tragedy that was the internment.

Heroes, another book that seeks to draw upon Japanese American history, tries mightily, but the result is weak. It's primary message that Asian Pacific Americans have and can be heroes or "the good guys" is an important one. Well meaning, it nevertheless misses a chance to explore the whole notion of heroism and winners. The protagonist's father and uncle appear before him and his friends in the uniforms they wore when they were in the service. It's a two-dimensional resolution that raises more questions than it answers: Is service in the armed forces synonymous with being a hero? Can women be heroic? Do all heroes get medals? If not, why not? Is recognition a necessary component to being a hero?

Hawaiian history has also proven to be a rich source for children's literature. *The Last Princess: The Story of Princess Ka'iulani of Hawai'i* by Fay Stanley, *Kalakaua, Renaissance King* by William N. Armstrong and *Liliuokalani, Queen of Hawaii* by Mary Malone are excellent examples.

Although other Asian and Pacific Island ethnic groups have not had as many stories based upon their histories in the United States published, in part because the history of some has not been very long, a few good examples exist, such as *Generation One Point Five* by Tanya Hyonhye Ko, *Quiet Odyssey: A Pioneer Korean Woman in America* by Mary Paik Lee, *Clay Walls* by Kim Rounyoung, *America Is in the Heart* by Carlos Bulosan, and *Bamboo & Butterflies* by Joan D. Criddle.

Cross Cultural Conflict

In reality, that which is considered "American" should, more likely than not, be more precisely identified as "European American." For those Americans whose cultural heritage does not derive from European roots, it is not uncommon for them to find some of the traditions, customs, and values inherent to their non-European culture to be at odds with European American culture. Asian Pacific Americans have encountered this cross cultural conflict all too often, so it is no wonder that it is a frequent theme in Asian Pacific American children's literature.

Some excellent examples of stories featuring cross cultural conflict are picture books *Char Siu Bao Boy*, about a Chinese American boy who introduces his classmates to his favorite ethnic food; *Ashok by Any Other Name*, about an Indian American boy with an ethnic name who wishes he had a more "American" name; *Nene and the Horrible Math Monster* by Marie Villanueva; and middle and young adult novels *Stella: On the Edge of Popularity* by Lauren Lee; *Halmoni and the Picnic* by Sook Nyul Choi; *Child of the Owl*, about a Chinese American girl trying to adjust to life in Chinatown with her grandmother; and *The Star Fisher*, about a Chinese American girl who moves to West Virginia, both by Laurence Yep; and *Children of the River* by Linda Crew.

Sharing Asian Pacific American Culture

Another popular theme in Asian Pacific American children's literature, particularly in picture books, is the introduction and sharing of elements of Asian and Pacific Islander culture. Some good examples are picture books such as *Dumpling Soup* by James Rattigan; *At The Beach* by Huy Voun Lee, which introduces children to the concepts underlying Chinese calligraphy; *Almond Cookies & Dragon Well Tea* by Cynthia Chin-Lee, which offers children a glimpse into the home of a family proud of its Chinese heritage through the friendship of two little girls; and *Thanksgiving at Obaachan's* by Janet Mitsui Brown, which shows the celebration of a traditional American holiday replete with both Japanese and American foods, and the integration of Asian culture into mainstream American culture.

The Search for and Acceptance of an Asian Pacific American Identity

The search for and acceptance of one's identity is a common theme in children's literature and Asian Pacific American children's literature is no different. Since "American" is often equated with "European American," children of Asian and Pacific Islander ancestry who are technically as American as their peers of European ancestry, encounter particular struggles and ordeals as they attempt to come to terms with their sense of their own identity. The writers of Asian Pacific American children's literature have found this theme a rich and provocative source of inspiration.

Among the better examples of this theme are Jennifer L. Chan's *ONE small GIRL*, *Ashok by Any Other Name*, *Stella: On the Edge of Popularity* by Lauren Lee, Marie G. Lee's *If It Hadn't Been for Yoon Jun* and *On My Own*, Elaine Hosozawa-Nagano's *Chopsticks from America*, *The Child of the Owl* by Laurence Yep, and *Wingman* by Manus Pinkwater.

ASIAN PACIFIC AMERICAN POETRY

Poetry is a time-honored form of literary expression in Asian culture. It has not lost its importance as a form of literary expression for Asian Pacific Americans. Since the early poetic musings of Angel Island detainees, poetry has continued to be a popular literary form. Most are written for an adult audience but quite a few can be accessible and appreciated by young adults. *Songs of Gold Mountain*, Marlon K. Hom's collection and translation of the Angel Island poems, is magnificent in its ability to capture the frustation, anger, despair, and agony of prospective Chinese immigrants waiting weeks, months, and sometimes years to gain admittance to the United States. Hom's translation loses none of the poignancy or subtlety of the original works.

Lawson Fusao Inada's *Before the War: Poems As They Happened* is a soulful examination of Japanese American identity and history. His writing requires a fair amount of familiarity with Japanese American history and culture, but those possessed of such familiarity will revel in his fluid use of language and imagery.

Expounding the Doubtful Points is a powerful and poignant collection of poems by Wing Tek Lum. Lum writes with a candor and insight that makes each of his poems a delight.

Dwight L. Okita's *Crossing Against the Light* offers a refreshing and sometimes humorous exploration of contemporary Asian American issues. He writes with an honesty and openness that makes his poetry easily accessible.

Good Luck Gold and Other Poems by Janet S. Wong is a poetic treasure. Wong's poetry is charming and endearing. She writes with a deft and sure touch. Her newest volume of poetry, *The Seaweed Suitcase*, confirms her skill as a poet. With each poem she swiftly but surely uncovers another facet of the Asian Pacific American experience. She skillfully uses humor and wry amusement as she offers poignant commentary upon the Asian Pacific American condition. Older children should enjoy both her books.

ASIAN PACIFIC AMERICAN ILLUSTRATORS

An interesting aspect of Asian Pacific American children's literature has been the emergence to prominence of Asian Pacific American illustrators such as Ed Young and Allen Say. Although both Young and Say write as well as illustrate, it is their exquisite, distinctive, and readily identifiable illustrations that make them especially noteworthy. Both draw heavily upon Asian themes, settings and styles for their images and their popularity, perhaps enhanced by their extraordinarily beautiful illustrations, may help acclimate mainstream America to a greater acceptance of and interest in Asian Pacific American culture. Indeed, it should be kept in mind that the works by Ed Young and Allen Say, while not definitive on the subject of Asian Pacific American children's literature, may be useful primers.

DEPICTION OF ASIAN PACIFIC AMERICANS IN CHILDREN'S LITERATURE

The persistently low numbers of Asian Pacific American children's books that are published each year have resulted in a correspondingly intense debate about how Asian Pacific Americans ought to be depicted in those same books. A variety of organizations, such as the Asian American Children's Book Project Committee and the National Association for the Education of the Young Child, and individuals, such as Esther C. Jenkins, Ginny Moore Kruse, Kathleen T. Horning, and Lyn Miller-Lachman, have attempted to develop standards and criteria by which to evaluate children's literature. Often, however, the criteria results in little more than guidelines or numerical rating systems that seek to be objective but to which subjective opinions must nevertheless be applied. While they are helpful, there is danger in too heavy a reliance upon them, for although they offer legitimate issues to be considered in evaluating children's books, they should not be used as or allowed to become a substitute for authentic and accurate knowledge of and insight into the intrinsic issues, concerns, and needs of the Asian Pacific American community and the individual ethnic communities that comprise it.

For example, consider the seven guidelines established by the Asian American Children's Book Project. The first says: "A children's book about

Asian Pacific Americans should reflect the realities and ways of an Asian Pacific American People."

While the sentiment is correct, it presupposes an intimate knowledge of Asian Pacific Americans. If someone applying this criteria has that knowledge, then there is almost no need to state it. But for someone lacking that knowledge, it simply opens the way for a host of other issues, such as which Asian Pacific Americans—Asian Pacific Americans in Hawaii, where they are not necessarily a minority group? Or Asian Pacific Americans in California, where they are still a minority, and frequently plagued by ethnic rifts, but have nevertheless achieved many firsts? Or Asian Pacific Americans in the Midwest or South, where they are such a minority that they are often overlooked in any discussion of minorities?

And just what are the realities and ways of an "Asian Pacific American People"? Certainly there are tremendous differences in the realities and ways of fourth and fifth generation Asian Pacific Americans who may no longer speak the language, or practice the customs or religion of their forebears, and new immigrants and refugees, struggling to adapt to life in the United States. And that is not to mention the differences between the cultures and customs of Asian and Pacific Islander ethnic and religious groups, and multi-ethnic and multiracial Asian Pacific Americans.

The second guideline of the Asian American Children's Book Project states: "A children's book about Asian Pacific Americans should transcend stereotypes."

Again, this is a noble sentiment. In practice, however, it may mislead by inspiring well-meaning, knee-jerk reactions to presumed stereotypes and allowing glib packaging and presentation to mask the perpetuation of more serious stereotypes.

A prime example is the controversy that surrounded the introduction of *Char Siu Bao Boy*. When the book was first introduced, there were those who felt the protagonist, a Chinese American boy named Charlie, was a blatant stereotype. Charlie was criticized for his name, his love for a "foreign" food (char siu bao—barbecued pork buns), and the way he looked— with glasses and a messy haircut.

While the name Charlie was chosen for its alliteration with char siu bao, criticism of the name resulted in a number of letters to the editor of Asian Week defending the choice and pointing to prominent (and not so prominent) Chinese Americans who also bear the name. The upshot seemed to be a realization that despite the stereotypic Charlie Chan of the movies and the U.S. military's wartime use of the name as a slang for the enemy, Charles and Charlie had been and continues to be a perfectly acceptable choice of a name within the Chinese American community.

Violet H. Harada, in her article evaluating Asian American picture books, criticized Charlie for his "foreign tastes."[14] Apparently, she feels char siu bao is "foreign." While it is true that it has its origins in Asia, it is a common and popular food item in Hawaii and throughout Asian and Chinese American communities across the country. Harada may think it foreign, but would she level the same criticism if Charlie's favorite food were tacos or burritos, or spaghetti, or gyros, or croissants, or pierogis, or strudel or tortes, or the multitude of other ethnic foods that all Americans now enjoy? In an age when Americans enjoy and appreciate cuisine from around the world, is there really still such a thing as "foreign" food? Certainly, different parts of the world still offer exotic delicacies that may not be readily available in the United States, but char siu bao, easily found throughout Hawaii and in Asian communities all over the mainland, and familiar to Americans of all ethnic backgrounds, is no more foreign than many popular foods that Americans have adopted.

As for Charlie's looks, Harada and others might find him unattractive or clumsy looking, but is he a stereotype? True, he wears glasses, but is that a bad thing? True, his hair isn't particularly neat, but is that stereotypic? Charlie suffers from a well-intentioned but ill-conceived reaction. While he may not be beautiful by classic European American standards, just what is so negative, so stereotypic, about the way he looks? Charlie doesn't speak in a sing song or pidgin accent. He has friends and is able to assert himself. He is generous and has a loving family. Is he truly a stereotype, or are the Haradas of the world allowing their own pre-dispositions, the negative connotations they associate with Asian Pacific American boys who wear glasses and have unruly hair, to color their reaction? If anything, Charlie is a warm and reassuring figure for children who may not be classically cute, who may wear glasses or have messy hair. (Thus the book ended up on the State of Hawaii's Department of Education recommended list.) Charlie neither suffers because of nor wishes to change his looks. *That* is a message children of all races need to hear.

Conversely, the knee-jerk reactions these guidelines may inspire may allow glib packaging to obscure more serious instances of stereotyping. Consider the book *Baseball Saved Us* by Ken Mochizuki. Acclaimed by mainstream reviewers for its stark illustrations, based upon the photographs of Ansel Adams, many less discerning readers may easily overlook the egregious stereotyping. The protagonist is a Japanese American boy, named stereotypically enough, Shorty. At the climax of the story, Shorty is playing baseball with some non-Japanese American boys after the end of the Second World War. As he comes up to bat, he is the victim of numerous racial epithets. Like a stereotypic Asian, he does not speak up. He simply hits a home run and becomes the hero of the game. While it is a dramatic ending, the message it sends is most disturbing. Shorty is unable or unwilling to speak up for himself. The reader receives no explanation about why racial insults and name-calling are harmful and not to be done, an issue of particular concern to the Asian Pacific American community given rising levels of anti-Asian hates crimes in this country. Mochizuki's solution (hit a home run) suggests that assimilation or acculturation as opposed to tolerance and respect for diversity is the route to success. For those children who cannot assimilate or acculturate, who are perhaps held back by an Asian accent, religious practices, or simply by preference for their own ethnic culture, hitting a home run is an oversimplified solution. Shorty may be attractive to look at, but he is a sad role model.

In their article, "Beyond Chopsticks and Dragons: Selecting Asian-American Literature for Children," Valerie Ooka Pang, Carolyn Colvin, MyLuong Tran, and Robertta H. Barba, propose a more realistic set of guidelines for evaluating Asian American children's literature, including "(a) a culturally pluralistic theme, (b) positive portrayal of characters, (c) settings in the United States, (d) authentic illustrations, (e) strong plot and characterization, and (f) historical accuracy."[15] In spite of their hyphenation of "Asian American," considered objectionable by many in the Asian American community, such as language expert and community activist Dr. David L. Liu,[16] the criteria they propose makes sense, although evaluating authenticity of illustrations and historical accuracy again presumes a more than passing familiarity with those issues.

So, if guidelines lack specificity, numerical rating systems rely too heavily upon making the subjective appear objective, and the opinions of reviewers too frequently suffer from the biases or ignorance or cultural insensitivity of the reviewer, how can the depiction of Asian Pacific Americans or any other group, for that matter, be fairly and accurately evaluated? Is such evaluation possible?

Yes, but it may require some new standards. In a genre such as Asian Pacific American children's literature, where the number of books published each year is so small, perhaps there needs to be greater emphasis upon what the Asian Pacific American community needs in children's literature and how a particular book serves that need. For example, rather than having a guideline advise the transcendence of stereotypes, it might be more useful and productive to identify stereotypes that Asian Pacific Americans would like to see dispelled and examine how effectively a particular book accomplishes that objective. If the model minority myth is a stereotype that needs to be dispelled, then perhaps we need to look at books and determine whether they indeed accomplish that. So, too, if being subjected to racial slurs and epithets is something the Asian Pacific American community wishes to overcome, again we need to look at books and determine how effectively they convey that need and the rationale for it.

Some might question why simply being a good story is not sufficient. Why not allow all stories to be judged on the same merits? The fact of the matter is that while it sounds egalitarian, it naively presupposes that what is a good story to one, is a good story to all. It ignores the very needs that underlie the demand for multicultural, especially Asian Pacific American, children's literature.

While addressing those needs necessitates greater understanding and appreciation of the Asian Pacific American community and others, it also allows us to put to rest the specious debates about the importance or unimportance of the race or ethnicity of authors of multicultural literature. There is a presumption that when an author of a particular racial or ethnic group writes about that same racial or ethnic group, the author's own race or ethnicity somehow should give him or her some greater degree of knowledge about or insight into that race or ethnic group. It sounds logical. Indeed, who should know about a race or ethnic group more intimately than a member of that race or ethnic group? The simplicity of that logic, however, overlooks the role that imagination and creativity play in writing and mistakenly reinforces the notion that racial and ethnic groups are monolithic. Knowledge of a community, its history, its accomplishments and problems, its expectations and fears, its dreams and aspirations, its similarities, diversity, and exceptions—these are among the elements necessary for any author writing about people. Race and ethnicity are no guarantee that an author embodies these elements.

Consider, for example, *Candle in the Wind* by Maureen Wartski. Although her name does not suggest it, Wartski is of Japanese descent. *Candle in the Wind* tells the story of a Japanese American family that suffers the tragic loss of its elder son. His car stalls and while he is asking to use a telephone, he is mistakenly shot by an elderly white man. The murder in the story is a thinly veiled account of the actual murder in Louisiana of a Japanese student named Yoshi Hattori. While Wartski does an admirable job of detailing the grief and anger of the surviving family members, she also explores issues of racial hatred and bigotry by introducing conflict between a neo-Nazi white supremacist group and their Asian American counterpart. It's fiction and certainly that gives Wartski license to tell her story any way she wishes. Yet anti-Asian violence is a very real problem for the Asian Pacific American community. And although Asian supremacist groups may exist in Asia, and some individuals may harbor feelings of ethnic supremacy, it is interesting to note that in the United States, within the Asian American community, there does not appear to be any such identifiable Asian supremacist group. For Asian American community leaders who advocate on behalf of victims of anti-Asian violence and hate crimes, Wartski's book creates some serious issues of concern. By suggesting to an uninformed reader that Asian American organizations that arrive in a community in the aftermath of a tragedy to help victims and their families may, in actuality, be an Asian version of the neo-Nazis, this story has the potential to undermine the very important and beneficial efforts of legitimate groups such as the Anti-Asian Violence Network, the Japanese American Citizens

League, the Organization of Chinese Americans, the National Asian Pacific American Legal Consortium, the Asian American Legal Defense and Education Fund, the Asian Law Caucus, and others.

In contrast, consider Lauren Lee, the author of *Stella: On the Edge of Popularity*, the book that the *Korea Central Daily News* proclaimed captured a realistic slice of what life was like for a Korean American adolescent and suggested that Korean American parents read to better understand their own children. Lee herself is not Korean (she describes herself as Korean American by marriage) but, through her husband and his family, she has spent over ten years immersing herself in the Korean American community. She spends time with her husband's family, but also tutors Korean American junior high and high school students, attends and actively participates in a Korean American church, has researched and written a non-fiction book about Korean Americans, and raises her children to be knowledgeable about and comfortable with their Korean heritage. Certainly Lee may be an exception; many authors are unwilling to devote the time necessary to thoroughly prepare themselves to write about a racial or ethnic group to which they do not belong, but she is living proof that it can be done and done well.

Too often the depiction of Asian Pacific Americans in children's literature is two-dimensional and uninspired. It does not begin to reflect the diversity of Asian Pacific Americans or the issues, realities, and experiences common to them. Issues of race and ethnicity, gender, class, religion, language, disability, and age are all too often ignored in favor of more familiar—that is, European American—and possibly more easily marketable themes, issues, topics, and subjects. In part, this is the result of ignorance about the Asian Pacific American community on the part of publishers, writers, reviewers, teachers, librarians, and booksellers. But it is also the result of a combination of Asian Pacific American confusion, apathy and naiveté, as well as a diversity of opinion about how they should be depicted.

EXEMPLARY AUTHORS AND WORKS

Thankfully, the regrettably low numbers of Asian Pacific American children's books being published each year is not indicative of the quality of the writing coming out of the Asian Pacific American community. While many of these authors have not achieved the fame or recognition of their European American counterparts, that is certainly not because of any lack of talent.

Of all the writers devoting their talents to the creation of stories about Asian Pacific Americans, author Laurence Yep surely sets the standard. His is a versatile talent. Whether he is writing historical fiction like *Dragon's Gate*, or contemporary young adult literature like *Ribbons*, or science fiction and fantasy like *Shadow Lord*, or non-fiction like his autobiography

The Lost Garden or the anthology *American Dragons*, he writes with warmth, humor, and profound insight. A Chinese American, Yep's writing captures the nuances and quirks of his community so as to make it recognizable to other Asian Pacific Americans and conveys stories, characters, settings, and the like, so as to make them understandable to all readers. Whether he is telling the story of his grandfather's life, or imagining his mother's girl-hood, or re-examining his own boyhood, Yep's writing is honest and his characters multi-dimensional people, motivated by both logic and emotions with which the reader cannot help but identify. Perhaps what makes Yep so extraordinary an author, however, is that like the old adage, he writes about what he knows . . . and he knows a lot. Consider, for example, his knowl-edge about the Chinese American community and its history. Yep grew up in San Francisco, but not in Chinatown. He attended a school in Chinatown and visited family and relatives who lived there, so that he is familiar with Chinatown, yet living outside it has apparently given him other perspec-tives with which to look at the Chinese American community. Yep's mother's family lived for years in West Virginia and Ohio, and Yep himself attended college in Wisconsin, giving him additional experience and insight into his own identity as a Chinese American, the Chinese American community in California and elsewhere, and Chinese American history. A prolific writer, perhaps even a genius, it is extremely difficult to point to just a few of his books as exemplary. Some favorites which merit particular attention are *Dragon's Gate*, *Dragonwings*, *The Star Fisher*, *Child of the Owl*, *American Dragons*, *The Lost Garden: A Memoir*, *Shadow Lord*, and *Later, Gator*.

Lensey Namioka is another talent whose writing should not be over-looked. Her *Yang the Youngest and His Terrible Ear* and *Yang the Third and Her Impossible Family* are a joy to read. Born in Beijing, she moved to the United States as a child and often uses her own childhood as inspiration for her stories. Thus, it is no wonder that her stories ring true-to-life. Clearly Namioka remains in touch with the feelings, worries, and perceptions of adolescents. She writes with a dignity and integrity that makes her char-acters three-dimensional and a clarity that makes each book a happy expe-rience for the reader.

Marie G. Lee is a young and promising author of Korean ancestry. In-terestingly, she grew up in Minnesota, where there is a sizable population of Southeast Asian refugees and Korean adoptees, but not necessarily a traditional Asian Pacific American community such as one would expect to find in California, Washington, or New York. Although she now makes her home in New York, Lee, like Yep, is obviously familiar with diverse experi-ences within her community, and writes about it in such a way as to make these experiences accessible by readers of any race or ethnicity.

Lee's first book, a young adult novel, *Finding My Voice*, introduced a warm and engaging heroine, Ellen Sung. A high school senior, Ellen finds herself questioning values and ambitions with which she has grown up, blindly accepting them as her own. On the verge of her own adulthood, Ellen begins searching for her own identity amidst the expectations of her self-sacrificing parents, her driven and over-achieving older sister, her less ambitious or otherwise directed classmates, and her unsympathetic, un-imaginative teachers. With humor and charm, she delicately allows the reader to follow Ellen's metamorphosis from her parents' daughter into her own self.

Saying Goodbye, the sequel to *Finding My Voice*, follows Ellen Sung during her freshman year at Harvard. In it, Lee shows real insight into the curiosity and interest in their ethnic heritage that many Asian Pacific Americans begin to develop as they enter adulthood.

If It Hadn't Been for Yoon Jun follows seventh grader Alice Larsen, a Korean adoptee, raised by an European American family in a predominantly European American town in Minnesota. Alice rejects any tie to her Korean heritage, embodied in the form of Yoon Jun Lee, a Korean boy who has moved to her town. Although not as natural as *Finding My Voice*, especially Alice's early disdain of Yoon Jun—perhaps because Lee herself is more com-passionate and less judgmental than Alice—Lee nevertheless has con-structed an interesting story that reaffirms her ability as a writer.

PROBLEMATIC TEXTS

Some of the most problematic texts in Asian Pacific American children's literature are also the oldest—stories written and published generations ago. Sadly, *Five Chinese Brothers* (and the updated version, *Seven Chinese Brothers*) and *Tikki, Tikki, Tembo* are still in print. What makes them prob-lematic is that they were created at a time when and in an atmosphere where the stereotypes they present were not even recognized as stereo-types, much less as inaccurate representations. In both *Five Chinese Broth-ers* and *Seven Chinese Brothers*, the brothers all look alike. It is not simply a case of a remarkable family resemblance. These brothers are identical. In spite of their differing talents and abilities, the message is clear: all Chi-nese look alike. They are not individuals; they are all fungible. *Tikki, Tikki, Tembo* purports to explain Asian names but in reality reinforces the stereo-type that Asian names sound like nonsense syllables. While Asian names may be distinctly different from European names, that is no reason to dis-miss them as some type of gobbledygook.

While modern stories generally have been more successful at avoiding the blatant stereotypes, some are still problematic. The problems are oftentimes more subtle but no less disturbing. *Baseball Saved Us* and *Candle in the Wind* have previously been discussed. *I Hate English!* by Ellen Levine relies upon the tired *deus ex machina* device of intervention by a European

American teacher to resolve its heroine's difficulty in learning English. *Chin Chiang and the Dragon's Dance* by Ian Wallace inaccurately links the dragon dance to the lunar calendar's Year of the Dragon. *Dragon Parade* by Steven A. Chin presents women whose attire is inconsistent with the setting and period and *Mrs. Sato's Hens* gives us Japanese American characters attired in Chinese clothing. While not as blatant as *Five Chinese Brothers*, *Seven Chinese Brothers*, or *Tikki, Tikki, Tembo*, these stories are nevertheless problematic.

ISSUES OF IDENTITY

What does it mean to be an Asian Pacific American? While books with universal themes reinforce notions of our common humanity, and fables and folk tales can convey insight into cultural values, there are still too few books being published that explore issues of identity for Asian Pacific Americans. Still, suitable books for all ages do exist.

Primary Grade Books

At the primary grade level, children are aware of physical differences but are not necessarily sure of what meaning to attribute to those differences. They can understand cultural identity and identify stereotypes. They are beginning to define people in terms of ethnicity and to understand group membership. As they become aware of racism directed against their own group, they want and need accurate information.[17] Books for this age group need to reassure children about who they and their families are and to suggest honest but not hurtful ways to react to others who may differ from them in some fashion. They need to introduce and instill values such as tolerance, appreciation and respect for diversity, and self-esteem, in children.

The primary grades are an appropriate time to acknowledge, recognize, and explore obvious physical, cultural, and religious differences so as to cultivate a greater level of comfort and acceptance than might otherwise exist. As children are exposed to and educated about those differences, they can then begin to examine the significance of these differences, and hopefully discern that the differences are not so great after all.

Among the books useful for exploring Asian Pacific American identity in the primary grades are stories such as *ONE small GIRL*, which asks children to think about whether people of a particular race or ethnic group all look alike and why some might think they do; *Char Siu Bao Boy*, which explores issues such as conformity, fairness, and fear of differences; and *Thanksgiving at Obaachan's*, which celebrates the diversity of America during a traditional American holiday. *Luka's Quilt*, about the melding of tradition and modernism, delves into our sense of roots and family. The inter-racial friendship story *Almond Cookies & Dragon Well Tea* and *Sam and the Lucky Money* are both nice treatments of the issue of integrating non-European cultural values in a matter-of-fact way. *Lights for Gita* and *Angel Child, Dragon Child* are charming stories about immigrant children adjusting to American life.

Intermediate Grade Books

At the intermediate grades, students become able to grasp more complex reasoning. Concepts like racism, prejudice, bigotry, and stereotypes can and should be introduced and discussed. By this age, children are interested in and aware of events in the world outside their immediate lives, as well as ancestry, history, and geography. At this age, children understand racism, can compare and contrast minority/majority perspective, and especially important, can use their own skills to take social action.[18]

Nene and the Horrible Math Monster is a wonderful book for this age group, and can serve as a good introduction to the concept of stereotypes. *Blue Jay in the Desert,* which explores the impact of the Japanese American internment through the eyes of a young boy, provides an excellent introduction to the deprivation of civil rights based upon race or ethnicity. In *Halmoni and the Picnic,* a Korean American girl struggles with her grandmother's difficult adjustment to life in America, and her classmates' perceptions about her Korean heritage. *In the Year of the Boar and Jackie Robinson* is somewhat dated, but nevertheless an entertaining glimpse at a Chinese American girl's first year in America. *Ashok by Any Other Name,* which looks at identity through an Indian American boy's confusion over his own obviously ethnic name, also introduces a new twist for readers: learning from the experiences of another racial or ethnic minority, in this case, an African American experience. *Yang the Youngest and His Terrible Ear* and *Yang the Third and Her Impossible Family* are delightful stories about balancing family and cultural values with American individuality.

Upper Elementary Grade Books

By the time students reach the upper elementary grades, they are able to examine and explore human relationships, alternative responses to racism, prejudice, bigotry, and stereotypes, and their own feelings about other people. Literature for this age group should help readers to examine, question, and re-evaluate their own perceptions about and attitudes toward others and the basis for and validity of those perceptions and attitudes.

Stella: On the Edge of Popularity explores an adolescent Korean American's Asian Pacific American identity through a variety of relationships with warmth, humor, and spirit. *Child of the Owl* follows a Chinese American's adjustment to life in Chinatown as she comes to terms with her Chinese heritage. *Dragonwings* is the captivating tale of two Chinese Americans coming to terms with their history and heritage as well as their ambitions and destiny. *Children of the River* is a compelling glimpse into the perceptions and experiences of a Cambodian refugee. *If It Hadn't Been for Yoon Jun*, about a Korean adoptee's struggle to develop a sense of identity that can incorporate her Korean heritage with her white, middle American upbringing, is an honest examination of one young woman's experience.

TEACHING / LEARNING STRATEGIES

When discussing teaching and learning strategies that can lead to meaningful discussions about Asian Pacific Americans and other racial, ethnic, and religious minority groups, the objectives of such discussion need to be kept in mind. Certainly discussion can focus upon common or universal themes in folk tales, such as the abundance of rabbit-in-the-moon stories from the various Pacific rim cultures, followed by exploration into and discussion about the reasons for any differences: geography, climate, social structures, religious beliefs, historical influences. Yet what information does such discussion really impart? How useful is such discussion?

Comparison of Universal Themes in Literature

First, this kind of discussion presumes the authenticity of the re-telling. Few Americans, including most Asian Pacific Americans, are well-versed in Asian mythology as it exists in the language, philosophy, psychology, and cultural memory of Asia. As author Frank Chin, the co-editor of the seminal Asian American literary texts, *Aiiieeeee! An Anthology of Asian American Writers* and *The Big Aiiieeeee! An Anthology of Chinese American and Japanese American Literature*, points out, some of the most popular Asian Pacific American writers, such as Maxine Hong Kingston, David Henry Hwang, and Amy Tan, create a non-existent cultural mythology that not only distorts and misrepresents Asian Pacific culture, but perpetuates and reinforces racist and misogynist images of and attitudes about it. They are inventing a cultural mythology that has no basis in the cultures into which they purport to give insight. As Chin succinctly puts it, "It's all a fake."[19]

When Chin talks about "the fake" in Asian Pacific American literature, he means that although they may be well-known, writers like Kingston, Hwang, and Tan "are not consistent with Chinese fairy tales and childhood literature. They are consistent with each other because (1) all the authors are Christian, (2) the only form of literature written by Chinese Americans that major publishers will publish (other than the cookbook) is autobiography, an exclusively Christian form; and (3) they all write to the Christian stereotype of Asia being as opposite morally from the West as it is geographically."[20] In other words, the stories, morals, and values they offer their readers, disguised as Chinese or Asian folklore, are nothing more than pseudo-folk tales that perpetuate damaging stereotypes about people of Asian ancestry.

By way of example, Chin points to the opening in Amy Tan's *Joy Luck Club*. There Tan purports to tell a Chinese fairy tale about a duck that wants to be a swan and a mother who dreams of her daughter being born in America, where she'll grow up speaking perfect English and no one will laugh at her and where "a woman's worth is [not] measured by the loudness of her husband's belch."[21]

Certainly it's an attention-grabbing opening, but, as Chin reminds us, it's fake. "Ducks in the barnyard are not the subject of Chinese fairy tales, except as food. Swans are not the symbols of physical female beauty, vanity, and promiscuity that they are in the West. Chinese admire the fact that swans mate for life; they represent romantic love and familial bliss. There is nothing in Chinese fairy tales to justify characterizing the Chinese as measuring a woman's worth by the loudness of her husband's belch."[22] Despite how entertaining a story such pseudo-folk tales may be, unfortunately they may also create and perpetuate grossly inaccurate views of Asian and Pacific Islander culture.

To be fair, the other side of the debate, however, argues that literary license encourages new and different interpretations, that variations on old themes that will allow that which is old to remain relevant is perfectly acceptable, and that the culture that cannot evolve will stagnate and die. What is real and what is fake can be very subjective, influenced not only by personal experience and interpretation, but even by that part of the country where one resides. As the Association of Asian American Studies and other national Asian Pacific American groups have discovered, there can be tremendous discrepancy between the experiences, values, attitudes, etc., of Asian Pacific Americans from California and those in other parts of the country. Still, the issue of accuracy is all too often glossed over in a zealous desire to be multicultural.

Second, the discussion of common or universal themes that may occur in fables and folk tales from diverse cultures encourages a reinforcement of stereotypes and misconceptions. While it may generate a great deal of discussion, it often fails to impart any significant insight or information about these diverse racial and ethnic groups, their histories or experiences.

Consider, for instance, the many varied renditions of Cinderella that have been published. In addition to numerous versions of the traditional western European Cinderella, including the Disney version, there have been *Egyptian Cinderella, Korean Cinderella, Yeh Shen* or *Yeh Hsien* (Chinese Cinderella), *Vassilissa the Fair* (the Russian Cinderella), *Little Burnt Face* or *The Rough Face Girl* (Native American Cinderella), and *Moss Green Princess* (African Cinderella), to name but a few. A discussion of their similarities and reasons for any differences can be interesting, but subconsciously, students are still presented with a message of European American cultural superiority. Even though a Chinese tale about Yeh Shen is believed to be the earliest of the so-called Cinderella tales, discussion is unlikely to be about the variations of "Yeh Shen tales" but rather about "Cinderella tales."

Furthermore, interesting or not, a discussion comparing the variations of Yeh Shen tales diverts some of the fundamental purposes of multiculturalism. These stories rarely provide an adequate amount of the information necessary to have a meaningful discussion. *The Korean Cinderella* (the Shirley Climo version), for example, tries through end notes to amplify the cultural context, but the illustrations and the text impart little of Korean or Korean American culture or history. Unless the author, illustrator, editor, graphic designer, and anyone else in a decision-making position is knowledgeable about the particular race, culture, or ethnic group from which they are attempting to tell a story, there is a strong likelihood that the story they produce, while it may be attractively packaged and even commercially successful, will do little to dispel stereotypes, and may even allow stereotypes to become further entrenched. Without authentic cultural representations, what we have with books like *Korean Cinderella* is Cinderella in yellowface.

Objectives in Incorporating Multicultural Children's Literature into Curricula

If conventional teaching / learning strategies such as discussion about common or universal themes in fables and folk tales fails to enhance the fundamental goals of multiculturalism, that does not mean effective strategies do not exist. They require education, open-mindedness, creativity, and hard work on the part of educators. As a starting point, we need to understand our objectives in incorporating multicultural children's literature into curricula. These objectives include:

1. The validation of minority experiences not commonly represented in literature, media, and the arts. This is crucial if the American educational system is to avoid the creation and perpetuation of feelings of alienation and bitterness among Asian Pacific American children and other children of color, and instead substitute the promotion of self-esteem and self-respect in these children, while sensitizing others about minority experiences.

2. Preparing students for life in a world characterized by diversity of race, ethnicity, culture, religion, gender so as to promote mutual respect, tolerance, and understanding, to foster greater appreciation of diversity, and to facilitate bases for clearer communication among all people.

3. Cultivating and instilling in students a greater appreciation of all people as valued and important individuals.

Understanding and appreciating the objectives behind the incorporation of multicultural children's literature into curricula is key to the development of innovative and effective strategies that will lead to meaningful discussions about Asian Pacific Americans and other minority groups. It allows a teacher to identify age-appropriate topics of discussion for a class that are designed to lead children to the conclusions that human beings are the same but individuals may be different and that being different is not necessarily bad. It allows a teacher to structure classroom exercises so as to expose children to different viewpoints and experiences while exploring the reasons for the differences. Do keep in mind that any strategies implemented need to be tailored to the age, maturity, and sophistication of the class.

For example, after reading *Ashok by Any Other Name* with the class, a discussion can be initiated about the names of the children in the class. How were the names chosen for the children in the class? Do the names have some significance? Are some names more common than others? Are some names perceived to be "better" than others? Why? What names would the children choose for themselves?

Or perhaps, after reading *Blue Jay in the Desert* or *Journey to Topaz* or *The Bracelet*, explore the history of the Japanese American internment by arbitrarily restricting privileges to one segment of the class, perhaps based on the month of birth or some other factor. Suggest that the restriction is because someone from this group might steal a test. Discuss the unfairness of targeting one segment of the class, emphasizing the fact that they are as legitimate a part of the class as the others. Encourage the children to draw parallels with the internment. Explore their feelings upon their "return" to the mainstream.

Or discuss the likely menu of the original Thanksgiving and how some of those items may have changed over time. Then use a book like *Thanksgiving at Obaachan's* to allow the class to share what "non-traditional" foods their family might enjoy as a family tradition at Thanksgiving. What does this kind of flexibility say about Americans?

Or try reading *Char Siu Bao Boy* to a class, followed by a discussion about similar experiences by class members. How did the students feel about it? How would the students handle being in Charlie's shoes? How do they feel about trying new foods? Perhaps some char siu bao can be brought into the class for the children to try.

Establish pen pal classes with students at schools in different racial or ethnic communities. Or ask the classes at different schools to exchange letters asking and answering questions on specific topics that are designed to explore and dispel stereotypes.

These are just some suggestions, but they can be used as a starting point in developing appropriate strategies for specific groups of students.

CONCLUSION

Teachers often say that there are so many multicultural titles being published that they would simply like to know which ones they need to offer in their classes. Many say they are afraid of choosing the "wrong" title; they fear misjudging the cultural authenticity of a book and are confused about which authority's opinion they should follow. That is not the right attitude. It presumes that a few select titles are sufficient to satisfy the need for multicultural materials. Certainly, if a teacher is only going to offer a single Asian Pacific American title, then the fear of making a poor choice is understandable, since that single title may have significant influence upon the class's perception about Asian Pacific Americans. Still, despite budgetary cutbacks and other fiscal constraints, it is unconscionable to allow students to believe that a single book can be representative of such a diverse community. Indeed, the more homogeneous a class or school or school district, the more the children there need to have a greater depth and breadth of multicultural materials made available to them.

Multiculturalism is more than just a fad. It is a recognition that diversity is a fact of life and that past efforts to address racial, ethnic, cultural, religious, and other differences among people have fallen short. Too often stereotypes and other misperceptions about different groups of people have been inadvertently reinforced. Too often we have shied away from serious exploration of our diversity. For too long, it has been difficult to find authentic multicultural materials. As a result, racial, ethnic, cultural, and religious strife continues to plague the world in which we live and, for all too many people, true tolerance and understanding remain elusive, a mirage. For Asian Pacific Americans and other racial and ethnic minorities, multiculturalism is crucial if they are to have more than just a theoretical opportunity to live their lives to their fullest potential.

That is where Asian Pacific American children's literature comes into play. It almost goes without saying that all children's literature should have strong plots, entertaining situations, engaging characters, and the like. But if children of all races and ethnic groups are to grow up recognizing that Asian Pacific Americans are Americans, they need to understand that there is nothing exotic or mysterious about Asian and Pacific Islander cultures, that names or customs or foods that have their origins in Asia or the Pacific are no more weird or strange or unpronounceable than those that have their origins in Europe, and that elements of Asian and Pacific Islander culture mix just as well as any other into the salad bowl that is American culture. Ideally, children would get to know and develop friendships with people from a variety of backgrounds so that they can see people as individuals, but in the absence of such opportunities, children's literature needs to fill the void.

Americans come in all sizes, shapes, colors, and accents. Unfortunately, even though we may accept this fact intellectually, stereotypes and other manifestations of racial biases often prevent us from accepting it emotionally and from expanding our perceptions about who Americans are. Perpetuating this situation is a disservice to future generations. Asian Pacific American and other multicultural children's literature offers at least a partial and hopeful solution.

NOTES

1. Interview with Senator Alphonse D'Amato by Don Imus.
2. *O.J.'s Legal Pad* by Henry Beard and John Boswell and illustrated by Ron Barrett (Villard Books, 1995).
3. *Washington Post*, March 4, 1993.
4. *1990 U.S. Census*.
5. This was the Asian American Children's Book Project of the Council for Interracial Books for Children.
6. Ibid.
7. *Publisher's Weekly*, May 16, 1994, p. 65.
8. *Korea Central Daily News*, June 1994.
9. *Asian Week*.
10. *Pan-Asian Panorama*, Vol. 1, No. 2, Spring 1994.
11. *School Library Journal*, August 1994, p. 126.
12. *San Francisco Examiner*, November 23, 1994.
13. *Special Edition Press*, Fall 1993.
14. "Issues of ethnicity, authenticity, and quality in Asian-American picture books, 1983–93" by Violet H. Harada, in *Journal of Youth Services in Libraries*, Vol. 8, No. 2 (Winter 1995).
15. "Beyond chopsticks and dragons: Selecting Asian-American literature for children" by Valerie Ooka Pang, Carolyn Colvin, MyLuong Tran and Robertta H. Barba, in *The Reading Teacher*, Vol. 46, No. 3 (November 1992).
16. "Asian American—No Hyphen, Please" by David L. Y. Liu, in *MAFBO Advocate* (March 1991).
17. *Stages of racial awareness* by Francis Aboud.
18. Ibid.
19. "Searching for Frank Chin" by Terry Hong, *A. Magazine*, February/March 1995, p. 68.
20. "Come all ye Asian American writers of the real and the fake" by Frank Chin, in *The Big Aiiieeeee! An Anthology of Chinese American and Japanese American Literature*, edited by Jeffery Paul Chan, Frank Chin, Lawson Fusao Inada, and Shawn Wong (New York: Meridian, 1991).

21. Ibid., p. 2.
22. Ibid., p. 3.

BIBLIOGRAPHY OF RECOMMENDED ASIAN PACIFIC AMERICAN CHILDREN'S BOOKS

There are far too few books by and about Asian Pacific Americans being published for children. Of those in print, certainly some are better than others—offering better writing, better plots, better character development, better insight, and better background into the Asian Pacific American experience. Too often, however, fear of selecting the wrong book, choosing the book with the stereotypes, or picking the unauthentic book has inhibited parents, librarians, and educators from providing children with the same abundance and variety of multicultural books as books featuring anthropomorphic animals and creatures of fantasy. It's a legitimate fear, but keep in mind that the potential for mistakes is compounded by a drastically limited selection of offerings. *Five Chinese Brothers* may suggest that people of Asian and Pacific Islander ancestry all look alike, but such a concept is far more damaging if that book is the only (or one of just a handful of) Asian and Asian Pacific American books in a classroom library. When it is one of forty or fifty or more Asian and Asian Pacific American books, then the impact of that one book is no longer quite so threatening. It is vitally important, therefore, that all of our children, regardless of their race or ethnicity, be provided with more than a token "Asian" book or two. If children are not given the opportunity to read multicultural books, we run the risk of condemning future generations of Americans to the perpetuation of the stereotypes, misperceptions, and misunderstandings that fuel the racial tensions and disharmony that have plagued our past.

Unfortunately, budgets and finances may require some selectivity, and with that in mind, the following are recommended:

Books for Primary Grades

Brown, Janet Mitsui. (1994). *Thanksgiving at Oboachan's*. Chicago: Polychrome Publishing.

Chan, Jennifer L. (1993). *One small girl*. Chicago: Polychrome Publishing.

Chin-Lee, Cynthia. (1993). *Almond cookies and dragon well tea*. Chicago: Polychrome Publishing.

Coutant, H.(1974). *First snow*. New York: Knopf.

Gilmore, Rachna. (1994). *Lights for Gita*.

Lee, Huy Voun. (1994). *At the beach*. New York: Henry Holt.

Lee, Huy Voun. (1995). *In the snow*. New York: Henry Holt.

McCunn, Ruthanne Lum. (1983). *Pie-biter*. San Francisco Design Enterprises of San Francisco.

Namioka, Lensey. (1992). *Yang the youngest and his terrible ear.* Boston: Joy Street Books.

Paek, Min. (1988). *Aekyun's dream.* Emeryville, CA: Children's Book Press.

Sakai Kimko. (1990). *Sachiko means happiness.* Emeryville, CA: Children's Book Press.

Say, Allen. (1990). *El chino.* Boston: Houghton Mifflin.

Say, Allen. (1993). *Grandfather's journey.* Boston: Houghton Mifflin.

Say, Allen. (1989). *Lost lake.* Boston: Houghton Mifflin.

Shigekawa, Marlene. (1993). *Blue jay in the desert.* Chicago: Polychrome Publishing.

Surat, Michele Maria. (1983). *Angel child, dragon child.* Milwaukee: Raintree.

Uchida, Yoshiko. (1993). *The bracelet.* New York: Philomel.

Yamate, Sandra S. (1992). *Ashok by any other name.* Chicago: Polychrome Publishing.

Yamate, Sandra S. (1991). *Char siu bao boy.* Chicago: Polychrome Publishing.

Books for Middle Grades

Children of Asian America. (1995). Compiled on behalf of the Asian American Coalition. Chicago: Polychrome Publishing.

Chop Sook Nyal. (1993). *Halmoni and the picnic.* Boston: Houghton Mifflin.

Hamanaka, Shelia. (1990). *The journey.* New York: Orchard Books.

Hosozawa-Nagano, Elaine. (1995). *Chopsticks from America.* Chicago: Polychrome Publishing.

Garland, Sherry. (1993). *The lotus seed.* New York: Harcourt.

Malone, Mary. (1975). *Liliuokalani, Queen of Hawaii.* Champaign, IL: Garrad Publishing.

Pinkwater, Manus. (1975). *Wingman.* New York: Dodd.

Uchida, Yoshiko. (1975). *The birthday visitor.* New York: Charles Scribners.

Uchida, Yoshiko. (1972). *Samurai of gold hill.* New York: Charles Scribners.

Villanueva, Marie. (1993). *Nene and the horrible math monster.* Chicago: Polychrome Publishing.

Books for Intermediate Grades and Above

American dragons: 25 Asian American voices (1993). Ed. Laurence Yep. New York: HarperCollins.

Choi, Sook Nyul. (1994). *Gathering of pearls.* Boston: Houghton Mifflin.

Crew, Linda. (1989). *Children of the river.* New York: Delacorte.

Lee, Lauren. (1994). *Stella: On the edge of popularity.* Chicago: Polychrome Publishing.

Lee, Marie G. (1992). *Finding my voice.* Boston: Houghton Mifflin.

Lee, Marie G. (1994). *Saying good-bye.* Boston: Houghton Mifflin.

Lee, Marie G. (1993). *If it hadn't been for Yoon Jun.* Boston: Houghton Mifflin.

Uchida, Yoshiko. (1981). *A jar of dreams.* New York: Atheneum.

Uchida, Yoshiko. (1991). *The invisible thread.* Englewood Cliffs, NJ: Julian Messner.

Uchida, Yoshiko. (1978). *Journey home.* New York: Atheneum.
Uchida, Yoshiko. (1971). *Journey to topaz.* New York: Charles Scribners.
Wong, Janet S. (1994). *Good luck gold and other poems.* New York: Simon and Schuster.
Wong, Janet S.(1995). *The seaweed suitcase.* New York: Simon and Schuster.
Yee, Paul. (1989). *Tales from gold mountain: Stories of the Chinese in the new world.* New York: Macmillan.
Yep, Laurence. (1977). *Child of the owl.* New York: Harper Trophy.
Yep, Laurence. (1993). *Dragon's gate.* New York: HarperCollins.
Yep, Laurence. (1975). *Dragonwings.* New York: Harper.
Yep, Laurence. (1991). *The lost garden.* Englewood Cliffs, NJ: Julian Messner.
Yep, Laurence. (1992). *Ribbons.* New York: Simon and Schuster.
Yep, Laurence. (1985). *Shadow lord.* New York: Pocket Books.
Yep, Laurence.(1992). *The star fisher.* New York: Puffin Books.

Note

A common complaint from parents and teachers is the difficulty they have in finding any but the most commercially popular Asian Pacific American children's books in their local bookstores. While this is a strong reminder about the importance of and need for public libraries, it is also a commmentary about booksellers' perceptions about what their clientele will buy. Any bookstore can order any of these titles. Or, you can order from the following (all of which publish fairly comprehensive catalogs of Asian, Pacific Islander, and Asian Pacific American books):

Asian American Bookseller
37 St. Marks Place
New York, NY 10003
(212) 228-6718
Fax: (212) 228-7718

Shen's Books and Supplies
821 S. First Avenue
Arcadia, CA 91006
(818) 445-6958
(800) 456-6660

Multicultural Distributing Center
800 N. Grand Avenue
Covina, CA 91724
(818) 859-3133
Fax: (818) 859-3136

Asia For Kids
P.O. Box 9096
Cincinnati, OH 45209-0096
(800) 765-5885
Fax: (513) 271-8856

Chapter 5

Mexican American Children's Literature in the 1990s: Toward Authenticity

Rosalinda B. Barrera and *Oralia Garza de Cortes*

More than twenty years ago, when the Council on Interracial Books for Children undertook a critical survey of Mexican American children's literature, only about 200 such books were found to have been published in the United States during the preceding 33 years, from 1940 to 1973. Not only was this miniscule number of books a disturbing finding, but even more distressing was the quality of the books' content. In fact, many books purporting to be about Mexican American life and culture were found to actually be about Mexico and the Mexican experience.[1] Stereotypes, distortions, and omissions characterized the books examined. On the eve of the twentieth anniversary of the Council's report (Council on Interracial Books for Children, 1975), we present here a critical analysis of how the Mexican American experience is presented/represented—qualitatively and quantitatively—in the "new" wave of multicultural books reaching schools, libraries, stores, and homes in the 1990s.

PAST AND CURRENT STATUS OF MEXICAN AMERICAN CHILDREN'S LITERATURE

We chose to study Mexican American-themed children's books published in the United States from 1992 to mid-1995, a period in which there was increased activity in multicultural publishing (Jones, 1991). Our total find was 67 books.[2] Additionally, we surveyed 50 books about the root culture, that is, Mexico and its people, published in the United States during the same time period.[3] Our purpose was not to focus on these latter materials, but to glean any salient observations from them that might be pertinent to our analysis of Mexican American content in children's literature. These root-culture materials will only be selectively discussed in this report.

Compared to the Council's book sample, the corpus of books which we assembled reflects a seeming improvement in Mexican American children's literature, quantitatively speaking: formerly, the average number published per year was about 6 books; now, the annual average is 19 books.[4] While this threefold publishing increase by itself might seem encouraging, it is still depressingly low in light of the increased production of multicultural children's literature in this country during the '90s, and of U.S. children's literature in general, not to mention the marked growth of the Mexican American population in recent years, particularly in the schools. In the following pages, we focus our attention on the content of these books.

Genre and Audience

Among the books examined, works of fiction outnumber nonfiction by a ratio of 2.35 to 1. Interestingly enough, the Council's sample of books—140 fiction and 60 nonfiction—yields a very similar ratio: 2.33 to 1.[5] Our data show that the number of fiction books about the Mexican American experience has increased gradually during the '90s, while the quantity of nonfiction books, biographies, and poetry has remained relatively steady and considerably lower. During this same time, folklore about/from the Mexican American community was not published, although folklore about/from the root culture, Mexico, apparently enjoyed publication as usual.[6]

A distribution of the total books by target audience shows that 33 books (49%) are for lower elementary students (Grades Pre-K to 3), 21 books (31%) are for middle elementary school students (Grades 4–6), and 13 books (19%) are for upper elementary readers (Grades 6–8). Of the fiction books, the majority (82%) are set in contemporary times, and the rest deal with the past. The gender distribution is fairly even among those works of fiction which feature children as main characters; 20 books have girls as main characters, 19 have boys in the main role.

Publishers

The books analyzed reflect a diverse group of publishers, ranging from large, "mainstream" companies to small, regional presses located mostly in the U.S. Southwest. In contrast, in the Council's study, "most (of the books) were published by large, commercial publishing houses" (p. 8).

Current publishers include companies historically involved in the production of multicultural and bilingual materials, such as Children's Book Press of California and Arte Público Press of Texas (which launched a children's literature imprint, Piñata Books, in 1994), and newer companies which seem to be focusing on Mexican American children's literature, such as Northland Publishing Company and Hispanic Books Distributors & Publishers, Inc., both of Arizona. Several New Mexico presses are also publishers in this field, among them Trails West Publishing, Red Crane Books, and New Mexico Magazine. In 1993, Hispanic Books, Inc. initiated a book competition called the *"Arroz con Leche* Award" contest that invites manuscripts on children's stories depicting Hispanic values, culture, and experience (that is, of the various Latino groups in the United States) and gives recognition annually to a new Hispanic writer of such material.

Our data show that in general the regional presses are producing mostly children's fiction, with little or no publication of nonfiction materials. Among the larger presses, only a limited group of companies are publishing biographies and historical works about Mexican Americans, most of which are parts of series, such as Chelsea House's *Hispanics of Achievement Series*, Millbrook Press's *Hispanic Heritage Series* and *Coming to America Series*, and Oxford University Press's *American Family Album Series*.

Authors

The proportion of Mexican American children's books written by "insiders," or persons of Mexican American background, has grown in the '90s and certainly in comparison to the years represented in the Council's study, when "with few exceptions the books were written and illustrated by Anglo Americans" (p. 8). About a third (34 percent), or 23, of the books examined were written by individuals of Mexican American descent. However, of this sub-total, almost half (48 percent), or 11 titles, are by *one* Mexican American writer, Gary Soto.

A number of the recent books are by Mexican Americans/Chicanos who previously have written mostly for adults; these include Gloria Anzaldua, Sandra Cisneros, and Juan Felipe Herrera. They joined Soto, Pat Mora, and Rudolfo Anaya, who began writing for children in the late 1980s and continue today. Other Mexican Americans/Chicanos also published in this area for the first time during the 1990s (for example, Alba & Peña, 1995; Avila, 1994; Stevens, 1993, 1995), primarily with smaller presses. Additionally, George Ancona, a Mexican American photographer with a long record of work in children's literature, recently began to write about the life and culture of Mexico and of U.S. Hispanics, including Mexican Americans.

Text Language

Recent books about the Mexican American experience reflect greater use of Spanish in a variety of formats. About 22 percent of the books analyzed are *bilingual editions* with parallel texts in English and Spanish within one volume; most of these are fiction. A few fiction titles have separate *Spanish-language editions* with accompanying English-language editions.

Mexican American children's literature published only in English appears to be making more *interlingual* use of Spanish, incorporating selected Spanish words and phrases within English text. Such interlingual usage can be natural and authentic—as in Soto's *The Skirt* (1992b) and *The Pool*

Party (1993b), in which the flow between English and Spanish is seamless and translation-free (that is, no glossary or back-to-back translations)—or unnatural and inauthentic in English-language texts in which the use of Spanish is strained, contrived, inaccurate, or random. Glossaries of Spanish words used interlingually are included in some of the English-language books.

As the use of Spanish has increased in U.S. children's literature, so, too, has the inclusion of different varieties of Spanish. Some books, however, contain explanatory information for the reader about such linguistic variation, apparently for both educational and political reasons, given the lesser prestige accorded to non-standard varieties of Spanish within the Spanish-language world. The end pages of *Friends from the Other Side / Amigos del otro lado* (Anzaldua, 1993) and *Carlos and the Cornfield / Carlos y la milpa de maíz* (Stevens, 1995) contain explanatory comments respectively about Chicano Spanish and linguistic authenticity.

It is encouraging that U.S. publishers are recognizing Spanish linguistic variation as a natural part of cultural authenticity in literature and are deciding to include it in books for children. Apparently, the long-standing concerns of teachers and librarians about the imposition of "Spanish from Spain" in children's books for the U.S. market are being heeded. But while the use of Spanish and Spanish dialects is increasing in U.S. children's literature, this positive trend is offset by two negative tendencies on the part of U.S. publishers, namely, (a) continued lack of editorial attention to Spanish print, and (b) a propensity for Spanish translations of English-language works, most of which are *not* culturally conscious as defined by Bishop (1993).

Publishers continue to show their editorial disregard for Spanish in a variety of ways: by applying differential quality controls to Spanish and English texts, for example, less rigorous editing and proofreading for the former often due to a lack of Spanish-proficient editorial staff; by indiscriminantly selecting Spanish-language translators as if the language and culture of Mexican Americans or other Latinos were monolithic; and by assuming that English texts can be easily and quickly translated into Spanish by anyone who is of Mexican American background, regardless of individual Spanish writing experience and ability. The results are Spanish texts of dubious quality, reflecting varying mechanical, structural, dialectal, and stylistic inconsistencies.

Currently, Spanish translations of English-language children's books are being marketed by some publishers as "multicultural" materials. Unfortunately, translations of English books with dominant-culture content are just that; a change in text language alone does not constitute a content change in perspectives and images. Apparently, some publishers view Spanish translations of mainstream books as "easier sells" than culturally-conscious Spanish-language materials, thereby according them higher publishing priority. It should be noted that Spanish-language materials imported from other countries also are not "multicultural" simply because they are in Spanish (Barrera, Liguori, & Salas, 1993). Incidentally, in its analysis, the Council excluded both translated and imported books, nearly 100 titles, because translated works failed to express "the Chicano viewpoint" and imported literature projected "the same racist and sexist stereotypes as the U.S. books. . . ." (p. 13).

RECURRING THEMES IN MEXICAN AMERICAN CHILDREN'S LITERATURE

Across the books examined, four thematic categories predominate: holidays/special days, migrants, immigrants (legal and illegal), and foods. In fact, more than one-third (36 percent) of the books reflect one or more of these themes. In some ways, this situation represents progress from 20 years ago when the Council found "certain themes, images and attitudes to be so prevalent in these books as to constitute characteristics of the *whole* (emphasis added) children's literature available" on the Mexican American experience (p. 7). In other ways, however, the thematic profile revealed in our analysis raises a number of significant concerns and questions about contemporary Mexican American children's literature which we will address in succeeding sections.

Holidays and Special Days

Christmas is central to four recently published works of fiction: *Maria: A Christmas Story* (Taylor, 1992), *Too Many Tamales* (Soto, 1993c), *Carlos, Light the Farolito* (Ciavonne, 1995), and *The Farolitos of Christmas* (Anaya, 1995), a newly expanded version of Anaya's 1987 story. Las Posadas, a multi-day Christmas celebration, is part of Ciavonne's *Farolito* and Anaya's *Farolitos*. Christmas is also the subject of at least an equal number of Mexican-focus books.[7]

Día de Los Muertos, another religious holiday, serves as the focus for *Day of the Dead: A Mexican American Celebration* (Hoyt-Goldsmith, 1994), a nonfiction book, and *Maria Molina and the Days of the Dead* (Krull, 1994a), a fiction story set mostly in Mexico. It is also the subject of several Mexican-focus books[8] and is the first of four holidays highlighted in Ancona's *Fiesta, U.S.A.* (1995). Interestingly enough, *Cinco de Mayo,* a historical holiday perennially featured in children's books about Mexico and Mexican Americans, is the subject of only one recent book of fiction, *Cinco de Mayo* (Riehecky, 1993).

Birthdays also fall within the holiday/special day theme. Birthday celebrations are at the center of two fiction books by Pat Mora—*A Birthday*

Basket for Tía (1992) and *Pablo's Tree* (1994c)—and one nonfiction work about the traditional fifteenth-birthday celebration for Mexican American girls, *Quinceañera: A Latina's Journey to Womanhood* (Lankford, 1994).

Migrants

The migrant experience is central to at least six recent books, four fiction and two nonfiction. The former are *Amelia's Road* and its Spanish edition *El Camino de Amelia* (Altman, 1993a & 1993b), *Radio Man: A Story in English and Spanish / Don Radio: Un cuento en inglés y español* (Dorros, 1993), *Lights on the River* (Thomas, 1994), and *Calling the Doves / Canto por las palomas* (Herrera, 1995); the latter are *Voices from the Fields: Children of Migrant Farmworkers Tell Their Stories* (Atkin, 1993) and *La Causa: The Migrant Farmworkers' Story* (de Ruiz and Larios, 1993). *Amelia*, *Radio Man*, and *Doves* deal with the migrant stream in the southwestern, western, and ostensibly the northwestern parts of the United States; *Lights* is set in Minnesota. Most of the parents and/or grandparents of the migrant children in these stories happen to be Mexican immigrants. All but one of the nine children featured in *Voices* are recent Mexican immigrants. *La Causa* focuses on the lives of Cesar Chavez and Dolores Huerta, leaders in the migrant farmworkers' struggle.

Immigrants

The immigration experience, legal and illegal, is the subject of five books: one nonfiction, *The Other Side: How Kids Live in a California Latino Neighborhood* (Krull, 1994b), which reports on the lives of two eight-year-old Mexican immigrant students; and four fiction, *Friends from the Other Side / Amigos del otro lado* (Anzaldua, 1993), *Sisters / Hermanas* (Paulsen, 1993), *Pablo y Pimienta* (Couvault, 1994), and *Lupe and Me* (Spurr, 1995). *Friends* involves a young Mexican boy and his family who are residing illegally in a Texas border community where he is befriended by a Mexican American girl; *Sisters*, a 14-year-old Mexican girl hiding in Texas and working as a prostitute, whose story is juxtaposed by the author with that of a White cheerleader; *Pablo y Pimienta*, a young Mexican boy crossing into Arizona where his father and uncle will seek jobs as documented workers; and *Lupe*, a Mexican woman illegally working in the U.S. as a maid for an Anglo girl and her mother. Immigration also figures into Krull's *Maria Molina*; by the end of the story, Maria and her family have immigrated to the U.S.

Food

Traditional Mexican American food/food products are recurrent themes, especially in books for younger readers. Such books include *Three Stalks of Corn* (Politi, 1994, 1976), *Green Corn Tamales* (Rodriguez, 1993), and *Tortilla Factory* and its Spanish edition *La Tortillería* (Paulsen, 1994a & 1994b).

The title of Paulsen's work is a misnomer of sorts, because the majority of the book focuses on the growing of corn for tortillas, as its introductory quote implies, rather than on the tortilla factory as such. The making of tamales is central to Soto's Christmas story, *Too Many Tamales*.

Recipes for sundry Mexican/Mexican American dishes are found at the end of the books by Politi and Rodriguez. Two bilingual fiction stories about a northern New Mexican boy, *Carlos and the Squash Plant / Carlos y la planta de calabaza* (Stevens, 1993), and its sequel, *Carlos and the Cornfield / Carlos y la milpa de maíz* (Stevens, 1995), similarly contain closing recipes.[9]

DEPICTION OF MEXICAN AMERICANS IN CHILDREN'S LITERATURE

In and by themselves, the recurrent themes identified above are not directly indicative of how Mexican Americans are depicted in today's children's books, but they are telling signs nonetheless. Generally speaking, what we found in our analysis was that recently published books are painting a relatively more favorable picture of Mexican Americans than twenty years ago when the Council concluded that the books "abound(ed) in the use of stereotypic symbols to identify Chicano or Mexican people and culture" and "fail(ed) to recognize the variety of Chicano life, work and achievement." However, in a throwback to the Council's findings, today's literature continues to suggest that: (a) Mexican Americans are an "exotic" and "foreign" people (partly via the emphasis on "surface" aspects of the culture such as holidays and foods) and (b) Mexican Americans are a readily identifiable group within a narrow band of society (partly via the emphasis on migrants and immigrants, two segments of the Mexican American population, but not its whole).

The Council's study showed that in works of fiction Mexican Americans were often depicted as poor, helpless, ignorant, passive, hopeless, friendless, selflessly sacrificing, surrounded by an unhappy family, and needing to learn English and to be acculturated. In nonfiction works, the image of all Mexican Americans as rural, migrant farm laborers was not uncommon. The Council pointed out that "this misrepresenting of a community, 85 percent of whose members are urban-based" was a major flaw, but also noted that on the whole, nonfiction materials were not "as pervasively racist or full of stereotypes" as their fiction counterparts. Two statements from the 1975 report serve to summarize how Mexican Americans were previously depicted: "Everywhere in the books, Chicanos exist on the periphery of a usually undefined, but implicitly Anglo, world. . . . The few Chicanos who are singled out for notice are those who have gained status within the Anglo world."

In the fiction books analyzed, Mexican Americans are depicted with more diversity and authenticity than in the past. For example, Mexican American book characters are not all hopelessly poor; about half of the fiction books show the main characters in poverty environments and the other half show better conditions. Many of the families are depicted in positive ways, as cohesive and supportive units, not fractured and non-supportive. Families are represented as having fewer children; in the 1975 study, the Mexican American child protagonist was found to have "at least half a dozen brothers and sisters" (p. 8). Presently, more families and children are represented as urban-dwellers, although some reflect a rural, farming background. The Mexican Americans portrayed live predominantly in the southwestern and western parts of the country, and some are bilingual.

In the nonfiction arena, the few children's books published in the '90s recognize the contributions of Mexican Americans to their community cultures as well as the national culture. The slim number of historical works recognize the fact that Mexican Americans are not "newcomers" to the United States. They are not presented simplistically as more Mexican than American nor as passive beings in a changing society.

Alongside these encouraging changes, however, are chronic tendencies to depict Mexican American life and culture in both limited *and* limiting ways for child readers. Although some stereotypic symbols may be fading (e.g., serapes, burros, and huaraches), new ones are taking their place (e.g., mariachis, Santa Fe furniture, religious icons), and others are just enduring (e.g., piñatas, fiestas, tacos). Questionable messages about Mexican Americans, their lives and culture, are conveyed by these overused symbols. One cumulative message is that Mexican Americans are a simple, fun-loving group of people, perpetually having fiestas and breaking piñatas. Another is that Mexican Americans are tied to the traditional past, in a form of arrested cultural development. Just as counterproductive are the messages given when Mexican Americans are repeatedly depicted in only one or two roles, namely, as migrants and immigrants. For the most part, the larger proportion of this population, which is neither migrant nor immigrant, is ignored and rendered invisible, keeping the literature from serving as a mirror for Mexican American children and a window for other children (Bishop, 1994).

EXEMPLARY AUTHORS AND WORKS IN MEXICAN AMERICAN CHILDREN'S LITERATURE

During the time period studied, the slow-growing body of Mexican American children's literature has been enhanced by the literary talent of several authors, all of whom have published works that have added much-needed breadth and depth to the field. Perhaps no one to date has contributed more than Gary Soto, whose multiple publications for children during the '90s have created greater awareness and understanding of contemporary Mexican American childhood. Spanning the K–12 spectrum, his fiction and poetry are characterized by skillful writing, sensitivity and humor, and a generous supply of cultural consciousness.

Soto's ability to capture the Mexican American experience is exemplified in two recent works: *Canto Familiar* (1995a) and *Chato's Kitchen* (1995b). *Canto* is a collection of poems with titles such as "Tortillas Like Africa," "My Teacher in the Market," and "Papi's Menudo" that reflect taken-for-granted, everyday experiences. *Kitchen* is a picture book about two low-riding East Los Angeles cats, Chato and Novio Boy, who have their eyes on a family of fat mice, but have to contend with the mice's dog friend, Chorizo. In both books, Soto's voice speaks clearly and confidently to children, and is filled with intimate knowledge about growing up Chicano.

In *Chato's Kitchen*, for example, we can hear the life and voices of the barrio speaking through the animal characters; in *Canto*, the sounds of family, friends, and other known people echo in the poet's words. Regardless of the setting—barrio, hometown, suburbia, or elsewhere—Soto's works as a whole are inhabited by richly textured Chicano characters who provide a beckoning vista of Mexican American diversity. Above all, his books for children show Soto to be a kid at heart, one for whom Hispanic-valued attributes such as *cariño* and *respeto* are still important even though he is an adult crafting stories and characters.

George Ancona, another author whose books are filled with a genuine affection and respect for the people he depicts, has published exemplary books on root-culture/Mexican content during the '90s. Originally from New York and now living in Santa Fe, Ancona has served as photographer for close to 50 children's books by other authors. However, it is the recent works in which he has been both author and photographer that have revealed his literary-artistic talents to maximum advantage. His keen sense of photography and design has resulted in fresh, sensitive treatments of all-too-familiar subjects in the field of Mexican and Mexican American children's literature in the United States.

Two recent nonfiction books by Ancona about Mexico and its people are exemplary root-culture materials, *Pablo Remembers: The Fiesta of the Day of the Dead* (1993b), with its Spanish-language edition, *Pablo recuerda: La fiesta del día de los muertos* (1993a), and *Piñata Maker/El Piñatero* (1994b), both of them standouts in a field in which fiestas and piñatas are worn-out images. Both books have the southern Mexican state of Oaxaca as their setting. In *Piñata Maker*, the subject is Don Ricardo, who earns a living by making and selling piñatas; in *Pablo Remembers*, it is Pablito, a young boy, and his family preparing to celebrate an important religious holiday.

Just as Ancona's works afford meaningful views of the root culture, two recent noteworthy books provide multifaceted, insightful views of the migrant experience, illuminating this recurrent theme with authenticity and realism. One book is *Calling the Doves/Canto por las palomas* by Juan Felipe Herrera (1995), a bilingual fiction story filled with Herrera's remembrances about his migrant childhood in California. His recollections include his mother's enchanting poetry recitations, their one-room house built on top of an abandoned railroad car, the workers in the fields who resembled colorful tropical birds, and especially his father's ability to make bird calls as if he had a "tiny clarinet inside his hand." Herrera the poet has infused his first children's work with a rich combination of realistic content and lyrical language that proves him to be a writer for adults who can also write skillfully for children.

The other exemplary migrant-themed work is *Voices from the Fields: Children of Migrant Farmworkers*, by S. Beth Atkin (1993), an informed and compelling nonfictional rendering of the lives of nine U.S. migrant children of Mexican background. With her skilled camera work and interviewing skills, photojournalist Atkin was able to capture powerful images and poignant stories of farmworker children in the California Salinas Valley. Another noteworthy aspect of this book is the literary contribution it garnered from California Spanish-language professor Francisco X. Alarcon, who translated and wrote poetry for its pages. Alarcon's ability to create and translate poetry is readily apparent in *Voices*. The closing poem in the book, "Tierra Prometida/The Promised Land" by Alarcon, is filled with expressions of cultural pride and human faith and is dedicated to students in Yo Puedo, a California migrant program.

Another nonfiction book that excels among the current crop of books on the Mexican American experience is *Day of the Dead: A Mexican American Celebration* by Diane Hoyt-Goldsmith, which offers a novel take on another recurrent theme. The book's clear explanations of the origins of this holiday, its vivid photography and page layouts, and its insights into cultural preservation and renewal efforts by contemporary Mexican Americans are exceptional. By focusing on Ximena and Azucena, ten-year-old twin daughters of Clara and Armando Cid, a Sacramento artist and community activist, the author is able to show how the entire Cid family and their ethnic community work to resurrect and preserve their heritage and culture.

Two recent books that provide children with selected, thought-provoking insights into Mexican American history are *Coming to America: The Mexican American Experience* by Elizabeth Coonrod Martinez (1995) and *The Mexican American Family Album* (Hoobler & Hoobler, 1994). Martinez's book is particularly notable for informing the reader about a previously excluded part of U.S. history not discussed in children's literature until now, namely, the past lynching of Mexican Americans in the Southwest when

when they refused to leave their lands during the process of Anglo take-over. The author notes that "between 1848 and 1948, the number of Mexican Americans lynched in the Southwest and in California was greater than the number of blacks lynched in the Deep South" (p. 32). Martinez also has published several recent biographies for children about Mexican Americans. The Hooblers' book is particularly worthwhile because of the diverse historical photographs of Mexican Americans that it provides, many of them reflecting scenes and images rarely included in children's literature. Like its counterparts in Oxford University Press's *American Family Album Series*, the book's heirloom quality invites readers young and old to take in its pages.

PROBLEMATIC CHILDREN'S BOOKS ON THE MEXICAN AMERICAN EXPERIENCE

Distortions of the Mexican American experience past and present continue to appear in U.S. children's literature, although not as blatantly or as frequently as documented by the Council in its 1975 report. In this section, we discuss several recent children's books that clearly perpetuate questionable views and information about Mexican American life and culture. Although these works are all stereotypical in a general sense, we have organized them into four types of prominent shortcomings: ethnocentricism, "overloading," romanticism, and "typecasting."

Ethnocentricism

A long-time ethnocentric perspective in U.S. children's literature, and adult literature, is the "myth of Anglo superiority" (Council of Interracial Books for Children, 1975; Duran, 1979; Rocard, 1989; TuSmith, 1993). A variant of this myth, which we call the "myth of U.S. opportunity" is clearly reflected in a recent book, *Maria Molina and the Days of the Dead* (Krull, 1994a). *Maria Molina* is the story of a Mexican child whose parents are seeking full-time work in the United States. The story line involves an invidious comparison between Maria's life in Mexico, which includes celebrating the Day of the Dead, and her life-to-be in the United States, which will include Halloween.

Most of *Maria Molina* takes place in Mexico; only the last four pages deal with Maria's new life in the United States. However, the comparison between Maria's Mexican existence and a better, more opportune life in the United States begins early in the story, with Maria musing: "If I lived in the United States, I, Maria Molina, would not be in a graveyard tonight. I would be out trick-or-treating on Halloween, with enough money to buy lots of candy and a fancy costume." Another reference to Maria's financially impoverished and culturally dutiful life follows shortly: "I had no money to buy anything, but I loved to look. Then it was time to get back to the grave-yard."

Later, Maria continues to compare her Mexican celebration with U.S. life: "I think the children had the most fun. Perhaps not as much fun as Halloween in the United States, but we were excited just to be out of school during these special days." Toward the end of the story, she awaits the re-turn of her parents, who have been working in the United States, contem-plating the better life she expects to find there: "They (parents) were com-ing home to fetch us children. We were *all* going to live in the United States. My aunt and uncle were coming, too. We would all be together again. We would be so much richer than we were in Mexico. *And* I, Maria Molina, would celebrate Halloween now. I began thinking of costumes already, and of the mountains of sugary candy . . . ."

"Overloading"

Some children's books on the Mexican American experience are a virtual collection of stereotypical symbols, a "cultural parade" of the worst sort, leaning heavily on customs and tradition but having little story or sub-stance (Barrera, Liguori, & Salas, 1993). One recent book that aptly fits this description and demonstrates graphically what we call "overloading" is *Cinco de Mayo* (Riehecky, 1993). The story is about a young Mexican American girl, Maria, who repeatedly but unsuccessfully tries to help her family prepare for Cinco de Mayo, until she finds a way to contribute by entering a drawing contest at the library. Participants in the story's cul-tural parade are Maria's mother, who cooks tacos, enchiladas, and tostadas (misspelled "tostados" in the book); her father, who makes painted straw animals; a brother and friends, who have a mariachi band; a sister, who decorates with traditional crafts; and party guests, who engage in the tra-ditional piñata-breaking ritual with a star piñata, of course.

More loading of stereotypic symbols occurs through the color and style of the artwork. Three colors dominate—red, white, and green, the colors of Mexico's flag. All the female characters wear ornate, traditional costumes in a pseudo-folk style that is probably more akin to Swiss traditional dress than Mexican. Flowers are everywhere; they decorate the house and are painted on almost every piece of furniture—mirror and picture frames, tables and chests, work benches, and guitar. They adorn the hair of the female characters and are part of their skirts' fabric. The story also includes not one but two fiestas, one in the city plaza and another in Maria's home. And as if this were not enough, crafts and food ideas are part of the end matter.

Another example of "overloading" is Politi's *Three Stalks of Corn*, origi-nally published in 1976 and reissued in 1994. It should be noted that some recent books depict a newer form of overloading, not Mexican but New Mexican in nature, evoking a Santa Fe style presumably symbolic of Mexican American life and culture in the Southwest. The text and illustrations of *Carlos, Light the Farolito* (Ciavonne, 1995) exemplify this newer strain of stereotyping.

Romanticism

Books that embellish and romanticize the Mexican American experience are part of contemporary literature for adults (Rocard, 1989; TuSmith, 1993) as well as for children. Books of this nature tend to "gloss . . . over the less colorful and more troublesome aspects of Mexican American reality" (Rocard, p. 38). One such book is *Frida María: A Story of the Old Southwest* (Lattimore, 1994), set in California in the late 1700s to early 1800s, presented as a time of aristocratic Spanish families, of "proper senoritas" and "caballeros," haciendas and missions, fiestas, music, and dancing. In essence, an idyllic time, or so the writer would have us believe.

Laden with stereotypical images and content, *Frida María* is offensive for multiple reasons, including an elitist perspective and a contrived story line. One glaring problem area involves characters' names. To begin with, "Frida María" is an unlikely name, because in the historical time in which the story is set, María would have been a likelier choice for a first name, and Frida, a German word/name, would have been unlikely unless the woman/girl were of German ancestry (which is the case with Mexico's well-known artist Frida Kahlo). Since the writer states in an author's note that she researched the historical period of the story, it is difficult to understand why this particular name was chosen.

"Narizo," the name of Frida María's uncle, also raises questions. Does it refer to the uncle's apparently large nose, and is it therefore a misspelling for "narizón/narigón" or "narizota," which in Spanish means a long and large nose? Although nicknames are not uncommon among Mexican Americans, Narizo in our estimation is a poor name choice and/or in bad taste. More disturbing, however, is the repeated reference to the indigenous-/mestiza-looking woman in the kitchen as simply "Cook." We were left to wonder why she does not have a name. Perhaps the writer was trying to make a sociopolitical statement by leaving her nameless. If so, more information on the social structure of the time, specifically the relationship between hacienda owners and their workers, might have been appropriate.

Other bothersome elements of the story include the repeated spelling of *fiesta* with a capital F without any mention of the fiesta's purpose, the repeated use of expressions such as *Ole! Hí-jo-le!* and *Viva!*, and the Diego Rivera-like images of indigenous women and lilies. Additionally, there is a hefty four-page spread of stereotypical images at the end of the book which only compounds its many problems.

Another recent example of a book that romanticizes the Mexican American experience is *Radio Man / Don Radio* (Dorros, 1993), which depicts the migrant experience of one boy as a virtual travel odyssey (" 'Now we'll go north, to new places,' said Papa."). The boy's migrant life includes traveling in a truck/van with personalized license plates ("PIC4U2"), staying in migrant camps with neat cabins, and having a family that sings at its most tired moments. One only has to compare this story with the children's narratives in the nonfiction book *Voices from the Fields* (Atkin, 1993) to detect the highly romantic treatment of the fictional story.

"Typecasting"

We use this term to refer to the repeated assignation of Mexican Americans to particular character types or roles. In films, some stereotyped roles of the past have included "bandidos, buffoons, dark ladies, caballeros, and gangsters" (Kanellos, 1994). Counterpart types/roles exist in literature, and Mexican American characters can be found in a variety of maligned roles, such as the undesirable half of the oft-told "good guy/bad guy" story. In a recent bilingual children's book with a "good gal/bad gal" story, an illegal Mexican immigrant teenager is the more despicable character compared to her white teenage counterpart. Although both 14-year-old girls in *Sisters/Hermanas* (Paulsen, 1993) are overconcerned with their appearance and beauty, Traci is merely an aspiring cheerleader while Rosa is a prostitute. Even the cover of this book suggests the "dark lady" stereotype.

   The Tortilla Factory/La Tortillería, another recent book by Paulsen (1994), reflects a more subtle form of typecasting. Within the sparse text of this picture book, the author describes the people who work in the *tortillería* as "laughing people." This two-word description downplays the back-breaking work actually involved in this line of work. The subtle message communicated is that Mexican Americans are happy doing grueling labor, a pervasive theme identified by the Council's study. This same message is evident in another book, *Lupe and Me* (Spurr, 1995), which contains the "happy Mexican housemaid" stereotype, plus an excessive amount of other stereotypical content. Lupe, who works for young Susan and her mother, loves to sing and to use the assorted electrical appliances in the house. Apparently, this softens the image of the work that Lupe carries out in Susan's house. Apart from the typecasting of the Mexican immigrant woman as a music-loving, appliance-worshipping maid, *Lupe* overall also exemplifies stereotypical "overloading" in a children's book.

   Stereotypical treatments of Mexico's people and culture are also evident in the Mexican-content books we surveyed. The four categorical shortcomings discussed above can be applied to these root-culture materials as well.[10]

ASPECTS OF MEXICAN AMERICAN IDENTITY IN CHILDREN'S LITERATURE

When the world of U.S. children's literature continues to include only a limited number of books about the Mexican American experience, such underrepresentation makes a *global*, *indirect* statement about what it means to be Mexican American. Quite simply, to be Mexican American means to be the "other," devalued and marginalized through exclusion in the literature. Apart from this collective statement, individual books make *particular*, *direct* (and indirect) statements about Mexican American life and culture, as the preceding two sections have shown. On this basis, one might say that Mexican American children's literature is qualitatively different and relatively better than 20 years ago because *at least some* books today are painting a more accurate picture of what it means to be Mexican American, affirming in the process Mexican American culture and heritage.

The more complex, informed picture of Mexican American identity emerging in the '90s, particularly as a result of the writing of insiders, is a welcome and long-overdue change from the knowledge conveyed by books of previous decades. More of today's books are providing young readers of Mexican American background and other backgrounds with authentic interpretations of what it means to be Mexican American, a positive development that no doubt will help nurture children's self-image and multicultural understanding. This is a significant improvement from the Council's findings of twenty years ago: "In short, there is very little in these books to enable a child to recognize a way of life, a history, a set of life circumstances—a culture—with which he or she can identify" (p. 7).

Within fiction and poetry, culturally conscious works are now providing valid, multifaceted views of what it means to be Mexican American. These books communicate to young readers that to be Mexican American is to be part of a diverse ethnic community, with tremendous intra-group differences but still bound by a common experience and heritage that have engendered a shared perspective. Part of this perspective includes a "communal ethos" that insists "on valuing the collective above the isolated individual" (TuSmith, p. 174). Not surprisingly, it is in books written by "outsiders" that individualism is accorded undue emphasis, with main characters striving to fulfill individual desires and the family and community either subordinated or missing. Above all, contemporary culturally conscious books reveal that to be Mexican American is to be normal in the best sense of the word, not maladjusted or pathological, even if financially poor.

Insiders' perspectives currently enriching Mexican American children's fiction and poetry are conspicuously absent, however, from the nonfiction and biography categories. No doubt, better informed historical and biographical works are being written than in previous years, mostly by outsiders, but overall, there is a palpable need for more substantive Mexican American histories and biographies, materials with built-in potential for transmitting valuable knowledge for children's identity development and multicultural understanding.

The few biographies published about Mexican American figures continue to be about the same individuals, although ostensibly written for readers of different age groups. Politician Henry Cisneros and the late labor leader Cesar Chavez are the subjects of more than half the recent biographies (Bredeson, 1995; Cedeno, 1993; Conord, 1992; Holmes, 1994; Martinez, 1993; Petrucelli, 1992); the rest are sports and entertainment figures. Apparently, only high-profile Mexican Americans are considered suitable subjects for biographies. It could be that publishers are creating pseudo-heroes on the basis of limited perspectives; certainly, many Mexican Americans living and dead who have made significant contributions to their ethnic community and the larger society are not reflected in existing biographies and histories (Cortes, 1995).

We doubt that children are getting an adequate understanding of what it means to be Mexican American when the biographies available do not reflect an ample variety of role models, including women, intellectuals, educators, authors, and others. Missing are biographical works on individuals such as Americo Paredes, George Sanchez, Emma Tenayuca, Dolores Huerta, Willie Velasquez, Antonio Hernandez, Ernesto Cortes, Gloria Molina, and others far too numerous to mention here. Just as unavailable are histories that do justice to the Chicano Renaissance, the Mexican American civil rights movement, C.O.P.S. (Communities Organized for Public Service), the contributions of Mexican American women, and innumerable other historical developments. It is nothing less than unfortunate that today's Mexican American children are more likely to know who Julio Cesar Chavez, the boxer, is than who Cesar Chavez, leader of La Causa, was (Cortes, 1995).

TEACHING/LEARNING STRATEGIES FOR MEXICAN AMERICAN CHILDREN'S LITERATURE

Increasingly, our professional service activities in the area of Mexican American children's literature have had a combined focus: teachers' learning-teaching and students' learning, via these materials. We have found it necessary to create and provide opportunities for teachers to interact with Mexican American children's literature in much the same ways students would in a literature-based, response-centered classroom (Cox & Zarrillo,

1993), due to the basically monocultural, rather than multicultural, education and preparation of most contemporary literature-related professionals, including teachers, teacher educators, librarians, and school administrators. In addressing the teacher's role, we have emphasized gaining knowledge *about* and *from* Mexican American children's literature *during* the process of teaching with it. Thus in this section, we will present pedagogical strategies for use with recent Mexican American-themed literature that emphasize learning by elementary students as well as their teachers.

Background Reading

Because the history and literature of Mexican Americans/Chicanos have rarely had a place in the school curriculum, it is important for teachers of all ethnic backgrounds, including Mexican American educators, to gain some sense of the sociohistorical development and literary endeavors of the Mexican American community. A recently published book, *The Hispanic Almanac: From Columbus to Corporate America* (Kanellos, 1994), is an excellent source for learning about the "Puerto Rican, Cuban, Mexican, or any of the other Hispanic manifestations of our American identity" (p. xii). Chapters focus on the Hispanic presence in history, business, labor, politics, media, art, literature, theater, film, music, and sports. Recent Hispanic/Latino anthologies that include the works of Mexican American writers are useful informational resources for teachers and students, for example, *Latino Voices* (Aparicio, 1994). Teachers seeking more in-depth information on the Hispanic contribution to American literature might wish to consult newly published books such as *Recovering the U.S. Hispanic Literary Heritage* (Gutierrez & Padilla, 1993).

Author Studies/Units

The works of Pat Mora and Gary Soto lend themselves to author studies by children in the lower elementary grades and children at the middle/upper elementary levels, respectively. Mora's *Pablo's Tree* and *Birthday Basket for Tía* invite young readers to respond with their own birthday accounts and to share stories about their grandparents and other elders in their lives. Children can then pursue other works by Mora, such as *Agua, Agua, Agua* (1994a) and *The Desert Is My Mother / El desierto es mi madre* (1994b), paying particular attention to their lyrical quality. Soto's diverse stories about Chicano boys and girls can be followed chronologically by older elementary students, as some of the works are serial in nature, for example, the adventures of Lincoln Mendoza which appear in the two novels *Taking Sides* (1991) and *Pacific Crossing* (1992a), or the two collections of short stories which form an entertaining whole about Chicano childhood, *Baseball in April and Other Stories* (1990) and *Local News* (1993a).

In the process of guiding students through these author studies, teachers could selectively pursue adult literature by Mora and Soto as a means of learning more about the Mexican American experience. Teachers are also encouraged to sample the adult literary works of other Mexican Americans who have recently published works for young children, for example, Rudolfo Anaya, Sandra Cisneros, Juan Felipe Herrera, and Gloria Anzaldua (Barrera, Liguori, & Salas, 1993). Teachers and their students might compare Cisneros's *Hairs/Pelitos* with its parent work *The House on Mango Street* (Cisneros, 1989) and Anaya's *Farolitos* with its earlier version, *The Farolitos of Christmas: A New Mexico Christmas Story* (Anaya, 1987).

Historical Studies/Units

Both elementary teachers and middle/upper elementary students can learn much about the writing of history as an interpretive and selective process by comparing "mainstream" historical works with recently published histories of the Mexican American experience, in particular Martinez's *Coming to America: The Mexican American Experience* and the Hooblers' *The Mexican American Family Album*. Mexican American educators and students with whom we have recently shared these books have had strong responses to them, ranging from high interest and enthusiasm (for example, even sharing these books in turn with others) to indignation at extant history books that have traditionally diminished or excluded Mexican American contributions. Some have described these two books as their *first* encounters with any historical material of an extended nature on Mexican American life and culture.

As an extension of the historical readings above, teachers can have students focus on a particular aspect of Mexican American history, for example, the farmworkers' labor movement, and trace the work to date of the United Farm Workers, with opportunity for students to reflect on how migrant farmworkers contribute to food production in the United States. Students can explore more fully the contributions of *La Huelga* leaders Cesar Chavez and Dolores Huerta by critically analyzing and comparing recent writings about them, for example, *La Causa: The Migrant Farmworkers' Story* by De Ruiz and Larios and the several biographies on Cesar Chavez cited in this chapter, including the one in Raintree-Steck Vaughn's misnamed American Troublemaker Series. Students might fill in the historical-biographical gap on Mexican American women by researching and writing accounts of the contributions of women to the farmworkers' strike and union.

Creative Studies/Units

Elementary school students and their teachers can take extensive and intensive looks at the creative processes of photography and writing through the work of Mexican American photographer and author, George Ancona, and the recently published nonfiction book, *Voices in the Field* by photojournalist S. Beth Atkin. Students might then employ the powerful combination of camera, interviewing, and writing (prose and poetry) to compile books on their communities' peoples, customs, and traditions.

Students can sample Ancona's works chronologically and trace the evolution of his photographic style for a quarter-century, from 1970 to 1995. We recommend having students analyze his photographic work for different books and authors, such as *Faces* (Brenner, 1970), *Spanish Pioneers of the Southwest* (Anderson, 1988), and *My Brother, My Sister* (Rosenberg, 1991). Students can also examine books in which Ancona is both author and photographer, such as *Powwow* (1992), *Pablo Remembers* (1993), *The Golden Lion Tamarin Comes Home* (1994a), *The Piñata Maker / El Piñatero* (1994b), and *Fiesta U.S.A.* (1995). Teachers might wish to show students a brief videotape of Ancona at work photographing material for a recent book project; the videotape narrated by Ancona and a 17-page autobiography of him are part of Scott Foresman's *Meet the Author* and *Something about the Author* materials accompanying the company's latest literature-based school reading series. The autobiographical account provides interesting details about Ancona's life and work, including his evolution from photographer to author-photographer.

Students can explore the creation of prose, poetry, and the photo essay during and after reading *Voices from the Fields*. On several occasions when we have shared this book, its stories and poems have elicited strong responses from adults and children, particularly Mexican Americans, some of whom have then written personal narratives and verse similar to those in *Voices*. Teachers might have students employ the photojournalistic processes of photography, interviewing, and reporting to collect and tell the stories of unheralded people in their community whose work and lives have been traditionally left out of the public's knowledge, as have those of migrant farmworker families and their children. Students might also interview community residents for oral histories. Teachers can read other personal accounts of the Mexican American migrant farmworker by means of *This Migrant Earth*, the English rendition by Rolando Hinojosa (1987) of Tomas Rivera's *. . . y no se lo tragó la tierra/ . . . and the earth did not devour him* (1971), or the latter work itself in Spanish, and *The Searchers: Collected Poetry / Tomas Rivera* (Olivares, 1990).

CONCLUDING REMARKS

It is important to note that in general the findings of our analysis reveal a somewhat improved picture for Mexican American children's literature than that reported by the Council on Interracial Books for Children two decades ago. Obviously, we did not find a worse scenario than the Council's, quantitatively or qualitatively speaking. Instead, there appears to be a discernible, albeit slow, move toward much-needed authenticity in text and pictures, particularly in fiction, buoyed by inclusion of insider perspectives. Additionally, there are other encouraging signs: low reissuance of objectionable, stereotypical literature; increasing understanding of intra-group differences (e.g., only one instance of overt confusion between the Mexican and Mexican American experiences); and growing use of illustrators from within the culture.

At the same time, however, it is necessary for us to point out that the results of our analysis are mixed at best. Less than positive developments include what appear to be a "one Chicano at a time" authorship pattern, a slow response by publishers to utilize and promote Mexican American authors overall, selection of Mexican American content and themes to fit "mainstream" perceptions, and continued underestimation of the potential need and market for Mexican American children's literature. The fact that we could easily find as many Mexican-content books as Mexican American-themed books without any effort to be exhaustive or comprehensive about the former was revealing by itself.

The preceding observations call for a hopeful but watchful stance with respect to Mexican American children's literature in the next few years. Authenticity in content and images will continue to be an important feature for critics, teachers, and students to expect *and* demand. Without authentic presentation of the Mexican American experience, any numerical gains in Mexican American children's books will be meaningless and needed improvement in quality will be impossible.

NOTES

1. The Mexican-themed books were included and evaluated by the Council's researchers nonetheless, given that publishers and bibliographers' definitions of Chicano/Mexican American were "so broad" (p. 7).

2. A cross-tabulation of the data by genre and year follows. It should be noted that bilingual editions (i.e., separate Spanish and English versions of a book) were counted as *one* title.

	1992	1993	1994	(mid-) 1995	
Fiction	5	14	14	11	(44)
Biography	4	3	2	1	(10)
Nonfiction	0	3	4	3	(10)
Poetry	1	0	1	1	(3)
Folklore	0	0	0	0	(0)
	10	20	21	16	67

3. By genre, the Mexican-themed books were distributed as follows: 17 nonfiction, 12 fiction, 9 folklore, 9 biographies, and 3 poetry. By year, the distribution was 9 in 1992, 13 in 1993, 18 in 1994, and 10 for the first half of 1995. Bilingual editions were counted as one title.

4. The actual annual subtotals above indicate a noticeable increase from 1992 to 1993, due to a higher number of fiction books published.

5. In computing this ratio, we treated genre broadly as the Council had: "fiction" encompassed poetry and folklore; "nonfiction" included biographies.

6. This included a 1992 reissuance of *The Boy Who Could Do Anything and Other Mexican Folk Tales* by Brenner (1970, 1942) and new editions of well-known myths, such as *How Music Came to the World: An Ancient Mexican Myth* (Ober, 1994) and *The Mouse Bride: A Mayan Folk Tale* (Dupre, 1993). Compare *All of You Was Singing* (Lewis, 1991) with the former and *The Little Ant / La Hormiga Chiquita* (Ramirez, 1995) with the latter.

7. These include *Pancho's Piñata* (Czernicki & Rhodes, 1992), *The Legend of the Poinsettia* (dePaola, 1994a), also available in Spanish, *La leyenda de la flor de nochebuena* (dePaola, 1994b), and *The Gift of the Poinsettia / El regalo de la nochebuena* (Mora & Berg, 1995), all fiction; and the bilingual poetry book, *La Nochebuena South of the Border* (Rice, 1993).

8. These include nonfiction books such as *Pablo Remembers: The Fiesta of the Day of the Dead* (Ancona,1993), available in English and Spanish editions, and *Days of the Dead* (Lasky, 1994). One half of the nonfiction book *Mexico* (Bailey & Sproule, 1992, 1990) is also devoted to the Day of the Dead. *The Spirit of Tío Fernando / El espíritu de tío Fernando: A Day of the Dead Story / Una historia del Día de los Muertos* (Levy, 1995) is a bilingual fiction story.

9. Food and corn are also central to two books about Mexico: *A Quetzalcóatl: Tale of Corn* by (Parke & Panik, 1992) and *A Taste of Mexico* (Illsley,1994), a nonfiction volume. The latter also contains several end pages of Mexican food recipes.

10. A blatant example of stereotypical images about Mexico and its people can be found in *Ashes for Gold: A Tale from Mexico* (Maitland, 1994, 1992).

REFERENCES

Barrera, R. B., Liguori, O., and Salas, L. (1993). Ideas a literature can grow on: Key insights for enriching and expanding children's literature about the Mexican American experience. In V. J. Harris (Ed.), *Teaching Multicultural Literature in Grades K–8*, pp. 203–241. Norwood, MA: Christopher-Gordon Publishers, Inc.

Bishop, R. S. (1993). Multicultural literature for children: Making informed choices. In V. J. Harris (Ed.), *Teaching Multicultural Literature in Grades K–8*, pp. 37–53. Norwood, MA: Christopher-Gordon Publishers, Inc.

Bishop, R. S. (1994). Introduction. In R. S. Bishop (Ed.), *Kaleidoscope: A multicultural booklist for grades K–8*. Urbana, IL: National Council of Teachers of English.

Cortes, O. G. de (1995). Cesar Chavez and La Causa: Books for children and teenagers. *MultiCultural Review*, 4:1, pp. 28–31.

Council on Interracial Books for Children (1975). Chicano culture in children's literature: Stereotypes, distortions, and omissions. *Interracial Books for Children's Bulletin*, 5, 7–14.

Cox, C. and Zarrillo, J. (1993). *Teaching reading with children's literature*. New York: Merrill/Macmillan Publishing Company.

Duran, D. F. (1979). The Latino literary renaissance: Its roots, status, and future. In D. F. Duran, *Latino materials: A multimedia guide for children and young adults,* pp. 3–12. New York: ABC-Clio Press, Neal-Schuman Publishers.

Gutierrez, R. and Padilla, G. (Eds.). (1993). *Recovering the U.S. Hispanic literary heritage*. Houston: Arte Público Press.

Jones, Jr., M. (1991). It's a not so small world. *Newsweek,* September 9, pp. 64–65.

Kanellos, N. (1994). *The Hispanic almanac: From Columbus to corporate America*. Detroit: Visible Ink Press.

Rocard, M. (1989). Translated by E. G. Brown, Jr. *The children of the sun: Mexican-Americans in the literature of the United States*. Tucson: The University of Arizona Press.

TuSmith, B. (1993). *All my relatives: Community in contemporary ethnic American literatures*. Ann Arbor: The University of Michigan Press.

CREATIVE LITERATURE CITED

Ancona, G. (1994a). *The golden lion tamarin comes home*. New York: Macmillan.

Ancona, G. (1992). *Powwow*. San Diego, CA: Harcourt.

Anderson, J. (1988). *Spanish pioneers of the Southwest*. New York: Dutton.

Aparicio, F. R. (1994). *Latino voices*. Brookfield, CT: Millbrook Press.

Brenner, B. (1970). *Faces*. New York: Dutton.

Cisneros, S. (1989). *The house on Mango Street*. Houston, TX: Arte Público Press.

Hinojosa, R. (1987). *This migrant earth*. Houston: Arte Público Press.

Olivares, J. (1990). *The searchers: Collected poetry / Tomas Rivera*. Houston: Arte Público Press.

Rosenberg, M. B. (1991). *My brother, my sister*. New York: Macmillan.

CHILDREN'S BOOKS REVIEWED

Mexican American/U.S. focus

Alba, J. and Peña, Jr., A. M. (1995). *Calor: A story of warmth for all ages*. Waco, TX: WRS Publishing.

Altman, L. J. (1993a). *Amelia's road*. New York: Lee & Low.

Altman, L. J. (1993b). *El camino de Amelia*. New York: Lee & Low.

Anaya, R. A. (1995). *The farolitos of Christmas*. New York: Hyperion.

Anaya, R. A. (1987). *The farolitos of Christmas: A New Mexico Christmas story*. Santa Fe: New Mexico Magazine.

Ancona, G. (1995). *Fiesta U.S.A.* New York: Lodestar/Dutton.

Anzaldua, G. (1993). *Friends from the other side / Amigos del otro lado*. San Francisco: Children's Book Press.

Atkin, S. B. (1993). *Voices from the fields: Children of migrant farmworkers tell their stories*. Boston: Little, Brown and Company.

Avila, A. (1994). *Mexican ghost tales of the Southwest*. Houston: Piñata Books.

Bredeson, C. (1995). *Henry Cisneros: Building a better America* (People to Know Series). Springfield, NJ: Enslow Publishers, Inc.

Cedeno, M. E. (1993). *Cesar Chavez: Labor leader* (Hispanic Heritage Series). Brookfield, CT: Millbrook Press.

Ciavonne, J. (1995). *Carlos, light the farolito*. New York: Clarion.

Cisneros, S. (1994). *Hairs / Pelitos*. Alfred A. Knopf/Apple Soup Books.

Conord, B. W. (1992). *Cesar Chavez*. New York: Chelsea Junior.

Covault, R. M. (1994). *Pablo and Pimienta / Pablo y Pimienta*. Flagstaff, AZ: Northland/Justin.

De Ruiz, D. C. and Larios, R. (1993). *La Causa: The migrant farmworkers' story*. New York: Steck-Vaughn.

Dorros, A. (1993). *Radio man: A story in English and Spanish / Don Radio: Un cuento en inglés y español*. New York: HarperCollins.

Herrera, J. F. (1995). *Calling the doves / Canto por las palomas*. Emeryville, CA: Children's Book Press.

Holmes, B. (1994). *Cesar Chavez: Farm worker activist* (America's Troublemaker Series). Austin, TX: Raintree/Steck-Vaughn.

Hoobler, D. and Hoobler, T. (1994). *The Mexican American family album*. New York: Holiday House.

Hoyt-Goldsmith, D. (1994). *Day of the Dead: A Mexican American celebration*. New York: Holiday House.

Krull, K. (1994a). *Maria Molina and the Days of the Dead*. New York: Macmillan.

Krull, K. (1994b). *The other side: How kids live in a California Latino neighborhood*. New York: Lodestar Books/Dutton.

Lankford, M. D. (1994). *Quinceañera: A Latina's journey to womanhood*. Brookfield, CT: Millbrook Press.

Lattimore, D. N. (1994). *Frida María: A story of the old Southwest*. San Diego: Browndeer/Harcourt Brace.

Maitland, K. (1994). *Ashes for gold: A tale from Mexico*. Greenvale, NY: Mondo Publishing.

Martinez, E. C. (1995). *Coming to America: The Mexican American experience*. Brookfield, CT: Millbrook Press.

Martinez, E. C. (1993). *Henry Cisneros: Mexican American leader* (Hispanic Heritage Series). Brookfield, CT: Millbrook Press.

Mora, P. (1994a). *Agua, agua, agua* (Let Me Read Series). Glenview, IL: Good Year Books/Scott Foresman.

Mora, P. (1992). *A birthday basket for Tía*. New York: Macmillan.

Mora, P. (1994b). *The desert is my mother/El desierto es mi madre*. Houston: Piñata/Arte Público.

Mora, P. (1994c). *Pablo's tree*. New York: Macmillan.

Paulsen, G. (1993). *Sisters/Hermanas*. Orlando, FL: Harcourt Brace.

Paulsen, G. (1994a). *The tortilla factory*. San Diego: Harcourt Brace.

Paulsen, G. (1994b). *La tortillería*. San Diego: Harcourt Brace.

Petrucelli, R. (1992). *Henry Cisneros: Alcalde trabajador*. Vero Beach, FL: Rourke Corp.

Politi, L. (1994, 1976). *Three stalks of corn*. New York: Macmillan.

Riehecky, J. (1993). *Cinco de Mayo*. Chicago: Children's Press.

Rodriguez, G. M. (1994). *Green corn tamales/Tamales de elote*. Tucson, AZ: Hispanic Books.

Soto, G. (1990). *Baseball in April, and other stories*. San Diego, CA: Harcourt Brace Jovanovich.

Soto, G. (1995a). *Canto familiar*. San Diego, CA: Harcourt Brace.

Soto, G. (1995b). *Chato's kitchen*. New York: G. P. Putnam's Sons.

Soto, G. (1993a). *Local news*. San Diego, CA: Harcourt Brace.

Soto, G. (1992a). *Pacific crossing*. San Diego, CA: Harcourt Brace Jovanovich.

Soto, G. (1993b). *The pool party*. New York: Delacorte Press.

Soto, G. (1992b). *The skirt*. New York: Delacorte Press.

Soto, G. (1991). *Taking sides*. San Diego, CA: Harcourt Brace Jovanovich.

Soto, G. (1993c). *Too many tamales*. New York: G. P. Putnam's Sons.

Spurr, E. (1995). *Lupe & me*. San Diego: Gulliver/Harcourt Brace.

Stevens, J. R. (1995). *Carlos and the cornfield/Carlos y la milpa de maíz*. Flagstaff, AZ: Northland/Justin.

Stevens, J. R. (1993). *Carlos and the squash plant/Carlos y la planta de calabaza*. Flagstaff, AZ: Northland/Justin.

Taylor, T. (1992). *Maria: A Christmas story*. San Diego, CA: Harcourt Brace Jovanovich. (Paperback, 1993, Avon Camelot)

Thomas, J. R. (1994). *Lights on the river*. New York: Hyperion.

CHILDREN'S BOOKS REVIEWED AND/OR CITED

Mexican/Mexico focus

Ancona, G. (1993a). *Pablo remembers: The fiesta of the Day of the Dead*. New York: Lothrop, Lee & Shepard.

Ancona, G. (1993b). *Pablo recuerda: La fiesta del día de los muertos*. New York: Lothrop, Lee & Shepard.

Ancona, G. (1994b). *The piñata maker/El piñatero*. San Diego, CA: Harcourt Brace.

Bailey, D. and Sproule, A. (1992, 1989). *Mexico*. (Where We Live). Austin, TX: Raintree/Steck-Vaughn.

Brenner, A. (1992, 1970, 1942). *The boy who could do anything and other Mexican folk tales*. Hamden, CT: Shoe String Press/Linnet Books.

Czernicki, S. and Rhodes, T. (1992). *Pancho's piñata*. New York: Hyperion.

dePaola, T. (1994a). *The legend of the poinsettia*. New York: G. P. Putnam's Sons.

dePaola, T. (1994b). *La leyenda de la flor de nochebuena*. New York: G. P. Putnam's Sons.

Dupre, J. (1993). *The mouse bride: A Mayan folk tale*. New York: Umbrella Books/Alfred A. Knopf.

Illsley, L. (1995). *A taste of Mexico*. New York: Thomson Learning.

Lasky, K. (1994). *Days of the Dead*. New York: Hyperion.

Levy, J. (1995). *The spirit of Tío Fernando: A Day of the Dead story / El espíritu de tío Fernando: Una historia del Día de los Muertos*. Morton Grove, IL: Albert Whitman.

Lewis, R. (1991). *All of you was singing*. New York: Atheneum.

Maitland, K. (1994). *Ashes for gold: A tale from Mexico*. Greenvale, NY: Mondo.

Mora, P. and Berg, C. R. (1995). *The gift of the poinsettia / El regalo de la flor de nochebuena*. Houston: Piñata/Arte Público.

Ober, H. (1994). *How music came to the world: An ancient Mexican myth*. Boston: Houghton Mifflin.

Parke, M. & Panik, S. (1992). *A Quetzalcóatl: Tale of corn*. New York: Fearon/Simon & Schuster.

Ramirez, M. R. (1995). *The little ant / La hormiga chiquita*. New York: Rizzoli International.

Rice, J. (1993). *La nochebuena south of the border*. Gretna, LA: Pelican.

Chapter 6 _____

Native Americans in Children's Literature

Debbie Reese

ဆ ဆ ဆ ဆ ဆ

> *Katie, a little girl with blonde hair and blue eyes looked across the snack table at the woman sitting there with her daughter, Elizabeth. Katie asked, "Why is your skin brown?" The woman replied, "Because I am a Native American—an Indian person and so is Elizabeth." Puzzled, the little girl said, "Indians aren't real. They're dead." Months later, the two girls and a few others played together. They decided to act out the movie Pocahontas, and Elizabeth said, "I'll be Pocahontas because I'm an Indian." Another child said, "You can't be Pocahontas. Your hair's not the right color. And your skin's not the right color." In the weeks to follow, Elizabeth would repeatedly assert her identity as an Indian child, and repeatedly, her friends would challenge her assertions.*

INTRODUCTION

The beginning of a chapter about Native American[1] children's literature is an odd place for a discussion about a movie to appear. Yet, the 1995 Disney movie *Pocahontas* must be addressed because the literary experiences of many children are based on movies. The spin-off books from Disney's *Pocahontas* have been listed among the best sellers in the Hardcover Frontlist Bestsellers in *Publisher's Weekly*. Indeed, of the 15 titles listed as having sold over 200,000 copies, five were variations of Disney's *Pocahontas* (Roback, 1996). As demonstrated in the vignette above, preschool children role play parts of the movie in their daily activities. In some ways, the movie is a positive representation of Native American people. For example, rather than the solitary and savage Indian, we see extended family members and the important connections that exist among them. The Indians are not one-dimensional, bad-guy warriors, but individuals who laugh with their children and lovingly embrace their wives. The main character, Pocahontas, is attractive to young children, such that they will argue over who "gets to be" her in role play. This is a first: most of the heroes and heroines in animated films are not minority or ethnic characters. Typically, the Indian is not positively presented, and Native children feel embarrassed and often deny their heritage because they don't want to be associated with these media images. Disney's Pocahontas is a positive character, affirms the identity of young Native children, and helps them feel pride, not embarrassment.

Unfortunately, the movie and spin-off books clearly begin by presenting the New World as a land with wide open spaces, largely uninhabited. This representation of the New World as a virgin land, ready to be taken by the Europeans, has permeated children's literature, in books written years ago (McCann, 1993), and, as *Pocahontas* demonstrates, in books that are published today. The *Pocahontas* movie and books also clearly place Native American people in this historical context and lead children to believe that all Native American people have black hair and dark skin.

Native Americans are often portrayed as barbarians and uncivilized savages who deserved to lose their land: the murdering redskin, the noble savage—the "Vanishing Redman" (Bruchac, 1987, p. x). In fact, the Native tribes of North America were territorial with respect to land, but did not claim individual ownership rights of specific plots of land as Europeans did. Land, like the air, was something to share with others. Native people were not solitary warriors roaming the land searching for someone to ravage; they were members of families and communities who fought against encroachment from the Europeans and defended their way of life. One popular image of the Native American is that of the savage who scalped innocent settlers. Scalping was actually introduced to Native Americans by Europeans who were paid 40 pounds for the scalp of an Indian male, and 20 pounds for scalps of Indian females or children under the age of 12. It was believed this would help clear the land of Native people (Council on Interracial Books for Children, 1981).

The most significant development in Native American children's literature is that more Native authors are becoming established as their work gains recognition and makes its way into libraries, bookstores, and homes. This is made possible through the efforts of Joseph Bruchac's Greenfield Press, and others who encourage Native writers. Writers often publish their work in collections such as Anna Lee Walters *Neon Pow-Wow: New Native American Voices of the Southwest.* Although many Native writers are publishing their work through small presses, access to larger populations will be accomplished when larger presses recognize and publish their work. Photo essay books that present the contemporary lives of Native people are being published in greater numbers and are often written and illustrated by Native authors, illustrators, and photographers, such as Rina Swentzel's *Children of Clay* (1995), Marcia Rendon's *Powwow Summer* (1996), and Gordon Regguinti's *The Sacred Harvest* (1988) from the We Are Still Here series collection published by Lerner Publications.

In the pages that follow, the authors will describe the past and current status of Native American literature and how Native people are depicted in children's literature. Exemplary authors and their work as well as problematic texts will be discussed in-depth. Strategies that lead to meaningful discussions about Native Americans, a resource list for professional reading, and a list of recommended books will be provided.

PAST AND CURRENT STATUS OF THE NATIVE AMERICAN IN CHILDREN'S BOOKS

Who are the Indian people of the United States?

Defining "Indian" is not an easy task. Ruoff (1990) cites The National Indian Education Association Bylaws, which state the following:

> For purposes of the NIE Constitution the term American Indian shall mean any person who: (1) is a member of a tribe, band, or other organized group of Indians, including those tribes, bands, or groups terminated since 1940 and those recognized now or in the future by the state in which they reside, or who is a descendent, in the first or second degree, of any such member, or (2) is considered by the Secretary of the Interior to be an Indian for any purpose, (3) is an Eskimo or Aleut or other Alaska Native, or (4) is recognized as an Indian by his community. (Membership, art. 3)

The bylaws refer to "tribes, bands, or groups." In the United States, there are over 500 different tribal groups, 308 of which are recognized by the U.S. Government. In addition to the nearly two million people who claimed American Indian status on the 1990 census, another five million indicated they were of Indian descent. Today, Native people live in urban and rural areas as well as tribal reservations or Trust Lands held by the U.S. Government. More than half of the Native population resides in six states: Oklahoma, California, Arizona, New Mexico, Alaska, and Washington. Their lifestyles range from those who retain most of their traditional activities to those who lead lives much like the mainstream American middle class, while still others weave together positive and productive elements of both lifestyles (Hodgkinson, 1992). Regardless of the rich diversity that exists, the Cooperative Children's Book Council (CCBC) documents that only 31 out of 70 books about Native Americans published during 1994 actually specify an Indian nation. In *CCBC Choices 1995*, the numbers are similar: Of the 83 books about Native American themes and topics located at the CCBC in 1995, only 32 are about a specific Indian nation. Although this is still less than half, it represents a significant change in children's books written about Native Americans. Typically, the Navajo and Cherokee nations appear most frequently in these books. Historically, most books about Native Americans did not indicate a specific tribe. Vizenor suggests that the homogenized, pan-Indian image that exists in literature and in the minds of Americans is preferable to one that looks at the complexities of actual Indian history (League of Women Voters, 1982).

Commenting on the books written about Native Americans, Byler (1982) writes that there are "too many books featuring painted, whooping, befeathered Indians closing in on too many forts, maliciously attacking 'peaceful' settlers or simply leering menacingly from the background; too many books in which white benevolence is the only thing that saves the day for the incompetent, childlike Indian; too many stories setting forth what is 'best' for American Indians" (p. 34).

Of these books, McCann (1993) notes that those "with a white bias vastly outnumber those expressing a Native American perspective" (p. 140). Unlike other cultural groups in the United States, there is an abundance of books about Native Americans. Writers are drawn to Native Americans as a theme. Sneve (1995) notes that, historically, the books and stories written about the Sioux could be divided into "good Indian" stories and "bad Indian" stories. The "good Indian" stories were well received by reviewers, were critically acclaimed, and were often used in classrooms. These good stories were about the Indian as a free child of nature, or the courageous and brave Indian. The "bad Indian" stories were not well received and their literary merit was never recognized. The focus of these stories was the "disintegration of the traditions and values and the extreme poverty and destitution of reservation life" (p. xv).

Given the popularity of the Native American as a theme, multiple issues surface. These issues include authorship, insider/outsider perspective, stereotyping, and ownership, age appropriateness of material, Eurocentric perspectives of women, and the issue of identity and self-esteem. A discussion of these issues follows.

The Issue of Authorship and Insider/Outsider Perspective

In 1995, 98½ percent of the books written about Native Americans published by mainstream publishers were written by non-Native authors (CCBC, 1995). Teachers and parents seeking materials written by Native American authors may have difficulty finding them as they peruse multicultural bibliographies. These bibliographies typically include three categories: African American, Asian American, and Native American. It is generally the case with these bibliographies that African American books are authored by African Americans and Asian American books are authored by Asian Americans. However, Native American books are rarely authored by Native Americans (Slapin and Seale, 1992).

Non-Native writers in America have frequently been drawn to topics and themes related to NativeAmericans. Scholars and authors may be drawn to this theme because they believe Indians are more honest and brave than other peoples (Dorris, 1994). Not being Native American themselves, they often rely on their own perceptions of what it might mean to be an "Indian," rather than conducting careful research or spending long periods of time with the tribe about whom they write.

Unfortunately, many of their perceptions are frequently based on the image of NativeAmericans presented by Hollywood's amalgamation of particular aspects of the Lakota Sioux, Crow, Cheyenne, and other nations of the Great Plains (Stedman, 1982). This generic Indian motif includes feathered headdresses, fringed buckskin clothing, tipis, war dances, pipes, and buffalo hunting. These images have their origins in George Catlin's paintings of Plains Indians, Buffalo Bill's Wild West Show, and the Plains nations resistance to encroachment of their lands in the 1880s (Council on Interracial Books for Children, 1981). Catlin's illustrations were used by illustrators of children's books and school textbooks (Ewers, 1982), thus perpetuating the idea that all Indians looked like the Plains Indians. Today, the general public believes Native people are warriors who lived in the Wild West during the 19th century, or are impoverished Natives living on reservations in the 20th century (Szasz, 1992).

There are many reasons why it is necessary for Native people to write and have their work published. A Native person who has grown up and/or lived in the context of tribal society knows that Indians are just "people" and are less likely to portray Natives as heroic or mystical individuals. Access to relatives and knowledge that comes from being raised among Native people means that their writings will accurately reflect the tribe they write about (Dorris, 1994). A work of fiction, Dorris writes, is "truly, at its heart, the product of an author's personal history. We can only draw with authenticity upon emotions we've known and tasted" (p. 142).

The Issue of Stereotypes

Derman-Sparks (1989) defines stereotype as "an oversimplified generalization about a particular group, race, or sex, which usually carries derogatory implication" (p. 3). In 1982, Hirschfelder wrote "Children in America regularly see images of Indians that are inauthentic, unrealistic, and often offensive" (p. xi). More than a decade has passed, but Hirschfelder's statement is as applicable today as it was then. Many of the beliefs about what it means to be an Indian form at an early age and are typically based on stereotypical images of Indians as presented in movies, television, children's books, toys, and various forms of advertising in which the Native American motif is used to sell products. The power of such images is demonstrated in McElmeel's study.

McElmeel (1993) surveyed approximately 250 elementary school students and asked them how they would know if an Indian walked into the room. Their typical response was "They'd be wearing feathers," "They'd have war paint on," and "They'd be carrying a tomahawk." Only one child mentioned that the Indian would look like a regular kid. Other school teachers and parents frequently report that children believe that Indians are an extinct, war-like people that existed only in the remote past (Shaffer, 1993; Kingsolver, 1995).

This stereotypical image permeates popular culture, and can be seen at sporting events where professional and college sports teams (Washington Redskins, Atlanta Braves, Cleveland Indians, University of Illinois' Chief Illiniwek) have "mascots" parading around the field during sporting events. Enthusiastic sports fans frequently attend the events dressed up like "Indians," exhibiting menacing behaviors they believe are typical Indian behaviors. This interpretation of what it means to be an Indian does not honor Native people, because the image the mascot presents is usually inaccurate, usually wears a hodge-podge of clothing from many different tribes, and mocks Native dancing, which is a form of prayer—not a form of entertainment. Lakota elder Matthew King comments on this distorted image which illuminates the ignorance that exists about Native people, and serves only to perpetuate this ignorance:

> He says we're warlike when we're peaceful. He calls us savages, but he's the savage. See. He calls this headdress a warbonnet. Sure we used it in war, but most of the time it was for ceremony, not war. Each feather stands for a good deed and I have thirty-six in mine. It's not about war; it's about who we are. When we sing songs he calls them war songs. But they're not war songs, they're prayers to God. We have drums, so White Man calls them war drums; but they're not for war, they're for talking to God. There's no such thing as a war drum. He sees how our warriors paint their faces, so he calls it war paint. But it's not for war, it's to make it so God can see our faces clearly if we have to die. So how can we talk to the White Man of peace when he only knows war? (Wall & Adren, p. 33)

The stereotypical image of Native Americans is introduced and reinforced in beginner and picture books depicting non-Indian people and animals dressed up like Indians as though "being Indian" was a role to be assumed rather than an inborn identity. The illustrations of children at play in *Blackboard Bear* (Alexander, 1969) include non-Native children who are being Indians and are drawn bare-chested, wearing feathered headdresses, fringed trousers, no shoes, and carrying tomahawks or bow and arrows. One of the children holds his hand over his mouth as he makes the woo-woo sound commonly associated with Indians. Two additional boys are shown, dressed as the cowboys. They are fully dressed, and carry lassoes and pistols. This illustration of playing Indian continues to be an extremely popular theme in young children's play, even today. Many people cannot understand why Native people object to this play theme. Mifaunwy Shunatona Hines, an Otoe-Pawnee-Wyandot woman offers this succinct response: "Nobody plays Italian or black—it's still only the Indian people who are referred to in that way" (Flaste, 1982, p. 5).

In addition to the "play Indian" theme, images of Indians are seen in alphabet and counting books. In these genres, the Native American is dehumanized and objectified. The ever-popular Richard Scarry books often include images of animals dressed up in buckskin and feathers, as seen in Richard Scarry's *Best Storybook Ever* (Scarry, 1968). In Maurice Sendak's alphabet book *Alligators All Around* (1991), alligators decked out in feathers and buckskin are shown on the "I is for Indian page." In *Clifford's Halloween* (Bridwell, 1986), Emily Elizabeth considers dressing Clifford in a feathered headdress as a Halloween costume. These books suggest to children that anyone or anything can put on feathers and "be" Indians.

Stereotypes are often found in material written and illustrated to accurately portray and inspire members of other ethnic groups. *Amazing Grace* (Hoffman, 1994) is the story of a young African-Anglo girl of Caribbean descent who enjoys playing various roles: Joan of Arc, Anansi the Spider, Helen of Troy, an explorer, a pirate, and Hiawatha, sitting crosslegged by the shining Big-Sea-Water. The image Grace projects as an Indian chief contains all of the stereotypical attributes associated with a noble Indian chief. She wears a multicolored-feathered headdress. Her head is held high, her back is straight, her legs are crossed, and her facial expression is decidedly stoic. Harris (personal communication), after long and careful reflection about *Amazing Grace,* decided to "give it up" as a favorite because she believes it wrong to celebrate one culture at the expense of another.

The Issue of Ownership

Many Native American folktales were gathered by anthropologists and ethnographers. Collections of the stories are fairly easy to obtain. These stories, however, were collected by individuals with little insight or respect for the spiritual needs of privacy and protection of Native religions. Frequently, a spiritual practice was taken out of context and recorded by an anthropologist as though it was simply a story free of religious and spiritual constraints and significance. A personal story told by one of the authors of this chapter, Debbie Reese, highlights this issue.

> Ever since childhood, my parents, grandparents, and elders
> told us repeatedly not to talk about this or that aspect of our

traditional practices. We were also told about a book written by a Pueblo Indian man trained as an anthropologist, that we were strongly admonished not to read because it contained secrets of our practices, many associated with gender roles. Although I have come across the particular book many times, I have always heeded the words of my elders, and have never opened the cover. However, in 1995, while preparing a bibliography about Pueblo Indians, I came across a collection of Native stories and poems. Innocently, I flipped through, found a poem attributed to the Pueblo people, and began reading. Too late, I realized the poem contained information that I as a Pueblo Indian woman, should not have access to. Deeply pained, I thought of my own young daughter and her cousins. Wanting to protect them from innocently reading printed words they should not read, I was in a dilemma whether or not to include the book in the bibliography. After consulting elders, we decided it was best to leave it out, as calling attention to it might attract more attention and further invade the privacy of the Pueblo people.

Whitt (1995) has written about "cultural imperialism and the marketing of Native America" (p. 1). Throughout the history of children's literature about Native Americans, most of the writers who have gained profit by writing Indian stories have been non-Native. The Indian motif has also proven financially lucrative for corporations that market clothing based on Native styles, and is exploited by organizations such as the Boy Scouts. This motif is recognized and promoted around the world as evidenced by Dorris's visit to a gift shop in New Zealand, where patrons could purchase a toy monkey wearing a brightly colored imitation headdress and carrying a plywood tomahawk. Native people do not benefit from these commercial ventures, and in fact are hurt by societies around the world that often reject a Native individual's claim to Indian identity because he or she does not meet with expectations of what is believed to be "a real Indian" (Dorris, 1994).

Sharing stories is described by Campbell (1988) as a universal experience that is common cross culturally. Native American people have a long and rich history as an oral society, passing stories from generation to generation. Through this oral tradition, history and other important cultural elements were taught. Historically, Native people did not write down their stories. They told them to their children. Today, some of what they said can be found in written sources, some of it is only in the memory of the people (Sneve, 1995). Many Native writers are currently writing and publishing these stories, but many non-Native writers have been doing so for years.

Many of these stories are folk tales, and have been retold, adapted, and copyrighted by non-Native people such as Joe Hayes, a prominent storyteller in the Southwestern part of the United States. In the introduction to *A Heart Full of Turquoise: Pueblo Indian Tales* (1988), Hayes writes that he is inspired by stories collected by anthropologists. He changes them for his own use, adding or dropping characters as he develops his own version. Hayes makes no claims that his stories are traditional, yet he attributes them to the Pueblo people, thus suggesting to his readers that the tale reflects the Pueblo culture. To illustrate the problems that often occur when non-Native authors revise traditional tales, it is useful to compare the Pueblo version of Cinderella, as told by Hayes, and the version told by Pablita Velarde, a Pueblo artist and author whose book *Old Father Storyteller* was first published in 1960 and reissued in 1989. Turkey Girl is an orphan. In Hayes' version, she lives alone, an outcast. However, there is no such thing as an outcast among the Pueblo people, who are very communal and readily take orphan children into their own homes. In Velarde's version, Turkey Girl lives with an unkind foster mother. This may seem like a small detail from an outsider perspective, yet it is not. Long-established family and communal living arrangements are basic elements of survival and are the foundations on which entire cultures are built, not just for Native people, but for people around the world. To casually sweep such a foundation away, as Hayes has done, is inexcusable.

Folk tales have long been a staple of children's literature (Hearne, 1993), and Native American folk tales have a place in children's literature. However, the prevalence and domination of folk tales in Native American literature prevents other important aspects of Native American culture from being presented to young children. Acoma Pueblo writer, Simon Ortiz (1990), writes that Native American symbols ". . . are taken and are popularized, diverting attention from real issues about land and resources . . ." (p. 112). Folk tales, like symbols, are only a part of the Native American reality, and, taken out of context, do not give children a full picture of the Native American living in the United States today. Although some authors and illustrators are producing books about Native Americans that are not folk tales, there is a great need for picture books and informational books that show other aspects of the lives of Native American people.

It is paramount that stories about Native Americans accurately represent the culture from which they originate or seek to emulate. Among Native American people, stories are understood to be both powerful and sacred. Indian people believe that stories can either enhance one's life or cause harm if they are not properly used (Howard, 1985). Native stories that are written without input from the people may produce an entertaining tale that may lend itself to beautiful illustrations, but often such retellings and illustrations provide children with a misguided and stereotypical view of Indian cultures (Keeshing-Tobias, 1992).

Age Appropriate Literature

Many scholars (Derman-Sparks, 1989; Ramsey, 1995) believe that young children are capable of learning about injustice and developing skills to act on their learning. They believe kindergarten children are learning to think critically and are able to speak up when they believe something is unfair. An opposing viewpoint, put forth by Spodek (personal communication), cautions teachers not to put too much emphasis on concepts such as social injustice in their curriculum for young children. Children frequently internalize events, believing they are personally responsible for an event's occurrence. (For example, young children often believe something they have done has caused the divorce of their parents.) Spodek points out that with respect to activism and political issues, the young child is not cognitively, emotionally or mentally able to sift through these complex issues.

Given these concerns, books selected for the youngest children should focus on providing information about contemporary Native children, presenting the traditional Native aspects of their lives, as well as the daily activities typical of other children in the United States (riding bikes, playing basketball, etc.). Books for older children can include the elements of historical tragedy and contemporary hardships of Native American people.

Books from Small versus Large Publishing Houses

Most Native American writers turn to small presses for the publication of their work, because it is difficult to break into the large presses. Given this, librarians and teachers seeking quality Native American materials often run into obstacles in trying to purchase the books. For example, small presses are often not able to fill book orders with the speed of larger publishing houses. Consequently, the order may be canceled by school business offices, which often maintain strict policies regarding the time period allowed for receipt of items ordered. In addition to this problem, books from small presses are frequently not available from the "jobbers" (suppliers of books) most schools use. Finally, librarians often do not have the time necessary to track down books from small presses that are listed in bibliographies.

Eurocentric Portrayal of Native American Women

The image of Native American women generally takes one of three forms: the hard working beast of burden, the helpful squaw, or the Indian Princess. When the English arrived in the New World, they discovered that Native American women were on a more equal footing with men than was the case in England. Finding this in conflict with the status accorded English women, Brant (1992), a Mohawk writer, suggests the "perjorative stereotype developed because the white men who came here so little valued their own women, one of their first missions was to reduce ours to the same status—beast of burden, important for the production of sons, but little else: squaws" (p. 102). Sneve (1995) notes that Indian women received attention by male historians "only if they were 'princesses' like Pocahontas or 'noble savages' like Sacagawea who in some way or another aided white men" (p. xiv).

Of greater concern in the context of children's books, however, is the theme of the Indian Princess, often embodied in the young Pawmunkey girl, Pocahontas. The image of the Native American Princess is very popular for thousands of young girls and boys in the United States. These children have added Disney's Pocahontas to their concept of the Indian Princess. The 1995 release of the film has generated the reprinting and publication of biographies based primarily on the writings of English men. Among them are: *Pocahontas* (D'Aulaire, 1936), *Pocahontas: Girl from Jamestown* (Jassem, 1979), *Pocahontas* (Fritz, 1993), *My Name is Pocahontas* (Accorsi, 1992), *Pocahontas: Princess of the River Tribes* (Raphael & Bolognese, 1993), and *Pocahontas* (Ingoglia, 1995).

The biographies of Pocahontas have been written by non-Native people, based on historical accounts kept by non-Native men who recorded events from a Euro-centric perspective. These documents portray Pocahontas in a positive light, but Reddish (1995) points out that these English accounts praised Pocahontas because they benefited the English colonists. The most famous episode of her life is the one in which she threw herself over John Smith's body to prevent his execution at the hands of her father. However, this event is not recorded in the diary Smith kept at the time, and historians speculate he may have fabricated the rescue story to gain court favor after his return to England (Lemay, 1993). By that time, Pocahontas had married and traveled to England with her English husband (John Rolfe) and their infant son. She received lavish attention from Queen Anne, became a favorite of the royal court, and was in demand to attend social functions. While returning to Virginia, she died of pulmonary disease in Gravesend, England. She was buried in an unmarked grave, and her remains have never been found. Mossiker's (1976) biography of Pocahontas includes a story that graverobbers stole her body to sell as a curiosity. This proved unsuccessful, and they reburied her in an unknown location.

The debate on whether or not the rescue actually occurred is based on two different arguments. Brant (1992) suggests that the execution was actually a mock execution that was part of an adoption ritual often held after the capture of enemies. Many historians now conclude that there is strong evidence to support the theory that Smith may have appropriated the story from an account by the Spanish explorer, Juan Ortiz. In the account recorded by Ortiz in 1528, he was saved by Ulele, a Timucua Indian who lived near what is now Tampa Bay, Florida. The Ortiz event occurred nearly 80 years before Smith arrived in Virginia.

The controversy surrounding the Disney version of the Pocahontas story focuses on Disney's decision to portray Pocahontas as a young, voluptuous woman rather than the 12-year-old child she actually was when Smith first met her. Although there is a vague suggestion in the Mossiker biography that Pocahontas and Smith may have spent a night together and that she may have been in love with him, there is no evidence that Pocahontas and John Smith were physically or emotionally involved with each other. Yet, Disney romantically linked the two. Many parents, teachers, and critics are quick to point out that the Disney story distorts history, but they fail to see its value to young Native American children. For the first time, there is a big-screen, animated Native American female with positive attributes that a young Native American girl can identify with. For the first time, these young Native children can say "I am an Indian like Pocahontas" and feel proud of this fact. Pocahontas stands alone among the multitude of embarrassingly simple and stereotypical images of Native women in children's literature and movies. The distortions of history in the Pocahontas movie provide an excellent opportunity to present more accurate information, and conduct a critical discussion about why Disney chose to present the story in this way.

Issues of Identity and Self-Esteem

Acoma poet Simon Ortiz writes about his belief, as a child, that he wasn't an Indian. Picture books showed him that Indians lived in teepees and rode ponies and hunted buffalo. At Acoma Pueblo, in the southwestern United States, there were no teepees and buffalo. Ortiz was not able to find himself or his people in a book. As a result, Ortiz writes, "In 1970, I went looking for Indians" (Ortiz, 1987, p. 220). His experience exemplifies how young children learn about Native Americans and the impact it can have on Native children.

During the preschool and elementary years, children develop their racial identity. This may be affected by current attitudes in one's own group as well as society in general (Ramsey, 1995). In the elementary years, children absorb more of the prevailing social attitudes, and the awareness of "us" versus "them" becomes more established (Katz, 1976). All children need books in which they see bits of themselves. Such books help them build feelings of success, achievement, and self-esteem (Burke, 1990). Books with stereotypes, as described by Ortiz, make Native children question their existence, and can cause feelings of embarrassment and shame about their identity. Books that portray contemporary Native children coping with issues all children identify with are becoming greater in number. For example, Bruchac's *Fox Song* (1993) is about a young girl who is coping with the death of her grandmother.

Books about issues specific to Native American identity are also available. *Less than Half, More than Whole* (Lacapa) is a story about a child who is struggling to understand the duality of his identity as a Native American/White child. This book can prove powerful to the self-esteem of a Pueblo child who knows that the word "saiya" means grandmother in the Tewa language, and who immediately recognizes the artwork as something he or she sees in their grandmother's home. Esther Sanderson's *Two Pairs of Shoes* (1990) is about the gifts Maggie, a young Indian girl, receives for her eighth birthday: a pair of black patent leather shoes from her mother, and a pair of moccasins from her grandmother. The two pairs of shoes symbolize modern times and time-honored traditions of Maggie's family, and how both can be included in Maggie's life. *Where Did You Get Your Moccasins?* by Brenda Wheeler is also a contemporary story about a Native child who tells his classmates how his grandmother made his moccasins. Both books are published by Pemmican Press, whose books are culturally accurate, include words from Native languages, and are written by authors who tend to be members of the nation they are writing about.

EXEMPLARY AUTHORS AND WORKS

With greater frequency, books written by NativeAmerican writers are making their way into classrooms, library bookshelves, and children's homes. Many of these authors attended government boarding schools designed to discredit their beliefs and values (Szasz, 1992) in an attempt to assimilate them, remove them from their "corrupting habits of savage homes" (Skinner, 1992, p. 54), and lead them to more easily "adopt the customs of civilized life" (Skinner, 1992, p. 54). Many young Native people were forbidden to speak their Native languages, and, as a result, only 206 of the 600 languages that once existed are currently in use (Skinner, 1992).The work of several outstanding Native American writers will be discussed in the following section. Many of them have a shared background as former students of government boarding schools where they were forbidden to speak their Native languages, and were even punished if they did so. Many include words from their Native language in their writings.

Luci Tapahonso (Navajo/Dine)

Navajo poet Luci Tapahonso's work is growing in popularity and is being received equally well among the Navajo people and non-Native people. She is in high demand as a speaker, and accepts engagements to speak to children in elementary schools as well as larger audiences through formats such as National Public Radio's program "All Things Considered" (Dunaway, 1995). Her work presents moving and realistic descriptions of Navajo tribal life (Ruoff, 1990).

Born in 1953 on the Navajo reservation, Tapahonso is careful to introduce herself in a traditional Dine (the Navajo name for their tribe) manner: she identifies her mother's clan, Too dik'oozhi (which means Saltwater Clan), and her father's clan To dichi'ii'nii (which means Bitterwater Clan). Both her parents were severely punished in school when they spoke Navajo, so they taught their own Navajo-speaking children English before they started formal schooling. In first grade, Tapahonso's parents enrolled her at a boarding school thirty miles from her home to nurture her natural talent for music. Her gift for writing blossomed, and she later edited the high school newspaper and began writing poetry. She attended the University of New Mexico, where she studied with Leslie Marmon Silko, Simon Ortiz, Joy Harjo, Paula Gunn Allen, and N. Scott Momaday, during the Indian renaissance that took place there (Dunaway, 1995).

Navajo ABC: A Dine Alphabet Book (1996) begins with a Foreword that eloquently introduces the reader to the Navajo people:

> We call ourselves T'aa Dine, which means "The People." We are also called the Navajo. There are about 220,000 Dine today. Our land is in Utah, New Mexico, and Arizona. We speak the Dine language, and many of our schools teach children to read and write Dine, as well as English. Our language is very important; because of it we are able to remember and practice many of the old ways that our ancestors taught us.
>
> We are happy to share some of our daily lives with our readers. All of the objects and words in this alphabet book are only parts of larger ideas, which are expressed through stories, songs, and prayers. Through these stories, songs, and prayers, we learn about animals and plants, we learn to respect one another, and we learn about the world around us. We also learn about our history, the land's history, and how to be responsible for the world we live in. The Dine language teaches us to be strong and have pride in all that we do.

In this book, every page contains a letter of the alphabet that represents an aspect of Dine life. Several pages contain Dine words. The word on the K page is "Keyah"; and the illustration is of a Southwestern mesa landscape. A glossary included at the back of the book indicates "Keyah" means "land." Although some pages contain English words, the illustration is culturally specific to the Navajo tribe. For example, the word on the D page is dress, but the illustration is of a Dine girl wearing a traditional woven rug dress that is worn on special occasions. In addition to providing a translation for Dine words, the glossary provides information on other words that may be unfamiliar to the general reader, such as "fry bread," which is a puffy, round bread fried in oil. Eleanor Schick's outstanding illustrations are rendered in the soft colors of the Southwest and her illustrations of the Dine people portray them as individuals.

The review in Booklist noted "the contemporary focus on a specific tribe is a welcome change from works that clump all Indians together in a historical context without mentioning individual languages."

Shonto Begay (Navajo/Dine)

As an Indian artist and writer, Shonto Begay has brought a more authentic representation of Navajo and other Native American cultures to the American public. In his childhood, Begay attended a boarding school operated by the Bureau of Indian Affairs of the U.S. Government. These schools were developed primarily as a means to assimilate Native American people into the dominant U.S. culture. He and other students were forbidden to speak Navajo or practice their religion and saw their families only during Christmas vacation. Yet, Begay recalls, "The experience at the boarding school only served to make us appreciate our culture more" (Begay, 1995). After graduation from the boarding school, Begay studied at the Institute of American Indian Arts, and later at the California College of Arts and Crafts, where he received a BFA with distinction. Begay tells an interesting story about an event preceding the invitation to develop the illustrations for *The Mud Pony* (1988). The offer came from Diane Hess, an editor at Scholastic, who had seen his art at a gallery. The day before her phone call, Begay had been with his nephew at a river bank, forming sculptures out of the mud on the river bank. *The Mud Pony* was Begay's first illustrated book for children.

Begay wrote and illustrated *Ma'ii and Cousin Horned Toad: A Traditional Navajo Story* in 1992. It features a traditional Navajo story about Ma'ii the coyote who visits his cousin Horned Toad in search of a free meal. Horned Toad is gracious to Ma'ii even though he realizes that the coyote is taking advantage of his good nature. To provide Ma'ii with food, Horned Toad travels to his corn field twice, but Ma'ii was still not satisfied. Before Ma'ii can ask for a third helping, Horned Toad angrily announces that Ma'ii will have to work in the field if he wants anything more to eat. Ma'ii works for a while, but then his laziness leads him to rest and he formulates a plan to trick his cousin, Horned Toad, out of the farm. He pretends to have corn stuck in his teeth, which can only be removed by Horned Toad climbing into his mouth. Ma'ii promptly swallows Horned Toad. Suddenly, Ma'ii hears someone calling his name. Searching for the source, he discovers his cousin is alive and well within his own belly, and demands that he come out. Horned Toad does not come out, choosing instead to move about inside Ma'ii, causing him much discomfort. Finally, Horned Toad tugs on Ma'ii's heart, causing him to faint. Horned Toad comes out, never to be bothered by Ma'ii again.

Throughout the story, Begay has been careful to include Navajo words: Ma'ii (which means coyote), ahehee (which means thank you), and shil na aash (which means my cousin). The inclusion of these words is significant and contrasts with Begay's experience in government boarding school, where he was prohibited from speaking his native language. It has been common practice not to include Indian language words in children's literature (which reflects non-Native writers access to knowledge of Native people), but they are being included more often in books published today. This technique may help readers understand that Indian languages spoken by Indian people are still used today.

The illustrations for the book are in the soft earth tones common in Begay's native land. Ma'ii and Horned Toad are drawn realistically with facial expressions and poses that enhance the text, allowing a non-reader to understand the story simply by studying the illustrations. This story is one of the many coyote stories told by the Navajo people. Begay's telling of it is filled with the suspense and humor common in traditional Navajo stories. The text is written in a style consistent with the oral tradition and the dialogue flows easily. This story is an excellent read-aloud.

Begay's *Navajo: Visions and Voices Across the Mesa* is the second book he has written and illustrated. It is a collection of twenty-one poems accompanied by acrylic paintings done in a series of small brush strokes and two mixed media water colors. The collection seeks to find a balance between living in the world of the Dine and living in contemporary white society. The book has been listed among the "Best Books for Young Adults, 1996" by the American Library Association.

Joseph Bruchac (Abenaki)

Joseph Bruchac's interest in and love for Native American stories was fostered by his Abenaki grandfather and grandmother, with whom he lived as a boy. Their influence led to a productive career for Bruchac as an award-winning storyteller, writer, editor, and author of over thirty books of poetry, fiction, folktales, and legends. His writing has appeared in over four hundred journals and anthologies and has been translated into many languages. He has an earned doctorate from Union Graduate School in Ohio.

As the founding editor of the Greenfield Review Press, a respected publisher of original works by beginning and notable Native American writers, Bruchac is actively working to preserve Native American cultures through print and recorded media for adults and young people. He seeks the wisdom of Native American elders and teachers, and, through the Greenfield Review Press, provides a way for other Native American writers to polish their craft, share their work, and attend workshops.

All of Bruchac's books are recommended as sources with accurate information from a Native American perspective. His work has been well received within the Native American community and by critics outside of the Indian community. Bruchac cautions teachers to avoid books that suffer from what he calls "The Dances with Wolves Syndrome," in which all Indians are noble, and all white people are bad. He reminds us that any children's book that builds up one culture at the expense of another ultimately keeps racial tension alive (website address: http://199.95.184.10/Instructor/hot/multicultural.html#bruchac).

In *The Milky Way: A Cherokee Tale* (1995), Bruchac and Gayle Ross (illustrations by Cherokee artist Virginia Stroud) share a traditional Cherokee legend about how the Milky Way came to be. In the story, cornmeal is being stolen from an elderly man and woman. Their grandson decides to catch the thief, and sees a giant dog stealing the cornmeal. The people turn to an elderly woman with great wisdom, and, under her guidance, come together to scare the great dog away.

Several aspects of the story reflect its authenticity. First, the tale accurately reflects the esteem Native people show toward the elderly. "Surely no one in the village would steal from the elders?" the text reads. Within Native American cultures, the elderly have always occupied a special place because of their wisdom and age. Tribal members accord them great respect. The elderly are typically brought to live with their children and grandchildren when they are no longer able to physically care for themselves, rather than living alone in the care of a nurse or being placed in a geriatric care facility. Second, because of the prevalence within Native communities of the extended family, the relationship between grandparents and grandchildren is often quite special. In this story, the grandson's desire to help his grandparents by catching the thief rings true. Third, the people work together to scare off the dog who is stealing the cornmeal. The lifestyle of Native people is highly communal in nature. Native people work toward the common good, sharing in work and play. Award-winning artist Virginia Stroud's Cherokee-Creek heritage and her knowledge of Cherokee culture is evident in the style of the colorful clothing the book's characters wear. Her illustrations include children, adults, and the elderly. Although it may seem a small point from an outsider point-of-view, Stroud is careful to show the people beating the drum with a drumstick. An inaccurate but very popular stereotype is that of the Indian beating a drum with the hands, which is not done by any tribe within the United States. The book is a winner of the Scientific American Award.

Iroquois Stories: Heroes and Heroines, Monsters and Magic (1988) is a collection of thirty-one stories from the tradition of the Haudenasaunee (People of the Long House). The stories were first recorded by J. N. B. Hewitt, Arthur Parker, Ray Fadden, David Cusick, and Jesse Cornplanter, all of Iroquois ancestry. The book begins with a valuable introduction about the history of the Iroquois Confederacy, which includes the Mohawk, Oneida, Onondaga, Cayuga, Seneca, and Tuscarora Nations. Bruchac discusses the role of the storyteller in Native communities. The stories in the collection are based on the oral tradition, and range from pourquoi to transformation tales.

Michael Dorris (Modoc)

Michael Dorris is an accomplished adult author who has successfully made the transition into writing books for children. Dorris began writing in 1977 while teaching at Dartmouth College and is well-known for his writings about Native Americans. Among his well-known books for adults are *The Broken Cord* (1989) and *Crown of Columbus* (1991), coauthored with his wife, author Louise Erdrich.

Dorris recalls that as a child, "I seldom identified with Indians in books because for the most part they were utterly predictable . . . They didn't remind me of anyone I knew, especially my cousins on the reservation" (p. 140).

Dorris's first book for young readers, *Morning Girl* (1992), is set on a Bahamian island in 1492. Written in the first person, twelve-year-old Morning Girl and ten-year-old Star Boy share their perspectives about themselves and their family members in alternating chapters. These Taino children provide a very realistic and well-balanced story about what life might have been like for Native people before Columbus arrived. The simple text is well written and provides ample information about the day-to-day activities of Taino families, and the strong family and community bonds that are typical of Native culture. The reader gains insight into practices such as the natural and respectful way in which Star Boy received his name.

Dorris is careful not to paint a picture of an idyllic Taino lifestyle free of hardship and tragedy. In the story, Morning Girl's mother loses a baby; Star Boy's friend, Red Feather, has parents who argue and fight; and the community experiences a fierce storm that destroys their homes. Each of these incidents is presented without being overly dramatic. Critics have praised and criticized *Morning Girl*. The review in Kirkus identifies the book as one to be cherished for its compassion and humanity. Thomas's (1992) comments echo those of others: "This novel avoids the coarse sermons that typify the flood of new books about the encounter between the Taino people and Columbus. It avoids the preaching and cuteness to which most writers of adult books resort when they turn to children's literature. Besides avoiding these pitfalls, it is brilliant, subtle fiction." Biglow (1994) writes "Dorris missed an opportunity to portray lives characterized both by personal freedom and social responsibility; second, because he leaves readers ill-equipped to reflect the full range of social consequences initiated by Columbus's arrival on Guanahani. Dorris's desire to tell a simple brother/sister story is understandable, but he does so at the expense of suggesting how a richer community life could nurture such a relationship" (p. 274).

In *Guests* (1994), Dorris writes about the first Thanksgiving, from the perspective of a pre-adolescent Indian boy named Moss. He questions why his father invited strangers to the village's special harvest meal. Moss is the only person in the village who senses that this event will bring unsettling changes. At the same time, Moss struggles with thoughts and feelings of personal uncertainty typical of adolescent children. Moss is caught up in a whirlwind of change and goes into the forest where he meets a porcupine who counsels him, and a girl, Trouble, who is also experiencing turmoil. This coming-of-age story, coupled with the theme of cultural conflict, has been favorably reviewed in *Publisher's Weekly,* Booklist, and Kirkus.

Virginia Driving Hawk Sneve (Sioux)

Sneve collected poems from several tribes across the country and published them in a critically acclaimed anthology, *Dancing Teepees: Poems of American Indian Youth* (1988). The poems in the anthology are authored by Native Americans, and Sneve is careful to record the author's tribal affiliation with each poem.

Most recently, Sneve has worked with Holiday House, writing the First Americans series of books. Each book focuses on a specific tribe. Sneve begins each book with the creation tale told among the people of whom she writes, provides information about historical life, initial contact with the white men, and conflicts with the U.S. Government. The final pages in each book give information about contemporary lifestyles. Among the titles in the series are the following: *The Sioux* (1993), *The Navajos* (1993), *The Hopis* (1995), *The Seminoles* (1994), *The Nez Perce,* and *The Iroquois.* Of *The Seminoles, School Library Journal* says that it is "An inviting and readable title, with plenty of information. Upon their publication, the Bulletin of the Center for Children's Books recommended the first two titles in the series The Sioux and The Navajo because Sneve successfully incorporates similarities among tribes such as reverence for land, while also highlighting differences such as the different creation stories specific to each tribe." Booklist identifies *The Sioux* and *The Navajos as* "excellent introductions" to these cultures. The illustrations are done by Ronald Himler. The Bulletin of the Center for Children's Books says "Himler's artwork balances the aesthetic with the instructive, the past with the present, in compositions that are steeped in plains or desert hues and are vibrant with action." Each book includes quotes from historical and contemporary members of the tribe and a map outlining the geographical location of the tribe.

Sneve was awarded the North American Indian Prose Award for her book, *Completing the Circle* (1995). In this young adult novel, Sneve explores the history of the women in her family. She beautifully weaves together autobiographical information and the vivid stories told by members of her family.

CONTROVERSIAL AND PROBLEMATIC BOOKS

Most of the books in the following discussions are books that have become favorites of parents, teachers, and librarians. Reasons for this status vary—perhaps the illustrations are beautifully rendered; perhaps the text is appealing because of its literary value; or perhaps the book has received a prestigious award like the Caldecott, or been featured on a children's literature program like Reading Rainbow. Many of the books have received favorable recommendations from children's literary journals. Specific objections to the books will be articulated, and background information provided to help others gain an understanding of why the book is problematic as a text about Native American people. The fact that these books are so popular and sell so well, even after being criticized by Native people, suggests that Native people, teachers, parents, authors, and scholars have a great deal of work to do in terms of informing and educating the public about appropriate representations of Native Americans. Before the general public can give up their false but dearly held concepts of what it means to be Native American, much education and understanding must develop.

In 1992, a rare event occurred: a children's book was among the top-selling books in the country. The book, *Brother Eagle Sister Sky* (Jeffers, 1991), carries a strong environmental consciousness message, and this may be the basis for its appeal. The text is a speech widely attributed to Chief Seattle of the Duwamish tribe of the Pacific Coast. The accompanying illustrations are done by Susan Jeffers. In an interview about the book, Jeffers stated she did not know what Seattle had said and that the speech in the book was written to illuminate the strong relationship the Indian people *had* with the environment. Although it is an award-winning picture book, there are two significant problems: one with the text, the other with the illustrations. First, the text presented in the book is actually a rewrite of the original speech delivered by Chief Seattle in January of 1854. The text in the book was the one composed by screenwriter Ted Perry for "Home," a historical epic about the Northwest rain forest, televised in 1971 (Jones and Sawhill, 1992). According to Nancy Zussy, state librarian at Washington State Library, different versions of the speech have appeared throughout history. The first version appeared in the *Seattle Sunday Star* on October 29, 1887, in a column written by Dr. Henry A. Smith. Since Seattle did not speak English, his words were translated into Chinook Jargon, and then into English. Smith reconstructed the speech from notes taken at the time. In the late 1960s, poet William Arrowsmith rewrote the speech in a more poetic style. The third version is the Perry composition, which was written as a letter to President Franklin Pierce. In truth, there was no actual letter from Chief Seattle to President Pierce. The final version was a shortened version of the Perry script, and was exhibited at Expo '74 in

Spokane, Washington. Many would argue that the beauty of the illustrations and the environmental message of the text overcome the stereotypical aspects of the book. However, other outstanding environmental awareness books are available, and teachers should select among them, especially if Native American students are in their class.

Ten Little Rabbits (Grossman, 1991) is beautifully illustrated by Sylvia Long. The book received numerous awards, including the International Reading Association Award for Children's Book of the Year. It has received favorable reviews in highly regarded children's literature journals and is often listed in catalogs of multicultural literature (Short and Fox, 1995). Each page depicts rabbits dressed in Native American clothing specific to a single tribe, supposedly engaged in a Native American activity. It includes a glossary, which seemingly adds to its credibility as a book providing accurate information about Native Americans. The glossary refers to each tribe depicted in the book, providing what Grossman believes to be information that supports the text and illustrations. However, the information she provides is culturally insensitive and works toward supporting popular stereotypes. For example, in the entry about the Tewa Pueblo Indians of New Mexico, Grossman writes that the Pueblo Indians "stage" a corn dance. The Pueblo people do not "stage" dances. The dance is actually a ceremonial prayer-in-motion offered to ask for a plentiful harvest. The dancers do not "leap and stamp to wake up the spirits." This phrase brings to mind the stereotype of the Indian wildly dancing about and leaping on one foot, not the quietly reverent and reflective repose of the Pueblo people participating in the dance. The illustration of the Pueblo Indian rabbits performing a corn dance is also inappropriate. Long's two lone rabbits dance facing each other. In reality, the dance is performed by many dancers, forming long rows in which they all face in the same direction. In addition to concerns about the book's authenticity, a strong objection to the text is that it is much too close to the chant "Ten Little Indians," which most teachers have stopped singing in their preschool classrooms. Finally, *Ten Little Rabbits* suggests to children that, simply by putting on Native American clothing, anyone or anything can become a Native American.

Award-winning author/illustrator Gerald McDermott's book, *Arrow to the Sun*, is a popular book often seen on bookshelves in early childhood classrooms. McDermott was awarded the Caldecott Medal for this book, and Horn Book hailed the book as visually eloquent. The tale is attributed to the Pueblo Indians, and is about a young boy who goes on a quest to find his father. He is fashioned into an arrow, and shot to the sun, who is his father. The sun tells the boy that only by successfully negotiating trials in four different kivas will he prove that he is the sun's child. The boy returns to the Pueblo and begins the trials. Emerging successfully, he brings a dance to the people, which they do every year to honor the sun. Like *Annie and the Old One,* it is a captivating story. However, kivas are places of ceremony and instruction—not places of trial. Thus, an important aspect of the story is totally inappropriate and provides incorrect information about the sacred nature of Pueblo kivas. In the early part of the story, the boy is ostracized by his friends because he has no father living in the Pueblo. This, too, is an inaccurate portrayal of the Pueblo people who do not ostracize members of their community.

One of the most popular series in which stereotypes of Indians appear is the *Little House on the Prairie* (Wilder, 1981). This series has been reprinted numerous times and is available in paperback. It has almost been immortalized on film in the long-running "Little House" television series now in syndicated reruns on many cable stations. The book series is a moving saga of a close-knit family: Ma, Pa, and Laura. Their family is portrayed as Christian, loving, and caring. Pa is brave, Ma is nurturing, and Laura is adventurous. They are fine, upstanding Americans. These images are juxtaposed with the images of Indians who aimlessly roam the land like animals and engage in "savage" dancing rituals under the darkness of night. They are uncivilized and cannot communicate well. They run around half naked, and worst of all, they smell horrible. They are not fine, upstanding Americans, and it is questionable if they are even human.

The reader accompanies Ma, Pa, and Laura on their journey as they encounter a land with wild animals and savage Indians. The reader comes away from this literary experience totally identifying with the white family. The Indians in the Little House series represent the standard negative stereotype and are so undesirable that no reader cares to identify with them. They are nothing more than an obstacle to the settlers who have a "God given" right to this land, and are therefore expendable. The subtle seeds of the doctrine of manifest destiny are planted by this series.

Written by two acclaimed children's author/illustrators, *Knots on a Counting Rope* (Martin & Archambault, 1990) is a popular book, easily obtainable in mainstream bookstores. Favorably reviewed by *School Library Journal*, it was featured on the television series, Reading Rainbow, and carries the Reading Rainbow logo on its cover. In the book, an elderly grandfather tells a young boy, "Boy-Strength-of-Blue Horses," about his birth. Although the story is engaging, Slapin and Seale (1991) criticize the writer/illustrator for failing to adequately research the culture they are attempting to depict. Primarily suggestive of the Navajo tribe, the illustrations are an inappropriate mix of artifacts from many different tribes. For example, the traditional Navajo men in the story are shown with hair styles typically worn by members of the Atsina, Blackfeet, Mandan, and Piegan tribes (a single braid near the brow, with the rest of the hair hanging lose about the shoulders). On two different pages, Pueblo people are shown attending a horse race wearing traditional clothing, as though it were common practice to walk about in these clothes which are worn only on ceremonial occasions.

Annie and the Old One (Miles, 1971) won several awards. It was a Newbery Honor Book, an ALA Notable Children's Book, and winner of the Christopher Award. *Horn Book Magazine* described it as "A poignant, understated story of a very real child, set against a background of Navajo traditions and contemporary Indian life." In the story, we meet a young Navajo girl, Annie, and her grandmother, the "Old One." Grandmother has told Annie and her family that she will die as soon as Annie's mother finishes a rug she is weaving. Annie does not want her grandmother to die and carries out plans to delay the completion of the rug and thereby prolong her grandmother's life: she misbehaves in school hoping her parents will be called to the school and away from the weaving; she turns the sheep out of the corral, thinking the family will spend the day searching for them. When these attempts to delay the weaving fail, she gets up during the night and removes the day's weaving from the loom. Her grandmother discovers her mischief and talks quietly with her about the circle of life. Annie understands and returns to the hogan, where she begins to weave, joining in the circle.

Although the book has several strong points, from an informed, Native American perspective, there are many aspects of the book which are objectionable. Slapin and Seale (1988) direct attention to the clothing Annie wears to school. Contemporary children reared in traditional ways would not wear traditional clothing to school—the child would wear jeans and shirts. Slapin and Seale (1988) also question the term "God's dog," which is used in the book to describe the coyote, who guards the hogan. God's dog is not a Navajo name for coyotes, and within the Navajo culture, coyotes cause feelings of unease—not comfort. A Navajo child reared in traditional ways would not be untruthful or dishonest, as Annie is. Navajo children are taught the virtues of truth and honesty. To be untruthful or dishonest brings shame to their relatives (Kluckhohn, 1974). Further, Slapin and Seale question the authenticity of the illustrations, which are not authentic representations of Navajo clothing, hair styles, or blanket designs.

This book is popular among librarians and teachers. The illustrations are beautifully rendered, with attention given to the details of land forms found in the southwest. The reader can recognize the shapes of the hogans and the garments of those depicted as Navajo. However, the premise of the story has been fashioned from a non-Navajo interpretation of how a Navajo child would react to the pending death of a beloved grandparent.

Friendship's First Thanksgiving (Accorsi, 1992) is a traditional story of the Pilgrims in the New World, with an unusual twist: it is told from the perspective of a dog named Friendship. Through his eyes, we learn of the difficult journey and hardships of the first winter. We learn about the meeting between Samoset and the Pilgrims, and how the Indians helped the Pilgrims learn to plant corn. Finally, Friendship tells the reader about the meal the Pilgrims invited the Indians to share with them. Friendship describes the dances the Indians did, and how he made friends with the Indian dog, with whom he eventually has a family. At the close of the book, Accorsi states that he relied heavily upon the freedom of artistic license when he illustrated this book, and that the characters are not portrayed with any accuracy. Evidence that Accorsi failed to conduct research before writing and illustrating this book is present in several instances. Friendship says, "It was exciting to see the Indians dressed in their finest clothing." But the "finest clothing" is not shown. The Pilgrims greet the barechested Indians, who arrive carrying food. They all wear one or two feathers in their hair. However, on the next page, where the Pilgrims and Indians are seated at a table, the Indians wear full headdresses and have painted their faces. Friendship says, "The Indians danced and told stories" as though the Indians were entertaining the Pilgrims. Indian dances are not performed to entertain, but are typically a form of prayer and spiritual worship. Further, the Pilgrims are shown with features that easily distinguish them from each other, such as variations in clothing and hair styles. The Indians all look exactly alike with no distinguishing facial features. In the final page of the book, Accorsi makes light of the solemn tradition of naming among Native people. Friendship and the Indian dog have six puppies. Three are given what Friendship calls "Indian" names: Chase the Bird, Chase the Rabbit, and Chase His Own Tail. The other three puppies are given "white" names: Pal, Spit, and Rover. Among Native people, the tradition of giving names is sacred. Much prayer and thought goes into the process, which is no less significant than a Jewish child receiving a Hebrew name, or a Christian child being baptized with a Christian name. That any author would trivialize the sacred naming traditions of any culture, as Accorsi has done, is offensive.

Finally, we examine *Indian in the Cupboard* (1995) by Lynn Reid Banks. Many view this story as a purely imaginative tale that captures the attention of children and encourages them to read. Others (Caldwell-Wood & Mitten, 1991; Slapin, 1994) are shocked and dismayed that the blatant racism in this book is overlooked, accepted, and promoted as required reading in many classrooms. *Indian in the Cupboard* is objectionable to most Native Americans because it promotes the stereotypical image of Native people, and because it presents Little Bear as an adult Indian man who is the plaything of Omri, a white child. Little Bear is simply identified as Iroquois, but there are six distinct Iroquois nations. He is portrayed as a savage as he grunts, raves madly, and approaches every situation with anger and violence. His speech patterns have the jaw-breaking quality from early Western movies. His dress is the typical headdress and fringed buckskin and he lives in a tipi. In all fairness to Banks, she has written a suspenseful story that holds one's imagination and curiosity. However, the profound image of a young white boy controlling the life of a grown Indian man serves to support and promote the notion of white superiority and domination at the expense of Indian people. The book is often part of whole language and/or literature-based reading instruction in schools. Teachers may be unaware of its problematic aspects for Native people. Or, perhaps, the issues are brushed aside because of its literary merits. But, as with *Brother Eagle Sister Sky*, other books are available that engage children without demeaning or demoralizing Native American people.

STRATEGIES FOR USING NATIVE AMERICAN LITERATURE

Teachers should continue to select both fiction and nonfiction Native American books to use in their classrooms, and should endeavor to select those recommended by individuals who are knowledgeable about Native culture. These individuals may be Native, but Native American identity is not necessary if the reviewer is knowledgeable. The books must be made accessible to the children, not only at specific times of the year (such as Thanksgiving), but throughout the school year. Books may be introduced as read-alouds, shelved in the recreational reading area, or may be assigned readings.

With Native American people and the multitude of ways American society uses Native icons, place names, and the prevalence of stereotypes in media and literature, the "teachable moment" occurs frequently. Teachers dedicated to providing children with accurate information about Native Americans will take advantage of these opportunities to correct prior learning.

Early Childhood and Elementary Education

This level includes children from birth through age eight, when children are typically in second or third grade. At this age, children prefer picture books on familiar topics such as children, families, and animals. Children who are learning to recognize the letters of the alphabet can use Tapahonso's *Navajo ABC* in addition to more mainstream alphabet books. As words from the Navajo language are introduced, children can be encouraged to provide words from their own Native languages, or talk about foods their families prepare. Using this book can convey to young children that the Native American cultures and languages, such as the Navajo, are not extinct. It can also serve to affirm not only the Navajo culture, but the culture of the children within the class. They may be prompted to design their own personal alphabet book with words and illustrations specific to their own culture and lives. A class project could involve finding out about all the different words that can be used to describe a garment worn by females, or perhaps the different precious and semi-precious stones and other materials used to make jewelry around the world.

Before reading several books about contemporary Native American children to the class, ask the children to brainstorm all they know about Native Americans, and make a list of their statements. After reading the books, make a second list. Compare and discuss the two lists.

Upper Elementary and Middle School

This level includes children from fourth grade through eighth grade, when children are ready to enter junior high school. Cognitive abilities of older children make it possible to engage them in discussions about stereotypes and the harmful effects they have, not only on Native children, but on all children. After reading several culturally specific books, these children will be able to look at a stereotyped illustration and identify the elements that are out of place. Teachers may want to pull together several books with stereotypes and develop a lesson on identifying stereotypes. A culminating collaborative activity can involve the students in a letter-writing campaign, in which they express their opinions and thoughts on books that contain stereotypes (Ramsey, 1995). These letters can be directed to book publishers. Other letters targeting stereotyped images in society can be directed to newspaper editors, television and movie producers, and toy companies.

Provide opportunities for non-Native children to correspond with Native children. The Internet can be used to locate individual children or entire classes who are willing to exchange letters to develop cross-cultural understandings. The classroom teacher can focus on a specific tribe, the children can read books about that tribe, and then, perhaps, an Internet pen-pal exchange can be established with children from that tribe. This activity will give the children the opportunity to verify the knowledge they gained from the books and engage in meaningful discussions with Native children about their lives.

After reading many books about Native Americans, create a chart that will facilitate discussion about similarities and differences among cultures. For each title, list the genre, character, conflict, and cultural value (Cullinan and Galda, 1994).

When creating cultural artifacts introduced in a children's book, conduct research to make certain the item is not sacred, thereby rendering its production sacrilegious. Standards of sensitivity applied to Christianity and other religions should apply equally to Native religions. For example, making a false mask is tantamount to making a chalice with glitter and styrofoam cups.

CONCLUSION

As noted earlier, the greatest need at this point in time is for more books that provide a contemporary perspective of Native American people, particularly Native American children. These books are best written by Native American authors (Cullinan and Galda, 1994), but non-Native people have demonstrated that careful research and sensitive writing can result in a quality children's book that should also be a part of the classroom library. Children must learn that, as Allen writes, ". . . Indians put Pampers on their babies! They watch T.V.!" (Allen, 1987, p. 6).

Teachers working toward building their collections of Native American children's literature must bear in mind that books about Native Americans recognized by the staff at Reading Rainbow or other such entities may be problematic. Books that become best sellers, as did *Brother Eagle Sister Sky*, and books written by giants in the field of children's literature, such as Bill Martin Jr. (*Knots on a Counting Rope*), can be fraught with problems. Knowing this may cause some teachers to become frustrated in their efforts to provide quality materials. The best tools a teacher can use to aid in selecting books about Native Americans are selection and evaluation guides written by Native people. It is also helpful to read book reviews written by Native people. There are alternatives to favorites that are of higher quality. One notable example is the 1996 book, *Giving Thanks: A Native American Good Morning Message* by Chief Jake Swamp, which has been favorably reviewed by Kirkus, the *San Francisco Chronicle*, the CCBC, and is among the books listed by the Bank Street College Children's Book Committee in "Children's Books of the Year."

Native children must learn that being Indian and being successful are not mutually exclusive (Szasz, 1992). Non-Native children must learn that Native Americans are alive and well in the 1990s. Quality children's literature can help both groups of children.

GUIDES FOR SELECTING NATIVE AMERICAN CHILDREN'S LITERATURE

Materials selected for classroom use should be carefully examined before using them with children. Because there are over 500 different tribes within the United States, the most authentic book, toy, or dramatic play materials will clearly identify a specific tribe. When the clothing, hairstyles, homes, modes of transportation, environment, and lifestyle are accurate, they can be described as "culturally specific" and will serve well to educate children about one tribe of the larger group identified as Native American people.

Educators must have a clear understanding of how to evaluate material about Native American people before using it with students. This understanding evolves out of a strong desire to develop critical thinking skills that can be used to evaluate material about Native Americans. Standard evaluation measures (a text must be well written, the material should be engaging and age appropriate, text and illustration should be accurate and should reinforce each other) must be used in combination with the following list of questions that specifically relate to material about Native American people.

The following evaluation criteria was adapted from *Unlearning Indian Stereotypes: A Teaching Unit for Elementary Teachers and Librarians*, by the Council on Interracial Books for Children; *American Indian Stereotypes in the World of Children: A Reader and Bibliography*, by A. Hirschfelder; and *Shadows of the Indian: Stereotypes in American Culture*, by R. W. Stedman.

Questions to ask yourself when looking at picture books and posters

In alphabet books, is I for Indian? Is E for Eskimo?

In counting books, are Indians—or animals dressed as Indians—objects for counting?

Are children shown dressed up with feathers, running around wildly, "playing Indian?"

Are animals dressed up like Indians?

Do characters have ridiculous names like "Indian Two Feet" or "Little Chief?"

Are Native people shown as menacing savages?

Do the illustrations contain a hodge-podge of artifacts from several different tribes?

In the text, are Native people referred to with adjectives conveying negative, derogatory traits that would cause fear in a young child?

Do all the Native people look exactly alike, with no variation in physical features?

Is the source of conflict identified in books that portray White and Native people in battle?

Do the Native people speak in short choppy sentences, or in gutteral tones?

In contemporary stories, are the Native characters "cute" or in need of rescue from their traditional way of life?

Are elders, who are significant family members in Native cultures, included in stories about family life?

Is the color selected for the skin color of Native people RED, rather than a more realistic hue?

Are Native characters dressed in buckskin and feathers, dancing wildly on one foot?

Are Native characters shown to have magical, mystical powers?

Is there evidence the author has researched the tribe of which he/she writes or illustrates?

Is the "living in harmony with the earth" environmental message of the Native characters overdone?

Questions to ask yourself when evaluating "Indian village" toy sets or dramatic play dress-up sets

Is the name of the tribe specified in the literature accompanying the set?

Do all the figures belong to the same tribe?

Are infant figures called papoose instead of baby?

Are the female figures called princess or squaw instead of woman or girl?

Are the male figures called chief, buck, or brave instead of man or boy?

Are the men shown with savage expressions, wielding tomahawks?

Do the human figures fold their arms over their chests or sit with crossed legs?

Are totem poles, buffaloes, teepees, and weaving looms all part of the same set?

Is the theme one in which settlers or cowboys must defend themselves from Indian attack?

Are the clothing items in the set from a single tribe?

Are the names for the clothing items included, and how/when the item is worn specified?

RESOURCES

Professional Books

Byler, M. G. (1973). *American Indian authors for young readers: A selective bibliography*. New York: Association of American Indian Affairs.

Council on Interracial Books for Children. (1977). *Unlearning Indian stereotypes: A teaching unit for elementary teachers and children's librarians*. New York: The Racism and Sexism Resource Center for Educators, a division of the Council on Interracial Books for Children.

Hirschfelder, Arlene B. (1982). *American Indian stereotypes in the world of children: A reader and bibliography*. Metuchen, NJ: Scarecrow Press.

Kuipers, B. J. (1991). *American Indian reference books for children and young adults*. Englewood, CO: Libraries Unlimited, Inc.

Rethinking Schools (1991). *Rethinking Columbus: Teaching about the 500th anniversary of Columbus's arrival in America*. Milwaukee, WI: Rethinking Schools.

Slapin, D. and Seale, D. (1992). *Through Indian eyes: The Native experience in books for children*. Philadelphia: New Society Publishers.

Internet (Information Superhighway)

Teachers and librarians can also find valuable information about children's literature on the Internet. The Cooperative Children's Book Center has a home page <http://www.soemadison.wisc.edu/ccbc/> that provides information about the Center, and links to other sites related to children's literature. CCBC also maintains a listserve which serves as an electronic forum to encourage awareness and discussion of issues in literature for children and young adults.

Teachers can visit a home page on the web called "Native American Sites" <http://www.pitt.edu/~lmitten/indians.html>. This site contains links to the home pages of individual Native nations, Native organizations and businesses, Native journals and newspapers, and a calendar of Native pow-wows and festivals.

"Native Web" includes journals, literature and bibliographies. The URL is <http://kuhttp.cc.ukans.edu/~marc/native_main.html>.

"NativeLit-L" is a listserve devoted to discussions about Native American literature. To subscribe, send an e-mail message to: listserv@cornell.edu. In the body of the message, include this line: subscribe NativeLit-L Your Name.

Native American Small Presses and Distributors

The following list was prepared with the assistance of information provided by the Center for Children's Books in Madison, Wisconsin. Other sources consulted include *Rethinking Columbus: Teaching About the 500th Anniversary of Columbus's Arrival in America*, published in 1991 by Rethinking Schools, Ltd., and *Through Indian Eyes: The Native Experience in Books for Children*, published in 1992 by New Society Publishers. As of press date, address information was correct.

Akwesansne Notes, Mohawk Nation, P.O. Box 196, Rooseveltown, NY 13683. Telephone: (518) 358–9531.

Anishinable Reading Materials, Indian Education Department, Central Administration Building, Lake Avenue & Second Street, Duluth, MN 55802.

Annick Press, 15 Patricia Avenue, Willowdale, Ontario, Canada, M2M 1H9. Telephone: (416) 221–4802.

Children's Book Press, 6400 Hollis Street, Emeryville, CA.

Choctaw Heritage Press, Mississippi Band of Choctaw Indians, Route 7, Box 21, Philadelphia, MS 39350. Telephone: (601) 656–5251.

Cross Cultural Education Center, P.O. Box 92, Welling, OK 74471.

Daybreak Star, P.O. Box 99100, Seattle, WA 98199. Telephone: (206) 285–4425.

Fifth House, 620 Duchess Street, Saskatoon, Saskatchewan, Canada S7K OR1.

Greenfield Review Press, 2 Middle Grove Road, P.O. Box 308, Greenfield Center, NY 12833. Telephone: (518) 584–1728.

Indian Country Communications. Rt. 2 Box 2900–A, Hayward, WI 54843.

Minnesota Chippewa Tribe, P. O. Box 217, Cass Lake, MN 56633.

Navajo Curriculum Center, Rough Rock Demonstration School, Chinle, AZ 86503.

New Seed Press, P.O. Box 9488, Berkeley, CA 94709. Telephone: (415) 540–7556.

OYATE, 2702 Mathews, Berkeley, CA 94702.

Pemmican Publications, Unit 2—1635 Burrows Avenue, Winnipeg, Manitoba Canada, R2X OT1. Telephone: (204) 589-6346.

Sierra Oaks Publishing Company, P.O. Box 255354, Sacramento, CA 95865-5354.

Sister Vision Press, P.O. Box 217, Station E, Toronto, Ontario, Canada M6H 4E2.

Theytus Books, Ltd., P.O. Box 218, Penticon, BC, Canada V2A 6K3. Telephone (604) 493-7181.

Waapone Publishing, Lakefield, Ontario, Canada KOL 2H0.

REFERENCES

Allen, P. G. (1987). I climb the mesas in my dreams. In J. Bruchac (Ed.), *Survival this way*. Tucson: Sun Tracks and University of Arizona Press.

Begay, S. W. (1995, June 24). Indians out of the cupboard: Native authors speak out. Program of the American Indian Library Association and the Office of Literacy and Outreach Services: Committee on Library Services for American Indian People, Chicago.

Brant, B. (1992). Grandmothers of a new world. In B. Slapin. and D. Seale (Eds.), *Through Indian eyes: The Native experience in books for children.* Philadelphia: New Society Publishers.

Bruchac, J. (1987). *Survival this way*. Tucson: Sun Tracks and University of Arizona Press.

Burke, E. M. (1990). *Literature for the young child*. Boston: Allyn and Bacon.

Byler, M. G. (1982). Introduction to American Indian authors for young readers. In A. B. Hirschfelder (Ed.), *American Indian stereotypes in the world of children: A reader and bibliography*. Metuchen, NJ: Scarecrow Press, Inc.

Caldwell-Wood, N. and Mitten, L. (1991). "I" is not for Indian: The portrayal of Native Americans in books for young people. Program of the ALA/

OLOS Subcommittee for Library Services to American Indian People, American Indian Library Association, Atlanta, June 1991.

Campbell, J. (1988). *The power of myth*. New York: Anchor Books.

Council on Interracial Books for Children. (1981). *Unlearning "Indian" stereotypes, A teaching unit for elementary teachers and children's librarians*. New York: The Racism and Sexism Resource Center for Educators, a division of the Council on Interracial Books for Children.

Cullinan, B. E. and Galda, L. (1994). *Literature and the young child*. Fort Worth: Harcourt Brace College Publishers.

Derman-Sparks, L. (1989). *Anti-bias curriculum: Tools for empowering young children*. Washington, DC: National Association for the Education of Young Children.

Dorris, M. (1994). *Paper trail*. New York: HarperCollins.

Dunaway, D. K. (1985). *Writing the Southwest*. New York: Plume.

Ewers, J. C. (1982). The emergence of the Plains Indians as the symbol of the North American Indian. In A. Hirschfelder (Ed.), *American Indian stereotypes in the world of children: A reader and bibliography*. Metuchen, NJ: The Scarecrow Press, Inc.

Flaste, R. (1982). American Indians: Still a stereotype to many children. In A. Hirschfelder (Ed.), *American Indian stereotypes in the world of children: A reader and bibliography*. Metuchen, NJ: The Scarecrow Press, Inc.

Hearne, B. (1993). Cite the source: Reducing cultural chaos in picture books, Part One. *School Library Journal*, July 1993, pp. 22–27.

Hirschfelder, A. (1982). *American Indian stereotypes in the world of children: A reader and bibliography*. Metuchen, NJ: The Scarecrow Press, Inc.

Hodgkinson, H. (1992). The current condition of Native Americans. *ERIC Digest*, ED 348202.

Horning, K. T., Kruse, G. M., and Schliesman, M. (1996). *CCBC Choices 1995*. Wisconsin: University Publications.

Howard, N. (1985). Crow ducks and other wandering talk. In D. M. Guss (Ed.), *The language of the birds: Tales, text and poems of interspecies communication*. San Francisco: North Point Press.

Jones, Malcolm Jr., and Sawhill, Ray. (1992, May 4). Just too good to be true: Another reason to beware of false eco-prophets. *Newsweek*.

Katz, P. A. (1976). The acquisition of racial attitudes in children. In P. A. Katz (Ed.), *Towards the elimination of racism* (pp. 125–154). New York: Pergamon.

Keeshing-Tobias, L. (1992). Not just entertainment. In B. Slapin, and D. Seale (Eds.), *Through Indian eyes: The Native experience in books for children*. Philadelphia: New Society Publishers.

Kingsolver, B. (1995). The spaces between. In *High tide in Tucson*. New York: HarperCollins.

Kluckhohn, C. and Leighton, D. (1974, 1946). *The Navajo*. Cambridge: Harvard University Press.

League of Women Voters. (1982). Children's impressions of American Indians: A survey of suburban kindergarten and fifth grade children: Conclusions. In A. Hirschfelder (Ed.), *American Indian stereotypes in the world of children*. Metuchen, NJ: Scarecrow Press.

Lemay, J. A. L. (1993). *Did Pocahontas save Captain John Smith?* Athens: University of Georgia Press.

McCann, D. (1993). Native Americans in books for the young. In V. Harris (Ed.), *Teaching multicultural literature in grades K–8*. Norwood, MA: Christopher-Gordon Publishers, Inc.

McCarty, T. L. (1995). What's wrong with *Ten Little Rabbits? The New Advocate, 8*(2), pp. 97–98.

McElmeel, S. L. (1993). Toward a real multiculturalism. *School Library Journal, 39*.

Mossiker, F. (1976). *Pocahontas: The life and the legend*. New York: Alfred A. Knopf.

Ortiz, S. (1990). Interview in L. Coltelli (Ed.), *Winged words: American Indian writers speak*. Lincoln: University of Nebraska Press.

Ortiz, S. (1987). The story never ends. In J. Bruchac (Ed.), *Survival this way: Interviews with American Indian poets*. Tucson: Sun Tracks and University of Arizona Press.

Ramsey, P. G. (1995). Growing up with the contradictions of race and class. *Young Children, 50*(6), pp. 18–22.

Reddish, J. G. (1995, Spring). Pocahontas. *Tribal College 6*.

Reyhner, J. (1992). Plans for dropout prevention and special school support services for American Indian and Alaska Native students. In P. Cahape and C. B. Howley (Eds.), *Indian nations at risk: Listening to the people: Summaries of papers commissioned by the Indian Nations at Risk Task Force of the U.S. Department of Education*. Charleston, WV: ERIC Clearinghouse on Rural Education and Small Schools, Appalachia Educational Laboratory.

Roback, D. (1996). The year of the paperback. *Publishers Weekly*, March 4, pp. 524–531.

Ruoff, A. L. B. (1990). *American Indian literatures: An introduction, bibliographic review, and selected bibliography*. New York: Modern Language Association of America.

Shaffer, Denise D. (1993). Making Native American lessons meaningful. *Childhood Education 69*(4), pp. 201–203.

Short, K. G. and Fox, D. L. (1995). Editors Note in "What's Wrong with *Ten Little Rabbits*." By Teresa L. McCarty. *The New Advocate, 8*(2), p. 97.

Skinner, L. (1992). Teaching through traditions: Incorporating Native languages and cultures into curricula. In P. Cahape and C. B. Howley (Eds.), *Indian nations at risk: Listening to the people: Summaries of papers commissioned by the Indian Nations at Risk Task Force of the U.S. Department of Education*. Charleston, WV: ERIC Clearinghouse on Rural Education and Small Schools, Appalachia Educational Laboratory.

Slapin, B. and Seale, D. (1992). *Through Indian eyes: The Native experience in books for children*. Philadelphia: New Society Publishers.

Sneve, V. D. H. (1995). *Completing the circle*. Lincoln, Nebraska: University of Nebraska Press.

Stedman, R. W. (1982). *Shadows of the Indian: Stereotypes in American culture*. Norman, Oklahoma: University of Oklahoma Press.

Szasz, M. C. (1992). Current conditions in American Indian and Alaska Native communities. In P. Cahape and C. B. Howley (Eds.), *Indian nations at risk: Listening to the people: Summaries of papers commissioned by the Indian Nations at Risk Task Force of the U.S. Department of Education*. Charleston, WV: ERIC Clearinghouse on Rural Education and Small Schools, Appalachia Educational Laboratory.

Wall, S. and Arden, H. (Eds.). (1990). *Wisdom keepers*. Hillboro, Oregon: Beyond Words Publishing, Inc.

Whitt, L. A. (1995). Cultural imperialism and the marketing of Native America. *American Indian Culture and Research Journal, 19*(3), pp. 1–31.

Zussy, Nancy. (1993). Memo to requestors of Chief Seattle's "Ecology" speech. Olympia, Washington: Washington State Library. (It can be found on the World Wide Web. The URL is: <http://www.cris.com/~nlthomas/history/seattle1.html>.)

Children's Books Cited

Accorsi, W. (1992). *Friendship's first Thanksgiving*. New York: Holiday House.

Alexander, M. (1969). *Blackboard bear*. New York: Dial Press.

Banks, Lynn Reid. (1995). *Indian in the cupboard*. New York: Avon.

Begay, S. (1992). *Ma'ii and Cousin Horned Toad: A traditional Navajo story*. New York: Scholastic.

Begay, S. (1995). *Navajo: Visions and voices across the mesa*. New York: Scholastic.

Bridwell, N. (1986). *Clifford's Halloween*. New York: Scholastic.

Bruchac, J. (1988). *Iroquois stories: Heroes and heroines, monsters and magic*. New York: Crossing Press.

Bruchac, J. (1993). *Fox song*. New York: Philomel Books.

Bruchac, J. (1995). *The Milky Way: A Cherokee tale*. New York: Dial Books for Young Readers.

Cohen, C. L. (1988). *The Mud Pony: A traditional Skidi Pawnee tale*. New York: Scholastic.

Dorris, M. (1992). *Morning girl*. New York: Hyperion.

Dorris, M. (1994). *Guests*. New York: Hyperion.

Grossman, V. (1991). *Ten little rabbits*. San Francisco: Chronicle Books.

Hayes, J. (1988). *A heart full of turquoise: Pueblo Indian tales*. Santa Fe, NM: Mariposa Publishing.

Hoffman, M. (1994). *Amazing Grace*. London: Magi.

Jeffers, S. (1991). *Brother Eagle Sister Sky*. New York: Dial Books.

Lacapa, K. and Lacapa, M. (1994). *Less than half, More than whole*. Flagstaff, AZ: Northland Publishing Co.

Martin, B. and Archambault, J. (1990). *Knots on a counting rope*. New York: Trumpet.

McDermott, G. (1987). *Arrow to the sun*. New York: Puffin.

Miles, M. (1971). *Annie and the Old One*. Boston: Little, Brown.

Regguinti, G. (1988). *The sacred harvest: Ojibway wild rice gathering*. Minneapolis: Lerner Books.

Rendon, M. R. (1996). *Powwow summer: A family celebrates the circle of life*. Minneapolis, MN: Carolrhoda Books.

Sanderson, E. (1990). *Two pairs of shoes*. Winnipeg, Manitoba, Canada: Pemmican Publications.

Scarry, R. (1992). *Richard Scarry's best storybook ever*. Racine, Wisconsin: Western Publishing Company.

Sendak, M. (1991). *Alligators all around: An alphabet book*. New York: Harper Trophy.

Sneve, V. D. H. (1988). *Dancing teepees: Poems of American Indian youth*. New York: Holiday House.

Sneve, Virginia Driving Hawk. (1995). *The Hopis*. New York, Holiday House.

Sneve, Virginia Driving Hawk. (1993). *The Navajos*. New York: Holiday House.

Sneve, Virginia Driving Hawk. (1994). *The Seminoles*. New York: Holiday House.

Sneve, Virginia Driving Hawk. (1993). *The Sioux*. New York: Holiday House.

Sneve, V. D. H. (1995). *Completing the circle*. Lincoln: University of Nebraska Press.

Swamp, Chief Jake. (1995). *Giving thanks: A Native American good morning message*. New York: Lee & Low Books.

Swentzel, Rina. (1995). *Children of clay: A family of Pueblo potters*. Minneapolis: Lerner Publications.

Tapahonso, L. (1996). *Navajo ABC: A Dine alphabet book*. New York: Simon and Schuster Books for Young Children.

Velarde, P. (1989). *Old Father Storyteller*. Santa Fe, NM: Clear Light Publishers.

Walters, Anna Lee. (1993). *Neon pow-wow: New Native American voices of the Southwest*. Flagstaff, AZ: Northland Publishing.

Wheeler, B. (1986). *Where did you get your moccasins?* Winnipeg, Manitoba, Canada: Pemmican Publications.

Wilder, L. I. (1981). *Little house on the prairie*. New York: Harper and Row.

List of Recommended Children's Books

Abenakew, F. (1988). *How the birch tree got its strips*. Saskatoon, Saskatchewan, Canada: Fifth House.

Abenakew, F. (1988). *How the mouse got brown teeth*. Saskatoon, Saskatchewan, Canada: Fifth House.

Alexander, B. and Alexander, C. (1995). *What do we know about the Inuit?* New York: Peter Bedrick Books.

American Indian stories. (1990). Milwaukee: Raintree.

Ancona, George. (1993). *Powwow*. San Diego: Harcourt Brace Jovanovich.

Ashabranner. B. (1984). *To live in two worlds:American Indian youth today*. New York: Dodd, Mead and Company.

Baylor, Byrd. (1976). *Hawk, I'm your brother*. New York: Macmillan.

Begay, Shonto. (1992). *Ma'ii and Cousin Horned Toad:A traditional Navajo story*. New York: Scholastic.

Begay, Shonto. (1995). *Navajo: Visions and voices across the mesa*. New York: Scholastic.

Bierhorst, J. (1993). *The woman who fell from the sky: The Iroquois story of creation*. New York: William Morrow & Company.

Bruchac, J. (1987). *Iroquois stories:Heroes and heroines, monsters and magic*. New York: Crossing Press.

Bruchac, J. (1995). *Glusabe and four wishes*. New York: Cobblehill Books.

Bruchac, J. (1995). *The Milky Way:A Cherokee tale*. New York: Dial Books for Young Readers.

Caduto, Michael J. and Bruchac, Joseph. (1988). *Keepers of the earth*. Golden, CO: Fulcrum.

Calloway, C. G. (1989). *The Abenaki*. New York: Chelsea House Publishers.

Cohen, C. L. (1988). *The Mud Pony:A traditional Skidi Pawnee tale*. New York: Scholastic.

Crum, Robert. (1994). *Eagle Drum: On the powwow trail with a young grass dancer*. New York: Four Winds Press.

Culleton, B. (1985). *April raintree*. Winnipeg, Manitoba, Canada: Pemmican Publications.

Culleton, B. (1986). *Spirit of the white bison*. Winnipeg, Manitoba, Canada: Pemmican Publications.

De Coteau Orie, S. (1995). *Did you hear wind sing your name?* New York: Walker and Company.

Dorris, M. (1992). *Morning girl*. New York: Hyperion.

Dorris, M. (1994). *Guests*. New York: Hyperion.

Erdoes, Richard. (1983). *Native Americans: The Pueblos*. New York: Sterling Publishing.

Girion, Barbara. (1987). *Indian summer*. New York: Scholastic.

Goble, Paul. (1992). *Crow chief*. New York: Orchard Books.

Goble, Paul. (1990). *Iktomi and the ducks*. New York: Orchard Books.

Goble, Paul. (1978). *The girl who loved wild horses*. New York: Scholastic.

Harvey, K. (Ed.). (1995). *American Indian voices*. Brookfield, CT: Millbrook Press.

Hirschfelder, Arlene B. (1986). *Happily may I walk*. New York: Scribner's.

Hoyt-Goldsmith, Diane. (1991). *Pueblo storyteller*. New York: Holiday House.

Hoyt-Goldsmith, Diane. (1992). *Arctic hunter*. New York: Holiday House.

James, B. (1994). *The mud family*. New York: G. P. Putnam's Sons.

Jennings, P. (1992). *Strawberry thanksgiving*. Cleveland, OH: Modern Curriculum Press.

Jones, H. (1971; 1993). *The trees stand shining: Poetry of North American Indians*. New York: Dial Books.

Josephy, A. M. (Ed.). (1989–). *History of the Native American*. Englewood Cliffs, NJ: Silver Burdett.

Keegan, Marcia. (1991). *Pueblo boy*. New York: Cobblehill Books.

Kendall, Russ. (1992). *Eskimo boy: Life in an Inupiaq Eskimo village*. New York: Scholastic.

King, Sandra. (1993). *Shannon, an Ojibway dancer*. Minneapolis: Lerner Publications.

Lacapa, Kathleen and Michael. (1994). *Less than half, More than whole*. Flagstaff, AZ: Northland Publishing Co.

Lacapa, Michael. (1992). *Antelope woman*. Flagstaff, AZ: Northland Publishing Co.

Lester, J. A. (1978). *We're still here: Art of Indians of New England*. Boston: Children's Museum of Boston.

Liestman, V. (1991). *Columbus Day*. Minneapolis, MN: Carolrhoda Books.

Meltzer, M. (1990). *Columbus and the world around him*. New York: Franklin Watts.

Momaday, N. S. (1969). *The way to Rainy Mountain*. Albuquerque: University of New Mexico Press.

Ortiz, Simon. (1977). *The people shall continue*. Emeryville, CA: Children's Book Press.

Pakarnyk, A. (1986). *My mom is so unusual*. Winnipeg, Manitoba, Canada: Pemmican Publications Inc.

Sanderson, E. (1990). *Two pairs of shoes*. Winnipeg, Manitoba, Canada: Pemmican Publications Inc.

Sekaquaptwa, E. (1994). *Coyote & the winnowing birds lisaw niqw tsaayantotaqam tsiròot: A traditional Hopi tale*. Santa Fe, NM: Clear Light Publishers.

Simmons, W. S. (1989). *The Naragansett*. New York: Chelsea House Publishers.

Sneve, Virginia Driving Hawk. (1989). *Dancing teepees*. New York: Holiday House.

Sneve, Virginia Driving Hawk. (1995). *The Hopis*. New York, Holiday House.

Sneve, Virginia Driving Hawk. (1993). *The Navajos*. New York: Holiday House.

Sneve, Virginia Driving Hawk. (1994). *The Seminoles*. New York: Holiday House.

Sneve, Virginia Driving Hawk. (1993). *The Sioux*. New York: Holiday House.

Steptoe, John. (1972). *The story of Jumping Mouse: A Native American legend*. New York: Scholastic.

Swamp, Chief Jake. (1995). *Giving thanks: A Native American good morning message*. New York: Lee & Low Books.

Swentzell, Rina. (1992). *Children of clay: A family of Pueblo potters*. Minneapolis: Lerner Publications Company.

Talashoema, H. (1994). *Coyote & little turtle liswa niqw yöngösonya: A traditional Hopi tale*. Santa Fe, NM: Clear Light Publishers.

Tapahonso, Luci and Schick, Eleanor. (1995). *Navajo ABC: A Dine alphabet book*. New York: Simon and Schuster Books for Young Children.

Turcotte, Mark. (1995). *Songs of our ancestors: Poems about Native Americans*. Chicago: Childrens Book Press.

Velarde, Pablita. (1989). *Old Father Story Teller*. Santa Fe, NM: Clear Light Publishers.

Walters, Anna Lee. (1993). *Neon pow-wow: New Native American voices of the Southwest*. Flagstaff, AZ: Northland Publishing.

Wheeler, B. (1984). *I can't have bannock but the beaver has a dam*. Winnipeg, Manitoba, Canada: Pemmican Publications Inc.

Wheeler, B. (1986). *Where did you get your moccasins?* Winnipeg, Manitoba, Canada: Pemmican Publications Inc.

Wood, T. and Numpa, W.A.O.H. (1992). *A boy becomes a man at Wounded Knee*. New York: Walker and Company.

Yamane, L. (1994). *When the world ended . . . and other Rumsien Ohlone stories*. Berkeley, CA: Oyaté.

NOTE

1. The terms used to refer to the indigenous population of North America includes Indian, American Indian, Native American, Amerind, and more recently, First Nation. Beyond using a specific tribal name, there is no general agreement among Native populations as to which term best describes who they are. In scholarly writing, the terms American Indian and Native American are used interchangeably. Native people frequently use the term Indian or people among themselves, choosing to identify themselves as American Indian or Native American in the broader social context. In this chapter, Native American is the term that we will use.

Chapter 7 _____

The Baby-sitters Club and Cultural Diversity: or, Book #X: *Jessi and Claudia Get Lost*

Christine A. Jenkins

ဢ ဢ ဢ ဢ ဢ

"I guess another thing you should know about the Walkers is that they're black. There aren't too many black families in our building. You know what's funny, though? When I'm with the Walkers, I don't think of them as *black*, just as *people*. I feel the same way when I'm with Jessi Ramsey, one of the new members of the BSC. I don't see her as black, just as an eleven-year-old baby-sitter who's Mallory Pike's best friend. I have never understood the big deal about black or white, Jewish or Christian, Irish or Polish or Chinese or Mexican or Italian or who knows what" (p. 6).

—*Stacey's Mistake*
(Baby-sitters Club Book #28), by Ann M. Martin

MASS MARKET SERIES BOOKS FOR YOUNG READERS

Series books have been perennial bestsellers in the U.S. children's publishing industry from the early years of this century to the present. Visit the children's section of any mass market bookstore in this country and you will most certainly see row upon row of series books, their uniform size and color and numbered spines acting as visual cues to the browser's eye. If you read series books as a young person, you may still recognize old favorites like the bright yellow backs of the Nancy Drew series or the black on white printing and mass market size of the Sweet Valley High series.

Series books have been and are uniform in other ways as well, as they are defined as having common elements of characters (Elsie Dinsmore, Nancy Drew, the Bobbsey Twins) and/or setting (Oz, Sweet Valley High). Their formulaic plots may include travel, mystery, missing objects, rescues, misunderstandings and reconciliations, problems and solutions, but generally end with loose ends tied up, questions answered, and the satisfaction of a happy ending, at least for the protagonists. Series books may be written by anonymous corporate authors (such as the Stratemeyer Syndicate's "Laura Lee Hope" [Bobbsey Twins], "Carolyn Keene" [Nancy Drew], "Frank Dixon" [Hardy Boys], or Victor Appleton [Tom Swift]), by a sequence of named authors (such as the writers of the Oz and Sweet Valley High series), or by a single author (such as Patricia Giff's Polk Street School series or Ann M. Martin's Baby-sitters Club). However, all exemplify the notion of the book not as a work of literature but as a commodity. The series concept, or package, is created much like other mass media forms. Such packages are written to order for publisher's identified markets and are known for their similar formats, which often includes predictable plots, sketchy characterizations, and bland prose. Like any other product, these books are designed to sell. If the series does not make a profit for the publishing company, the product line is discarded. If it does make money, the same formula is recreated (and occasionally modified to meet new consumer requirements) again and again and again.

It is a fact that series books are perennially popular with young readers. Each generation of young readers has had them; Elsie Dinsmore's sacchrine religiosity, the Rover Boy's gentlemanly adventures, Nancy Drew's dauntless female heroism, Sweet Valley's high school antics, and Goose Bumps' predictable shivers have all had their fans. Yet each generation's adult critics have voiced similar criticisms of the ubiquitous series book as mass-produced products of popular culture, and parents, teachers, and librarians have expressed concern about the potential ill effects of series books upon the literary taste, intellectual growth, and emotional health of vulnerable young readers. The fact remains, however, that young readers have been choosing to read and enjoy this type of reading for generations. The ubiquity and popularity of series books are often decried, but reading researchers have frequently noted that series book reading is a common and significant element in the reading autobiographies of avid adult readers (Carlsen & Sherrill, 1988, pp. 87–94).

Reading researchers interested in the development of reading fluency point to the essential element of reader interest in the development of literacy. The element of choice in reading is critical (Carlsen & Sherrill, 1988, pp. 145–155; Krashen, 1993). Beginning readers need the reading practice inherent in independent silent reading, particularly free reading—that is, the reading of books that students choose for themselves (Anderson et al. 1985, pp. 76–79). Once reading skills develop beyond simple decoding, fluent readers are able to move beyond efferent reading—reading for information—and begin to develop the ability to read aesthetically—reading as a "lived through" event or experience (Rosenblatt, 1968). Fluent and avid readers develop a sense of story structure through reading and hearing many stories with plots and action that introduce and reinforce an understanding of elements of story and narrative structure. As researcher Stephen Krashen has insisted, "we learn to read by reading" (Krashen, 1995), and it makes intuitive sense that the best incentive for the development of literacy is in the choice of materials that children are genuinely interested in reading. It is time, then, to take another look at series books and see what they have to offer young readers.

The reading of series books—reading materials that we know that great numbers of children are genuinely interested in reading—provides a valuable incentive for the reading practice that young readers need. Common reading of series fiction also provides social connections between readers and contributes to the creation of communities of readers who discuss texts and further reinforce readers' understandings of story and narrative structure (Mackey, 1990). There is much to be learned from the study of popular genres and the communities of readers that gather around them, whether juvenile series fiction, romance, science fiction, fantasy, westerns, mysteries, horror, or others (Radway, 1991; Tompkins, 1992). Instead of dismissing series fiction as mass market schlock, adults interested in children's reading would be better served by a thoughtful examination of what series books can (and cannot) offer young readers. This examination may be used to inform students' responses and enrich their discussion and evaluation of these and other reading genres. Many negative portrayals of series fiction have focused on the books' predictability and consistency of characters, setting, and plot. It is time to accept these elements as unquestionably attractive to young readers (just as they are to adult readers) and look instead at the actual content of the books in relation to the world they purport to portray. What we find in current series fiction for young readers is a reading of contemporary social interactions that appears to have room for multiple interpretations by multiple readerships. Reading and discussion can bring out these multiple interpretations and help children and young adults read their chosen texts both efferently and aesthetically (Rosenblatt, 1968).

While many aspects of series books for young readers have remained consistent from generation to generation, other aspects have changed. For years, the world of the series book was an all-white middle-class, urban/suburban setting of Euro-American names and faces (Sufrin, 1975). The few characters who were members of racial or cultural minorities included faceless and/or clownlike African American servants (such as Dinah and Sam, the Bobbseys' cook and handyman, or Eradicate, Tom Swift's carman), long-suffering victims (inscrutible Orientals, impulsive Italians, noble Indians), or stereotypic villains (shifty-eyed gypsies, vulgar Jews, bloodthirsty Indians) (Deane, 1972, p. 117; Prager, 1971, p. 85).

INTRODUCING THE BABY-SITTERS CLUB

In 1986, however, the Scholastic Publishing Company began a new series for girls, the Baby-sitters Club, by Ann M. Martin. On the shelf the spines create a rainbow of pastel colors. The covers picture the baby-sitters and their charges in middle-class suburban settings: a backyard with a badminton net, a spacious kitchen with wood cabinetry, a colonial-style living room with a television and VCR, a carnival on a grassy field, and other similar scenes. But a closer examination of the covers reveals a visual note of difference from the older series books. There are several Asian and African American faces included in the predominantly white landscape of the Baby-sitters Club books. In reading them, one meets seven baby-sitters: five are Euro-American, one is Japanese American, and one is African American. In a country that is becoming more multicultural by the day, these covers may not seem worth commenting upon. However, given the overwhelming whiteness of children's series books of the past, "breakthrough" may not be too strong a word to describe this new trend toward a cautious inclusion of young people of color as series books' main characters. Since 1986 and the extraordinary popularity of the Baby-sitters Club books, several more series have appeared featuring one or more Asian American or African American main character(s). Some are from mainstream presses, such as Sharon Dennis Wyeth's Penpals series (Dell), Elizabeth Levy's Gymnasts series (Scholastic), Betsy Haynes' Fabulous Five series (Bantam), Dean Hughes' Angel Park All-Stars series (Knopf), and Walter Dean Myers' 18 Pine Street series (Bantam); others are from independent presses, such as Connie Porter's Addie series (Pleasant Company), Michelle Y. Green's Willie Pearl series (W. Ruth Company), Debbi Chocolate and Wade Hudson's N.E.A.T.E. series (Just Us Books), and Sharon Droper's Ziggy series (Just Us Books).

Alongside the pleasure of seeing the homogeneous world of series books become slightly more inclusive, however, there is the necessity for a thoughtful evaluation of these books. What, if any, are the messages for readers about the lives of people of color? More specifically, in looking at the Baby-sitters Club books, what are images of and messages about Japanese Americans and African Americans and their place in American society? What can readers glean from the lives of the members of the Baby-sitters Club? How may these books be read?

The Baby-sitters Club books, written by Ann M. Martin, published by Scholastic Books, and targeted to 8- to 12-year-old girls, are an extremely successful series package. At first glance, the Baby-sitters Club has a great deal in common with other series books, particularly series marketed to girl readers. They are set in a fictional middle-class suburb populated by nuclear families. Just as Nancy Drew and the Hardy Boys are preoccupied with sleuthing and Cherry Ames is preoccupied with nursing, so the main characters of the BSC are preoccupied with baby-sitting. The first book in the Baby-sitters Club (or BSC) series, *Kristy's Big Idea*, came out in 1986 and the series has been a bestseller ever since. In mid-1988 it was noted in *Publishers Weekly* that at least one BSC book had been on the Dalton weekly bestseller list since the series began (Fleischer 1988, p. 37). Since that time the list has grown longer, the sales stronger, and the cover of the eightieth book in the series, published in mid-1994, announced that 100 million copies of Baby-Sitters Club books had been sold. Scholastic also publishes several spinoff series ("Baby-sitters Little Sister," and "Baby-sitters Mysteries"), and the current BSC product line includes T-shirts, games, calendars, date books, videos, dolls, and a fan club. A feature-length movie based on the Baby-Sitters Club books was released in August 1995.

Baby-sitter Club author Ann M. Martin is a former copywriter and book editor for Scholastic Book Services. In early 1986 she wrote an article for *Publishers Weekly* on book packaging for children, in which she described the business of marketing the book series (Martin, 1986). Precisely because the BSC books are written by a publishing-savvy author who is aware of her target audience, the Baby-sitter Club books may be examined to discover the meaning(s) and message(s) that the publishers wish to send, and believe will sell, to the targeted audience. And they certainly do reach their audience. The sales figures, plus the 10,000 letters the author receives from children annually, prove that the books are being bought, read, and presumably enjoyed. In an interview in the *Milwaukee Journal*, Martin said that she sees her books as primarily entertainment, but added, "I hope that kids will learn something from every book. I think I'm trying to make a point in each book, but in a light-handed way" (Demet, 1990). This comment, plus the evidence of the series' enormous popularity with young readers, invites a closer examination of the series and its messages.

THE NOT QUITE ALL-WHITE WORLD OF STONYBROOK

Although these books contain rich material for analyses using the lens of gender and of class, in this chapter I explore the messages about race and racial difference in contemporary U.S. society as expressed in the Baby-sitters Club series. As mentioned earlier, one of the most unusual—but least commented upon—features of the Baby-sitters Club is the inclusion of two people of color among the seven-girl cast of main characters—Claudia Kishi, a Japanese American, and Jessi Ramsey, an African American. This chapter focuses primarily on book #14, *Hello, Mallory*, the title that introduces Jessi and issues of race and difference into the series, and secondarily on those books narrated by either Jessi or Claudia. What are the messages about African American and Japanese American lives as portrayed in these books?

How do their lives compare to the lives of their white friends? How does the author portray differences within the club, between the members, and between the minority individuals and society as a whole? What are the messages of racial difference in the BSC books? According to the Baby-sitters Club, how are racial equality and social harmony to be achieved?

Baby-sitters Club books are set in Stoneybrook, Connecticut, a fictional middle- to upper-middle-class white suburban community which appears to be a bedroom community for nearby Stamford, where many of the characters' parents work. All the full members of the Baby-sitters Club attend Stoneybrook Middle School and most live in the same neighborhood:

> [We] would form a club to do baby-sitting. We would tell people (our clients) that at certain times during the week we could all be reached at one number. We would hold our meetings during those times. That way when someone needed a sitter, he or she could make one phone call and reach three different people. (#1 *Kristy's Big Idea*, pp. 14–15)

Thus the Baby-sitter Club is born. Kristy, Claudia, Mary Anne, and Stacey are the founders, Dawn joins in #5 (and moves away—at least temporarily—in #67 and permanently in #88]), Stacey moves away in #13 (and moves back in #28), and Mallory and Jessi join in #14.

Each book is narrated primarily by the girl named in the title in an informal, confiding tone, addressing the reader as directly as she would a friend in a telephone conversation or a letter. When other narrators are included, cursive excerpts from the BSC logbook indicate a change in voice. Every book begins with a lengthy introduction describing each of the club members, usually in the context of a club meeting, and each girl's personality is denoted by a consistent signature collection of personal characteristics (likes and dislikes, style of dress, and character traits), plus a description of her family:

Kristy Thomas: BSC president; age 13, white, brown hair and eyes, short; dresses in jeans and practical clothes; lives in a large blended family with her mother, millionaire stepfather, grandmother, and six siblings; outspoken, sometimes bossy ("a loudmouth"); the only one of the babysitters who enjoys sports

Claudia Kishi: BSC vice-president; age 13, Japanese American, long black hair and dark eyes; dresses in trendy, sophisticated clothes; lives with her parents, grandmother and older sister; does poorly in school; loves junk food; artistic

Mary Anne Spier: BSC secretary; age 13, white, brown hair and eyes, short; dresses conservatively; lives with her widowed father (who marries Dawn's mother in #30); quiet; the first BSC member to have a boyfriend

Stacey McGill: BSC treasurer; age 13, white, blond hair and blue eyes;

dresses in trendy, sophisticated clothes; lives with her parents (they separate in book #28); diabetic; New York City native

Dawn Schafer: BSC alternate officer; age 13, white, long blond hair and blue eyes; dresses "like California girls"; lives with her divorced mother (who marries Mary Anne's father in #30), father and brother live in California; vegetarian

Mallory Pike: BSC junior officer; age 11, white, curly red/brown hair, wears glasses; dresses in casual clothes; lives with her parents and seven younger siblings; writes

Jessi Ramsey: BSC junior officer; age 11, African American, long black hair and dark brown eyes; dresses in casual clothes; lives with parents, aunt, and two younger siblings; serious ballet student

WHAT DIFFERENCES MAKE A DIFFERENCE?

The Baby-sitter Club is a utopian community in the melting pot American tradition. Individual differences are acknowledged, but the common interests and goals of the group are given more importance. As Jessi says, "It's funny that us six club members work so well together, because boy, are we different. We have different personalities, different tastes, different looks, and different kinds of families" (#22 *Jessi Ramsey, Pet-sitter,* p. 4). However, within the club some differences are considered worth discussing, others are stated and then ignored, and still others are never mentioned at all. Predictably, the differences that are discussed extensively are precisely those differences that are considered the most beneficial and least threatening to both the BSC members and (not incidentally) to contemporary U.S. society. Thus, the stylistic differences of clothing and hair (which are the foundation of the teen advertising industry) become the arenas in which the girls can express their differences in a way that does not threaten group harmony. A typical account of these friendly BSC style wars begins as Claudia describes her current trendy outfit and then notes:

> We are so different, it is amazing. Dawn, Mary Anne, and
> Stacey arrived a few minutes later. Actually, as you might
> guess, we are *all* different—but some of us are more different
> than others. Stacey is kind of like me. She wears trendy
> clothes and is always getting her hair permed or something,
> but she's not as outrageous as I can be. I did notice that day,
> though, that she had painted her fingernails yellow and then
> put black polka dots all over them. Mary Anne, who is quiet
> and shy, dresses more like Kristy (who's a loudmouth). But
> Mary Anne is beginning to pay some attention to what she
> wears. Dawn falls in between Stacey and me, and Kristy and
> Mary Anne. She's just an individual. She's originally from

California and tends to dress casually, but with flair. (#12
Claudia and the New Girl, pp. 16–17)

Outside activity is another area of difference. All seven girls have interests besides babysitting, with several members involved in other activities
to such an extent that they must sometimes choose between the club and
ballet (Jessi), art (Claudia), or coaching softball (Kristy). Even so, schedul-
ing jobs around these activities is not seen as a problem by the club members and BSC members willingly attend Jessi's dance performances,
Claudia's art exhibits, and (at least some of) the games of Kristy's Krushers.
Family configuration—nuclear, single parent, adopted, and blended—is
another place where differences are tolerated, even celebrated, though only
up to a certain (unacknowledged) point; thus far, there are no gay or lesbian
families in Stoneybrook, and same-sex romantic attractions are never mentioned. Like the norm of clothing style differences, there is also a norm of
family and residence change among the club members: in the course of the
series, each member's family experiences significant changes and five of
the seven members move into, out of, or within Stoneybrook.

The differences that are important to the outside world are emphatically *not* the differences that "make a difference" to the BSC. These include
religion, class, and race. Club members attended church weddings, funerals, and christenings, but religious affiliations or differences were unstated,
except in the fact that these events never took place in any religious building *not* described as "a church" (see Afterword). There are *no* gender differences between the seven female BSC officers. When a boy, Logan, is admit-
ted as an associate member (in #10 *Logan Likes Mary Anne!*), it is with the
understanding that there's *no* difference between boys and girls in baby-
sitting skill, although all are relieved when they decide that Logan doesn't
have to attend meetings due to the conversational inhibition club members
feel with a boy's presence. Class differences are nonexistent due to the similarity of BSC family incomes. There is the contrast club members see between middle-class and upper-middle-class as exemplified by the wealthy
neighborhood where Kristy's new stepfather's nine-bedroom mansion is
located. Club members view the rich with mixed envy and pity—envy because the rich can afford backyard swimming pools and pity because when
someone *does* have a backyard swimming pool, it's hard to tell who likes
you for yourself and who only likes you for your pool. Mallory's father is
laid off in book #39 *Poor Mallory!* but his unemployment is seen as temporary and club members declare that her father's job loss makes *no* difference to them. Indeed, although the BSC *is* a money-making venture, the
girls emphatically reject the importance of money in their lives except as a
means to buy the items their parents won't purchase for them. Likewise,
they reject racial differences as unimportant, not making a difference, indeed, not even being noticed. Over and over, the message here is that *every-*

one experiences differences, and that these differences are roughly comparable. Sometimes differences cause problems, but then, *everyone* has problems. Even so, the BSC books' treatment of racial difference is far more
deliberate than their treatment of religious, class, and gender differences,
beginning with the 14th book in the series, *Hello, Mallory*:

> I wondered what being the only black student in your grade
> would feel like. I guessed it would feel no different from being
> the only anything in your grade. I was the only one in our
> grade with seven brothers and sisters, including ten-year-old
> triplets. But I knew that wasn't quite the same. The kids
> couldn't tell that just by looking at me. But Jessica's coffee-
> colored skin was there for the world to see. However, I didn't
> think nearly as much about Jessica's skin as I did about the
> fact that a new girl was finally in our class. I'd been waiting
> for this. I needed a best friend. (#14 *Hello, Mallory*, pp. 14–15)

INTRODUCING JESSI RAMSEY

Jessi Ramsey, the Baby-sitters Club's only Black member, is first introduced
in #14 *Hello, Mallory*, which traces Mallory's progress from baby-sittee to
baby-sitter. The cover blurb focuses on Mallory's efforts to be accepted into
the Baby-sitters Club and ends: "Maybe with her new friend Jessi she'll
start a club of her own . . . It's time to show those Baby-sitters what a couple
of new girls can do!" Thus Jessi's first identity is as Mallory's new friend.
Many books later, Jessi is still introduced as Mallory's sidekick, the perennial new girl and, not incidentally, still the only Black sixth grader at
Stoneybrook Middle School.

The two girls meet through an alphabetical chance when Jessi **R**amsey
is seated next to Mallory **P**ike. This begins the first in an endless pairing of
Mallory-and-Jessica, with Mal almost always first and Jessi second. In *Hello,
Mallory*, however, the first-second relationship seems more natural, as Jessi
is the new girl being shown the ropes by Mal, and all the action is seen
through Mallory's narrator eyes. "She was long-legged and thin, and even
sitting down she appeared graceful. Also, she was black. There are no black
students in our entire grade. This new girl would be the only one. . . . Wow.
This was pretty interesting" (pp. 12–13). Right from the beginning, Jessi is
put into the position of not simply being a newcomer, but of stepping into
someone else's space. Jessi's family has moved into Stacey's old house and
Jessi lives in Stacey's old room. Her homeroom teacher assigns her to a
classmate's desk, forcing the entire back part of the alphabet of students to
change seats. During lunch, the displaced classmate and her friends further emphasize Jessi's interloper status:

> "Well, she doesn't, you know, belong here."
> "Where?" I challenged them. "She doesn't belong where?"

> Sally shrugged.
> ". . . Where do you think Jessica moved from—Africa?"
> For some reason, the other girls thought this was hysterical.
> "I bet her real name is Mobobwee or something," added
> Sally. (p. 18)

Mallory doesn't challenge them further, but instead directs her energy into getting to know this intriguing new girl, seeing in Jessi a potential best friend. Her initial hunch that Jessi might be a kindred spirit is proved correct, and the girls find many common interests, including a shared love for baby-sitting. Mallory aspires to the Baby-sitters Club membership, but her 6th grade status and inexperience result in her initial rejection by the club. When she tells Jessi, Jessi in turn relates her own feelings of rejection with a naively sympathetic Mallory:

> "Tell me about it," said Jessi bitterly. "At least the only
> place you don't belong is in that club. I don't belong in this
> school, or even this *town*. Neither does my family."
> "You mean because you're, um . . ."
> "You can say it," Jessi told me. "Because we're black." (pp.
> 69–70)

During Jessi's first visit to the Pike's house, Mal's younger sister Claire asks if Jessi has come to clean the house, and Mrs. Pike looks "just a teeny tiny bit surprised" when Mal introduces Jessi, but then recovers her composure and shakes Jessi's hand, which both pleases and surprises Jessi (pp. 77–78).

Later Jessi gets into the advanced ballet class she auditions for, and her adjustment to Stoneybrook is complete when Mallory successfully challenges the Baby-sitters Club to admit them into the club together as a package of Mal-and-Jessi. In the first two pages of their first BSC meeting, Mal speaks directly five times, while Jessi is given direct speech only once, when she finally asks whether the girls think her membership will hurt the club's business because of the possible prejudice of customers. The girls talk over "Jessi's problem" (as they call it) and Kristy finally states that although she doesn't think any of their regular customers will reject Jessi, "If it does happen with anyone, though, I'll tell you one thing—I wouldn't sit for them, either" (p. 126). The others immediately agree, and Jessi is thrilled by this show of solidarity. It is still troubling, however, that in this book, containing as it does the first treatment of racism in the BSC series, the word "racism" is never uttered, the problem of prejudice is identified by the club as Jessi's problem, and none of the other girls—including Mallory—believe that prejudice is any more than faulty prejudgment that is simply rooted in ignorance and equally simply erased by contact and getting to know each other.

Mallory is Jessi's best friend, but even Mallory's initial naivete never appears to lessen, and twenty-five books later she understands racism as simply a matter of white community members being unreasonably phobic of those of other skin colors: "[Jessi's dark skin] doesn't matter to us or to our BSC friends, but it's been hard to ignore since, when the Ramseys first moved here, some people were not very nice to them. For reasons I haven't figured out entirely, they didn't want another black family in our community, which is almost all white" (#39 *Poor Mallory!* p. 14).

In the books following Jessi's admittance to the Baby-sitters Club, Mallory and Jessi are introduced as a pair, generally first described as best friends and as the club's two junior officers. In many of the books, particularly the earlier ones, there is a consistent pattern in the description of the two girls within the tandem description of Mallory-and-Jessi. First, the narrator talks about the similarities between the two of them: both like to read, both are the oldest children in their families, both are in sixth grade, and so on. Then (and only then) are their differences brought up, and Jessi's race is mentioned in opposition to Mallory's, and again, the narrator reminds the reader that Jessi's race *doesn't matter*, not a bit.

> Another difference is that Jessi is black and Mal is white. This doesn't matter to them, or to any of us in the BSC, but Jessi's skin color bothered a lot of people in Stoneybrook, I'm ashamed to say. The Ramsey's neighbors gave them a really hard time at first, although they've calmed down now. They've found that there's not a thing to dislike about the Ramseys. Oh, I forgot one other similarity between Jessi and Mal. Each of their families has a hamster! (#32 *Kristy and the Secret of Susan*, pp. 21–22)

Jessi's racial identity—usually described as "black" (uncapitalized), occasionally referred to as "African American"—is often introduced as a conversational afterthought. Even when Jessi herself is the narrator, she mentions her race in one sentence but in the next says that being black wasn't so important in her old racially diverse community in New Jersey, but being black has become important now that her family is one of the only black families in Stoneybrook.

INTRODUCING CLAUDIA KISHI

While Jessi has some conflicted feelings about her role as the only black sixth grader at Stoneybrook Middle School, Claudia Kishi, who is Japanese American, never admits any feelings or experiences of isolation or racial discrimination, despite being the only person of color in the club until Jessi's appearance in book #14. Claudia inhabits the contradictory position of Asians, particularly the Japanese, within U.S. culture. On the one hand, Asians are part of a "model minority." They are seen as quiet, mannerly, and academically successful immigrants who share the same culture, aspirations, and goals as "real Americans" and whose only desire is to assimilate and become part of mainstream American culture. At the same time, these "model minority" attributes are turned into negative stereotypes of Asians in general and of the Japanese in particular. They are *too* successful (they take jobs and scholarships away from "real Americans"), *too* hard-working (they become math and science nerds who emphasize rote learning over creativity), and *too* competitive (they are driving "real Americans" out of business). The stereotype of Japan in particular has taken on attributes of acquisitiveness, greed, and materialism, and the desire to buy all of the United States. The image of Asian women also suffers from a two-sided stereotype of ruthless and aggressive Dragon Ladies or childlike and submissive Fragile Flowers. In all cases, their beauty is described as exotic. No matter how long Asians live in the United States, they are viewed as foreign, inscrutable, Other (McCann & Woodard, 1977, pp. 83–96).

The character of Claudia contradicts some of these stereotypes, but reinforces others. Furthermore, the very stereotypes she contradicts are embodied in other members of her family. Claudia does not do well in academics—indeed, she's the only club member who gets poor grades—but her older sister Janine is a socially maladept genius who is rarely seen anywhere except in front of her computer screen or harrassing club members for their ungrammatical language. Claudia is not passive or submissive, but her grandmother Mimi is consistently described as sweet, shy, soft-spoken, and delicate. Claudia is brash, forthright, and likes making an impression, but the rest of her family is rarely seen in public, except for her mother, who is a public librarian. Claudia's talent lies in visual arts, both in terms of creating artwork and creating her own appearance, and Claudia's appearance is made much of by all the club members. As Kristy says:

> There is nothing, and I mean *nothing*, typical or average or ordinary about Claudia. To begin with, she's Japanese-American. Her hair is silky and long and jet-black. Her eyes are dark and almond-shaped and exotic. And her skin, well, I wish it were mine. I'm sure her skin doesn't even know what a pimple is. (#24 *Kristy and Mother's Day Surprise,* p. 6)

Almost every introduction of Claudia describes her dark, "almond-shaped" or "exotic" eyes, her perfect complexion and her long, jet-black, fashion-accessory hair, with Jessi reporting admiringly that Claudia fixes her hair "a different way every time I see her. You wouldn't think there could be so many ways to fix hair" (#27 *Jessi and the Superbrat,* pp. 13–14). Then there are her clothes, which are both trendy and plentiful. Claudia makes her first appearance in the series wearing short, baggy lavender plaid overalls, a white lacy blouse, a black fedora, and red high-top sneakers without socks (#1 *Kristy's Big Idea,* p. 25). In a later book, she wears "a wonderful Claudia outfit—a purple-and-white striped body suit under a gray jumper-thing. The legs of the body suit stretched all the way to her ankles, but she was wearing purple push-down socks anyway. Around her middle was a wide purple belt with a buckle in the shape of a telephone. And on her feet were black ballet slippers" (#13 *Goodbye Stacey, Goodbye*, pp. 125–26). Claudia is never seen in the same outfit twice and only she and New Yorker Stacey are consistently described by the unusual clothes they wear, although even super-shopper Stacey sometimes admits Claudia's fashion superiority. Claudia herself confides, "I love to mess around with clothes and jewelry. I might as well just come out and say it—I'm one of the coolest-looking kids in Stoneybrook Middle School. I know that sounds conceited, but everyone agrees it's true" (#19 *Claudia and the Bad Joke*, pp. 6–7). While Claudia's clothing taste is seen as super-sophisticated by her friends, it also reflects a consumer-oriented more-is-better approach to clothing, as typified by her ensemble in #24 *Kristy and the Mother's Day Surprise*:

> She had on these new, very cool roll socks. When she pushed them down just right, they fell into three rolls. The top roll was red, the middle one was peacock blue, and the bottom one was purple. She looked as if she were wearing ice-cream cones on her feet. In her hair was a braided band of red, blue, and purple, like her socks. And dangling from her ears were—get this—spiders in webs. Ew. (but they were pretty cool). (p. 34)

In fact, on BSC trips she insists on bringing a large wheeled suitcase to carry all her clothes, which is a source of irritation to her friends *until* they need to borrow an outfit or accessory. And, luckily for them, Claudia is endlessly generous with her possessions.

Kristy narrates the first book and introduces Claudia by saying that although Kristy, Mary Anne, and Claudia have always been close neighbors, "somehow Claudia has never spent as much time with us as Mary Anne and I have spent with each other. For one thing, Claudia's really into art and always off at art classes, or else holed up in her room painting or drawing. Or reading mysteries. That's her other passion. She's much more grown-up than Mary Anne and I" (pp. 7–8). As Kristy sees it, Claudia is responsible for the lack of contact between her and Kristy-and-Mary Anne. However, art lessons, mystery reading, and being "much more grown-up" are older child activities that don't explain (at the very least) what kept the girls apart for the first six to eight years of their lives.

The club members elect Kristy to be president of the club because it was her idea, Mary Anne to be secretary because she's good at writing things down, Stacey to be treasurer because she's good with numbers, and Claudia to be vice-president "mainly because we hold our meetings in her room. Plus she has her own phone with a private line—very important for the club" (#35 *Stacey and the Mystery of Stoneybrook*, p. 12). Claudia is chosen not for her ability, but for her possessions. The stereotype of Japanese materialism is also manifested in Claudia's obsession with junk food, which she keeps stashed in her room. Japanese are polite and hospitable and Claudia is hostess to the club three afternoons a week, welcoming them into her room and serving them junk food snacks. Japan makes trinkets, Claudia wears trinkets and clothing as "with-it" clothing statements of the latest fashion. Her friendship with Stacey has its roots in their similar trendy clothing and hairstyles. Only once in the first fifty-five books does Claudia refer to possible discrimination against Asian Americans. In the scene in which Jessi asks the club what they will do about possible racial prejudice, Claudia does draw a parallel between herself and Jessi, but negates the possibility in virtually the same breath. "*We* don't care that you're black. After all, I'm Japanese. Well, Japanese-American. No one minds that" (#14 *Hello, Mallory*, p. 124).

"SHADOW AND SUBSTANCE" IN THE BABY-SITTERS CLUB

What messages may be taken from these two seemingly contradictory portrayals of people of color in a mass market girls' series? What template may be laid on these books to understand the characters and contexts of Jessi Ramsey and Claudia Kishi? Rudine Sims [Bishop], in her book *Shadow and Substance: Afro-American Experience in Contemporary Children's Fiction* (1982), proposes a three-part model of the treatment of African American characters in children's books. I believe that this model can be used to evaluate the treatment of both Jessi and Claudia in the Baby-sitter Club books. Sims' model is based on a historical progression of twentieth-century U.S. children's literature dealing with African American characters. First, "social conscience" books appeared, books in which race was the problem and desegregation the solution. Next came "melting pot" books, in which racial diversity was present but unacknowledged and integregation was a given. Finally, "culturally conscious" books began to be published, books in which African Americans are portrayed in a culturally accurate manner.

In portraying characters of two different racial backgrounds, Martin has drawn an interesting and problematic distinction between the African American and Japanese American experience. Jessi's African American experience is portrayed in the manner of the "social conscience" books, books which had their heyday in the late 1960s. Like the Black students of that time, Jessi finds herself in the position of desegregating Stoneybrook Middle School, and Mallory and the other members of the BSC are forced to deal with the potential racism of their customers. The story of Jessi's first weeks in Stoneybrook is told from both Jessi's and Mallory's point of view. Thus this story fits into both a white-viewing-black plot of "guess who's coming to dinner" and a black-viewing-white plot of "learning how to get along with whites" as described by Sims (Sims, 1982, pp. 19–21). In the former, the protagonist is a white person who befriends a Black person who has moved into a white community and encountered hostility and prejudice. "The protagonist is able to convince the prejudiced adults and young people to be at least tolerant of the Afro-Americans, and the lives of all concerned are richer and sweeter" (p. 20). In the "getting along with whites" books, the same desegregtion story is seen through the eyes of the Black newcomer. He or she encounters problems, but comes to realize that *everyone*, Black and white, has problems and whites' behavior that Blacks have interpreted as racism may actually be a manifestation of some other personal unhappiness. This equation of the effects of racism with the effects of personal problems is unfortunate because, while personal problems are important, "they are very different from the problems caused by the effects of individual and institutional racism. Thus, the issues are oversimplified" (pp. 30–31). Social conscience books rarely speak of racism, but instead relate discrimination in terms of prejudgment based on faulty information. Thus, prejudice can be remedied by education and contact with members of the prejudged group. As illustrated above in the account of Jessi's experiences in *Hello, Mallory*, Sims' definition of "social conscience books" is an almost startlingly accurate description of the treatment of the African American experience found in the Baby-sitters Club books.

In contrast with the treatment of Jessi, Claudia's experience as a Japanese American is portrayed in the manner of the "melting pot" books. Melting pot books recognize the universality of the human experience to such an extent that they "ignore all differences *except* physical ones: skin color and other racially related physical features" (Sims, 1982, p. 33). They do not concern themselves with the problems of racism, but instead focus on common human experiences that are shared by all children. It follows that all children in melting pot books speak standard English, wear mainstream clothes, and live mainstream lives.

> As a group, they [melting pot books] create that imaginary, racially integrated social order . . . [in which racial minorities have been] assimilated into the larger white cultural milieu. Within that milieu, the personal problems and experiences shared are those of other American children—sibling relationships, growing pains, and so forth. On one level, to project such a social order is a positive act. On some other level, however, one must ask at what point the ignoring of differences becomes a signal that the recognition of them makes people uncomfortable or unhappy. (Sims, 1982, p. 45)

The word "racism" is rarely spoken in the Baby-sitter Club books. Racial discrimination is consistently referred to as "prejudice," with the emphasis on the element of prejudgment. According to Baby-sitters Club logic, racism is simply a collection of ignorant assumptions and is best fought through information and experience that contradict those assumptions. As Stacey says, "The people of Stoneybrook did not exactly accept the Ramseys right away. They didn't look closely enough to see what a nice family they are. They only saw their dark skin. (Well, that was at first. Things are better now.) But in the beginning, it would have helped if they'd kept their minds open" (#28 *Welcome Back, Stacey!* pp. 29–30). In good people, racism is a natural (though lamentable) aversion to the unfamiliar. Thus defined, these middle-class white people's racism can be cured by contact with middle-class people of color. Once Mrs. Pike gets over her initial surprise at having a Black person enter the house as an equal, once Mal's younger sister is told that Jessi is not the cleaning woman, all will be well. Once people see how nice the Ramseys are, things will get better for them, and they will adjust to the white world of Stoneybrook. And they do. Racism is reduced to an old-fashioned malady that can be cured by education and the simple passage of time.

In examining the BSC books' framing of racial prejudice as old-fashioned, it is instructive to look at the treatment of the three older women who are live-in members of BSC members' families. Mimi, Claudia's grandmother, is Japanese. Nannie, Kristy's grandmother, is white. Cecelia, Jessi's aunt, is African American. Despite their similarity of age, their roles within the books are set up to preclude any contact between them, thus reflecting the bad old days of racial segregation. The descriptions of the three women and the contrast between the three is illustrative of racial stereotyping. Mimi, Claudia's grandmother, is small and birdlike, "quiet, soft-spoken and endlessly patient" (#2 *Claudia and the Phantom Phone Calls*, p. 4). Her voice has "a gentle Asian accent" (#5 *Dawn and the Impossible Three*, p. 17). She is seen entirely within the confines of the Kishi home, cooking, making tea, nurturing Claudia and her friends, and—between her stroke in book #7 and her death in book #26—being cared for by her family.

In contrast, Kristy's grandmother Nannie is an independent woman who moves into Kristy's household not to be cared *for*, but to take care *of* Kristy's newly adopted two-year-old sister, Emily. Nannie is primarily seen outside the home and "doesn't seem like a grandmother at all. Her hair is barely gray, she has tons of energy, and is always off bowling or visiting friends or something, and she drives this rattly old car, which she painted pink and named the Pink Clinker" (#32 *Kristy and the Secret of Susan*, p. 5). Nannie is sporty, vivacious, and always on the go, the image of the modern white American woman. Although Mimi and Nannie are from the same generation (and would no doubt have been polite to each other had they met), they have little in common besides their age. Their characters embody contrasts in racial and national stereotypes: Mimi is the fragile and sequestered Japanese woman and Nannie is the hearty white American pioneer woman. Old-fashioned racists could very well use these two to illustrate the inevitability and essentially benign quality of racial segregation.

The portrayal of the third older woman, Jessi's Aunt Cecelia, is far more troubling and less benign. This is particularly true in her initial appearance in #36 *Jessi's Baby-sitter*, in which she embodies a host of unfavorable stereotypes of African American women. When Jessi learns that Aunt Cecelia is moving in, Jessi expresses her dismay in a series of negative words that also describe stereotypes of African Americans: "[she's] absolutely awful. I can't tell you how many things are wrong with her. She may be Daddy's older sister, but she smells funny. Bad perfume, probably. . . . This is my Aunt Cecelia: bossy, strict, mean" (#36 *Jessi's Baby-sitter*, pp. 7–8). True to Jessi's expectations, life with Aunt Dictator (as Jessi refers to her) is miserable. She is an intrusive and overbearing woman who is obsessed with obedience, cleanliness, and punctuality, the kind of adult teens love to hate. The Ramseys eventually have a family meeting during which Jessi and Becca air their grievances and Cecelia explains apologetically that her dictatorial manner has been her way of showing her concern that they be "kind, responsible, neat, and polite . . . [because] it's awful to have to say, but sometimes black people have to work twice as hard to prove themselves. It isn't fair, but that's the way it is—sometimes" (pp. 125–26). And Jessi, spokesperson for the melting pot generation, responds by making the melting pot equation of racism with personal problems by describing the prejudice one of her (white) babysitting charges suffers from because of his physical clumsiness: ". . . he's a klutz, and that's how most people see him. So he has to work twice as hard to prove himself" (pp. 126–27). Aunt Cecelia eventually mellows, but the stereotype of the ignorant, domineering Black woman (and the negative value assigned to those who acknowledge the existence of racism) lingers in this reader's mind long after Jessi makes peace with her aunt.

When Jessi tells her friends about Aunt Cecelia's imminent arrival, they themselves make the comparison between the three older women.

> But then [Kristy] said, "Really, Jessi. How bad could having your aunt move in actually be? Nannie moved in with my family, and it's been great. We love having her around."
> "And Mimi lived with us for as long as I can remember," added Claud. "You know how I felt about her. She was like another mother."
> I knew. And I knew that Nannie was wonderful, too. But Aunt Cecelia would not be wonderful, and my friends wouldn't understand that until they personally saw Aunt Cecelia in action. (pp. 28–29)

Jessi's last statement directly contradicts all earlier get-to-know-them strategies in dealing with racial differences, and further divides African Americans into Good Black People and Bad Black People. Good Black People are the junior Ramseys—they're good because they are just like whites and act as if skin color doesn't make a difference. They are rewarded for their apparent disbelief in racism by having whites feel comfortable around them. Bad Black People are the ones like Aunt Cecelia who believe that skin color *does* make a difference and that racism *does* exist. They become defensive and make whites uncomfortable. Thus the only real "solution" to racial discrimination is the white middle-class melting pot offered by the members of the Baby-sitters Club, with Claudia as the model for this melting-pot way of acting as if a racial harmony is a current reality. Although Claudia is subtly insulted by teachers who assume she should be a superior student and friends who value her for her possessions and her difference from her more traditional Japanese American family, the BSC approach of ignoring racial and cultural differences is seen as the winning strategy. And, as shown in her conflation of attitudes toward race with attitudes toward clumsiness, Jessi appears to be learning this as well.

IS THE BABY-SITTERS CLUB "CULTURALLY CONSCIOUS"?

As stated earlier, Rudine Sims' model includes three categories of multicultural literature: social conscience books, melting pot books, and culturally conscious books. Sims describes "culturally conscious" books as follows:

> They are books that seek to reflect, with varying degrees of success, the social and cultural traditions associated with growing up Black in the United States. In contrast to the social conscience books, they are not primarily addressed to non-Blacks, nor are they focused on desegregating neighborhoods or schools. They differ from the melting pot books in that they recognize, sometimes even celebrate, the distinctiveness of the experience of growing up simultaneously Black and American. . . . At a minimum, this means that the major characters are Afro-Americans, the story is told from their perspective, the setting is an Afro-American community or home, and the text includes some means of identifying the characters as Black—physical descriptions, language, cultural traditions, and so forth. (p. 49)

This definition can be expanded to include other historically oppressed minority groups as well. A thoughtful reading of the Baby-sitter Club books reveals very little of the cultures in which Jessi and Claudia were raised. The stories in two out of every seven books in the series are told from either Jessi's or Claudia's point of view. However, the treatment of neither Jessi nor Claudia could be described as "culturally conscious" except in the most superficial of ways.

Jessi calls her parents Mama and Daddy and at one point her father addresses her as "baby," terms commonly used in African American families (Sims, 1982, p. 71). However, in large and small ways, Jessi appears to be a white girl in a brown mask. She is devoted to ballet, and says at one point that to her it is the most beautiful of all art forms. Ballet has its origins in white European court dancing, and African Americans have historically had great difficulty gaining acceptance in this field. No mention, however, is made of this extra hurdle Jessi could face in her goal of becoming a professional ballerina. She also states that she "keeps her hair long for ballet," with no mention, however fleeting, of the problematic relationship African American women have traditionally had in regards to hair. Historically, Black features, including hair, have been judged by white standards of beauty and thus Black hair—too curly, too dry and too short—was considered "bad" hair. Jessi's hair, however, never poses any problems until Aunt Cecelia moves in. It is only the troublesome Aunt Cecelia, whose first words to Jessi are a request that she *please* tidy up her hair (#36 *Jessi's Baby-sitter*, p. 50), who makes Jessi's hair into a problem. Later in the book, she fixes Jessi's hair in a way that she believes will be suitable for ballet:

> She got out a jar of cream, a brush, and some other things,
> and gave me the most awful hairdo possible . . . severe, so it
> was great for ballet. My hair would *never* be in my eyes.
> "There," said my aunt. "Now you're someone I can be proud
> of." Because of my *hair*? (p. 110)

At age eleven, Jessi talks as if she had never before thought about hair styles and hair care. For a middle-class African American girl raised in an African American family, this seems highly unlikely. But, most significantly, despite the recency of the Ramsey's move away from their home community and extended family, there is no talk of seeing, speaking with, or corresponding with family members, let alone returning to Oakley for a visit. After only a few months away from her home in Oakley, Jessi appears willing to trade the lifelong connections of that community for the excitement of membership in the Baby-sitters Club, talks about her extended family as a past phenomenon instead of a present reality, and is never seen interacting with any of the other African American students at Stoneybrook Middle School. Each of the specific details taken separately is not necessarily critical to an authentic portrayal of a middle-class African American girl, but taken together they indicate that the author's treatment of the character of Jessi is not a culturally conscious one.

Claudia's character and family is likewise ungrounded in any significant form of Japanese American culture aside from acknowledging that Japanese objects/people/ language may be different than American majority culture objects/people/language. However, the difference is generally described solely in terms of that difference, thus giving the reader a picture of what the object is *not* rather than what it *is*. For example, Mimi and Claudia drink "special tea" in "cups without handles," both descriptions defining the tea and the cups by their difference from the norm—the tea is special (as opposed to the usual, the norm) and the cups are without handles (as opposed to normal cups *with* handles). Claudia's parents speak English with "no accent whatsoever" (#2 *Claudia and the Phantom Phone Calls*, p. 4), while Mimi's accent is due to the fact that she "didn't come to the United States until she was thirty-two" (#3 *The Truth About Stacey*, p. 5); that is, Mimi lived in not-the-U.S. until she was thirty-two. Claudia says that she and her sister Janine consider themselves "not just Japanese, but Japanese-American, meaning that we're full-blooded Asian but we've lived all our lives in the U.S." (#26 *Claudia and the Sad Good-bye*, p. 4).

"Issei" is the Japanese term for Japanese who, like the older Kishis, emigrate from Japan to the United States. "Nisei" is the term for Japanese who, like Claudia and Janine, are of the first generation born in the United States. Claudia, however, uses only English terminology to describe the cultural identity of herself and her family. Even when Claudia is narrating, the point of view is from within mainstream American culture, and the Kishis' Japanese identity is seen only as a thing of the past. Mimi reads Japanese books, has a haiku written in Japanese hanging over her bed, and gets Japanese and English words confused in the course of her recovery from a stroke. However, none of the Kishi family members ever talk to Mimi in Japanese, and when Claudia is helping Mimi with speech therapy, she responds to Mimi's correct Japanese identification of a picture by reminding her to speak in English. While it has not been uncommon for foreign-born Americans to incorporate the melting pot ideal to such an extent that they teach their children no language but English, it seems highly unlikely that Mimi's daughter and son-in-law would not respond to a confused stroke patient in her (and their) first language.

The Japanese were subject to exclusionary U.S. immigration laws during this century; from 1924 to 1952, no Japanese were permitted to immigrate to the United States (Banks, 1987, pp. 425–26). There are few specific references to current events or people to date the Baby-sitter Club books in real time, but they appear to take place in more-or-less the same time period in which they were published. In tracing the chronology of Mimi's life, the thirty-two-year-old Mimi could have come to the United States no earlier than 1952, which would mean she was born no earlier than 1920. When she dies in #26 *Claudia and the Sad Good-bye*, which was published in 1989, she would have been sixty-nine years old. Sixty-nine is not considered extraordinarily old, but the Kishis say several times that Mimi's heart was too old to go on any longer, that her body was simply worn out. While this scenario is not impossible, it is more likely a reflection of the author's unfamiliarity with Japanese immigration history. This lack of familiarity is unfortunate but not surprising.

What *is* surprising in this past decade of Japan-bashing is Claudia's denial of ever having experienced racial discrimination until the brief appearance (in #56 *Keep Out, Claudia!*) of a new (white nuclear) Stoneybrook family that shuns members of all racial, cultural, and religious minority-status groups and all single-parent, adoptive, and blended families. Even in this extreme case, however, Claudia does not recognize the racism directed toward her until it is named by Kristy and confirmed by Jessi (" 'The Lowells are prejudiced,' said Kristy in a rush. 'Claud, they didn't like you because you're Japanese.' . . . . 'So—so what does being Asian have to do with being a good sitter?' I sputtered. 'Nothing,' replied Jessi. 'Prejudice doesn't make sense' " [p. 85]). Shortly after this revelation, Claudia has a brief (and apparently first) conversation with her father and sister about racism, in which she is astounded to learn that Japanese Americans were interned during World War II.

In the absence of such overt discrimination as the Lowells', Claudia takes responsibility for her earlier isolation from her neighbors Kristy and Mary Anne, chalking it up to her interest (and their disinterest) in clothing and make-up, despite the fact that they had been neighbors from birth. Even her problems with overly high teacher expectations are blamed by Claudia on her older sister Janine's genius status, rather than acknowledging the possibility that her teachers might be making assumptions based on their stereotypes about the superior academic performance of Asian students. Although Claudia sees herself as a thoroughly assimilated American, her strong relationship with her beloved Issei grandmother makes it unlikely that she would be so thoroughly divorced from her cultural roots.

"Fiction about Afro-Americans[/Asian Americans] seems to have had one of three major socializing purposes: to promote racial harmony, to promote American cultural homogeneity, or to provide self-affirmation for Afro-American[/Asian-American] children" (Sims, 1982, p. 103). The messages of racial understanding in the Baby-sitters Club books are primarily toward the first two purposes of promoting racial harmony and cultural homogeneity. The third purpose of providing self-affirmation may be met in the eyes of individual white readers, but it is unlikely that many African American or Japanese American children will find in Jessi or Claudia a culturally conscious reflection of themselves.

USING BABY-SITTERS CLUB BOOKS IN THE CLASSROOM

Despite the inclusion of non-white protagonists, the Baby-sitters Club series remains a commodity written for and about and marketed to white middle-class readers. Conversely, despite the BSC's status as a mainstream mass market commodity, young readers of various backgrounds continue to seek out further engagement with the female-friendly, racially heterogeneous, utopian world of the BSC. The cover of #78 *Claudia and Crazy Peaches* announces "The Baby-sitters Club: 100 Million Books / 100 Million Friends," and there is certainly reason to appreciate the series for successfully stimulating its vast audience to read more (and more and more) about the members of the BSC. Considering the limited worldview of most mass market series fiction and the rampant racial and cultural stereotypes that typified series fiction published earlier in this century, the BSC's Stoneybrook is indeed a remarkably diverse community and Jessi and Claudia remain two of the more interesting and lively members of the Baby-sitters Club.

The questions the BSC poses for librarians and teachers is how to evaluate and use these and other contemporary series books that include multicultural casts in library and classroom settings. Given their proven popularity, they certainly encourage voluntary free reading among vast numbers of young people, including many who are not generally interested in recreational reading. In addition to the BSC's invaluable encouragement of voluntary free reading, however, it may be possible for students to engage in critical readings and analyses of these and other contemporary series. As illustrated above, the BSC series is a rich source of fictional representations of race, class, gender, and cultural differences in American society. Thus, these mass market books could be the subject of extensive discussion using the same questions and techniques employed in discussions of series television, films, MTV, and other productions of mass and/or popular culture.

Generally speaking, plots in all genres of fiction are driven by problems and their resolution. Among the problems faced by BSC members are the ongoing negotiation of parental expectations, differences among friends, and communication between older and younger siblings, as well as explorations of problems and conditions such as autism, anorexia nervosa, learning disabilities, and hearing impairment. Thus, the books in the BSC series could be read, discussed, and compared with literary works that feature more multi-dimensional, ambiguous, or nuanced approaches to these and similar problems.

In addition to noting the ways in which BSC characters and plots differ in complexity from those found in contemporary realistic fiction, there is also value in examining the Baby-sitters Club for the utopian model that it is. While each BSC member encounters problems in the books she narrates, as a group the club members share and maintain a small utopian community in which young women continually negotiate difficulties and bridge differences in an atmosphere of mutual support and affirmation. The creation and implementation of utopian visions is a centuries-old theme in a body of literature devoted to the exploration of various fictional and actual "Cities on the Hill." As such, the BSC could usefully be discussed in the context of other Utopias that have appeared in literary, historical, and contemporary American societies.

The final question in this exploration of the Baby-sitters Club and other series that include multicultural casts will be the extent to which culturally conscious content might be incorporated in the future. Perhaps they will continue to reflect in some small way the changes that continue to occur within a society that is continually—and increasingly—resistant to all changes that challenge the cultural hegemony of the status quo. It may be that the promotion of racial harmony and cultural homogeneity will be as far as mainstream publishing companies can go before upsetting their marketing departments. If this is the case, it may well be up to the non-mainstream and small press publishers to create future series book characters, plots, and messages that provide self-affirmation to non-white readers. At present, the Baby-sitters Club books continue to appear on children's bestseller lists, and their ambivalent and contradictory messages regarding race and culture continue to be a more-or-less accurate reflection of the myriad racial and cultural assumptions present in contemporary American society.

AFTERWORD

The Baby-sitters Club series was recently revised and updated, beginning with #89, *Kristy and the Dirty Diapers*. The series' new look (with a redesigned cover and format) includes some significant changes in the content as well. When Dawn moves back to California and takes permanent leave of the Baby-sitters Club, BSC members invite twins Abby and Anna Stevenson, new arrivals to Stoneybrook, to join. With the addition of Abby (Anna declines membership in favor of violin and orchestra practice), the BSC has its first Jewish member. Wise-cracking, brash, and athletic, Abby introduces an element of difference to the BSC membership that appears to signal a new approach to difference within the series as well. As noted above, the earlier books portrayed BSC members' individuality through the relatively unproblematic variations in appearance, interests, and family configurations, while the differences of race, class, and culture (such as those raised in *Hello Mallory* and *Keep Out, Claudia!*) were acknowledged but ultimately dismissed. In the revised and updated series, the overall approach has shifted, and differences that do indeed "make a difference" in contemporary American society are no longer purposely ignored but are instead explored and even celebrated. Representative books in the new series include #91: *Claudia and the First Thanksgiving*, the story of Claudia's involvement in the historically accurate—and controversial—version of the traditional Thanksgiving story, and #96: *Abby's Lucky Thirteen*, a story centered around the celebration of Abby and Anna's Bat Mitzvah. Just as the BSC's original social conscience / melting pot approach represented a small but striking change from the racial homogeneity of earlier series books, it is possible that the revised BSC may represent another small step toward more culturally conscious—and even complex—portrayals of diversity within mainstream series fiction for young readers.

BABY-SITTERS CLUB SERIES: 1986 to 1996

1. *Kristy's Great Idea*
2. *Claudia and the Phantom Phone Calls*
3. *The Truth About Stacey*
4. *Mary Anne Saves the Day*
5. *Dawn and the Impossible Three*
6. *Kristy's Big Day*
7. *Claudia and Mean Janine*
8. *Boy-Crazy Stacey*
9. *The Ghost at Dawn's House*
10. *Logan Likes Mary Anne!*
11. *Kristy and the Snobs*
12. *Claudia and the New Girl*
13. *Good-bye Stacey, Good-bye*
14. *Hello, Mallory*
15. *Little Miss Stoneybrook . . . and Dawn*
16. *Jessi's Secret Language*
17. *Mary Anne's Bad-Luck Mystery*
18. *Stacey's Mistake*
19. *Claudia and the Bad Joke*
20. *Kristy and the Walking Disaster*
21. *Mallory and the Trouble With Twins*
22. *Jessi Ramsey; Pet Sitter*
23. *Dawn on the Coast*
24. *Kristy and the Mother's Day Surprise*
25. *Mary Anne and the Search for Tigger*
26. *Claudia and the Sad Good-bye*
27. *Jessi and the Superbrat*
28. *Welcome Back, Stacey!*
29. *Mallory and the Mystery Diary*
30. *Mary Anne and the Great Romance*
31. *Dawn's Wicked Stepsister*
32. *Kristy and the Secret of Susan*
33. *Claudia and the Great Search*
34. *Mary Anne and Too Many Boys*
35. *Stacey and the Mystery of Stoneybrook*
36. *Jessi's Baby-sitter*
37. *Dawn and the Older Boy*
38. *Kristy's Mystery Admirer*
39. *Poor Mallory!*
40. *Claudia and the Middle School Mystery*
41. *Mary Anne vs. Logan*
42. *Jessie and the Dance School Phantom*
43. *Stacey's Emergency*
44. *Dawn and the Big Sleepover*
45. *Kristy and the Baby Parade*
46. *Mary Anne Misses Logan*
47. *Mallory on Strike*
48. *Jessi's Wish*
49. *Claudia and the Genius of Elm Street*
50. *Dawn's Big Date*
51. *Stacey's Ex-Best Friend*
52. *Mary Anne + 2 Many Babies*
53. *Kristy For President*
54. *Mallory and the Dream Horse*
55. *Jessi's Gold Medal*
56. *Keep Out, Claudia!*
57. *Dawn Saves the Planet*
58. *Stacey's Choice*
59. *Mallory Hates Boys (and Gym)*
60. *Mary Anne's Makeover*
61. *Jessi and the Awful Secret*
62. *Kristy and the Worst Kid Ever*
63. *Claudia's Freind / Friend*
64. *Dawn's Family Feud*
65. *Stacey's Big Crush*
66. *Maid Mary Anne*
67. *Dawn's Big Move*
68. *Jessi and the Bad Baby-sitter*
69. *Get Well Soon, Mallory!*
70. *Stacey and the Cheerleaders*
71. *Claudia and the Perfect Boy*
72. *Dawn and the We [heart] Kids Club*
73. *Mary Anne and Miss Priss*
74. *Kristy and the Copycat*
75. *Jessi's Horrible Prank*
76. *Stacey's Lie*
77. *Dawn and Whitney, Friends Forever*
78. *Claudia and Crazy Peaches*

REFERENCES

Anderson, R. C., et al. (1985). *Becoming a nation of readers: The report of the Commission on Reading*. Washington, D.C.: National Institute of Education.

Banks, J. (1987). *Teaching strategies for ethnic studies*. 4th ed. Boston: Allyn & Bacon.

Carlsen, G. R. and Sherrill, A. (1988). *Voices of readers: How we come to love books*. Urbana, IL: NCTE.

Colborn, C. "Kristy's Great Idea" (review). *School Library Journal,* 33 (March 1987), 163.

Deane, P. C. (1972). The persistence of Uncle Tom: An examination of the image of the Negro in children's fiction series. *The Black American in books for children*. D. MacCann and G. Woodard, eds. Metuchen, NJ: Scarecrow, 116–23.

Demet, M. Alison's adventure: Tosa girl finds famous penpal. *Milwaukee Journal* (May 6, 1990): G2.

Fleischer, L. Talk of the town: One-woman industry. *Publishers Weekly,* 233 (June 17, 1988), 37.

Jenkins, E. C. and Austin, M. C. (1987). *Literature for children about Asians and Asian Americans*. New York: Greenwood Press.

Krashen, S. D. (1993). *The power of reading: Insights from the research*. Englewood, CO: Libraries Unlimited.

Krashen, S. D. The reading hypothesis, the expanded reading hypothesis, and the greatly expanded reading hypothesis. *School Library Media Quarterly,* 23 (Spring 1995), 187–192.

"Kristy's Great Idea" (review). *Publishers Weekly,* 230 (October 31, 1986), 69.

Lindgren, M. Telephone interview. 14 November 1990.

MacCann, D. and Woodard, G., eds. (1972). *The Black American in books for children*. Metuchen, NJ: Scarecrow.

MacCann, D. and Woodard, G., eds. (1977*). Cultural conformity in books for children: Further readings in racism*. Metuchen, NJ: Scarecrow.

Mackey, M. Filling the gaps: the Baby-Sitters Club, the series book, and the learning reader. *Language Arts*, 67 (September 1990), 484–89.

Martin, A. Packaging for children. *Publishers Weekly*, 229 (February 21, 1986), 94–96.

"Martin, Ann M(atthews)." (1986). *Something about the author,* vol. 44. New York: Bowker.

McGrath, J. Paperbacks for children. *Emergency Librarian*, 15, (November–December 1987), 53–55.

Prager, A. (1971). *Rascals at large, or The clue in the old nostalgia*. Garden City, NJ: Doubleday.

Radway, J. (1991). *Reading the romance: Women, patriarchy, and popular literature*. Chapel Hill, NC: University of North Carolina Press.

Rosenblatt, L. (1968). *Literature as exploration*. Rev. ed. New York: Noble and Noble.

Sebesta, S. L. and Neeley, J. L. Literature for children. *Reading Teacher* (March 1989), 536–539.

Sims, R. (1982). *Shadow and substance: Afro-American experience in contemporary children's fiction*. Urbana, IL: NCTE.

Sufrin, M. Yesterday: Boys' sports books portrayed an idealized world of manly virtues. *Sports Illustrated*, 43 (September 1, 1975).

Tangorra, J. Beyond Disney. *Publishers Weekly*, 237 (July 27, 1990), 195–97.

Tompkins, J. (1992). *West of everything: The inner life of westerns*. New York: Oxford University Press.

Chapter 8

Creating Good Books for Children: A Black Publisher's Perspective

Cheryl Willis Hudson

ॐ ॐ ॐ ॐ ॐ

Three quotes are noteworthy as a framework for discussion of the contents of this chapter and the thoughts that follow:

"A tree cannot stand up without its roots."

—proverb from Zaire/Africa

"We wish to plead our own cause. Too long has the public been deceived by misrepresentation in the things which concern us dearly."

—editorial from *Freedom's Journal*, 1827
Samuel Cornish and John Russworm, publishers

"Knot in de plank will show thru de whitewash."

—ante-bellum slave aphorism

Part of the goal of Just Us Books is to share the story of the Black experience in literature for children and, in so doing, create good books for all children. Creating books of quality and substance is a tough job in any publishing institution, but publishing good *children's* books has added challenges. The demands of the audience are great and the broadening context of a multicultural world means looking at literature for children from varying perspectives.

As a publisher of books for children, I'd like to discuss some of the issues Just Us Books has attempted to address as they relate to *imagery, information, authenticity* and *access*. What we do and how we do it relates directly to the growth of independent or "alternative" publishing, the changing demographics of the United States of America, and the highly charged issue of "Multiculturalism." Although our focus is grounded in African American history and culture, we believe that many of our tenents apply to publishing "good" children's books in general. Specific references will be made to titles on the Just Us Books list in order to illustrate what good books are rather than to point out what many books lack.

I. BACKGROUND

"We want to plead our own cause . . ." As a publisher, Just Us Books is a relatively new kid on the block. We were incorporated in 1988, a year after my husband Wade and I self-published our first title, *AFRO-BETS® A B C Book*. This was a major undertaking for us because although each of us had experience in the publishing industry (writing, editing, and art directing), we produced the *ABC Book* in dozens of little steps over a period of several years, in the early morning, after hours and on weekends while holding down our "real" 9 to 5 jobs. It is important to note that we turned to independent self-publishing for several reasons.

1. Our ideas and proposals for Afro-centric books were rejected by a number of "mainstream" children's book publishers. "Not universal, limited audience, not easily marketed" were some of the reasons given for these rejections.
2. We believed in the value of our materials for a wide audience including African Americans and all other Americans.
3. Very few outlets were focusing on books for children—especially with Black children at the center. Books produced by Third World Press, the Associated Publishers, and others were primarily targeted for adult readership.

From "mainstream" publishers we received form letters, some personal notes, some verbal comments—all of which said in some measure . . . "not right for our list"; "limited audience"; "not easily marketed"; "a novel idea and cute concept, but . . . "; or "not enough Black people buy or read books." As parents, our experience was quite the contrary. Good Black books were hard to find!

Even though books have always been a passion for both of us, having grown up in the fifties and sixties in the segregated South, we rarely saw anything positive in print about people who looked like us. Overall, the images were either absent or distorted or somehow didn't ring true. So, with the establishment of Just Us Books in 1988, we began to create something that we didn't have or own as children. And we began to fulfill a life-long dream—that is, producing books that showed and related our experiences realistically and authentically as African Americans.

II. PROVIDING INFORMATION: WHY WE PUBLISH BLACK BOOKS

"A tree cannot stand up without its roots."

—proverb from Zaire/Africa

Just Us Books is an independent publishing company that produces children's books focusing on the Black experience. In this multicultural world of ours, books say so much about our lives and our mores and our concerns. *Not* seeing diversity in books has a major impact on how all children relate to ideas about race, class, literature and ultimately, civilization. All children need to see themselves reflected positively in books, magazines, movies, ads, and so on. Ours is an image-driven age and images transmit ideas. A major part of our publishing philosophy involves addressing the historic dearth of positive African-American imagery in children's literature.

Marian Wright Edelman writes about her childhood experiences in the Deep South. In *The Measure of Our Success*, she says:

> The outside world told [B]lack kids when I was growing
> up that we weren't worth anything. But our parents said
> it wasn't so and our school teachers said it wasn't so.
> They believed in us and we, therefore, believed in our-
> selves.

Apart from providing information about African American history and culture, a key element in the publication of our books is an "affirmation of the value of African American children to themselves." Although it has happened quite often in the past, Black children need not be marginalized in literature. Black children have strong roots, but the published body of literature does not reflect this. Black children do not have to be compared to other groups to prove their value. Black children are valuable because they *are*. Just Us Books, therefore, produces books that are culturally specific, yet relevant to a wide range of readers from backgrounds that are not African American. All children should be able to read the words and delight in their content. The children in *Bright Eyes, Brown Skin* are presented forthrightly, with pride and without apology. There is no fear of later being categorized as a story that is exclusive because it "leaves out" white children or other ethnic groups. (quotes are mine)

Bright eyes, brown skin
A heart-shaped face
A dimpled chin—
Bright eyes, cheeks that glow
Chubby fingers, ticklish toes . . .
Bright eyes, brown skin
Warm as toast
And all tucked in.

In *Jamal's Busy Day*, Jamal relates his school day to his parents' day at work. He says,

My daddy is an architect. He makes drawings to guide the people who build houses. He works hard. My mommy is an accountant. She's always busy with numbers. Mommy works very hard. I work hard, too.

The reader can see through the story line and the imagery that Jamal is a part of a nuclear, two-parent, African American family and that he appears well-adjusted as he goes about this regular routine. Jamal's race is an integral part of what he is, but he is *not* an exception to a more "universal" rule. What Jamal does during his busy day can apply to children of all colors and ethnic groups in this country. Jamal's experiences are authentic and they are real and Jamal is African American.

III. ACCESS AND AUTHENTICITY

According to data collected by the Cooperative Children's Book Center in Madison, Wisconsin, in 1988, the year Just Us Books began operation, less than one percent of the 5,000 books published for children were written and/or illustrated by African Americans. Did this mean that Black folks didn't know how to write? That they didn't know how to draw? That they didn't know how to read? That they weren't interested in books? Or that African-American book creators were not worthy of being published? Of course not. What the statistics *did* reflect was something more about *who* was publishing the books and *who* was making them available to be read. What Just Us Books has attempted to do is to create a body of work that reflects the diversity of the Black experience in this country. Although we began as "self-publishers" without the benefit of "mainstream," commercial distribution, Just Us Books quickly grew into what is referred to now as a small press or an independent publisher of children's books. Through niche marketing, creative advertising and word of mouth, Just Us Books was able to give African American consumers broader access to books rather than limit the Black interest books that were made available to them through traditional retail and library channels. Part of our mission was to expand access to African American writers and illustrators. In 1994 the numbers had increased somewhat.

IV. PUBLISHING POLICY AND PRACTICE

Our policy and practice is to publish Black writers and illustrators and to look, actively, for the talented among both published artists and emerging ones. In this way, we feel we can offer a great deal of authenticity about the Black experience as well as provide access for writers and illustrators who may not always be sought out by "mainstream" publishers. We believe that there are a number of key ingredients that are useful in evaluating prospective titles that deal with Afro-centric themes for children. Many publishers do not share our perspective, but we have found these ingredients useful in producing good multicultural books. It is also interesting to note that although many major publishers were reluctant to publish our material ten to fifteen years ago because of their perception of "limited marketability," many of the same publishers have begun to seek out the advice and referrals of publishers such as Just Us Books for artists, writers, and marketing angles in presenting their new "multicultural lists" for the nineties. Following our list of key ingredients are specific examples taken from titles which incorporate them.

V. KEY INGREDIENTS TO LOOK FOR IN AFRO-CENTRIC BOOKS FOR CHILDREN

1. *Positive images that leave lasting impressions*   The images that are projected should reflect positive aspects of our community in order to give children visual objectives to achieve. What we do not see, we usually do not believe. Negative images and pathology, to be sure, do exist, but they should not be considered the norm in literature which is formative for the very young.

2. *Accurate, factual information that's enjoyable to read*   Too long have our children been bombarded by distorted or biased information, or pure misinformation. Our goal and mission are to provide the facts, and to present them in a fun, age-appropriate and appealing manner.

3. *Cultural authenticity/cultural specificity*   The cultural references in children's material should reflect the authentic experiences and background of people of African descent. Children should be able to see that the material is specific to them.

4. *Meaningful stories that reflect a range of African American values and lifestyles*   Stories should include an attitude of respect for our ancestors, as well as give respect and accountability for our audience.

5. *A clear and positive perspective for people of color in the 21st century*   The material should highlight a clear path of positiveness and progress, being fully oriented toward self-realization and the community spirit necessary for continued success in the future.

6. *Nonfiction that is relevant to today's issues*   Topics covered should be timely and germane to those issues affecting us presently or in the future.

7. *Material that is self-affirming*   If we do not affirm and define ourselves, who will? And do we trust others to do a fair, unbiased, and realistic job?

8. *Strong three-dimensional characters*   Characters should be well-rounded and fully developed, showing the multifaceted nature of people in general.

9. *Attractive graphics*   The graphics must be pleasing to the eye, culturally accurate, and able to capture and maintain the attention of children of various ages.

10. *Durability and affordability*   Children's books, by nature, will be subject to stress and continual use. The quality of materials used should reflect this need for durability, and should also take into account the economics of many households with children.

11. *A vehicle that opens the windows of knowledge, information, and self-discovery*   Speaks for itself, doesn't it? It is important to make sure that the printed material is designed to open the young reader's mind and to guide him or her on a journey toward knowledge and awareness of self and others.

VI. TYPES OF BOOKS

Just Us Books publishes books for children in several categories and our criteria are applied to all of them.

Concept Books

Alphabet and counting books fall into this group. Because there are so many of them in the marketplace, concept books need to have a unique slant if they are to compete successfully. The AFRO-BETS[R] Kids are six Black characters with a range of hairstyles, complexions, personalities, and interests. Originally, they were designed as graphic devices for displaying the letters of the alphabet, thus the coinage of the term "AFRO-BETS"[R]. In our books, however, they have evolved into learning tools identified with presenting aspects of African-American history and culture. They are used to show positive, energetic children with high self-esteem, doing what kids do—playing, learning, relating to their families and peers, going to school, growing up and having a future. At the same time, they introduce Afro-centric words and phrases. In *AFRO-BETS[R] A B C Book*, for example, A is for apple but also for Africa, B is for ball and brown baby, and C is for car and for cornrows.

The unique slant is embodied in the letters themselves in the introduction of words not commonly found in other alphabet books: for example, cornrows, Egyptians, kente cloth, Nefertiti, and sphinx. Furthermore, illustration examples are used for African animals such as alligator, camel, elephant, (mud)fish, giraffe, hippo, jaguar, lion, monkey, rhinoceros, turtle and zebra. Self-affirmation for Black children is also demonstrated by using African features for baby, doll, lips, mask, and nose. The *AFRO-BETS*[R] *A B C Book* is a clear example of presenting accurate information about a wide variety of subjects within a culturally specific milieu. The material has been enthusiastically received by parents, teachers, and most importantly, young children.

Picture Books

Books in this category are designed primarily for children aged two to five or up to age seven. These are books in which the pictures or illustrations occupy a far greater proportion of space than does the text. Although the pictures appear to carry the text, the two are in fact complementary. The text must be well written and carefully structured in order for the illustrator to capture precise emotions and ideas the writer wants to convey. In picture books, each word counts and each image counts. For picture books on our list, a great deal of attention is paid to imagery in order to avoid stereotypes and to present culturally accurate illustrations. It is not enough to take what might have been a white child, color her brown (a medium brown at that), and say that a publisher has printed a "multicultural" book, that is, *"Knot in de plank will show thru de whitewash."*

Editors at Just Us Books examine the following: the content, the context, the culture, the cosmetology, the classics, the "canon," and the status quo. A number of questions are asked when we give consideration to an unsolicited manuscript. These questions and their answers help us to determine if the manuscript is a good fit for our list. Among the questions are:

1. Whose story is being told?
2. Who is going to tell the story?
3. What assumptions is the writer bringing to the task?
4. How will the story be illustrated? photos? artwork?
5. In what style? In what colors? In what size? By whose design?
6. What are the historical facts?
7. Who will interpret these facts?
8. How much latitude is there for interpretation? (i.e., Can illustrated classics have a multicultural cast?)

9. What are the technical considerations? (How does one maintain quality control?)

10. How will the children respond? For example, is the story appealing to children? Will is satisfy their literary and aesthetic needs? Is the story a "good read"?

Annie's Gifts by Angela Shelf Medearis, illustrated by Anna Rich, is a picture book whose main character is an African American girl whose home is filled with music. Through a series of attempts at playing various musical instruments, Annie discovers her own special gifts which are, surprisingly, not in the area of music. Although mother, father, sister, and brother are integral to the story line, there are other personalities in the story from obviously different racial backgrounds. The story evolves naturally and at an even pace. It incorporates various elements of a middle-class African American family lifestyle without resorting to "preachiness," artificial effects, or a contrived story line.

Story Books

These picture books are designed for slightly older readers and involve a greater proportion of text than the previously noted picture book format. They may be read aloud to younger children, or some children from age six to eight or nine may find that they are able to read them alone. *Land of the Four Winds* by Veronica Freeman Ellis, illustrated by Sylvia Walker, and *When I Was Little*, written by Toyomi Igus and illustrated by Higgins Bond, fall into this category. *Land of the Four Winds* incorporates fantasy and folklore and *When I Was Little* is a work that is both historical and intergenerational in nature.

Animal fantasies frequently make up a large body of literature for children. They are very instructive, largely non-threatening, and are excellent vehicles for teaching about strong emotions such as anger, jealousy, and fear. African folktales about Anansi abound in children's literature. Brer Fox and Brer Rabbit tales are often retold as a part of African American folklore. To date, Just Us Books has made a conscious decision *not* to republish any of these traditional tales, yet we have made an effort to include folklore and elements of the oral tradition in our works. *Land of the Four Winds* combines elements of Bassa folklore (from Liberia, West Africa) in a modern setting (Massachusetts) within a Liberian family who has settled in the United States.

It also utilizes a Liberian dialect, and the voice of the Winds to appeal to the imagination of the child. This approach is an alternative to the assumption often made that there is very little in the way of contemporary stories about African cultures outside of nonfiction stories about specific communities.

When I Was Little uses the device of graphic flashbacks in black and white and color to illustrate the "good ole days" of the Grandfather whose voice is heard in this intergenerational story. The result is a realistic portrayal of a video-age child who can get a glimpse of a by-gone history that is difficult for him to imagine otherwise.

Biography and Nonfiction

Offerings in this area include *AFRO-BETS^R Book of Black Heroes From A to Z; Book of Black Heroes, Vol. II: Great Women in the Struggle;* and *AFRO-BETS^R First Book About Africa*. The first two titles are short entry biographies of historical and contemporary Black personalities. They were created out of a demand for a range of materials about people other than stand-alone titles about Martin Luther King, Jr., George Washington Carver, and Mary McCleod Bethune. Both books have been extremely well received by librarians because of the short entry format, large black-and-white photos used, and the variety of contemporary and historical personalities included. *Great Women in the Struggle* was selected as a Reading Rainbow selection in 1994.

AFRO-BETS^R First Book About Africa falls into the nonfiction area but includes instructional storytelling as well. It uses the device of a visiting griot to present new information to the reader in a classroom setting. It also incorporates an animal story and the legend of the Golden Stool from the Ashanti people. *First Book About Africa* attempts to address the erroneous perception of Africa as a homogeneous place populated by animals and "uncivilized" people who inhabit a largely jungle-like area. Producing this title presented a tremendous challenge for the author, illustrator, and editor. There was so much information that could have been included, and yet the publisher did not want to include broad strokes of information which could be equally distorted because they contained too little substance.

Books for Middle Readers

This category of books is one that is often requested by librarians and teachers who are looking for material for the child who considers himself too old for picture books but who is not completely ready for longer novels. Contemporary fiction and biographies are included here. *Ziggy and the Black Dinosaurs* by Sharon M. Draper is an example of such a chapter book written with Black boys in mind. It is a contemporary action-filled adventure about four friends who form their own club. In the course of a few days in the summer, they uncover part of the community's past history and learn something about building character as well. We chose to illustrate this 80-page book with 8 black-and-white illustrations to provide a transition for readers from our picture book audience more familiar with illustrated titles. Although the story itself is fiction, the storyline offered the publisher an opportunity to include authentic photographs of a recently discovered African burial ground in New York City and relevant information concerning it as an epilogue to the text. Other titles in this middle reader category include *The Twins Strike Back* by Valerie Flournoy and *Susie King Taylor: Destined to Be Free* by Denise Jordan.

Books for Older Readers

This category includes series books such as *NEATE to the Rescue*. Five middle school friends, male and female, are central to stories in this series. Placed in a multicultural, suburban setting, the five friends, **N**aimah, **E**lizabeth, **A**nthony, **T**ayesha and **E**ddie, attempt to deal with contemporary issues that concern them and their peers. As the Just Us Books' original readership grows older, so have the children who people the books that we have published.

Poetry

On Just Us Books' list, books of poetry fall into a special category since so few are published. *From a Child's Heart,* a book of prayer-poems by Nikki Grimes with pictures by Brenda Joysmith, is the title of note for this group.

YA Books

Young Adult books are being developed for Just Us Books' 1997 fall list.

VII.   RESPONSES IN THE MARKETPLACE

The response has been excellent for the titles published by Just Us Books. Because our initial efforts focused on marketing directly to Black book stores, day care centers, and institutions in various African American communities, our readership in these areas has seen solid and steady growth. After the first six months of publishing, we expanded efforts into trade channels and followed this by selling to school libraries. Shortly afterwards, our books were distributed to the chain bookstores such as B. Dalton and Waldenbooks, and mass market outlets such as Toys R Us. On a more personal level, we have received hundreds of letters from children, parents, teachers, and librarians applauding our efforts. Knowing our audience has made it easier to access it. Our books are grounded in African American history and culture so they are well rooted and relevant for extended periods of time. *"A tree cannot stand up without its roots."*

VIII.   CRITICAL AND ACADEMIC REVIEWS

Our titles have been reviewed by a number of trade journals (*Booklist, School Library Journal, Publishers Weekly, Instructor Magazine, NEA Today, The*

Multicultural Review, Hungry Mind Review, Quarterly Black Review of Books and others). Reviews have also appeared in a number of newspapers such as the *Boston Globe* and the *Newark Star Ledger*, and in magazines such as *Essence* and *Black Enterprise*.

IX. AWARDS

Sources such as Parent's Choice, Reading Rainbow, Publisher's Marketing Association, Multicultural Publisher's Exchange (now known as MPEC) and others have honored some of our titles (see the following list).

SELECTED AWARDS AND NOTABLES

♦ **BRIGHT EYES, BROWN SKIN**
Publishers Marketing Associates
Ben Franklin Award–1991
Starred Review—*Booklist*

♦ **AFRO-BETS® First Book About Africa**
Multicultural Publishers Exchange
Book Award of Excellence—1991
Starred Review—*Booklist*

♦ **JAMAL'S BUSY DAY**
The Boston Globe's Top 25 in Multicultural
    Reading, Spring 1992
National Council of Social Studies
Children's Trade Books in the Field of Social
    Studies Honor—1992
Multicultural Publishers Exchange
Book Award of Excellence—1992

♦ **AFRO-BETS® BOOK OF BLACK HE-ROES FROM A TO Z, VOL. I**
United Brothers and Sisters Communications
    Systems' Best Selling Book of the Year Fi-
    nalist—1992

♦ **FROM A CHILD'S HEART**
Publisher's Marketing Association
Ben Franklin Award—1994
NAACP Image Award Finalist—1992
"Thirteen subtly cadenced, accessible poems
    . . . A lovely, deeply felt book."—*Kirkus
    Review*

♦ **WHEN I WAS LITTLE**
Multicultural Publishers Exchange
Book Award of Excellence—1993

♦ **BOOK OF BLACK HEROES: VOL. II, GREAT WOMEN IN THE STRUGGLE**
New York Public Library Best Books for the
    Teenage—1993
Multicultural Publishers Exchange
Book Award of Excellence—1992
A Reading Rainbow Review Book—Fall 1993

♦ **ANNIE'S GIFTS**
Parents' Choice Selection
Approved 1995 Black History Month

X. EXTENDING OUR VISION

As of March 1995, Just Us Books had 24 titles on our list with well over one million copies in print. In addition to publishing our own titles, we have also established relationships with other publishers through the sale of subsidiary rights for book clubs, big books, and classroom packages. We have entered into relationships with Scholastic, Scott Foresman, and Sundance in this regard.

Just Us Books has also created and packaged a number of titles which are published by Scholastic Books. These include four baby board books in the WHAT-A-BABY Series (*Good Morning, Baby, Good Night, Baby, Let's Count, Baby* and *Animal Sounds for Baby*), two Hello Readers (*Five Brave*

Explorers and *Five Notable Inventors*) and other trade books and compilations such as *My First Kwanzaa Book, Kwanzaa Sticker and Activity Book, I Love My Family, Pass It On: African-American Poems for Children, How Sweet the Sound: African American Songs for Children* and *Hold Christmas in Your Heart: African-American Songs, Poems and Stories for the Holidays*. Given the tremendous expense of producing full-color books for children, working in the capacity of a packager has afforded Just Us Books the opportunity to produce over one dozen additional titles that reflect its publishing philosophy within a more condensed period of time than it would have taken had the projects been mounted independently. (A packager is an independent company sub-contracted by a publisher to create books from concept, editorial development, and design usually through to mechanicals in lieu of the traditional author/publisher arrangement.) There are also opportunities on the horizon for licensing Just Us titles in the electronic media.

XI. COMPETITION AND COOPERATION

There exists within the independent press movement, a number of opportunities for networking with other companies with similar visions and challenges. The Multicultural Publishing and Education Council (formerly The Multicultural Publisher's Exchange) is a national networking and support organization for independent publishers of multicultural books and materials. NABBP (The National Association of Black Book Publishers) has been organized to address needs and concerns particular to Black book publishers. The Center for Multicultual Children's Literature (housed at HarperCollins) is an organization formed to assist talented multicultural writers and illustrators to enter the field of children's literature. PMA (Publisher's Marketing Association) is another organization which provides valuable information and guidance to members of the independent press movement. Just Us Books has been active in some capacity in all of these organizations and each association has provided valuable services through its newsletters, conferences, seminars, marketing programs, and personal networks.

XII. BUILDING AN INSTITUTION

Building a company and producing good books present challenges on both the business and editorial side. To a large extent, Just Us Books has published books we believe *need* to be published in order to share Black children's stories. We have taken into consideration information, imagery, authenticity, and access. We have not looked only toward making money or simply at the bottom line. Rather, we have proceeded with some measure of risk in doing things unconventionally in order to get the word out. We are convinced that good books *do* make a difference in children's lives and the feed-back we get from the Black community and other areas is that our books are achieving the desired effects. A tremendous amount of work still needs to be done, however, to meet the needs of school-age children in order to adequately reflect this country's diversity.

Publishers, like movie makers, have tremendous power to present ideas and images. In today's multicultural world, publishers have the power to question many assumptions without resorting to either propaganda or pabulum. Somewhere between these two extremes are stories and pictures reflecting authentic cultural substance which should form the basis of truly multicultural literature for children.

XIII. CONCLUSION

An editorial "bite" from a once best-selling title, *Megatrends 2000,* by John Naisbitt and Patricia Auburdene, notes with some measure of insight:

> *The more homogeneous our lifestyle becomes, the more stead-fastly we shall cling to deeper values—religion, language, art and literature. As our outer worlds grow more similar, we will increasingly treasure the traditions that spring from within.*

In this statement, the authors are speaking of a time only a few years away—of an internationalized world where nations borrow trends liberally from one another, through Japanese technologies, French Concords, German-made cars, Third World resources, Italian fashion, English language, poly-cultural slang and, of course, U.S. marketing.

But what is the "lifestyle"?

Who is the "we"?

What are the "traditions"?

What is the "outside"?

What is "within"?

Are the authors talking about a global marketing phenomenon, or multicultural equity? Are they speaking of surface imagery or substantive information? And who controls what kind of information is transmitted?

Through its publishing efforts, Just Us Books' goal is to broaden access to information and imagery about the Black experience and thereby to enrich the reading experiences of all children.

Chapter 9 _____

Reading Multiculturally

Daniel D. Hade

ॐ ॐ ॐ ॐ ॐ

We were talking, my two daughters and I, about the Disney movie, *The Lion King*. As the story goes, a young lion cub, Simba, heir to the throne of the Lion King, goes into self-exile when his wicked Uncle Skar convinces Simba that he is responsible for the death of his father, Mustafa. With Mustafa dead and Simba gone, Skar assumes the throne, maintains power by allying himself to hordes of hyenas, and commands the many lionesses of the pride to supply him and his hyenas with food. A chance encounter with Nala, who implores Simba to return to claim his throne (and by implication marry her), creates doubts about exile for Simba. A brief, mystical reunion with his father convinces Simba that he must accept his destiny to be king and return to fight Skar and claim what is rightfully his. While the lionesses beat back the hyenas, Simba defeats Skar and the kingdom is made whole again.

A question had been troubling me since I had seen the movie. "If Nala is stronger than Simba (she twice defeats him in tests of physical strength)," I asked, "why don't she and the other lionesses attack Skar, why do they have to wait for Simba to return and defeat Skar?" It seemed to me that *The Lion King* was suggesting that being able to govern was only a birthright. Simba was the legitimate heir to the throne, Skar followed him in the line of succession. With Mustafa dead and Simba presumed dead, the pride had no choice but to accept Skar as their leader, even though his leadership was cruel, even though the movie made clear that the lionesses could physically defeat him. I thought the movie was suggesting that the role of women is to do what the men tell them to do, even if it means living under a cruelty they have the power to overcome. I wondered if my daughters had noticed this also.

Anna, who is nine, replied, "This is not exactly my point-of-view, but I think the story is trying to say that Skar took Simba's power from him and it was Simba's to take back. The lionesses couldn't do it, because it was Simba's job to get back what Skar took."

"But couldn't the lionesses overthrow Skar?" I asked.

"You don't understand, Dad, it's Simba's story, not the lioness's."

Anna had a point. The story is Simba's story, a story of his coming of age. And helpers such as Nala and the other lionesses are common motifs in coming of age stories. However, when women are the helpers and the victims, the story suggests more than a simple male quest for identity.

Nonplused but undaunted, I turned to Rebecca, age 15. "I see what you mean, Dad, but I really liked the movie and I really like the music and I don't like to let the details get in my way of enjoying a story."

"But, isn't that the point?" my wife and I said at the same time.

"You guys are wrecking the story for me," she objected.

Rebecca's stance was all too familiar. I have encountered it often from students in my children's literature classes—a view of discussion as potentially ruining the pleasure one has received from a story.

Though I was frustrated with my daughters' inability or refusal to see what I thought were troubling and obvious messages in the movie, I had to admit that Anna and Rebecca were good "readers" of this film in that they displayed many of the characteristics that educators and critics hope readers will display. They suspended their disbelief and received the movie on the movie's terms. They kept their minds open to the movie's possibilities and enjoyed their "lived-through" experience. Critics and teachers have prized such readings. Tolkein and Coleridge wrote that for a reader to appreciate a work the reader must suspend disbelief and accept the work. Lewis (1961) heaped scorn on readers who "used" literature, rather than being open to "receive" what the author might be doing. Chambers (1985) noted that children need to become "yielding readers," readers who will change themselves to fit the book rather than expecting the book to change to fit them. And no less an authority than Wayne Booth (1983) has stated that the best readings are those in which the reader reads as the author intends.

But texts are multilayered and can have implicit as well as explicit meanings. While *The Lion King* may indeed be about the male Simba's coming of age, it is the lionesses who suffer under the unjust rule of Skar and it is the lionesses who do nothing even though they have the physical power to overcome their oppression. It may be Simba's story, but do the women in the story need to be portrayed as acquiescent? The story and the music may amuse its audience, even provide pleasure, but this does not change the implication that if one is a female in *The Lion King*, one suffers injustice quietly and patiently, waiting for the rightful male heir to claim what is his.

A person who knows something about lions might counter that Disney's lions are behaving as one might expect lions to behave—females hunt and take care of the young, and males eat and sleep. This argument would hold weight if one reads this story as one about how lions actually live in the wild. This would also mean that one would have to accept that a monkey will walk with a staff, use the tools of a juju man, paint pictures, and call up the spirits of the dead. One would also have to accept as factual all the animals gathering to bow down to a newly born male lion cub, acknowledging that he is at the top of the food chain, accept that lions would befriend a warthog and a meerkat and sing songs with them, believe that lions could exist on insects, that a weaker male lion could plot with hyenas to create a stampede of wildebeests that would slay the leader of the pride, and that hyenas will march in step, Nazi-style. I could go on, but I trust I've made my point. *The Lion King* isn't really about how lions behave, it's about people, especially boys growing up facing their destiny, and accepting the responsibility that accompanies it.

It is these implied meanings or assumptions of meaning in children's stories that interest me. In particular, how do authors seem to understand race, class, and gender? How do race, class, and gender, as *signs* to be interpreted, mean in the stories we put before children? I am using *sign* in the sense that the semiotician C. S. Peirce (1931–1935) used it. A sign is comprised of an indivisible and triadic relationship of symbol (what appears on the page), referent (the object that is represented by the symbol), and an interpretant (the meaning brought *to* the sign which mediates between the symbol and the referent). This means that we do not think to get meaning, but rather we use meaning to think. Interpretation is the means by which we understand text. For example, looking at the presence of Native Americans in a children's book in this *semiotic* manner, we have the manner in which a Native American is presented (the symbol), the real Native American to whom the symbol refers (object), and the meaning the reader assigns (interprent). Reading is inherently social and is dominated by culture. And the meanings we hold about race, class, and gender (many of which may be stereotypes) mediate how we interpret text.

My daughters and I read the signs of the lionesses in *The Lion King* differently. This is because a sign is a product of a relationship that is laden with experience, meaning, and value. The relationships my daughters and I have with the sign of the lionesses in *The Lion King* are not the same. We read the sign of gender differently and assigned different values to it.

I've been involved with children's literature for over 20 years as a teacher, school librarian, teacher educator, and now as a professor of children's literature. I currently teach persons who want to be teachers and persons who are teachers about children's literature. I publish articles and chapters in books about children's literature, and I edit a journal, the *Journal of*

Children's Literature. Most of my professional work has been in rural and suburban areas, but I've also spent some time in urban classrooms as well.

For much of my professional life, I've held a tourist's conception of multiculturalism. I saw multiculturalism as an issue that could best be dealt with by addressing a lack of knowledge and understanding we have about one another, that whatever problems might exist among groups could be resolved if we only understood each other better. The culture in which we lived was essentially fair, I believed; education, or the lack of it, denied some full participation, but a little learning could fix that. As the vast majority of the children with whom I worked were white and middle class, I saw my job as making available to them books about persons different from themselves, helping them and myself gain understanding and tolerance.

Likewise, the vast majority of the preservice and inservice teachers with whom I work are also white and middle class. I saw my task here as acquainting these adults with a variety of works by persons of color, because demographics indicated that they would likely be working with children of diverse backgrounds and all children had the right to see themselves in the stories they read. So we looked at books by Virginia Hamilton, Mildred Taylor, Patricia McKissack, John Steptoe, Laurence Yep, and Gary Soto.

But acquainting my college students with multicultural books did little. Students laughed at the dialect in Eloise Greenfield's poetry or in Patricia McKissack's *Flossie and the Fox.* Many students would comment that they would not share such books because children would learn bad grammar. Students were amused at the African American families in *Tar Beach* and *Roll of Thunder, Hear My Cry* eating watermelon. African American students would refuse to read *Roll of Thunder, Hear My Cry*, because the word, "nigger" was in it. It was becoming clear to me that for my students a "normal" person looked like them, someone who was black was exotic and someone who was poor was disgusting. Teachers from white, rural areas would often comment that though the stories about persons of color or the poor were compelling, they couldn't see using books showing persons of color in their classroom, because their students could not relate to characters different from themselves. Of course the characters they were thinking about were white and middle class or wealthy. It didn't seem to occur to them that large percentages of their classrooms were comprised of children who lived in poverty.

I believed, like many of my colleagues in children's literature, that the power of literature could work miracles, that all I had to do was to bring children together with the right book (Hade, 1994). What my college students were telling me was that what they were bringing to the text was vital to their readings of multicultural books. My students' responses showed me that I held a naive view of culture and the power culture played in how my students read.

The problem with this tourist view of multiculturalism that I held is that it absolved educators (such as me) of responsibilty other than to create access to certain stories. To be more forceful in raising questions would raise the issue of me denying my students' freedom to make their own meaning. If I truly believed that readers played a major role in the meanings they make of stories, then I couldn't ignore the contributions readers made to their understandings of text. I couldn't count on the text alone to do the job. Nor could I maintain a purely learner-centered view of education, where I create the opportunity to learn by bringing the proper books into contact with readers, who, if left on their own, would look at their own assumptions about human diversity. That was a negative view of freedom, a view that freedom is a list of things we do not do, rather than a postive view of freedom, where we have the responsibility to confront and act upon injustice. Confronting my students' (and my own) assumptions about race, class, and gender became critical to my teaching. Why did you laugh at the reference to watermelon? Why do you feel that the language Flossie speaks is bad grammar? Why do you not want to read a book that has the word "nigger" in it? Why are you repulsed by the poor? And in my own case, why was I defensive about issues of gender in children's books?

At the same time I was reading scholars such as Toni Morrison, Cornel West, Cameron McCarthey, Joel Taxel, Henry Giroux, Paulo Freire, bell hooks, Donaldo Macedo, Edward Said, Maxine Greene, Howard Zinn, Noam Chomsky, and Henry Louis Gates. These scholars gave me a language with which to name my thoughts and beliefs. And this naming helped me understand much better that our culture is not inherently fair, but rather is inherently unfair. Our culture distributes wealth and privileges unevenly among the rich and poor, persons of color and whites, males and females. Now multiculturalism wasn't merely about learning about others and tolerating difference. Toleration implied that even though some members of society might hold more power than others, if the powerful merely tolerate the presence of difference, the situation will be fine. But this view doesn't address the injustice of privilege. For me, multiculturalism was about justice, it was about critiquing the world of which I was a part and how this world denied persons of certain groups the opportunities afforded so easily to rich, white males.

Learner-centered educators would respond to me and say that what I was proposing was an imposition on children, a forcing of my political values upon them. I was told that children don't "naturally" read for race, class, and gender, and I mustn't impose my agenda upon them. But what I am after isn't *imposing meaning*, it is *exposing injustice*. To ignore the injustice implied in children's stories is a far more insidious way of imposing ideas than to challenge these ideas openly. Silence is the oxygen of racism and bigotry. Silence allows the dominant assumptions about the inferiority of the poor, women, and persons of color to remain unchallenged.

We've know for some time that reading isn't natural—it's learned (Barthes, 1974; Howard, 1974; Fish, 1980; Heath, 1982, 1983; Meek, 1987; Scollon & Scollon, 1981, 1982; Bauman, 1977, 1986; Bloome, 1983, 1985; Michaels, 1986; Collins & Michaels, 1986; Cook-Gumperz & Green, 1984). Studies of parents reading to infants have shown how, from the beginning, adults are showing children how to attend to text, where to look, how to make meaning, and what kinds of meaning to make (Ninio & Bruner, 1978; Snow & Goldfield, 1983; Teale, 1984; Cochran-Smith, 1985; Roser & Martinez, 1985). My own research (Hade, 1989, 1992) suggests that children "read" the social context in which they interpret literature and produce readings according to what they believe their teacher wants in that particular situation. The richness of the readings in the classroom appeared to be influenced heavily by the kinds of readings the teacher values. Interpretation is a cultural product. If children do not read in a certain way, it is not because they do not read that way naturally, it is because they are not taught how to read that way (Hunt, 1991). To view what children do with books as natural is to allow the influence of culture and the manner in which certain signs are interpreted to go unchallenged. This is imposition by omission.

I am convinced our pedagogy must accommodate learning how to read race, class, and gender. I hold that our pedagogy must enable children to critique what they read and the world around them. Of course we do not want to force meaning upon students like a medicine, but we do want them to think about their assumptions about race, class, and gender, about the assumptions texts seem to suggest, and how they use these assumptions to interpret text. Perhaps we can begin to do this by choosing stories in which the discussion of issues of race, class, and gender do not appear forced, but rather integral to understanding the story.

For example, two recent books, *Brother Eagle, Sister Sky* by Susan Jeffers (1991) and *A River Ran Wild* by Lynne Cherry (1992) use Native Americans to advance a theme of environmental responsibility. *Brother Eagle, Sister Sky* spent many weeks on *The New York Times* Best Seller List. The book is an illustrated version of a speech made by Chief Seattle, and was much praised for its detailed illustrations and for its message of environmental responsibility. The book was also severely criticized for depicting the Suquamish people of the Pacific Northwest and the plants and animals of that area inaccurately. Lost in the controversy about the accuracy of Jeffers' book was discussion of how Jeffers used Native Americans as a sign to convey meaning. The cover of *Brother Eagle, Sister Sky* provides some clues. We see on the cover a Native American chief, presumably Chief Seattle, in traditional dress (though not necessarily the traditional dress of the Suquamish people) with hands placed gently upon the shoulders of a contemporary, blue-eyed, Anglo boy. The boy is gazing at a dragonfly, seemingly unaware of Seattle's presence. We can see the colors of the boy's shirt through Seattle's hands, suggesting that Seattle's presence is spiritual, not physical. Seattle's headdress and body blend into clouds and mountains, suggesting that he is connected to the natural world. Seattle seems to be there to guide the boy into an appreciation of the natural world.

Inside the book, Jeffers continues this theme. As we read the words attributed to Chief Seattle, Jeffers shows Native Americans living in an unspoiled environment. The Native Americans illustrated by Jeffers are clearly not Suquamish. They are shown with the wrong clothing (in fact the clothing doesn't match that of any known Native American people), the wrong canoe, and riding horses, though the Suquamish didn't ride horses. Even the words attributed to Seattle are suspect—a film maker claims to have written them in the 1970s for an Earth Day celebration (Murray, 1993). At the end of the book, Jeffers shows a forest that has been clear cut, a family of European Americans planting trees, and a mystical Native American family watching approvingly. Seattle's words become a prophecy spoken on behalf of all Native Americans to European Americans, respect the land or you will lose it.

If *Brother Eagle, Sister Sky* is viewed as a book about Seattle and the Suquamish people, the book is a failure. But the book isn't really about Native American life. Rather, Jeffers uses the association of Native Americans with living environmentally responsible lives to send a message to European Americans. The presence of Native Americans in *Brother Eagle, Sister Sky* means something other than a particular culture. Their presence represents to whites an attitude about the environment many whites admire and want children to adopt.

Lynne Cherry uses Native Americans in a similar fashion in *A River Ran Wild*. Cherry describes how the Nashua River was respected by Native Americans, polluted by European Americans, and cleaned up through the efforts of many people. Significantly, Cherry uses two Native Americans, Oweana and his long-deceased ancestor, Weewa, as counterpoints to the Europeans who despoil the river. Weewa appears in a dream to Oweana. In the dream Weewa sheds tears for the polluted Nashua River and his tears cleanse the river. This dream inspires Oweana to join with Marion Stoddard to work for the clean-up of the river.

When Native Americans appear in a book about the environment, their appearance means something and it has little to do with the particulars of a Native American culture. Jeffers and Cherry borrow from dominant culture its image of Native Americans as a sign of environmental responsibility. What is stated explicitly in *A River Ran Wild* and implicitly in *Brother Eagle, Sister Sky* is that Native American responsibility should be juxtaposed with European American irresponsibility. In the views of many these may be flattering, albeit romantic images of Native Americans. But neither book is really about Native American culture. The meanings implied for the images of Native Americans in these two books are white meanings— that is, the signs are used as the dominant culture would normally use them. White America has appropriated Native Americans as a sign that white America will use to convey meaning about environmental responsibility.

How race, class, and gender mean in a story is vital to the reading of children's literature. These meanings are not fixed messages, lying dormant until the reader comprehends them. Viewing reading as an act of *comprehension* places authority outside the reader. A semiotic view of reading focuses upon *interpretation* and interpretation is reader-based. If we view reading not as comprehending existing messages, but interpreting certain signs with which we have a relationship that includes experience, culture, and value, we can see readers as becoming more powerful interpreters of their reading and of their world.

For me, multiculturalism as a social movement has three aspects. First, multiculturalism is a systematic critique of the ideology of westernness. This means we challenge the domination of assumptions held by our western culture. Second, multiculturalism is also the challenge of living with each other in a world of difference. Multiculturalism means searching for ways to affirm and celebrate difference, while also seeking ways to cooperate and collaborate across different groups of people. Third, multiculturalism is a reform movement based upon equity and justice. Goods and privileges are concentrated with white, wealthy males; they are not distributed justly across race, class, and gender. Multiculturalism is about social change and social justice.

Too often in practice multiculturalism is something students learn about. This practice suggests that we all become tourists, traveling to other cultures, learning what we can from them, and then returning, perhaps wiser in knowledge of the ways of another group, perhaps a bit more aware of the effects of bigotry, but no less ignorant in how to effect real change. The role of children's literature in a tourist approach to multiculturalism is to provide lists of books about underrepresented groups. Classifying books as authentic or culturally conscious (Sims, 1982; Cai & Bishop, 1994) is vital for tourists. Such efforts at classification usually key into the origin of the author and have invited spirited debate on whether white authors can write authentic books about persons of color. The origin of the author is also vital to the identification and development of the literature of a specific group. It is ludicrous to argue that books written by whites (e.g., *Sounder, The Cay*) be included in the body of work we would call African American children's literature. But some books written by white authors, such as *Nightjohn* (Paulsen, 1993), are honest descriptions of an African American experience. It is not proper to refer to *Nightjohn* as African American children's literature, but it would be unfortunate if *Nightjohn* was ignored because its author, Gary Paulsen, is white. These lists are also useful in identifying what publishers are doing or in evaluating the balance of a reading list. And scholars (see Sims, 1982, for example) have used this information to call for the development of a body of literature that better represents the experiences of the diversity of children in this country. However, the categories are less useful to describe what readers actually do with books.

The point I wish to make is simple. The way we teach reading has to change if multiculturalism is the reform movement so many have claimed it to be (Banks, 1993; Cai & Bishop, 1994; Perry & Fraser, 1993; Sleeter & Grant, 1993; McCarthy, 1993; Bishop, 1994; Harris, 1994; Nieto, 1992). Multiculturalism isn't something we study or learn about. It isn't a bibliography of good books about underrepresented groups. It isn't a month or week of focused study on a particular group. *Multiculturalism is a perspective we take on and struggle to understand, a stance we take to our reading that race, class, and gender matter in the way we interpret stories.*

Toni Morrison (1992) has argued brilliantly in her book, *Playing in the Dark: Whiteness and the Literary Imagination,* that we live in a racialized society. Racialized does not mean the same as racist, though they are not incompatible terms. Racialized means that race matters in how we think about one another. Race is a category into which we slot people and that category has meaning. Our culture has taught us that there is meaning in the identity of someone as black or white, male or female, rich or poor. By examining how race, class, and gender mean in our stories, we begin to understand how we live our lives according to these meanings. This is a big step beyond multiculturalism as tourism. Race, class, and gender are social semiotics—they mean—they are *signs* to be interpreted. If we deny that race, class, and gender are not signs to be interpreted, then we also deny what is obvious, that literature is a cultural product and that race, class, and gender do not matter in our lives. By making the racialized, classed, and gendered nature of our culture explicit, by making the signs visible, reflecting upon the sign, we can teach children to become readers not just of the word but also of the world.

RACE MATTERS

If readers take a stance that race matters (West, 1993, 1994), that is, if readers attend to the signs of race and how authors and illustrators use race to convey meaning, then readers often make interesting and provocative readings of children's books.

Charlie Parker Played Be Bop (Raschka, 1992) and *Ben's Trumpet* (Isadora, 1979) are both about jazz and making music and were created by European Americans. Each book uses the association of jazz with African

Americans to create mood. Raschka keeps his book focused solely upon the sound coming from Parker's saxophone, the book stays focused upon the music. His illustrations of Parker are caricature, a style that can easily become offensive, but seems appropriate to the funky, be bop tone of the book.

Isadora's book would seem to have a similar purpose of conveying the idea of jazz in print and picture, but she chooses to attempt a culturally conscious book (Sims, 1982) and in the process uses a stereotype of the dysfunctional black family. Since this family is shown ignoring Ben, gambling, and drinking through illustrations and these facts are not commented on but rather are accepted by the narrator, Isadora gives the impression that she is portraying the way black families are. Because Isadora is white, her race also becomes a sign, the book becomes a white woman's vision of what black city life in the 1920s is like. Family and friends ignore Ben, they look disinterested. Dad is seen gambling and drinking, irresponsible acts given the family's economic state. Perhaps this is why many whites find criticisms by African Americans of the book so puzzling. The dysfunctional black family is a sign many white readers accept without question. This illustrates how race matters and what living in a racialized society means. The typical argument among some whites that *Ben's Trumpet* doesn't stereotype black families is that, "surely, there are black families like that." Yes, surely there are. And surely there are African Americans who enjoy eating watermelon. But if a white illustrator shows African Americans eating watermelon, that person would justifiably be accused of using a stereotypical image of African Americans. That one or some African American families are dysfunctional doesn't negate the impact of a white illustrator drawing a poor black father drinking and gambling and presenting this sign out into a culture where race matters. While Isadora's book is a stunning blend of word, picture, and music, its use of race needs to be questioned.

In *Tar Beach* (Ringgold, 1991) we have a much different use of race as a sign. Like Isadora's book, *Tar Beach* is set in the city, but unlike *Ben's Trumpet*, *Tar Beach* is a celebration of African American life and an emancipation from the discrimination her family faces. Ringgold weaves a fantastic element of flying with the realities of life for an African American family in the city. Cassie, the protagonist, realizes her dreams by flying over, and thus owning, structures such as the George Washington bridge, the building that houses the union that excludes her father, and the ice cream factory. The book is thoroughly conscious of race and uses this sign as well as others to show us the dreams, desires, pains and pleasures of a struggling black family. It is a racialized book, as is *Ben's Trumpet*, but its use of race is far different.[1]

A common complaint against readings such as I have done is that they are too political and that political readings overwhelm other aesthetic qualities of the text (see Gill, 1995). This argument conceals an unwillingness to examine the dominant political agenda. The argument that political readings overwhelm the beauty of the literature is a straw argument (Taxel, 1995; Taxel, 1994; Saul, 1995; Saul, 1994; Kelly, 1985). Certainly the manner in which the book uses race to make meaning ought to be one characteristic of what makes a book a good book. We cannot deny that content is part of literary quality.

These signs of race, class, and gender are not just in the books, it takes a reader to make them come alive. In other words if a reader does not attend to race in these books then these meanings based upon a critical reading of race do not exist for that reader. What I am suggesting is that we need to examine how we read and how we teach children to read. I am aware of no set of prepared lessons that asks children to examine how an author uses race (or class or gender) to mean. Yet reading children's literature from a multicultural stance demands such a reading. Anything else smacks of tourism.

The Moves Make the Man by Bruce Brooks (1984) is the story of two boys, one black and one white, living in North Carolina in the 1960s. The story is narrated by Jerome Foxworthy, an African American boy, who desegregates the white high school and later is denied a place on the basketball team even though he is clearly the best player in the school. Brooks raises these two serious and important racial issues in the book and then ignores them. It is bewildering that a story narrated by a character who is the first black student in a North Carolina high school and is unjustly kept off the basketball team wouldn't be dominated by these events. That is, it is shocking if you are expecting Brooks's story to be about a black character's life. If we hold that Jerome's race matters, Jerome's race, in the story Brooks chose to tell, serves a much different function than to comment on racial issues. Why is Jerome black if Brooks isn't going to explore seriously issues of race? Brooks needs the character of Jerome to offset Bix Rivers, a messed-up white boy. Jerome may be the narrator, but the story is Bix's. Both Jerome and Bix are outcasts and loners—Bix because he is mentally unstable, Jerome because he is the only African American in the school. The characters need each other and in the process Jerome serves as a foil for Bix. Though as outcast and as alone as Bix (though for different reasons) unlike Bix, Jerome is totally sane. Jerome's blackness and saneness contrast sharply with Bix's whiteness and mental instability. It is Jerome's ability to use fakes and deception on the basketball court that serves as a comment on Bix's revulsion to anything false, including a basketball move. Brooks's book is an example of how a white imagination uses race.

Another basketball book, *Hoops,* by Walter Dean Myers (1981), takes a different perspective on race. Race in this book is a subject, that is, the book tells a story about being black in Harlem, compared with *The Moves Make the Man,* where race serves as object or metaphor of sanity and contrast to whites. A gritty book, *Hoops* shows the struggles of talented black athletes trying to find success in a world that has excluded them. Basketball is a means of escaping the inner city, but it is not a metaphor for life, such as Brooks uses it. Myers looks at race and class issues, daring to take on issues such as different shades of blackness and upper-class African Americans.

By comparing books with similar themes, the differences between a white and a black imagination can become stark. *Maniac Magee* (Spinelli, 1990) and *Roll of Thunder, Hear My Cry* (Taylor, 1976), each winners of the Newbery medal, offer contrasting views of tensions between blacks and whites. The main characters of the two books, Jeffrey "Maniac" Magee and Cassie Logan, are, at the beginning of each book, naive about the importance of race. The books describe how Maniac and Cassie each struggle to understand how race matters in their world. Cassie has been shielded from contact with whites so that she might develop a self that is not defined by the more powerful and racist white society. Cassie doesn't understand why being black should force her into being very careful in her dealings with whites; why she must defer to whites; why whites should have privileges that she does not have. Cassie loses her naiveté through a careful, yet tense, introduction into black/white relationships. Mama takes Cassie to visit the Berrys, who were burned by white hooligans, and Cassie learns about the hate and violence of her white neighbors. Big Ma takes Cassie to the farmer's market located in the small town named Strawberry, and Cassie learns that the whites expect her to act with deference when she is around them. But by the end of the book, Cassie also has learned how to fight back, how to struggle for the respect and justice she deserves from the world. By the end of the book she knows better how to read the white and black worlds she lives in, how to survive in them, and where she can join others to struggle for a more just world.

In contrast, Maniac Magee doesn't understand why race matters. He believes that if the whites and blacks of Two Mills will only learn about each other, racial animosity would disappear. While living in the black community, Maniac Magee ponders differences in color. While living in the white community, he passes on knowledge. Eventually Maniac Magee's idealism forces both blacks and whites in the town to reconsider their prejudices. Both books are racialized books, but the characters in *Maniac Magee* and *Roll of Thunder, Hear My Cry* understand race differently. *Maniac Magee* is a fantasy. What *would* happen if people could put aside their notions about race; what if race didn't matter in the way we interact with one another? The book is a product of a white, liberal imagination. *Roll of Thunder, Hear My Cry* cannot afford such fantastic elements—it would compromise Taylor's story of how race (and class) matters to the lives of African Americans. In vivid contrast to Maniac Magee's idea that breaking down walls of ignorance will end discrimination, Taylor has David Logan offering this advice to his children who are playing with Jeremy Sims, a poor, white boy: "Far as I'm concerned, friendship between black and white don't mean that much 'cause it usually ain't on a equal basis. Right now you and Jeremy might get along fine, but in a few years he'll think of himself as a man but you'll probably still be a boy to him. And if he feels that way, he'll turn on you in a minute . . . . We Logans don't have much to do with white folks. You know why? 'Cause white folks mean trouble . . . . May be one day whites and blacks can be real friends, but right now the country ain't built that way" (pp. 119–120). Taylor has a different story to tell—how being black mattered in rural Mississippi during the Depression.

GENDER MATTERS AND SO DOES CLASS

It's easy to understand why *The Secret Garden* (Burnett, 1911, 1987) remains popular after nearly 100 years in print. Adults, such as Archibald Craven, his brother Dr. Craven, and Mrs. Medlock, are unsympathetic characters. The children, Mary, Colin, and Dickon, keep secrets from the adults about the garden and about Colin's physical recovery and the children do things that adults do not know about. There is a sense of subversion in the book, as Lurie (1990) and Paul (1990) have noted, that is characteristic of children's literature that endures across generations. *The Secret Garden* is a triumph of children over adults.

A multicultural stance—one that seeks to understand how race, class, and gender mean in a story—taken to *The Secret Garden* shows a different meaning. A reading that accounts for class and gender makes it clear that the poor and women, though apparently each with more sense than rich males, have been put on earth to serve rich males. The working-class people in *The Secret Garden* exist for the upper class. Dickon and Martha happily serve. Dickon's mother, who is poor, buys a jump rope out of pity for the spoiled rich girl. The narrator of the story seems upset that Colin and Mr. Craven are ungrateful, that they are poor custodians of the privilege to which they were born. But the story doesn't question their right to be privileged. Once Colin is well, Mary's place in the story gives way to Colin. Her task is finished once Colin is well and the garden (and the story) become his. Martha's and Dickon's tasks are to awaken Mary. Mary's task is to awaken Colin. Colin as male heir to his father's fortune has no task or responsibility to anyone except to himself.

A romantic view of class pervades the book. The poor are noble savages. They don't need modern medicine or money, just fresh air and starchy food. They are uncorrupted by wealth; innocently happy in their destitution.

While these attitudes may be genuine to the time and the privileged class to which Mary and Colin belong, this does not mean these attitudes should be received by readers unquestioningly. This isn't a matter of arguing whether Burnett should have written the book the way she did. It is a matter of *reading* the book she did write. This is a reading issue—not a writing one.

If I were to use *The Secret Garden* in an upper elementary school grade, I would contrast it with books that explore class and gender from a different perspective—a perspective that challenges the assumption that rich white males deserve the privileges society has bestowed upon them. Books such as *Prairie Songs* (Conrad, 1985), which explores the lives of women on the Nebraska prairie (though the depiction of Native Americans as savages in this book ought to be explored as well); *Working Cotton* (Williams, 1992) and *Voices from the Fields* (Atkin, 1993), books that describe the lives of children of migrant farm workers living today; *Mother Jones: One Woman's Fight for Labor* (Kraft, 1995), the biography of the fiesty labor organizer who confronted some of the richest and most powerful men of her time; *Kids at Work* (Freedman, 1994), which documents child labor at the turn of century (the same time period as the setting for *The Secret Garden*); *Lyddie* (Paterson, 1991), the story of a girl working in the textile mills of early 19th-century New England; *Farmer Duck* (Waddell, 1991), a razor sharp, humorous book about workers and landlords; and *Children of the Dust Bowl* (Stanley, 1992), an account of migrant children in the 1930s. These books show the lives of women and working poor, the Dickons, Marthas, and Ben Weatherstaffs, from their perspective rather than the perspective of the rich and powerful.

At the beginning of each semester, I ask my students to list the children's books they remember fondly from their childhood. Without exception, Shel Silverstein's *The Giving Tree* (1964) is mentioned. This book is about a tree (who is identified as a "she") who loves a boy. As the boy grows into adulthood and then into old age, the boy asks the tree for her apples, her branches, her trunk, and the tree happily grants each request until all that remains of the tree is a stump. The story ends with the boy, now an elderly man, resting on the stump and the tree is happy. My students tend to see this book as a statement of unselfish love, the kind of love a parent would give a child. Often readers do not notice the gender of the tree. But if a reader takes the gender of the tree into account in the reading of this story, another meaning emerges—that of a male exploiting the female—taking all that the tree has to offer and giving little in return. Gender must matter in this book. Silverstein could have made the tree an "it" if gender did not matter.

Though my students tend not to notice the gender of the tree when left on their own, when I ask my students to read *The Giving Tree* alongside Anthony Browne's *Piggybook* (1986), the sign of gender in *The Giving Tree* becomes more apparent. The cover of *Piggybook* strikingly shows the theme:

A mother is shown holding up her husband and two sons piggyback. As the cover suggests, the story is about Mrs. Piggot becoming tired with the demands of her husband and two boys that she serve them and do all the housework for them. She leaves her male chauvinist pig family to fend for themselves. After many disastrous attempts to do the cooking and weeks of neglecting the cleaning, the male Piggots come to realize the inequity of the arrangement of work at home. Mrs. Piggot returns and household jobs are divided up equally among the members of the family. By reading a book that takes a different view of gender alongside *The Giving Tree*, it problematizes Silverstein's book. Mrs. Piggot's situation is similar to that of the tree in *The Giving Tree*. By comparing the two books, new meanings become possible—meanings that explore the signs of gender.

At a workshop, I asked a group of teachers to read *The Giving Tree* and *Piggybook* together. The teachers were familiar with *The Giving Tree*, less so with *Piggybook*. After reading the two books, they commented that they had never considered the gender of the tree as important to the story until they had read *Piggybook* alongside it. For them, *The Giving Tree* had been a story of unconditional love. Reading it side-by-side with *Piggybook*, the gender issues became much more obvious. They were taken with *Piggybook*, but very reluctant to bring the book into their classroom. They were afraid that some vocal parents would make mischief for them because of the obvious feminist theme of the book. They also expressed doubt that children would pick up on the gender themes.

Challenged by that remark, I read the two stories to a fourth grade class. After a discussion in which I asked the children to share their initial reactions to the stories, I asked the children to make pictures comparing the two stories. With one exception, the children's pictures showed the boy in *The Giving Tree* and Mr. Piggot and his two sons from *Piggybook*. They noted that each of these characters were takers who had "no feelings" for the tree and the mother. The group that was the exception showed the tree giving the boy her apples and the mother working in the kitchen while Dad and the boys watch TV, commenting that the tree and the mother were taken advantage of by others. Then I asked, "Should we make anything of the fact that the mother and the tree are females and the boy and Mr. Piggot and his sons are males?" Many, but not all, of the boys thought, "no," while many, but not all, of the girls thought, "yes." They discussed their differences of opinion, formed no consensus, and finished, having aired their thoughts without forcing their views upon anyone. And they had considered gender as an appropriate sign to consider in their reading. This, I argue, is not *imposing*, but *exposing* assumptions about gender by *opposing* different points of view.

"WHO HAS SET THIS TABLE?"

BROWN HONEY
My mother says I am
Brown honey in broomwheat tea
My father calls me the sweetwater
          of his days
Yet they warn
There are those who
Have brewed a
Bitter potion for
Children kissed long by the sun
Therefore I approach
The cup slowly
But first I ask
Who has set this table

—Joyce Carol Thomas (1993)

Issues of race, class, and gender often become more visible when books are compared. Books that appear simple and sweet when read by themselves become problematized in the company of a book that takes a different perspective. My suggestion for a multicultural curriculum is to let traditions debate each other—explore the assumptions of race, class, and gender—ask what person is the author asking me to become? This is what I have tried to do with *The Moves Make the Man* and *Hoops, Maniac Magee* and *Roll of Thunder*, and *The Giving Tree* and *Piggybook*. Reading multiculturally isn't about censoring bad books. It is about reading the signs of race, class, and gender in the books we have. These texts and the readings we give them say much about how we view each other. This isn't about censoring books, rather this is about learning to read our world, it is asking the question Joyce Carol Thomas asks, "Who has set this table?"

By comparing books, the range of readings for each book increases. For example, compare a *Flossie and the Fox* (McKissack, 1986) with *Santa Calls* (Joyce, 1993). In *Flossie and the Fox,* Patricia McKissack uses race, class, and gender as political satire of the powerful. Flossie is poor, black, and female. She speaks in a rural Tennessee, black dialect. Flossie is sent by her mother to deliver a basket of eggs and is told to beware of the fox who will surely try to steal the eggs. Shortly after she enters the forest, the fox appears. The fox is male and his use of "King's English" suggests he is also white and rich.[2] When Flossie shows no fear, the fox insists that she be afraid of him. Flossie replies that she will not be afraid of him until he can prove he is a fox. A bold statement, it disarms the fox and their positions become reversed—it is Flossie who is in control and the fox becomes more and more desperate as he is unable to respond to the challenge to his authority. Flossie, using her cunning, out-smarts the fox. She refuses to grant the fox the privileges the fox believes are his birthright.

On the surface, *Santa Calls* (Joyce, 1993) would seem to have little in common with *Flossie and the Fox*. A closer look, though, shows that Joyce used race, class, and gender differently to tell a story than the way McKissack used these signs in *Flossie and the Fox*. Art Atchinson Aimesworth is the protagonist of *Santa Calls*. Though an orphan raised by his aunt and uncle, his name and his dress of sweater and tie suggests he belongs or aspires to the upper class. His best friend is a "young Comanche brave," named Spaulding Littlefeets, a hyperbolic mix of names that suggests upper-class and Native American roots. (Though Littlefeets strikes me as a product of a white imagination rather than an authentic Comanche name.) Art also has a little sister to whom he is often mean. One day a large crate is delivered to Art from Santa Claus, who beckons Art to assemble the contents and come north. A flying machine is assembled. The basket for passengers arrived broken, so Spaulding lends his "beloved canoe to the cause." The illustrations show Spaulding dressed in attire similar to Art's, with the exception of a leather headband and a long, braided ponytail. Art, Spaulding, and his sister Esther climb aboard the canoe and fly north.

At the North Pole they meet Santa's captain of the Santarian Guards, Ali Aku, and help him fight the Dark Elves and their evil Queen. During the fight the evil Queen abducts Esther, and Art must rescue his little sister. The adventure over, the children are returned to their home in Abilene, Texas, and Art wonders why Santa called him in the first place. At the end of the book, we are shown two letters, one from Esther to Santa asking for her brother to be nicer to her and a response from Santa saying he is happy the adventure has done the trick. Much of the humor of the book comes from the positioning of "exotic" elements, that is, non-western names and artifacts in places where a white audience would not expect them. The story is resolved through the worn-out trick of the adventurous boy rescuing the hapless girl. This book is brilliant in many ways, but its use of race and gender belie a white, male imagination at work. While McKissack uses race, class, and gender to comment (humorously, I should add) on social conditions, Joyce in *Santa Calls* uses race and class as hyperbole and gender as stereotype.

Few books have raised as much controversy as Ouida Sebestyen's *Words by Heart* (1979). The book tells of the Sills family which has moved west from an all-black community to a new place where they are the only black family in the area. Immediately, the family is threatened with violence, but Ben Sills, the Bible-quoting father, urges his family to remain calm and not rush the white folks. Eventually, Ben is wounded fatally by a white boy who was angry at Ben for taking a job that once belonged to his father. Incredulously, the dying Ben begs his daughter Lena not to press charges against his murderer but to forgive him. Reportedly, this story is one that comes from Sebestyen's family history. Interestingly, Sebestyen changes the race of her characters from white to black to great effect. Her story is one of forgiveness and plays to the Christian tradition of Christ as the suffering servant. Ben Sills is put into the Christ-like role, suffering the racism of the town with patience and an understanding that his tormentors cannot do otherwise. The act of forgiving a murderer is accentuated by the races of those involved, the victim being African American and the perpetrator being white. In a move similar to one Brooks used in *The Moves Make the Man*, Sebestyen has played upon the sign of African Americans as victims to make her point about forgiving one's enemies. What greater act of forgiveness could there be than an African American family forgiving the white boy who has killed their father?

It is oppressive when someone from a dominant group uses a less powerful group as a sign. This use of race objectifies, that is, it makes the African American characters objects rather than subjects. Real issues of race, class, and gender are ignored when the sign is appropriated for other reasons by dominant groups. However, we are rarely taught to read in such a fashion. I've had more than one white colleague defend *Words by Heart* as brilliant and as accurate. "Surely there were black families like that and surely there were men like Ben Sills," they argue. When I reply that I've yet to have an African American student read that book and find it anything but abhorrent, my colleagues seem stunned. This is a stark difference in how race is read by different readers.

Roll of Thunder, Hear My Cry is an excellent book to read alongside *Words by Heart*. The differences in how the Logans and the Sills understand racism and respond to it are striking. Another book that is interesting to compare with *Words by Heart* is *The Star Fisher* by Laurence Yep (1992). Like *Words by Heart*, *The Star Fisher* is a story that comes from the author's family. The book tells of the Lees, a Chinese American family that moves from a secure community where they were not racially isolated, into a new community that promises greater economic opportunity but also racial isolation. The Lees are the victims of much prejudice and it takes much patience and courage on their part to persevere in their attempt to convince the town that they are Americans, too. A breakthrough seems to occur when Joan Lee's mother learns to make delicious apple pies that catch the attention and admiration of members of the local church. Though Yep's view of the Lees is much more sympathetic than Sebestyen's description of the Sills, *The Star Fisher* offers many of the same solutions to bigotry as *Words by Heart*—patience, forgiveness, and a willingness to blend in (what could be more American than apple pie?). The story seems to suggest that the resolution of tensions among peoples occurs when the less powerful show that they can fit in and become "real" Americans. It isn't the definition of what an American is that is elastic, in the case of *The Star Fisher;* that definition cannot accommodate the Asian American Lees. It is the identity of the Lees that must assimilate into American culture.

READING MULTICULTURALLY

This is a reading issue—we afford great freedom to writers—therefore we need crafty readers who can interpret the signs—examine the rhetoric. Sartre (1988) wrote that literature can only exist in a true democracy— where readers have the freedom to respond, to argue, to choose.

Though I have been critical of the politics of *Brother Eagle, Sister Sky, A River Ran Wild, The Moves Make the Man, The Secret Garden, The Giving Tree, Maniac Magee, Santa Calls,* and *Words by Heart,* this does not mean I don't think they are well-written and well-illustrated books. They are and Jeffers, Cherry, Brooks, Burnett, Silverstein, Spinelli, Joyce, and Sebestyen are talented creators of books for children. But just because they are good artists doesn't excuse their works from criticism of their content. Likewise, I have praised *Hoops, Tar Beach, Piggybook, Roll of Thunder, Flossie and the Fox* and others for their content. That doesn't mean I overlook the aesthetics of these books. Indeed, the artists who created these books are talented as well, and their works show virtuosity in crafting of text and image. Politics and art are inseparable, and the responsibility for identifying a work as a work of quality literature lies with readers. Suzanne Langer (1953) wrote quite some time ago that the two questions the critic must answer are, "What has the author made?" and "How did the author make it?" This means that readers should seek and name books as well written and well illustrated, *and* ask what is being represented in these books. There can be no difference between a literary reading and a multicultural reading.

What I am suggesting is not what has been derisively called by some as "political correctness"—a dismissive term that reduces discussion to name calling. Reading multiculturally is a challenge to the status quo. The challenge of multicultural education is a challenge to reform.

Like most school children, my daughters live in a dominant culture that does not encourage them to account for gender (or race or class) in their reading. They are taught the opposite—that stories have no political meaning or that to make a political meaning will overpower the aesthetic value of literature. We were taught and we continue to teach in our schools that, under the laws of the United States, race, class, and gender do not matter; we are equal. This myth is useful only for hiding what we all know: wealth, power, privilege, and justice are distributed unequally among the rich and poor, whites and persons of color, males and females. Unlike Jeffrey "Maniac" Magee, we cannot afford the belief that justice will happen naturally if people just learn about each other. Eichmann, the Nazi leader who supervised the death camps that murdered millions of Jews and other human beings the Nazis deemed to be "undesirable," spoke fluent Hebrew and Yiddish.

Doesn't reading a book in the context of another book interfere with the meaning a reader might otherwise make? Absolutely! But not to make the signs visible is to cede the meaning of the sign to the orthodoxy of a dominant and popular culture. This is imposition by omission—a far more insidious interference than directly confronting our assumptions. There cannot be a context free of cultural and social influence. Every day mass media, popular culture, religion, and school textbooks "interfere" with the meanings children make. Multiculturalism disappears without the challenge of critique.

Multiculturalism, at least in part, is about challenging mainstream discourse. Even if desired, it is impossible to purge reading of social interference and influence. Culture sets the meaning for signs. If we are not satisfied with how certain groups of people are treated, then society's assumptions must be challenged. There cannot be true reform if the meaning of signs is not challenged. The sign itself must be reviewed. This means we may need to be explicit with children that race, class, and gender are signs to be read and interpreted in stories. We will need to show children how to read in this manner, just as we demonstrate other possible readings to children.

Multiculturalism is about reform, as so many have suggested (Banks, 1993; Cai & Bishop, 1994; Perry & Fraser, 1993; Sleeter & Grant, 1993; McCarthy, 1993; Bishop, 1994; Harris, 1994; Nieto, 1992). We need to teach reading accordingly. Challenging assumptions about race, class, and gender must be at the core of multicultural education; our reading needs to do the same. How do authors use race, class, and gender to mean? What assumptions about race, class, and gender do they ask us to take on? What assumptions do we bring to text? We do not always need to read *with* an author; we can also read against an author, questioning and even refusing to become the kinds of sympathetic readers of their stories that authors ask us to become. And we can read authors against each other. Looking at reading children's literature in elementary schools this way moves us from a naive pedagogy of tourism to a pedagogy of critique, change, and justice. This is not an easy or safe pedagogy, but it is the one with which I believe we are all called to struggle.

ENDNOTES

1. A book that uses the sign of African Americans in a way similar to that used in *Tar Beach* and serves as a contrast to *Ben's Trumpet* is *Cornrows* (Yarbrough, 1979). The book is also a good antidote to "cultural literacy" (Hirsch, 1988) zealots.

2. If you are still skeptical that race, class, and gender are signs to be interpreted and that they matter in the meanings we make, try changing the character of Flossie into a rich, white boy and the fox into a poor, black girl. I suspect most readers would switch their allegiance to the fox and hope that the rich, white boy loses the basket of eggs.

BIBLIOGRAPHY

Atkin, S. B. (1993). *Voices from the fields: Children of migrant farmworkers tell their stories.* Boston: Little, Brown.

Banks, J. A. (1993). Multicultural education: Characteristics and goals. In J. A. Banks and C. A. M. Banks (Eds.), *Multicultural education: Issues and perspectives,* second edition (pp. 3–28). Boston: Allyn and Bacon.

Barthes, R. (1974). *S/Z.* New York: Hill and Wang.

Bauman, R. (1977). *Verbal art as performance.* Prospect Heights, IL: Waveland Press.

Bauman, R. (1986). *Story, performance, and event: Contextual studies of oral narrative.* Cambridge: Cambridge University Press.

Bishop, R. S. (1994). A reply to Shannon the canon. *Journal of Children's Literature,* 20, 6–8.

Bloome, D. (1983). Reading as a social process. In B. Hudston (Ed.), *Advances in reading/language research,* Vol. 2. (pp. 165–195). Greenwich, CT: JAI Press.

Bloome, D. (1985). Reading as a social process. *Language Arts,* 62, 134–142.

Booth, W. C. (1983). *The rhetoric of fiction,* second edition. Chicago: University of Chicago Press.

Brooks, B. (1984). *The moves make the man.* New York: Harper & Row.

Browne, A. (1986). *Piggybook.* New York: Knopf.

Burnett, F. H. (1911, 1987). *The secret garden.* New York: Bantam.

Cai, M. and Bishop, R. S. (1994). Multicultural literature for children: Towards a clarification of the concept. In A. H. Dyson and C. Genishi, *The need for story: Cultural diversity in classroom and community* (pp. 57–71). Urbana, IL: National Council of Teachers of English.

Chambers, A. (1985). *Booktalk: Occasional writing on literature and children.* New York: Harper & Row.

Cherry, L. (1992). *A river ran wild.* San Diego: Harcourt Brace Jovanovich.

Cochran-Smith, M. (1985). *The making of a reader.* Norwood, NJ: Ablex.

Collins, J. and Michaels, S. (1986). Speaking and writing: Discourse strategies and the acquisition of literacy. In J. Cook-Gumperz (Ed.), *The social construction of literacy*. Cambridge: Cambridge University Press.

Conrad, P. (1985). *Prairie songs*. New York: Harper & Row.

Cook-Gumperz, J. and Green, J. (1984). A sense of story. In D. Tannen (Ed.), *Coherence in written and spoken discourse* (pp. 201–218). Norwood, NJ: Ablex.

Fish, S. (1980). *Is there a text in this class? The authority of interpretive communities*. Cambridge, MA: Harvard University Press.

Freedman, R. (1994). *Kids at work: Lewis Hine and the crusade against child labor*. New York: Clarion.

Gill, S. R. (1995). A reader responds: Children's literature and political correctness. *The New Advocate*, 8, vii–viii.

Grant, C. A. and Sleeter, C. E. (1993). Race, class, gender, and disability in the classroom. In J. A. Banks and C. A. M. Banks (Eds.), *Multicultural education: Issues and perspectives*, second edition (pp. 48–67). Boston: Allyn and Bacon.

Hade, D. D. (1989). *Events and stances as foundations of children's responses to literature: An ethnographic study of a second and third grade literature-based reading classroom*. Unpublished dissertation. The Ohio State University, Columbus, Ohio.

Hade, D. D. (1992). The reader's stance as event. In J. E. Many and C. Cox (Eds.), *Reader stance and literary understanding* (pp. 191–215). Norwood, NJ: Ablex.

Hade, D. D. (1994). Aiding and abetting the basalization of children's literature. *The New Advocate*, 7, 29–44.

Harris, V. J. (1994). No invitations required to share multicultural literature. *Journal of Children's Literature*, 20, 9–13.

Heath, S. B. (1982). What no bedtime story means: Narrative skills at home and school. *Language in Society*, 11, 49–76.

Heath, S. B. (1983). *Ways with words: Language, life and work in classrooms and communities*. London: Cambridge University Press.

Hirsch, E. D. (1988). *Cultural literacy: What every American should know*. Boston: Houghton Mifflin.

Howard, R. (1974). A note on *S/Z*. In R. Barthes, *S/Z* (pp. ix–xii). New York: Hill and Wang.

Hunt, P. (1991). *Criticism, theory, and children's literature*. Exhard, UK: Basil Blackwell.

Isadora, R. (1979). *Ben's trumpet*. New York: Greenwillow.

Jeffers, S. (1991). *Brother eagle, sister sky*. New York: Dial.

Joyce, W. (1993). *Santa calls*. New York: HarperCollins.

Kraft, B. H. (1995). *Mother Jones: One woman's fight for labor*. New York, Clarion.

Langer, S. (1953). *Feeling and form*. New York: Scribners.

Lewis, C. S. (1961). *An experiment in criticism*. Cambridge: Cambridge University Press.

Lurie, A. (1990). *Don't tell the grown-ups: Subversive children's literature*. Boston: Little, Brown and Company.

McCarthy, C. (1993). After the canon: Knowledge and ideological representation in multicultural discourse on educational reform. In C. McCarthy
and W. Crichlow (Eds.), *Race, identity, and representation in education*
(pp. 289–305). New York: Routledge.

McKissack, P. C. (1986). *Flossie and the fox*. Illustrated by Rachel Isadora.
New York: Dial.

Meek, M. (1987). *How texts teach what readers learn*. Great Britain: The
Thimble Press.

Michaels, S. (1986). Narrative presentations: An oral preparation for literacy with first graders. In J. Cook-Gumperz (Ed.), *The social construction of literacy*. Cambridge: Cambridge University Press.

Morrison, T. (1992). *Playing in the dark: Whiteness and the literary imagination*. New York: Vintage.

Murray, M. (1993). The little green lie. *Reader's Digest*, 100–104.

Myers, W. D. (1981). *Hoops*. New York: Dell.

Ninio, A. and Bruner, J. (1978). The achievement and antecedents of label-
ling. *Journal of Child Language*, 5, 5–15.

Paterson, K. (1991). *Lyddie*. New York: Lodestar.

Paul, L. (1990). Enigma variations: What feminist theory knows about
children's literature. In P. Hunt (Ed.), *Children's literature: The development of theory* (pp. 148–166). London: Routledge.

Paulsen, G. (1993). *Nightjohn*. New York: Delacorte.

Peirce, C. S. (1931–1935). *Collected papers* (Vols. 1–6). (P. Weiss and C.
Hartshorne, Eds.). Cambridge, MA: Harvard University Press.

Perry, T. and Fraser, J. W. (1993). Reconstruction schools as multiracial/
multicultural democracies: Toward a theoretical perspective. In T. Perry
and J. W. Fraser (Eds.), *Freedom's plow: Teaching in the multicultural
classroom*. New York: Routledge.

Raschka, C. (1992). *Charlie Parker played be bop*. New York: Orchard.

Ringgold, F. (1991). *Tar beach*. New York: Crown.

Roser, N. and Martinez, M. (1985). Roles adults play in preschoolers' response to literature. *Language Arts*, 62, 485–490.

Sartre, J. P. (1983). *"What is literature?" and other essays*. Cambridge, MA:
Harvard University Press.

Saul, W. (1994). Notes from the guest editor. *The New Advocate*, 7, vii–xi.

Saul, W. (1995). Practical reflections: Notes from the associate editor. *The
New Advocate*, 8, xv–xvii.

Scollon, R. and Scollon, S. B. K. (1982). Cooking it and boiling it down:
Abstracts in Athabaskan children's story retellings. In D. Tannen (Ed.),
Spoken and written language (pp. 173–197). Norwood, NJ: Ablex.

Scollon, R. and Scollon, S. B. K. (1981). *Narrative, literacy and face in inter-
ethnic communication*. Norwood, NJ: Ablex.

Sebestyen, O. (1979). *Words by heart*. Boston: Little, Brown.

Silverstein, S. (1964). *The giving tree*. New York: Harper & Row.

Sims, R. (1982). *Shadow and substance: Afro-American experience in contemporary children's fiction*. Urbana, IL: National Council of Teachers
of English.

Snow, C. E. and Goldfield, B. A. (1983). Turn the page please: Situation specific language learning. *Journal of Child Language*, 10, 551–570.

Spinelli, J. (1990). *Maniac Magee*. Boston: Little, Brown.

Stanley, J. (1992). *Children of the dust bowl: The true story of the school at Weedpatch Camp*. New York: Crown.

Taxel, J. (1994). Political correctness, cultural politics, and writing for young people. *The New Advocate*, 7, 93–108.

Taxel, J. (1995). Notes from the editor. *The New Advocate*, 8, ix–xii.

Taylor, M. D. (1976). *Roll of thunder, hear my cry*. New York: Dial.

Teale, W. H. (1984). Reading to young children: Its significance for literacy development. In H. Goelman, A. Oberg, and F. Smith, *Awakening to literacy*. Portsmouth, NH, Heinemann.

Thomas, J. C. (1993). *Brown honey in broomwheat tea*. Illustrated by Floyd Cooper. New York: HarperCollins.

Waddell, M. (1991). *Farmer duck*. Illustrated by Helen Oxenbury. Cambridge, MA: Candlewick.

West, C. (1994). *Race matters*. New York: Vintage.

Williams, S. A. (1992). *Working cotton*. Illustrated by Carole Byard. San Diego: Harcourt Brace Jovanovich.

Yarbrough, C. (1979). *Cornrows*. Illustrated by Carole Byard. New York: Coward McCann.

Yep, L. (1992). *The star fisher*. New York: Morrow.

Chapter 10

Toward Developing a Multicultural Perspective

Dierdre Glenn-Paul

ಹಿ ಹಿ ಹಿ ಹಿ ಹಿ

As a teacher educator in literacy, with a publicly acknowledged commitment to multicultural education, I am often confronted by both pre-service and in-service educators who say, "I know that I am supposed to be 'multicultural' in my classroom and I am familiar with the theories, but what does a multicultural classroom in which literacy development is fostered look like?" There are a number of ways in which the question can be interpreted. I take the question at face value and acknowledge the teacher's quest for some degree of understanding, regardless of motivation.

Yet, for me, the question is problematic for other reasons. First, the educator regards me as an expert, a role in which I am somewhat uncomfortable. Developing a multicultural perspective is an on-going, life-long process; thus, I will never achieve the status of an expert. Second, in a number of instances, it appears as if these educators are seeking simplistic, expedient recipes such as "read a book featuring a racial and/or ethnic character, celebrate students' diversity by asking them to bring their favorite home dishes to class, or share biographies of racial/ethnic heroes and heroines." If one considers James Banks' "Approaches to Multicultural Curriculum Reform" (1988), which outlines the four types of multicultural content integration, the recipes sought relegate multicultural curriculum to the lowest level of integration, the *Contributions* approach.

In wrestling with my response to such questions and in an attempt to display that one journeys toward a multicultural perspective rather than merely implements multicultural practices, I have chosen to reflect upon my six-year experience in the intermediate school classroom and year-long stint as an elementary school Communication Arts Teacher Trainer in this chapter. I specifically wish to share with other educators the way in which my classroom experience—the context in which I taught, the students in my classes, and my need to ensure their literacy—helped me to develop my present level of multicultural awareness. I will simultaneously attempt to share the process of my growth as a literacy educator.

It should additionally be noted that I use the term *Black* throughout this piece in contrast to African American because I am not only referring to American students, but to those whose families migrated from African and Caribbean geographic locations as well. Furthermore, I do not find the term *Black* offensive or less appropriate than African American. As Haki Madhubuti (1990) has suggested before me in *Black Men: Obsolete, Single, Dangerous?: Afrikan American Families in Transition: Essays in Discovering Solutions and Hopes,* I view the term with the same reverence with which it was used in the late 1960s and early 1970s. In reference to use of the term at that time, Black theologian Howard Thurman (as quoted in Hooks, 1989, p. 115) asserts that:

> "Black is Beautiful" became not merely a phrase—it was a stance, a total attitude, a metaphysics. In very positive and exciting terms it began undermining the idea that had developed over so many years into a central aspect of white mythology: that black is ugly, black is evil, black is demonic.

Similarly, I descriptively use the term *Latino/a* to reflect the "deep connection among all . . . in the Americas who are descendants of native inhabitants, Spanish and other European colonizers, and enslaved Africans, or any combination of these groups" (Nieto, 1992, p. 177). I do not use it to suggest that the group is monolithic.

BEGINNINGS

As a child, I loved to read. Some of my earliest and fondest memories include my grandparents reading picture storybooks to me that my mother had sent. Then, the books served as the lifeline between my mother and me as we were temporarily separated and I lived with my grandparents in Birmingham, Alabama. I vividly remember sitting on my grandmother's lap (or my mother's when she visited) and being read to. I can still feel the skin of the reader against my own and the smell of the reader's perfume and warm breath. Thus, for me, the affective qualities of these readings were as consequential as the content. With such positive experiences with reading behind me, it is no wonder that I continue to foster the love of reading.

As I entered the New York City Board of Education as a first-year teacher in a Bronx intermediate school, however, I was confronted by 5th, 6th, and 7th grade students who unashamedly boasted "I hate to read." This antipathy was somewhat baffling to me; it just didn't fit my existing schema of reading. Some of my students were alliterate. They could read, meaning they could both decode and comprehend. Yet, reading proved to be a bore, especially when there was Nintendo, Sega Genesis, television, rap star MC Lyte, Arnold Schwarzenegger and Jean Claude Van Damme videotapes with which to contend.

Other students hated reading because it was a source of both difficulty and embarrassment. It had caused, in their minds, other students to laugh at them during those famed round-robin reading sessions. It had caused teachers to saccharinely smile and say "That was nice reading," when the snickers in the back of the classroom clearly indicated that it was a far cry from "nice." It had also caused teachers to yell, "Can't you read?" Sometimes I wonder what would have happened if a student had yelled back at that very instant, "What's wrong with you . . . can't you teach me to read?"

Holdaway (1979, p. 16) asserts that:

> . . . Learning theory would predict that if literacy is taught in an environment in which competition decides the nature and levels of individual rewards for learning, an over-reinforced elite will excel [slanting use away from understanding toward performance]; a large minority subjected to intensive punitive feedback will fail [with appalling effects on mental health]; and a majority, treated to years of indifference and low levels of reinforcement, will use literacy as little as possible outside the instructional setting.

In the spirit of fairness, however, it must be acknowledged that these students' problems with literacy did not evolve solely from formalized educational experiences.

Some students' problems resulted from a lack of commitment to formal education in their homes. This attitude could be gleaned from comments made by both parents and children in this working-class and poor, Black and Latino/a community. For example, some parents shared that, as per the dictates of their socio-economic reality, work was the priority. Everything else, including their children's academic performance, was of secondary importance.

A possible outcome of such sacrifice, however, is children who cannot read. It has been solidly established that children from backgrounds in which school is given little merit do not exhibit the same degree of literacy as children from school-oriented households (Heath, 1983).

There were other parents who harbored antipathetic feelings about the school culture as a result of their own experiences and/or the antagonistic nature of interaction they experienced with school officials regarding their children. In many ways, these parents were rebelling against the premise of the school culture as the dominant culture and the implications surrounding that premise. As alluded to and/or discussed by Delpit (1988), Edelsky and Harman (1991), and Willis (1995), these parents from traditionally marginalized cultures were painfully aware that the school culture was unresponsive and unable to cope with the needs of their children as evidenced by the curriculum addressed, discipline used, and educational materials selected.

Truthfully, I was concerned about both sets of students, the alliterate and the illiterate. I hoped to spark an interest in reading in all of my students. Yet, my most prominent concern was to expose the students in my remedial classes to a wide variety of books and to establish a comfort zone for them in which books played a part in their schooling.

This concern was engendered as a result of growing up and attending school in the same community in which my students presently lived and then receiving the opportunity to attend boarding school in Massachusetts. This experience permitted me to see the disparity between education for the White elite compared with education for the working class and/or poor people of color. The difference could be seen in everything from the educational materials used to the instructional format.

I also realized that without the ability to read and understand the power inherent in the written word, a number of my students (as happened to many of my public school classmates) would be relegated to existences in which drugs, prison, dropping out, and poverty played inevitable roles. In my estimation, there is a strong connection between insufficient literacy development and dropping out. Wacquant and Wilson (1989) extend the connection by identifying the ties between dropping out and poverty, asserting that "Not finishing secondary education is synonymous with economic redundancy" (p. 18).

As a result of the perceived gravity of this matter, determining an educational plan that would enhance my students' facility with language, provide them with greater access to society, and counter these social ills was of utmost importance to me.

THE BEGINNINGS OF READING INSTRUCTION IN A BRONX CLASSROOM

How could I go about turning my concern and desire into a feasible educational plan? I had commenced teaching through the alternate certification route that was created out of necessity. There simply weren't enough teachers to meet the demands of the growing New York City student population. Yet, at 21 years of age, with a degree in English/Journalism and without the benefit of an education, literacy, or children's and adolescent literature course, this first-year teacher wasn't experienced or knowledgeable enough to develop a full instructional plan that emphasized literacy development. Examining the experience retrospectively and according to Gordon's (1974) Skill Development Ladder that outlines the stages of a teacher's professional development, I was both unconsciously unskilled and unconsciously talented.

In regard to on-site staff development, the Communication Arts Teacher Trainer provided me with the basal series used by a number of teachers and the assistant principal reviewed my lesson plans for content. I was given few concrete suggestions regarding effective teaching for the three classes in my charge. I had even fewer ideas for teaching the approximately 80 to 100 students I encountered each day; after all, I had been licensed as a Day High School teacher of English. I began my career with the vision that I would teach Shakespeare, Milton, and Chaucer, as opposed to basal selections.

By and large, I felt as though I was on my own and I sensed that the children were bored with the basal selections. I also felt that the basal reader used, although considered literature-based, contained stilted, basalized language and did not intellectually challenge the students for the most part. Even at this early stage of my career, I knew that students should be actively engaged with text. At the time, however, active engagement was relegated to their acknowledged enjoyment of text primarily, as opposed to their ability to critically analyze, interpret, and interact with it.

As a result of my perceptions and beliefs, I initiated a component of a literacy plan . . . read-aloud. I believed that this activity would, at least, spark my students' interest in reading. Thus, one can imagine that I was somewhat dismayed by their less-than-glowing reactions to this innovation. "This is boring," I heard from some. Others clearly voiced their opinions by placing their heads on their desks and sleeping. I had not yet heard the cliched admonition about being "a guide on the side rather than a sage on the stage." In my mind, my readings were as stirring and provocative as those given by poets Nikki Giovanni and Maya Angelou. My students' responses helped to remind me that perception is not necessarily reality.

Discouraged and quite concerned about upcoming standardized reading tests and their possible effect on the administrative decision to rehire me, I discontinued the read-aloud component for the remainder of that academic year and spent much of my time completing test-taking drills with the students. In fact, I spent the majority of the class periods (40 minutes each) that were allotted per week to Communication Arts, completing such drills.

During summer vacation, I made time to reflect upon the read-aloud component that I had initiated and subsequently discontinued. I considered the possible reasons for some students' obvious boredom and decided to re-implement the program with a few modifications, in an effort to make these sessions more listener-friendly and pleasurable.

The first modification involved my questioning of students during read-aloud sessions. Previously, I stopped frequently to ask them questions so that I would be able to ascertain whether they followed the plot and understood certain literary conventions. I decided that I would no longer ask questions during read-aloud, yet I would answer students' "burning questions," meaning that the listener just couldn't continue with the story if the question wasn't answered.

Second, I stopped being so ambitious with my book choices. Previously, I relied on classic selections (as cited below) that I had read in high school and college because I found the selections inspiring. I wanted to expose my students to literature's finest, a number of which were considered by many to be "the canon." Yet, I didn't consider the fact that the language used in these texts was quite sophisticated. I was also totally unaware of the wealth that children's literature offered.

During my first-year teaching experience, a couple of the first books I had tackled were Bronte's *Jane Eyre* and Twain's *The Adventures of Huckleberry Finn*. A number of my 6th grade students and I engaged in exciting discourse regarding the difference between the way the term "nigger" was used then in comparison to the way they used it today as slang. We also discussed child abuse and writing styles of the past that were considered to be "linguistically convoluted" (Hooks, 1989) by these contemporary listeners. The students who were most actively engaged were usually those who enjoyed reading and Communication Arts or had developed an affinity toward my instructional style and/or personality. For this group, reading for sheer pleasure was lost. We often spent so much time discussing issues contained within the books that we only read three or four pages during one 40-minute period.

For those who were traditionally disengaged from reading, Communication Arts, school and/or me, they continued to be so during these read-aloud sessions. Thus, their needs seemingly remained unmet.

The third change involved timing. Any successful program implementation must be supported by organizational structures (Jacobs, 1989); thus, reading for enjoyment was scheduled on Fridays, no-homework days for my classes.

As a result of attending a few workshops, evening classes, and investigating, I found more appropriate books for read-aloud. One such book was Blume's *Tales of a Fourth Grade Nothing*. Now, there might be some educators who would find such a selection inappropriate for a group of sixth grade Black and Latino/a remedial students. There are some who would claim that the book lacks intellectual challenge. I might agree, especially if my initial concern that basal selections lacked intellectual challenge is considered. Others, including The Council on Interracial Books for Children, have quite vocally claimed that Blume's work is racist, sexist, and classist (anonymous, 1977).

Presently, I may agree with some of the claims. At the time, however, the humor it contained served as my primary reason for selecting the text.

I also believed that the experience of having a difficult younger sibling was universal in many ways. Further, I had not been introduced to the possible criticisms of the book in the workshops and classes I attended. Instead, there seemed to be a focus upon the universal qualities of children's trade books.

Whatever my reasoning, I began reading the book aloud and noticed, to my surprise, that some of those slumbering had awakened. Children were listening and laughing. As predicted, they appreciated the humor and easily related to the plight of Peter, the protagonist. With each subsequent chapter, I noticed that my students became more actively engaged with the text. They were soon requesting that I read more often than once a week in order to uncover the plot or the latest antic of the story's antihero, Fudge.

Soon, even some of my most reluctant readers were asking if they could borrow the book and whether it was in the school library. I eventually saw several with copies of the book. I even had to request that they refrain from revealing the plot to other students who had elected not to read ahead. The students' newly acquired interest in reading led me to establish a classroom library in an effort to make the texts more readily accessible. Chapter I/PCEN funding, used to support efforts to develop reading scores of students who failed the standardized reading tests, and the school's principal assisted me in accomplishing this goal.

Yet, I should also acknowledge that a number of those whom I had previously identified as disengaged from reading, Communication Arts, school and/or me remained so. I recall asking some of these students to cite reasons for their dislike of the trade books that were read. They told me the books were "corny," "real people don't act like the people in the books." I also knew that a number of these students had adult responsibilities and concerns. Quite simply, school was losing them to the streets. I kept searching for appropriate reading selections that would meet their needs as well.

Over the next four years, I steadily worked toward refining the read-aloud component that I used in conjunction with the basal series I was required to use and class sets of trade books and newspapers that I was learning to integrate. I attempted to provide students with as many opportunities with text as I could and I attempted to engage the disenfranchised.

I was also becoming more proficient at selecting books that were more relevant to my students' lives. This proficiency was acquired through my participation in more children's literature courses and workshops, as well as by reading many children's and adolescent trade books and children's literature journals such as *The Horn Book Magazine* and *Interracial Books for Children Bulletin*.

Blume's *Tales of a Fourth Grade Nothing, Superfudge, Blubber;* Barthe DeClements' *Nothing's Fair in Fifth Grade, Sixth Grade Can Really Kill You;* Beverly Cleary's *Ellen Tebbits, Ramona the Pest, Ribsy;* and Roald Dahl's *Charlie and the Chocolate Factory* were consistently read as standards because they were funny and the students found them to be so. They truly enjoyed listening to these stories. Yet, by carefully examining the students' reader response entries on these books, I determined that while the level of involvement with text had increased with the use of these books, it hadn't developed to a sufficient point. It could still be considered minimal. Some of the response entries read:

> The best book I read was "Superfugde [sic]." It's funny.

> Today we read the story Ramona the pest. This book is hilariously funny . . . I read slow, some fast. But this book its like Im sciming [sic] through the pages.

> I don't know why they call Ramona a pest for, but she is a funny little girl. She should go on comedy if she was real. Because her arguments have me goin [sic].

> . . . "Superfudge," written by Judy Blome [sic] . . . became my favorite book because it had comedey [sic], adventure, etc.

Oftimes, they summarized the plot and commented on the humor, but there were very few signs revealing that they were making attempts at personal meaning making, character and plot involvement, and literary criticism (Hancock, 1993).

In an attempt to reconcile the lack of depth expressed in their written responses to the readings, I began to examine the fact that the protagonists contained within the texts used were predominantly middle-class, Anglo, and had lifestyles that were dramatically different from those of my students. For example, Blume's *Tales of a Fourth Grade Nothing* was set in New York City, but few of my students were able to identify the setting. The New York City presented by Blume was one with which many of my students (who also lived in the City) were unfamiliar.

I desired to find books that touched my students because they related to their everyday experiences and the characters mirrored them. In essence, I wished to present, as June Jordan (quoted in Horning and Kruse, 1991, p. 10) so eloquently put it, "a multicolored mirror of an honest humankind."

Aware of the fact that all books have the capability of touching the human heart and that there are many "melting pot" books (Sims, 1982) that present universal themes, I specifically sought books with Black and Latino/a characters who lived in urban centers. I believed that my students might be better able to become actively engaged, as would be evidenced in their response entries, with characters whose life experiences more accurately reflected their own.

Eventually, I began incorporating Joyce Hansen's *The Gift Giver* and *Yellow Bird and Me*, Cruz Martel's *Yagua Days*, Walter Dean Myers' *Scorpions*, Nicholasa Mohr's *Felita* and *Going Home*, and Camille Yarbrough's *The Shimmershine Queens*, as well as adding these selections to the classroom library. I also included books featuring marginalized White characters such as Gilly in Katherine Paterson's *The Great Gilly Hopkins*. I discovered that even some of my most streetwise students, who were basically unresponsive to every instructional strategy I employed, listened attentively during our read-aloud period and went to the classroom library to read ahead. Their response entries indicated that they were more actively involved as well. For some, the entries on the "new" books were the first assignment they had completed in any class for the year.

I especially recall a school emergency during which the bell system was malfunctioning and students were required to remain with their homeroom teachers throughout the day for three days consecutively. During those three days, my 7th grade class began to read Myers' *Scorpions*. Each student appeared spellbound. They completed the class assignments in an orderly and efficient manner, in an effort to provide more time for reading. The students also energetically discussed and wrote about the realistic way that Jamal and Tito were portrayed in the text and stated that *Scorpions* was the best book that they had read in school. One student, who was having a number of problems in regard to seeing the relevance of schooling to his life and consistently expressed low opinions of teachers, wrote in reference to the book:

> The best book I read this hole [sic] year was "Scorpions." It was wrating [sic] by Walter D. Meyers [sic]. I all way's [sic] say that it was like the movie "Juice" [an urban drama featuring Omar Epps and Tupac Shakur].

I was also surprised when a number of my students approached me and said, "We wish that we didn't have to go back to our other classes. You could teach us all day, we'd read good books, talk about them, you do all our subjects and we'd really learn."

Upon hearing Hansen's *The Gift Giver*, one of my more vocal students who quite frequently rebelled against the school culture enthusiastically responded, "Thank God, I.S.—finally got a Black book."

In another instance, when I was employed as a teacher trainer, a teacher to whom I recommended Hansen's books related that her students really became excited, because a number of them lived in the same area of the Bronx that Hansen wrote about and they were able to clearly identify the region.

In reference to Mohr's *Going Home*, two of my seventh graders wrote these powerful entries:

> I've read books on White people, Black people, Indian people and different races, but this year was the first time that I ever read a book about Puerto Ricans and its [sic] just not a little part in the story it's the whole book. It's a fact that not many latino and blacks are in books too many times, but

> when they are in books I like to read them. How come there
> are not many books written and published. Is it racism or
> could it just be their style of writing? It's true that when your
> work is criticized you begin to give up, some don't get right
> back on there [sic] feet and keep trying.

> The reason I like "Going Home" more than any other book is
> because I can relate to it . . . because I have a brother who is
> a pest, just like Falita [sic], and also because my parents are
> from Puerto Rico. When Falita found out she was going to P.R.
> she became very excited. The same thing happened to me . . .
> If I do not finish the book with the class, I plan to read the
> whole book on my own. I think I take it out from the library.

During classroom discussion of this book, another of my students coura-
geously stated that she was tired of hearing everyone else's story, those of
Blacks and Whites. She desired to hear Latino/a stories. Soon after, she
entered a piece on her experiences as a Latina in a writing contest, won,
and was published in a local newspaper.

In a read-aloud session with a group of seventh grade ESL students
(during which we had just concluded Mohr's *Going Home*), my group decided that too many questions that they generated about the text had remained unanswered. Thus, they decided to write a play that would continue the plot and answer their questions.

Seemingly, once my students felt that their own lives and cultures had
been validated through the texts presented and used in the classroom, they
were more willing and interested in examining texts that featured characters, both Anglo and from other diverse groups, and that dealt with serious
subject matter. For example, after reading Greene's *Summer of My German
Soldier*, a student's journal entry read:

> She tried to help him hide from the authorities because she
> admired him no matter who or what he was . . . it shows us
> children to overcome our hate for different people no matter
> what the conciquences [sic] are.

Following a reading of Cormier's *The Chocolate War,* a student wrote:

> In this book conformity is the issue. Those who don't conform
> with the majority are shuned [sic] away. Some things in this
> book caused controversy for some of the people in this class
> which is another reason that I liked it better.

In reference to *The Chocolate War,* students also seemed to pay greater
attention to details like style. For example, students wrote:

> I liked this book because of the way the words structure the
> book. This book is very descriptive. It makes you think that
> you are right there in the book.

> This book contained qualities that the other books didn't
> have. One of these qualities was action . . . another qualitie
> [sic] was suspense . . . This book is also very detailing about
> everything.

It appeared as if, in their minds, humor was no longer the only criterion for enjoying a book. It seemed as if they now understood the premise that art mirrors reality and the books they read related information about the society in which we all live. In essence, the trade book could be considered a cultural product. Yokota (1993, p. 156) asserts that:

> Cultural information can be present in virtually every aspect
> of a story: the description of the setting, the events in the
> plot, the actions and words of the characters and the treat-
> ment of the overall theme.

While books are no substitute for human interaction, they can serve as the vehicles through which sensitivity can be increased, empathy developed, and consciousness raised (Banks, 1994).

Another meritorious result of reading the multicultural books in class was that students were seeking such books on their own, as reflected in their response entries. For instance, some wrote:

> The book the learning tree is a book that inspired me very
> much. It is a good experience to read a book with characters
> of your own race especially during racial times in the
> world . . . About a year ago my mother bought the book for me
> but I never decided to read that particular book because I did
> not think it would interest me. Then I had a assignment to
> read a book of your choice and come up to the front of the
> class and then discuss the book with your classmates, but I
> was told the book had very tiny print and it was long plus the
> vocabulary might be difficult. After reading this book, I
> learned that it was one of my best book choices and I hope to
> make another one.

> I really liked . . . a book called "Children of the River," it was
> a Khemer family that moved to the United States . . . I like
> this book because it has to do with love, history and that if
> you have hope your wish can come true.

> "I Know Why The Caged Bird Sings" by Maya Angelou . . . is
> not fiction or fairy tale. It's an autobiography of her life . . .
> She gave the reader a clear image of her life. She also was
> able to express her feelings without over-doing it.

TOWARD DEFINING A PERSONAL PHILOSOPHY

As I relate this attempt to implement a component of an instructional plan that fostered students' literacy development, I believe that the reader is able to detect the degree of my inexperience, my quest toward personal and professional growth, and the impact of those factors on my teaching.

As I have reflected upon that particular point in my career development, I have realized that I, like many new teachers, was much more concerned with the implementation of practices than the development of a personal philosophy on education and literacy. As a result of time, experience, and exposure to innovative approaches to reading and language arts such as Whole Language, literature-based, interdisciplinary, and thematic teaching, I was able to develop my read-aloud component into one aspect of an integrated, well-planned, and efficacious Language Arts/Reading program. Effective Language Arts programs have been defined as those that evolve from a sound research knowledge base, are learner-centered, emphasize both language products and processes (illustrating their interdependence), are integrated with other subject areas, and are efficaciously assessed (Wood, 1994).

I should provide a caveat, however, concerning the listing of Whole Language as an approach. I am presently aware that Whole Language is considered a philosophy for many. Yet, I personally found that when it was introduced in my school system to my colleagues and me, it was introduced top-down (via administrative mandate) as an amorphous set of strategies that were to be immediately implemented in the classroom. Thus, I refer to it as an approach, in this context.

As a result of experience and exposure to the aforementioned practices, students in my classes were regularly provided with books and times during which they could engage in paired readings, book discussion groups, whole class (shared and guided) readings, as well individualized reading. The reading/writing connection practices of freewriting reader response journals and dialogue journals (in this instance, defined as engaging in a written dialogue with students and making certain that my responses focused solely on emotion and content) were also incorporated in the classroom.

I chose to focus students on the way specific texts made them feel and toward constructing their own meanings rather than merely summarizing and relying upon the teacher (as authority figure) to provide the "right" answer. I wished to move them toward a different mode of thought. I desired that my students would become comfortable selecting events and characters to discuss and write about that were personally significant.

As was also found by Atwell (1987), Applebee (1978), and Whitehead (1977), many of my students had rarely taken the time to think about what they read or attempt to decipher how the text made them feel and the ways in which it related and applied to the lives they led.

In addition to the use of reading and writing as student exercises in constructing meaning, I provided students with opportunities to cook and experiment, using the novels read in class as a base. For example, there was an occasion when I asked students to interview a family member and ask that family member to share a family tradition—one they wouldn't mind sharing with our class. After a number of students returned with "secret" recipes, the class decided to sponsor a celebration. All of the students brought in favorite family dishes that they assisted their family members in making and the accompanying recipe. The recipes were subsequently compiled and each student received a class cookbook. A number of students reported back that they had used the cookbook and made some of the dishes they first tasted at the celebration.

I would also like to share another observation regarding this specific celebration. At some class parties and other teachers' "multicultural days," I noticed that some children were cruel to others because their contributions didn't meet the level of expectation or the children placed value judgments on the dish and the culture. With our class-sponsored celebration, I noticed that such cruelty was not present. The children tasted everything and clearly understood that each person was sharing the most personal of things, something considered precious within their respective families.

After reading Dahl's *Charlie and the Chocolate Factory*, a number of students created food inventions (such as an M & M cake at which I still marvel and an improved Rainbow "Gobstopper") that they'd attempt to sell to Willie Wonka. They brought the inventions to class and we all benefited from taste-testing. Once again, many students involved family members in the production, thereby making the experience intergenerational and even more personally significant.

By providing such classroom-based opportunities with literacy that extended into students' homes, I was attempting to provide my students with as many chances as possible to connect text to their daily lives, to make text both relevant and meaningful.

I also attempted to expand their concepts of literacy so that they would be inclusive of the "story" in both film and music. I wished to enlighten them to the possibility of "reading" these literary forms as well. Previously, they believed that the art forms of film and music were diametrically opposed to the literary form of the book.

The children were encouraged to compare film adaptations to original texts. They sometimes used the Siskel and Ebert Thumbs Up/Thumbs Down approach to critique. The group was split in half on whether Dahl's *Charlie and the Chocolate Factory* was better than its film adaptation *Willie Wonka and the Chocolate Factory*. Some students shared that they were able to form mental pictures of the characters and the settings as we read and they liked having the freedom to do so. They related that if they had seen the movie prior to reading the text, the reading process would have been hindered. Other students claimed that the film produced greater visual images than they could ever have imagined. They discussed the way in which the film pulled the story together for them.

Students were introduced to other genres in our classroom as well, such as expository text, historical fiction, and poetry. In relation to poetry specifically, students were provided with the opportunity to explore the question, "What is poetry?" In my experience, many students appeared to bring limited knowledge of the topic to discussions and to limit the scope of the genre to the works of a few traditional poets like Shakespeare and Edgar Allan Poe. At the beginning of my teaching career, I tended to focus students' attention on such poets, while expanding the concept of traditional by the inclusion of poets like Langston Hughes and Gwendolyn Brooks. With this approach, I discovered that my students seemed to associate poetry with boredom and antiquity.

Through discussion, exposure, and more teaching experience, I was able to assist students in establishing a broader conceptualization of poetry. They were encouraged to collaboratively define poetry in cooperative learning groups, as well as to define it through exploration of the "poetry" in various media forms, such as art, song, rap, greeting cards, motion, dance, and nursery rhymes (Paul, 1994).

I was most excited by their enthusiasm over their discovery that rap music, an aspect of urban culture with which many of the students were familiar, was a valid poetic form that included rhyme, meter, figurative language, and significant theme (Paul, 1994; Purves, 1993). Legitimately, rap could be classified as poetry because "regardless of a poet's culture, that poet uses rhythm, imagery, typography, grammar and syntax as the medium of the poem" (Purves, 1993, p. 358).

While it may have proven more beneficial to use Eloise Greenfield's *Nathaniel Talking* or a more recent publication, Frances Minters' *Cinder-Elly,* with younger students, it was most beneficial to use authentic, appropriate rap selections with these older students, such as a number of those by Arrested Development, MC Serch, KRS One, Public Enemy and A Tribe Called Quest (Paul, 1994).

By using rap in this manner, I felt that I was simultaneously introducing a traditional genre and validating the culture of my students in the classroom. Thus, the genre became more accessible (Paul, 1994).

Yet, to reiterate, the opportunities that I was providing students fell under the auspices of instructional strategy and those strategies were not yet guided by any clearly defined and acknowledged beliefs about literacy instruction. At the time, my actions weren't guided by a philosophy on literacy development, even though I considered myself to be a Whole Language teacher, as based upon the descriptions I received in the aforementioned administrative mandates.

It was only through a course I attended at Columbia University's Teachers College that I came to the realization that I wasn't a Whole Language

purist, even though a number of the practices in my instructional reper-
toire were literature-based and I attempted to place literacy learning into a
meaningful context. I believed that there was a great deal of benefit to the
integration of skills and explicit instruction. I found that, in a number of
instances, my Black and Latino/a students needed and craved such instruction because it was consistent with their cultural views on education and
those of their families.

In essence, I believed in balance and wished to move my students toward the ability to accept diverse conceptualizations regarding literacy and
thought, without declaring any better or more significant.

I saw the value in both literature-based instruction and the explicit
teaching of skills in meaningful contexts. While I found literature-based
practices innovative and motivating, I couldn't negate the fact that traditional decoding and comprehension strategies employed in meaningful contexts was also essential. This need for strategy has also been discussed by
Strickland (1994) and Gersten and Jiminez (1994).

Students needed chances to learn strategies that would help them to
successfully navigate through text, such as establishing purposes for reading, surveying text, decoding unfamiliar words, assessing comprehension,
and de-mystifying text considered linguistically dense.

They needed opportunities that would enable them to facilely manipu-
late the written and spoken word, so that they would operate from a posi-
tion of strength in society. I desired to "make the secrets of reading public"
(Gersten and Jiminez, 1994). For far too long, in my estimation, Black and
Latino/a youngsters have been denied such keys to access (Delpit, 1988;
Reyes, 1992).

Audre Lorde once said "the master's tools will never dismantle the
master's house" (hooks, 1989, p. 36). As I reflect upon this quote, however,
one must know the master's tools before one can even envision the disman-
tling of the house.

I eventually determined that in regard to selecting a single philosophy
regarding literacy and instruction, I could not choose one at that particular
point in my career development. My philosophy on literacy development
and my role, as instructor and/or facilitator, in students' development could
most accurately be defined as eclectic. There was no one approach (that is,
Whole Language, Competencies-based Language Arts instruction) that proved
sufficient and inclusive of all learners. According to Kameenui (1993, p. 382),

> the standard of always searching for the single right best
> method for literacy development may be misguided. The
> search instead should be for multiple perspectives of right-
> ness guided by the diverse needs of learners and sound in-
> structional principles, practices, and craft knowledge.

During this process of defining my personal philosophy on literacy development and instruction that facilitated growth, however, I came to a much

more significant revelation regarding education, my students, multiculturalism, politics, and me.

EDUCATION, STUDENTS, MULTICULTURALISM, POLITICS, AND ME

Presently, I remain consistent on not adhering to any one philosophy concerning literacy development and my instructive role, yet I have come to the realization that I had unknowingly adopted a philosophy on education that has, in many ways, impacted upon the way I approach literacy instruction. It has also been instrumental in assisting me in developing a multicultural perspective rather than merely implementing multicultural practices.

The progression toward adopting this philosophy (which encompasses both critical pedagogy and critical literacy) was quite natural for me. In a number of ways, it was as if the philosophy found me. Throughout this chapter, I have sought to convey the way in which the life experiences and cultures of my students greatly affected my views of education, literacy, and the instruction I offered to them in my classroom. In fact, those factors impacted just as significantly as my own life experiences and the cultures to which I belonged (Black, female, belonging to a single-parent family, an urban dweller, attending private and public school). This composite of considerations grew to affect every instructional decision I made and the texts I used.

For me, understanding and acknowledging the cultures of students in the classroom was and remains essential, especially as I consider that (for many of my students) their life experiences had left them feeling disempowered. In many ways, the school culture perpetuated those feelings of disempowerment and disenfranchisement. In many ways, the school culture was deemed oppressive in regard to issues of race, class, and gender. I wished to help my students shift their paradigms from powerlessness to power. I believed that such a shift would have an impact on the way they interacted with text, the way they mediated the school culture, and the way in which they viewed life.

As a result, I adopted an educational philosophy that centered on critical pedagogy and critical literacy as conceptualized and defined by Paulo Freire, Ken Goodman, Yetta Goodman, Henry Giroux, bell hooks, Donald Macedo, and Peter McLaren. Critical pedagogy focuses on the translation of knowledge gained within the classroom to revolutionary change outside of it (McLaren, 1988). The classroom learnings affect the students' perception of themselves, the world, and their respective places within the structure. Critical literacy is defined as focusing upon

> . . . the interests and assumptions that inform the generation
> of knowledge itself. From this perspective all texts, written,
> spoken or otherwise represented, constitute ideological weap-
> ons capable of enabling certain groups to solidify their power
> through acts of linguistic hegemony. (McLaren, 1988, p. 218)

At last, I discovered a philosophy that seemed to speak directly to me, a
philosophy that seemed to validate my concerns and consider my students'
needs.

In my estimation, it was at this point that I *truly* understood that the
mere implementation of practices and selection of multicultural books was
not enough. It was understanding the dynamics underlying that implementation and selection that was most significant. I realized that I hadn't
chosen books featuring racial and ethnic characters because it was man-
dated or suggested that I should be "multicultural" in my selections. I
incoporated such books because I fervently believed that my students should
see themselves represented in our classroom and within the school. I also
hoped that they would see that, even in books that featured characters that
they perceived were like them and lived in settings such as theirs, there
was diversity. I desired that they would realize that within the diverse
voices expressed through these texts, there were "multiple, complex and
often contradictory discourses" (Giroux, 1990, p. 91).

Similar reasoning and concern for my students increased the importance of motivating them to actively interact with text, analyzing and interpreting, as opposed to passively accepting text as authority. I wished to
lead them to the understanding that the texts they were accustomed to
reading in school were to "be viewed as someone's story, one that is never
innocent and, consequently, has to be interrogated for its social and political functions" (Giroux, 1990, p. 89). An example illustrating this point could
be found in the class reading of Dahl's *Charlie and the Chocolate Factory*,
which I've mentioned several times in this chapter. While I've mentioned
the students' enjoyment of the fantasy and my attempts to bring the text to
life for them, I have not mentioned that I also deemed it necessary to discuss with my students seeming problems in the text and in certain representations. We discussed that the version we read was revised because the
original portrayal of the Oompa Loompas was perceived as racist. We also
talked about the implications of such a portrayal, the portrayal's power,
and the power inherent in text in all of its forms.

We, as a class, consistently engaged in an on-going, non-threatening
dialogue about text, images, and messages (Paul, 1994). According to Edelsky
(1994, p. 255), teachers and students should "talk about the positions people
are put in by texts, what premises we're positioned to accept, and how we
accept or resist those." These points appear especially significant if we con-

sider that we're preparing citizens who will eventually participate and live in the emerging American democracy. In my mind, one of the primary purposes of education is to create a new social order—an order in which a significant number of those from traditionally marginalized groups have the opportunity to *fully* participate in the infrastructure currently labeled the American democracy.

LESSONS LEARNED

A number of people to whom I have spoken and have encountered on this quest toward a multicultural perspective have criticized me for being "too political about education," "racist," and "laying too much on children in these books rather than just accepting that a book can just be a book." In my mind, some of these criticisms are a result of society's discomfort with acknowledging difference and discussing issues of race, class, and gender. The criticism seems grounded in the desire of many to focus on universality and racelessness. Unfortunately, such denial doesn't negate the constructs of race, gender, and class or minimize their effects, even in something deemed as undefiled as children's literature. Toni Morrison asserts that "a criticism that needs to insist that literature is not only 'universal' but also 'race-free' risks lobotomizing that literature and diminishes both the art and the artist" (1992, p. 12).

I have attempted and continue to attempt to bring the issues of race, class, and gender to the forefront as they relate to education. I additionally try to enable my students to work from positions of strength as opposed to those of weakness. It is nearly impossible for me to determine the long-term effects that I have had on students. I do know, however, that they had a significant impact upon me and an intangible something tells me that I had some effect upon them as well. I continue to strive toward making an impact in the lives of students, helping them to live life on their terms rather than terms defined for them by others.

REFERENCES

Anonymous. (1977). All values surface in Blume country. *Interracial Books for Children Bulletin,* Vol. 7, no. 5: 8–10.

Applebee, A. (1978). *A child's concept of story.* Chicago: University of Chicago Press.

Atwell N. (1987). *In the middle.* Portsmouth, NH: Boynton Cook Publishers.

Banks, J. A. (1993). Approaches to multicultural curriculum reform. *Multicultural Leader,* Vol. *1*, no. 3: 1–3.

Banks, J. A. (1994). *An introduction to multicultural education.* Boston: Allyn and Bacon.

Delpit, L. (1988). The silenced dialogue: Power and pedagogy in educating other people's children. *Harvard Educational Review,* Vol. *58*, no. 6, 280–298.

Edelsky, C. and Harman, S. (1991). Risks and possibilities of whole language literacy: Alienation and connection. In C. Edelsky (Ed.), *With literacy and justice for all: Rethinking the social in language and education.* London: Falmer Press.

Edelsky, C. (1994). Education for democracy. *Language Arts, 71*(4), 252–257.

Gersten, R. and Jiminez, R. T. (1994). A delicate balance: Enhancing literature instruction for students of English as a second language. *The Reading Teacher*, Vol. *47*, no. 6, 438–447.

Giroux, H. (1990). Reading texts, literacy, and textual authority. *Journal of Education,* Vol. *172*, 84–103.

Hancock, M. (1993). Exploring and extending personal response through literature journals. *The Reading Teacher*, Vol. *46*, no. 6, 466–474.

Heath, S. B. (1983). *Way with words.* New York: Cambridge University Press.

Holdaway, D. (1979). An open approach to literacy. In *The foundations of literacy* (pp. 11–23). Sydney: Ashton Scholastic.

hooks, b. (1989). *Talking back: Thinking feminist, thinking Black.* Boston: South End Press.

Horning, K. T. and Kruse, G. M. (1991). Looking into the mirror: Considerations behind the reflections. In M. Lindgren (Ed.), *The Multicolored mirror: Cultural substance for children and young adults.* Fort Atkinson, Wisconsin: Highsmith Press.

Jacobs, H. H. (1989). *Interdisciplinary curriculum: Design and implementation.* Alexandria, Va.: Association of Supervision and Curriculum Development.

Kameenui, E. J. (1993). Diverse learners and the tyranny of time: Don't fix blame; fix the leaky roof. *The Reading Teacher, 5*, 376–383.

Madhubuti, H. (1990). *Black men: Obsolete, single, dangerous?: Afrikan American families in transition: Essays in discovering solutions and hopes.* Chicago: Third World Press.

McLaren, P. (1988). Culture or canon? Critical pedagogy and the politics of literacy. *Harvard Educational Review,* Vol. *58*, no. 2, 213–235.

Morrison, T. (1992). *Playing in the dark: Whiteness and the literary imagination.* New York: Vintage Books.

Nieto, S. (1992). We have stories to tell: A case study of Puerto Ricans in children's books. In V. Harris (Ed.), *Teaching Multicultural Literature in Grades K–8.* Norwood, MA: Christopher-Gordon Publishers, Inc.

Paul, D. G. (1994). *A comparative analysis of Black and White heroines in children's and young adult text.* Doctoral Dissertation. Teachers College, New York.

Paul, D. G. (1994). Exceptionality and poetry. *New Jersey English Journal.* New Jersey: NJCTE, 46–48.

Purves, Alan C. (1993). Toward a reevaluation of reader response and school literature. *Language Arts 5,* 348–361.

Reyes, M. de la Luz (1992). Challenging venerable assumptions: Literacy instruction for linguistically different students. *Harvard Educational Review,* Vol. *62,* 427–446.

Sims, R. (1982). *Shadow and substance.* Urbana, Illinois: NCTE.

Strickland, D. (1994). Educating African American learners at risk: Finding a better way. *Language Arts,* Vol. *71,* no. 5, 328–336.

Wacquant, L. J. D. and Wilson, W. J. (1989). The cost of racial and class exclusion in the inner city. In W. J. Wilson (Ed.), *The Annals of the American Academy of Political and Social Science.* Newbury Park, CA: Sage Publications.

Whitehead, F. (1977). *Children and their books.* London: Macmillan.

Willis, A. I. (1995). Reading the world of school literacy: Contextualizing the experience of a young African American male. *Harvard Educational Review,* Vol. *65,* no. 1, 30–49.

Wood, M. (1994). *Essentials of classroom teaching: Elementary language arts.* Boston: Allyn and Bacon.

Yokota, J. (1993). Issues in selecting multicultural literature. *Language Arts,* Vol. *70,* no 3, 156–167.

CHILDREN'S BOOKS

Blume, J. (1972). *Tales of a fourth grade nothing.* New York: Dell Publishing.

Blume, J. (1974). *Blubber.* New York: Dell Publishing.

Blume, J. (1980). *Superfudge.* New York: Dell Publishing.

Cleary, B. (1951). *Ellen Tebbits.* New York: Avon Books.

Cleary, B. (1964). *Ribsy.* New York: Dell Yearling.

Cleary, B. (1968). *Ramona the pest.* New York: Dell Yearling.

Cormier, R. (1974). *The Chocolate War.* New York: Pantheon.

Dahl, R. (1973). *Charlie and the chocolate factory.* New York: Bantam Skylark.

Greene, B. (1973). *Summer of my German soldier.* New York: Bantam.

Hansen, J. (1980). *The gift giver.* New York: Clarion Books.

Hansen, J. (1986). *Yellow bird and me.* New York: Clarion Books.

Martel, C. (1976). *Yagua days.* New York: Dial Books for Young Readers.

Mohr, N. (1979). *Felita.* New York: Bantam Skylark.

Mohr, N. (1986). *Going home.* New York: Bantam Skylark.

Myers, W. D. (1988). *Scorpions.* New York: Harper and Row.

Paterson, K. (1977). *Bridge to Terabithia.* New York: Harper and Row.

Paterson, K. (1978). *The Great Gilly Hopkins.* New York: Harper Trophy.

About the Authors

Violet J. Harris received her Ph.D. from the University of Georgia. She is currently an Associate Professor at the University of Illinois at Urbana-Champaign. Her research interests include children's literature, multiethnic children's literature, and literacy materials created for African-American children prior to 1950.

Rosalinda B. Barrera received her Ph.D. from the University of Texas at Austin. She is currently Professor of Curriculum and Instruction at New Mexico State University at Las Cruces, specializing in literacy education. Her many journal articles and book chapters reflect her interests in Mexican-American bilingual elementary students, and the socio-cultural foundations of literature based literacy education.

Rudine Sims Bishop received her Ed.D. from Wayne State University in Detroit. She is Professor of Education at The Ohio State University, where she teaches course in children's literature. She is author of ***Shadow and Substance: Afro-American Experience in Contemporary Children's Fiction*** and ***Presenting Walter Dean Myers***.

Oralia Garza de Cortes   earned a bachelor's degree in social work and a master's degree in library science from the University of Texas at Austin. She is an active member of the American Library Association (ALA) and its affiliate, REFORMA, the National Association to Promote Library Services to the Spanish Speaking. She chaired the joint task force of REFORMA and the Association for Library Services to Children (ALSC), an ALA division, that established the Pura Belpre Award in 1996, to honor exemplary works about the Latino cultural experience by Latino/a writers and illustrators. Formerly a librarian in Austin and San Antonio, she is now a free-lance consultant in Latino children's literature, while also serving as a column editor for *Multicultural Review* and publishing professionally in the field of multicultural children's literature. She was recently appointed to the Caldecott Award Committee.

Daniel D. Hade   is an Associate Professor of Education and Professor in charge of Language and Literacy Education at the Pennsylvania State University. He has published articles in ***Research in the Teaching of English***, ***Children's Literature in Education***, and ***The New Advocate***. His research interests include issues of social justice, children's literature, and the manners in which adults influence children's readings of literature.

Cheryl Willis Hudson   is a founder of **Just Us Books, Inc**. The independent publishing company specializes in books for children and young adults that focus on the Black Experience and is now recognized as one of the leading publishers of Black interest books, garnering them many awards and honors.

Christine A. Jenkins   received her Ph.D. from the University of Wisconsin-Madison. She is an Assistant Professor at the University of Illinois at Urbana-Champaign, where she teaches library and information science. She is a long time member of the American Library Association (ALA).

Sonia Nieto   received her Ed.D. from the University of Massachusetts where she is Professor of Education. In addition to numerous articles and book chapters, she is author of *Affirming Diversity: The Sociopolitical Context of Multicultural Education*. She has published articles in The Harvard Educational Review, The Educational Forum, and Multicultural Education, among others. Her research focuses on multicultural and bilingual education, the education of Latinos, and Puerto Rican children's literature.

Dierdre Glenn Paul received her Ed.D. from Teachers College, Columbia University. She is currently an Assistant professor in the Department of Literacy and Media Studies at Montclair State University. Her research interests include multiethnic and multicultural children's literature, African American girls and popular culture as it relates to education.

Debbie Reese is a Pueblo Indian woman, currently enrolled in a doctoral program in Curriculum and Instruction at the University of Illinois. Her primary research interests focus on the ways in which Native people are presented to young children in the media, the school environment, children's books, and society in general. She teaches workshops on issues related to teaching young children about Native Americans

Sandra Yamate earned her A.B. in Political Science and History from the University of Illinois at Urbana-Champaign, where she graduated Phi Beta Kappa. She is a graduate of Harvard Law School. For almost ten years, she was an attorney in private practice, specializing in civil litigation. In 1990, she helped found Polychrome Publishing Corporation, the only company in the nation dedicated to producing children's books about Asian-Americans and their experiences.

Subject Index

ಸ್ಥ ಸ್ಥ ಸ್ಥ ಸ್ಥ ಸ್ಥ

G

Gender, meaning of, in children's literature, 235, 238, 240, 245–247, 248
Ghost stories, 32
Goosebumps series, 51
Greenfield Review Press, 156, 170

H

Harlem Renaissance, 46
Hawaiians
children of, depicted in books, 100
history of, 107
Hernandez, Antonio, 144
Hines, Mifaunwy Shunatona, 161
Hispanic Books, Inc., 130, 131
Hispanic Heritage series (Millbrook Press), 131
Hispanics of Achievement series (Chelsea House), 131
Horning, Kathleen, 110
Huerta, Dolores, 134, 144
Hughes, Langston, 50

I

Illness, 39
Imamu Jones series (Guy), 34–35
Independent press movement, 230
Indian Americans, 98
Internet, use of, 180, 184
Ito, Lance, 95

J

Japanese Americans
history of, 107
internment during World War II, 96, 97, 107
Jenkins, Esther C., 110
Journal of Children's Literature, 235–236
Just Us Books, 102
Just Us Books approach to creating good books, 219–231
access and authenticity, 222–223
awards, 229
background, 220–221

building an institution, 230–231
competition and cooperation, 230
critical and academic reviews, 228–229
extending our vision, 229–230
key ingredients to look for in Afro–centric books for children, 223–224
providing information: why we publish Black books, 221–222
publishing policy and practice, 223
responses in the marketplace, 228
types of books, 224–228
biography and nonfiction, 227
books for middle readers, 227–228
books for older readers, 228
concept books, 224–225
picture books, 225–226
poetry, 228
story books, 226–227
YA books, 228

K

King, Martin Luther King, Jr., 35, 50
King, Matthew, 160
Korea Central Daily News, 101, 115
Korean Americans, 98, 101, 115
Kruse, Ginny Moore, 110

L

Latinos, 60–61
Loo, Ming Hai "Jim," 96

M

Magic Attic series (Reed), 30
Melting pot books, 206, 207, 210, 264
Mexican American children's literature, 129–153
aspects of Mexican American identity in children's literature, 143–144

Author, Illustrator, Title Index